MODERN EUROPEAN HISTORY Made Simple 1871–1979

K. Perry, BA, MA, ARHistS

Made Simple Books
HEINEMANN : London

Printed and bound in Great Britain
by Richard Clay (The Chaucer Press) Ltd, Bungay, Suffolk
for the publishers William Heinemann Ltd,
10 Upper Grosvenor Street, London W1X 9PA

First Edition, September 1976
Reprinted, July 1980
Reprinted, January 1983

British Library Cataloguing in Publication Data

Perry, K.
Modern European history made simple 1871–1979.
—(Made simple books)
1. Europe—History—1871–1918
2. Europe—History—20th century
I. Title II. Series
940.2′8 D395

ISBN 0-434-98569-4

Foreword

This book has been written during a period in which Europe has suffered an energy crisis and Irish affairs have taken on a deeper seriousness. These developments illustrate two of the chief themes of this book: the downward spiral of European power and the enormous influence of Nationalism in the last hundred years.

It is hoped that the reader will be helped to an awareness of the impact of these and other developments which have determined Europe's—and Britain's—place in the world today. The book should prove of value to schools, colleges and universities as it covers the syllabuses of various G.C.E. examining bodies as well as degree courses at university level. It should also be of interest to any layman seeking a greater understanding of the world in which he lives. The selection of maps reproduced in the Appendix will improve the reader's grasp of the major developments.

Of the many people who have given valuable aid in the preparation of this book, three individuals stand out. Mr Robert Postema of Heinemann gave willing guidance on many points of procedure while my colleague Dr Frederick Jones made many searching criticisms which were of especial help in the several areas of debate where we patently disagreed! My deepest debt of gratitude is due to my wife, who in the intervals of a very busy life found time to type the manuscript and give constant encouragement.

K. PERRY

Table of Contents

MODERN EUROPEAN HISTORY

CHAPTER ONE

PRELUDE TO MODERN EUROPE: 1815–71

Introduction: Versailles, January 1871

On January 18, 1871, an event of immense importance occurred in the Hall of Mirrors at Versailles. At twelve o'clock the King of Prussia entered with a train of German princes. Proceedings opened with divine worship and the old King walked down the long gallery to a platform at the end. There he read out a declaration that he accepted the new title of German Emperor. The heavy figure of the Prussian Chancellor, Bismarck, then stepped forward in the blue tunic and great boots of a Prussian Cuirassier. After he had proclaimed the German Empire the cheers of the German princes rang through the gallery and echoed to the ceiling painted in celebration of the victories of Louis XIV two hundred years before. The noble mirrors on the French king's walls reflected a forest of German swords and spiked helmets lifted in honour of the German Emperor. After a round of presentations the first ceremony of the German Empire ended.

Its creation was made possible by the defeat of France in the Franco–Prussian war and was the most significant event of the whole epoch. In many ways 1871 represented the end of one era and the beginning of another. Before we discuss why this was the case, it is necessary to examine certain crucial themes in the development of Europe in the nineteenth century.

The Impact of the French Revolution and the Napoleonic Wars

'The generation or more which separates the 1780s from the battle of Waterloo saw the beginnings of modern history in Europe,' asserts M. S. Anderson. During the eighteenth century the continent was still closer to the twelfth century than to the twentieth century in its everyday life. Industrial organisation remained highly traditional and technology advanced only slowly. Society almost everywhere continued to be dominated by tradition and privilege and was divided into the 'orders' of the Church, nobility, burghers and peasantry.

The governments of continental Europe before the French revolution were, as they had been for generations, monarchies of a more or less absolute kind. No major continental state possessed an effective parliament, while republicanism was a remote classical tradition rather than a living idea. Even the armed forces were traditional; techniques had not changed fundamentally for two centuries and armies remained small and often dynastic rather than national in their outlook.

By 1815 this traditional structure had changed almost beyond recognition over much of western Europe and had been seriously eroded in central Europe. In part this was the work of the British example. Britain's wealth and her ability to sustain the burden of the long wars with France which dragged on from 1793 to 1815 were, in Anderson's phrase, 'a spectacular advertisement for industrialisation and parliamentary government'. Much more important, however, was the example of revolutionary France. Her elimination of the old inequalities aroused much admiration and sympathy in the educated classes over much of Europe.

The French revolutionaries were not content to preach merely by example. By the spring of 1792 the Messianic element in the Revolution contributed to the outbreak of war between France and the powers of old Europe. The expansionist tendencies of the new France became even more evident after 1799 when Napoleon Bonaparte seized power. Under him the sheer military power of the country, based to a large extent on its superiority in population to most other European states, appeared to threaten the permanent subordination of most of the continent to French rule. The Habsburg Empire, Prussia and even Russia fell before Napoleon in the campaigns of 1805–7. Therefore Napoleon's lack of moderation destroyed his power for, as the able Dutch historian Pieter Geyl rightly says, he was 'a conqueror with whom it was impossible to live'. As a result France's enemies were forced to make common cause against him in an effective coalition. Yet his career had shown with frightening clarity the power of the new forces, which to a large extent had eliminated privilege in France and replaced it with equality of opportunity and rational efficient government. But the most important consequence of the French wars was the stimulus that they gave to the development of nationalism.

The Growth of Nationalism

The most important political fact of the nineteenth century in Europe was the growth of nationalism. It has been defined by Hans Kohn as a state of mind in which the supreme loyalty of the individual is felt to be due to the nation-state. Many elements combined to distinguish one nation from another—like common descent, language, territory, religion and traditions—but none of these factors was essential to the existence of a nation. The most essential element was the belief of a large majority of the population that the nation-state was the ideal and only legitimate form of political organisation and that nationality was the source of all cultural creativity and economic advance. If nationalism in its early stirrings seemed like Sleeping Beauty to people in the nineteenth century, by the early years of the twentieth century it appeared as a Frankenstein's monster capable of causing total war.

Before the French Revolution wars did not as a rule arouse deep national emotions. National consciousness was weak among the peasantry and, for the educated few, learning in Europe was rooted in the cosmopolitan tradition of classical civilisation. It was the impact of the French Revolutionary and Napoleonic wars that aroused national passions from Ireland to Serbia and made nationalism the dynamic force it was to become in the following century. In France itself a new emphasis on national unity was visible during the revolution. The Declaration of the Rights of Man of 1789 proclaimed that 'the principle of all sovereignty resides essentially in the nation'. The French victories during the long wars did much to stimulate national feeling in the rest of Europe. Positively, they displayed the military and political power which a great nation could possess once it was united. Negatively, French conquest and exploitation provoked a hostile reaction.

In central Europe the strength of the new national feeling lay in cultural movements, in the dreams of scholars and poets who looked back with nostalgia to the past glories of the nation. In Italy the most influential writer was Mazzini. To him nationality was truly a religion; national unity must be based upon religious belief and be itself a form of religious belief. He was not a parochial nationalist; he believed that not only Italians but all nationalities should create their own sovereign nation-states which would then unite voluntarily and spontaneously in an association of free peoples. In Mazzini's view, therefore, the nation was 'the God-appointed instrument for the welfare of the human race'.

In the first half of the nineteenth century all the arts in Italy were mobilised for the objective of stimulating national feeling. A constant theme was the struggle against the foreign overlord, as in Manzoni's novel *The Betrothed* and in Rossini's opera *William Tell*.

The call to political action through a grievance against the foreigner was also the case in Germany. Here national consciousness was given a lead by the epoch-making ideas of Herder. He developed the theory of the folk-soul (*Volkgeist*). Men were, above all, members of their national communities and only as such could they be really creative through the medium of their folk language and their folk traditions. His ideas sparked off much research into long-neglected folklore and songs, the best known researchers being the brothers Grimm. Herder was not a nationalist in the modern sense of the word. He hated Prussian militarism and respected all nations, regarding the peaceful Slav peasant peoples as more civilised than the Germans.

In contrast, the next generation of German nationalists like Fichte and Arne asserted that Germans were superior to all other nations because they had succeeded in maintaining the purity of their race and language. To the concept of racial superiority was added Hegel's idea of the state. Only through service to the state would the individual find fulfilment. 'All the worth which the human being possesses—all spiritual reality—he possesses only through the State. . . . The State is the Divine Idea as it exists on earth . . . morality is duty.'

It was Prussia's defeat at the hands of Napoleon at the Battle of Jena in 1806 which made German nationalism noisy and explicit. Though Napoleon had reduced the number of German states from nearly 300 to 39, Germany was still a geographical expression. Nevertheless, Prussia's defeat was felt as a German humiliation and there developed among students and teachers a desire for revenge and national unity.

The nationalists played only a small part in the liberation of Germany from the French. The anti-Semitic Friedrich Jahn formed military free-corps but the real fighting was done by the Prussian army. In 1815 a loose confederation of the 39 states was set up in Germany, each state being in practice independent. National feeling remained weak among a largely passive peasant population. During the 1848 revolutions, when the German middle-class liberals attempted to unite Germany through the Frankfurt Parliament, one of the chief reasons for their failure was lack of mass support.

By the 1860s, however, German nationalism had become an important force. Germany had become more of an economic unit by then through the success of the national customs union, the *Zollverein*, which acclimatised the rest of Germany to Prussian leadership. As in other countries, historical writing became less cosmopolitan and more narrowly patriotic. Historians like Ranke and Treitschke used history as a means of firing German patriotism. Ranke wrote in 1836, 'Our fatherland is with us, in us. Germany lives in us.'

There were two media through which nationalism could be fostered: the school and the press. It is significant that the growth of primary education in the nineteenth century developed at the same pace as popular nationalism. The second could hardly have existed without the first. It is equally significant that in Germany, as in many other countries, education, previously the preserve of the Church, fell more and more under governmental control.

Similarly, the emergence of weak nationalities depended in its early stages on the development of some national literature, above all in newspapers in the national language. Vernacular literature and newspapers did much to generate national feeling and all too often national antagonisms. In Germany the first great political daily, the *Allgemeine Zeitung*, was founded in 1798. By the 1840s the growth of a popular press had helped to produce something like a genuine national public opinion.

National sentiment was further stimulated by the progress made by Italy towards unity between 1859 and 1861. In 1859 a national conference of democratic leaders at Eisenach set up a national association, the *Nationalverein*, pledged to supporting the concentration of military and political power in the hands of Prussia. In 1862 a politician capable of exploiting this sentiment became Minister-President of Prussia, Otto von Bismarck.

Governments and Societies (1815–71)

In 1815 governments and societies over much of Europe were still traditional and backward. With the exception of France there was still universal acceptance of hereditary monarchy as the normal constitutional form. The power of the monarchy varied from state to state. At one extreme lay Britain, where the power of the monarchy had been in obvious decline since the seventeenth century and was now limited and constitutional. At the other extreme lay Russia, where since the reign of Peter the Great (1689–1725) the autocratic power of the tzar had increased. In practice several factors drastically limited the tzar's influence: the sheer size of his empire, its diversity of nationalities, poor communications and the backward feudal nature of his realm. Since Peter's reign the tzar had been forced to work in partnership with the privileged landowning class. He gave the landowners complete control over their serfs and in return expected the landowners to serve in the bureaucracy or the armed forces. These factors combined to create a system of intolerable inefficiency.

The other great monarchies of Europe fell between the British and Russian extremes. In France the restored Bourbon Louis XVIII had to govern as a parliamentary monarch and when his brother Charles X later tried to restore the old monarchical powers the revolution of 1830 drove him into exile. The old mystique of the monarchy was dead beyond recall and the next king, Louis Philippe (1830–48), had to cooperate with a middle-class dominated parliament.

In the Habsburg Empire and Prussia the monarchy was essential as a unifying force because both states had developed in a haphazard way over centuries, with different territories, possessing no common interest or history. Therefore the dynasty with the army and bureaucracy was required to hold the territories together. The role of the monarchy as a unifying force was particularly vital in the Habsburg Empire. It was a multinational agglomeration which had evolved partly through war, mainly at the expense of Turkey but more through dynastic marriage and diplomatic shrewdness. As the fifteenth-century Hungarian wit Matthias Corvinus had put it, 'Let other powers make war! Thou, happy Austria, marry'. However, the multinational state was ill-suited to a century which saw the growth of a dynamic nationalism. The Habsburg lands lacked any national religious or geographical unity. In effect they were, in Taylor's words, 'a collection of entailed estates, not a state; and the Habsburgs were landlords not rulers'. Inside the Empire were many important nationalities, including Germans, Magyars, Czechs, Italians, Slovaks, Ruthenes, Rumanians, Poles, Serbs, Croats and Slovenes. The supporters of the monarchy were well aware that as nationalism and liberalism developed, then the dissolution of the Habsburg lands was imminent. Metternich, Austrian Chancellor from the Napoleonic Wars to 1848, was obsessed by this threat and referred to his task as that of 'propping up the mouldering edifice'.

In general, however, monarchy was still very popular because rule by one man was the most comprehensible to ordinary people. Secondly, it was widely believed that only a hereditary monarchy could rise above sectional interests and govern for the general good of all groups in society. Finally, even the autocratic monarchies were not as a rule oppressive, at least by the standards of the twentieth century, because most rulers were still traditional in outlook and methods.

Nevertheless the conservative régimes came under attack from two main directions between 1815 and 1848. They were challenged by secret societies like the *Carbonari* in Italy. Such societies proliferated in the two decades after 1815 but they were not a serious threat because they lacked unity. A more serious challenge to the conservative monarchies came from middle-class demands for effective parliamentary government. The example of the British parliament was an important stimulus to such demands but even more important was the French Revolution with its idea of popular sovereignty. Parliamentarianism made only modest headway. In France, the 1814 Charter set up an elected Chamber of Deputies side by side with a Chamber of Peers nominated by the king, but the franchise remained narrow even after the Bourbons were replaced by Louis Philippe in 1830. Progress in the rest of Europe was even more disappointing. The Constitution of the German Confederation, established in 1815, was essentially illiberal and in the two most important members of the Confederation, Prussia and Austria, constitutional government made no progress at all. Nor did it in Russia, which was ruled by a dedicated reactionary, Nicholas I. Only in Belgium in 1831 was a genuine limited monarchy created.

The pressure for change grew and came mainly from two directions: the universities, which grew in number at the same time as their students became more radical; and the growth of a significant public opinion which owed much to the growth of newspapers. In 1848, the general political stability of Europe was shattered by revolutions which at first seemed to demonstrate the fragility of conservatism. They caused a great upheaval in France, Germany, Italy and Austria but were essentially middle class, lacked mass support and suffered from acute divisions over methods and objectives. Once the authorities recovered their nerve and used their trump card—their armies—the revolutionary movements collapsed quickly. Ironically governments became stronger after 1848 than before. In France, Louis Napoleon overthrew the Second Republic in 1851 and as Napoleon III set up a dictatorship, the Second Empire, in 1852. The reality of government power was also seen in Prussia when liberal opposition to army reform was crushed by Bismarck in the 1860s.

An important reason for the increased strength of governments was their appreciation that revolution was possible and that their authority was based on the consent of the governed. Therefore they tried as never before to win the positive loyalty of their subjects. In France, Louis Napoleon made genuine attempts from 1859 to convert his autocratic government to a more liberal régime. In Austria, Francis Joseph attempted a number of constitutional experiments in 1860–61 and finally consented in 1867 to the Compromise (*Ausgleich*). This reform divided the Habsburg lands into two political entities, one a Hungarian-dominated state, the other a German-ruled federation. Except for questions of foreign policy defence and finance, the two parts of the monarchy were independent of each other, each with its own parliament. Thus after 1867 the Empire had a constitution and as A. J. May has pointed out the Compromise was probably the best arrangement that could be worked out at the time because it went far towards achieving the immediate object, that of conciliating the Magyar ruling class. In time the defects of the Compromise became clear; it was a deal between the German minority in the western half of the empire and the Magyar minority in the east at the expense of all the other nationalities. Nevertheless, the Compromise lasted for 50 years, which was a long period of life for any central European settlement.

It was, however, in Russia that the most striking reforms were found. By 1850 the inefficient Russian system was being criticised by two groups from the growing Russian intelligentsia. The Westerners believed that as Russia was so backward she must learn from the more advanced West European countries. The Slavophils disagreed with this thesis. To them Holy Russia with its unique institutions like the peasant commune (the *mir*) and the Orthodox Church had a mission—that of revitalising Western civilisation. It was, however, Russian defeat in the Crimean War that made change inevitable. Nicholas I died in 1855 and his successor Alexander II, though conservative, had the commonsense and courage to initiate major reform. In 1861 his famous Edict of Emancipation granted serfs on private estates immediate freedom and this was soon followed by similar enactments for serfs in Russian Poland and on state lands. The complexity of the legislation reflected the complexity of the situation in a huge multinational empire with vast variations between the different areas in climate, soil and density of population. The reform had its weaknesses—chiefly the failure to endow the former serfs with sufficient land—but the grant of individual freedom to 20 million people previously in legal bondage is probably the greatest single liberating measure in modern European history. Hugh Seton-Watson notes that serfdom was abolished peacefully in the same year in which the failure to abolish slavery in the United States became a principal cause of one of the most bloody wars of the nineteenth century.

Important judicial and military reforms followed the emancipation of the serfs but perhaps the most significant reform after 1861 was the creation of local councils (*zemstvos*) in 1864. Unfortunately, Alexander became the object of bitter criticism in Russia, though he had in fact merited the gratitude of his people. Some of the reforms failed and in 1866 Alexander was nearly assassinated by a young student revolutionary Dmitri Karakozov. Karakozov's action is a landmark in Russian history for Alexander now gave up liberal reform; but though he became more conservative as his reign progressed, it is still true that no European state in the nineteenth century attempted so much so quickly as Russia to enter fully the modern world.

Warfare 1815–71: Transition and Transformation

The long period of peace after 1815 meant that for 40 years military factors did not maintain the importance which they had possessed in the days of Napoleon. Most powers were in fact glad to cut expenditure by reducing the size of their armies and navies. Conscription was applied in only a limited way, except in Prussia, yet a slow evolution of organisation was general. Armies became increasingly officered by professionals who regarded their military service as a permanent career. The same professionalism can be seen in the central organisation of the great European armies. In Prussia was evolved what became the most admired military institution in Europe: the General Staff, which was to be the brains of the army. Established by Scharnhorst after the defeats of 1806, it replaced the war minister as the main adviser to the king on operational matters. Only after 1870, however, was there full imitation of the Prussian model by the other powers.

Vast and accelerating changes took place in military technology. The old smooth-bore muzzle-loading musket of the Napoleonic period was replaced by breech-loading weapons which allowed a much higher rate of fire to be achieved. The introduction of rifled barrels made possible a far greater range and accuracy than ever before. By the 1840s the Prussians had adopted on a large scale the Dreyse needle-gun, which was accurate up to 500 yards and had a rate of fire over three times as fast as the muzzle-loaders. By the 1860s the French were also using a breech-loading rifle, the *chassepôt*, which was superior to the needle-gun in range and accuracy. Such fire-power implied that in future frontal attacks on well-defended positions would be terribly costly and the end of the cavalry as a major force in warfare was foreshadowed.

Changes in artillery took longer to evolve, but by Bismarck's wars in the 1860s the Prussians were using breech-loading cannon while the French were still using muzzle-loaders. As Basil Liddell Hart has stressed, the Prussian superiority in artillery was a vital factor explaining Prussia's victory in the war of 1870. It more than compensated for the superiority of the French rifle over the needle-gun and the French possession of the *mitrailleuse*, an early form of machine-gun. German artillery broke up French infantry attacks at ranges of over a mile, and at the crucial Battle of Sedan the French army was ringed by 600 Prussian guns which shattered the brave attempts of the French forces to break out of the trap.

By the middle of the nineteenth century armies were gaining a new mobility in speed of decision and movement by the use of the telegraph and railways. Helmuth von Moltke was keenly alive to the use of the railways from the 1830s. After he became commander of the Prussian General Staff in 1857, he equipped the army with a railway section. Specialised units from this section were to repair railways destroyed by the enemy in the later wars. Moltke exploited the Prussian railway system for military purposes superbly and in 1866 he was able to transport the Prussian armies into Austrian Bohemia so rapidly that the Austrian armies were encircled and destroyed.

It was the Crimean War that first saw the use of the accumulated technological developments of the previous four decades and the defeats suffered by Russia drove home the lesson that for a state to be a great military power it would need to be industrially progressive as well. The revolution in warfare was revealed even more clearly by the Prussian triumphs against Denmark, Austria and France between 1864 and 1871, which were based on superior mobility, strategy and artillery.

The Diplomatic Scene (1815–71)

The Concert of Europe (1815–50)

The Vienna peace settlement of 1815 at the close of the Napoleonic Wars attempted with considerable success to restore in Europe an effective balance of power and hence paved the way to a long period of peace. France enjoyed lenient treatment but was effectively restrained by the strengthening of both Prussia and Austria. It was a peace based on fear—fear of a renewal of revolution and war—and the three eastern powers, Russia, Prussia and Austria, combined in the

Holy Alliance to carry out the repression of liberal and national movements in Europe even if such a policy required intervention in the domestic affairs of other states.

The motives of the powers were not wholly selfish. The years after 1815 saw a genuine though limited impulse towards some form of European unity in the form of congresses of heads of state at Aix-la-Chapelle (1818), at Troppau and Laibach (1820–21) and at Verona (1822). The Congress System was short-lived; it was undermined by the opposition of Britain to interventionist policies and by the widespread fear of Russian strength felt by the other powers.

The fear of Russia was in fact exaggerated. The unwieldy empire was to remain for another century relatively backward compared to other powers but during the decades after 1815 this was largely hidden from contemporaries who recalled the Russian victories against France from 1812. Only one power seemed capable of holding its own against Russia: Britain. She was the greatest colonial power in the world and her naval strength gave her a degree of security matched by no continental state. Above all, her industrial development gave her economic resources far superior to those of her political rivals.

Other powers seemed far inferior to Russia. The ramshackle nature of the Austrian Empire was generally despised, while Prussia, the other major German state, seemed even less equipped to combat Russian power. At the Vienna Settlement she had ranked as a great power by courtesy title only and even after her territorial gains in Saxony and the Rhineland her small territory and population scarcely fitted her for great power status. The conservative and unobtrusive character of her foreign policy in the generation after 1815 meant that she was very much overshadowed by Austria and Russia.

Even France after 1815 scarcely seemed the equal of Russia or Britain. Her reputation as the centre of revolutionary thought made her distrusted by conservatives everywhere. Their suspicion seemed justified by France's persistent political instability, which resulted in revolutions there in 1830 and 1848. Moreover, her military reputation had not recovered from the defeats of 1812 to 1815. Economic stagnation made her lag far behind Britain in iron production and railway-building and by the middle of the century her status as a great economic power was menaced not only by Britain but by rapid development of the German economy.

The political events from 1820 to the 1850s reflected British and Russian superiority to the other states, the two cooperating in support of the Greek rebels in their war of independence against Turkey in the1820s and again in the Middle East crisis of 1839–40. The 1848 revolutions left Russia virtually unscathed and her armies, by crushing the Hungarian national revolt in 1849, re-established Habsburg rule over Austria's most turbulent subjects. Such action led to acute russophobia in Western Europe, especially in Britain, where Russia was hated even more as the gendarme of Europe.

Britain too enjoyed great diplomatic success during these decades. In the 1830s the British Foreign Secretary, Palmerston, became the main creator of an independent Belgium after the Belgian revolt against Dutch rule. In 1840–41 he achieved a personal triumph in the Middle Eastern crisis which saw France isolated and humiliated and her protégé, Mehemet Ali of Egypt, forced to make peace with his overlord the sultan on moderate terms which ensured the continued existence of the Turkish Empire, one of the prime aims of British foreign policy.

Despite these rivalries, the years from 1820 to 1850 did not see the idea of European cooperation—the Concert of Europe—die altogether. There was still a widespread feeling that important territorial changes in Europe should only be made with the general consent of the great powers. The emergence of an independent Belgium after long negotiations and the Straits Convention of 1841, which laid down a set of internationally agreed rules regarding the passage of ships of war through the Bosphorus and the Dardanelles, were both triumphs for the concert idea.

The Revolution in the Balance of Power (1850–71)

The increased competitiveness in international relations after 1850 and the revolutionary changes in the European states system that resulted may largely be explained by three factors. Nationalism, which had been gathering strength for almost a century, was by 1870 the most dynamic force in the political life of most of Europe. Less spectacularly, but with an almost equal significance, economic and military changes were influencing relations between states in a manner not hitherto seen. A third factor was the collapse of the idea of the Concert of Europe, which in turn was largely the result of the defeat of Russia by Britain and France in the Crimean War (1854–56).

No power had wanted this war but it was this struggle far more than the upheavals of 1848 which ended the Europe of 1815. In Britain, anti-Russian hysteria had been growing for decades and it was the British government which pressed for severe peace terms on Russia at the Congress of Paris in 1856. The Russians, having already suffered military reverses, now had to stomach diplomatic humiliation. The Black Sea was neutralised and as a result Russia was unable to build forts on the coast or maintain a navy in the Black Sea. The demilitarisation of the Black Sea, writes Anderson, was 'extremely harsh and unprecedented. Not until the even more stringent restrictions imposed on Germany in 1919 was a state to be forced to submit to so obvious and flagrant a limitation of its military freedom of action.' Russia became a revisionist power, the major objective of her foreign policy being the abrogation of the hated Black Sea clauses.

Above all, the war brought about a decisive breach between Russia and Austria. The entente between them that had endured for over a generation was destroyed by the Austrian refusal to side with Russia in the war and then by the Austrian threat in December 1855 to intervene in the war on the side of the Western powers. This Austrian ultimatum forced Russia to make peace and henceforth relations between the two empires were dominated on the Russian side by bitter resentment. Under the guidance of the new foreign secretary Gorchakov, who was vehemently anti-Austrian, Russia moved towards a rapprochement with France. These developments constituted a genuine diplomatic revolution.

The real importance of the Crimean War as a dividing line in the history of Europe lay in the isolation and weakening of Austria. It paved the way for the defeat of Austria by Franco–Piedmontese forces in 1859 and by Prussia in 1866. So did the policies of Napoleon III. This ruler had a sincere sympathy with the national idea and he championed the creation of a Rumania independent of Turkey after the Crimean War. While his fundamental objective was the safeguarding of French interests, he was quite willing to see a Prussian-dominated north Germany and a Piedmont-dominated north Italy. In 1859 he made an essential contribution to Italian unification by his support of Piedmont against Austria in the war of that year.

Since 1815 the Italian peninsula had been divided into separate states each with its own laws and traditions. It was under the sway of Austria, which after the Vienna Settlement gained Lombardy–Venetia, and Metternich was therefore correct in calling the Italy of this period merely a geographical expression. Yet by the 1850s the north Italian kingdom of Piedmont–Sardinia was in a position to take the lead in the expulsion of Austria from the peninsula. It was the most advanced state in Italy and had borne the brunt of the fighting against Austria during the 1848 revolutions. In 1852 the shrewd opportunist Count Cavour became prime minister and contributed much to the modernisation of Piedmont. His greatest single achievement was, however, the securing of the alliance with France. It took real shape in July 1858, when Napoleon III and Cavour met at Plombières to define the arrangements by which Austria could be driven out of Italy. Piedmont was to annex Lombardy–Venetia, Modena, Parma and the Romagna, with France receiving Nice and Savoy from Piedmont. But Austria had to be seen to be the aggressor and Cavour was singularly fortunate that in April the next year the Austrian government allowed itself to be provoked into declaring war on Piedmont unnecessarily. As a result the Austrians found themselves fighting France as well as Piedmont.

The war of 1859 was of short duration. After hard-won victories at Magenta and Solferino, Napoleon made peace with the Habsburgs because he was horrified by the slaughter and alarmed by the hostile attitude which Prussia had taken on the Rhine. To Cavour's rage, Piedmont only received Lombardy and not Venetia. Yet the way had been opened for great changes in central Italy. In Tuscany, Modena and Parma the rulers had been driven out with ease in the spring of 1859 and by the end of the year Napoleon had decided to allow the union of these states with Piedmont, France being compensated with Nice and Savoy. Then the Italian soldier-hero Garibaldi took advantage of a revolt in Sicily to overthrow Francis of Naples between May and September 1860 in the most spectacular episode in the whole history of Italian unification. He then proceeded to hand over his conquests to Piedmont and the first Italian parliament met in Turin the following year, after the acquisition of the new territories had been confirmed by plebiscite.

The whole process of Italian unification was, however, in a sense artificial. The movement for national unity was not one of the mass of the population but one of the urban middle classes and to a lesser extent of the nobility. Cavour himself was realistic and far from being a nationalist. Only after Garibaldi's successes in the south did he accept the idea of a united Italy which he had previously despised as impracticable. Cavour believed that Italy was not ready for unity and he was right. In the south there was widespread indifference to the idea and only 15 per cent of the male population voted in the plebiscite held in the Kingdom of Naples. A deep gulf continued to divide the prosperous urban north from the poor rural south and it precluded real unity in the years after 1861. Diplomatic and military reverses in the 1860s drove the same lesson home. When Italy joined in the Austro–Prussian war to gain Venetia, the Italians suffered a series of humiliating disasters on land and sea, though they were ceded Venetia by the Treaty of Prague.

In contrast, the process of German unification has about it a certain inevitability. By the 1860s national feeling and industrial growth were making more and more unavoidable the creation of some kind of unified, powerful German state. But no historical process is inevitable until it happens and German unification required the diplomatic skill of Bismarck. His personality and achievements have always exercised a magnetic attraction for historians of the twentieth century because of the need to assess his responsibility for the German tragedies in the modern period. Were the seeds of these disasters planted by Bismarck, as Meinecke and Eyck believe? Many German historians have repudiated this. Gerhard Ritter stated that Bismarck was a man of moderation and reason, that the empire which he created was a healthy body and that therefore there could be no direct relationship between Bismarck and Hitler. Yet there can be little doubt that he exploited nationalism for imperial and authoritarian purposes. 'What moved him,' asserts Otto Pflanze, 'was not the ideal of German unity but the quest for greater internal stability for the Hohenzollern monarchy and the greater external power for Prussia in Europe.' His alliance with the nationalists allowed him to outflank the liberal opposition at home and create a united Germany dominated by Prussia. This was a blow to the development of parliamentary government, especially as Bismarck's manipulations fragmented the liberals and reduced the possibility of stable majorities. Perhaps most significant for the future was his use of expediency and military power, which set an unfortunate precedent that men of lesser ability were to follow.

Bismarck was fortunate in coming to office at a most favourable moment for Prussia. The Crimean War had resulted in the defeat of Russia and the isolation of Austria, while in 1863 French sympathy for the Polish revolt against Russia ended the Franco–Prussian entente. The only stable feature in diplomatic affairs was, therefore, the friendship of Russia and Prussia. The two powers had been traditional allies since the days of Napoleon and were both conservative, monarchical states with identical interests over Poland. Bismarck was to cultivate this friendship by supporting Russia in her aim of abrogating the Black Sea clauses.

It would be wrong to believe that Bismarck came to power in 1862 with a master plan for German unification, just as it would be wrong to imagine that he fumbled his way through events caused by other statesmen. He had his long-term objectives but they were achieved by a combination of dexterous expediency and good fortune. His first success came in the Danish war of 1864, which led to the Prussian gain of Schleswig and prepared the way for the confrontation with Austria in 1866. The Austro–Prussian war lasted only seven weeks as three Prussian armies invaded Bohemia and defeated the main Austrian forces at Sadowa. Bismarck exercised a wise restraint by imposing moderate peace terms on Austria in the Treaty of Prague but Prussia now controlled all northern Germany in a new North German Confederation and only the four southern German states—Baden, Württemberg, Saxony and Bavaria—retained any real independence.

The Prussian success in 1866 came as a disagreeable surprise to the French and Franco–Prussian relations became tense. In 1870 the French government objected to an offer of the vacant Spanish throne made by the Spanish *Cortes* to a member of the Prussian royal family, Prince Leopold. Bismarck had plotted such a move as a means of putting diplomatic pressure on France and he was disappointed when King William acceded to the French demand to withdraw Leopold's candidature. However, the French now sent their ambassador Benedetti to place before William a demand that the candidature would never be renewed in the future. William refused this unreasonable démarche and sent Bismarck a telegram from Ems notifying him of the development. Bismarck, now converted to the idea of war, sent an edited version of the telegram to the press and he is supposed to have made it more offensive to the French in order to provoke war. In fact, as A. J. P. Taylor has shown, the French wanted war anyway and declared war without waiting to learn from Benedetti what had really happened at Ems. If the Franco–

Prussian war was a trap for the French, it was largely one of their own making.

The French went to war in 1870 with 'light hearts', assuming that their professional armies would sweep aside Prussia and the four south German states, now linked by a military alliance with Prussia. But the French army was unprepared for the challenges of a new age and in September McMahon's army was surrounded at Sedan and destroyed by the Prussian artillery. 'The success of the German gunners,' states Michael Howard, 'showed that a new age of applied technology in war had begun.' Napoleon's defeat led to the fall of his régime and its replacement by a republican government which by January 1871 was forced to sue for an armistice.

The Consequences of the Franco–Prussian War

The war of 1870 was not merely a military and political, but even more a psychological dividing line in European history. For the first time two great European peoples had fought a war using against each other all the resources provided by developed economies, mass armies and mass hates. French primacy was ended and the balance of power revolutionised. All the other powers now felt apprehensive of the new German Empire. Her military might was now indisputable; her economic might, already considerable in 1871, was to grow at an unprecedented rate in the final decades of the century.

Nevertheless, the war built into German history a fatal insecurity by ensuring the permanent hostility of France. By the Treaty of Frankfurt that ended the war, France was forced to cede Alsace, most of Lorraine, and the fortresses of Strasbourg and Metz. She was to pay an indemnity of 5,000 million francs within three years, maintaining an army of occupation in the meantime. The fortress of Belfort was kept by France only at the cost of a victorious German parade through Paris. C. J. H. Hayes claims that the insistence on such acquisitions was inspired by military and economic considerations. The Vosges mountains would indeed provide a stronger frontier than the River Rhine and Lorraine's mineral wealth would help the growth of German armaments, but Bismarck's desire for Alsace–Lorraine was also caused by his need for a symbol of victory which would unite both the north and the south together in the new Germany. He underestimated the resentment which the French people felt over the loss of their national territory; yet they would have been bitter even if defeat had not been followed by annexations, for the defeat itself rankled.

The onset of the Franco–Prussian war gave the opportunity to two states to make adjustments in their favour. Gorchakov, with Bismarck's support, notified the powers that Russia would no longer be bound by the Black Sea clauses of the Treaty of Paris. A conference in London in January 1871 formally endorsed this unilateral Russian action and Russia again appeared as a threat to the stability of the Middle East. Another sign of a new age occurred in September 1870 when the Italian army invaded the Papal Enclave around Rome. After token resistance, Rome became the Italian capital and the Pope retired to the Vatican, refusing to accept the situation. Relations between Church and State in Italy remained rancorous until the advent of Mussolini.

The war brought about a decisive change in the policy of the Habsburg monarchy. After Sedan, Francis Joseph gave up all hope of revenge on Prussia and accepted the loss of Austrian leadership of Germany. The way was now open for a reconciliation with Bismarck's Germany, for both powers were conservative and had no vital clash of interests. Austro–Hungarian foreign policy was to be increasingly anti-Russian as the two empires became bitter rivals in the Balkans.

Finally, the Franco–Prussian war drove home the lesson that a new age of materialism had arrived. Science and material progress seemed to prove Germany's superiority to France. Other nations sought to imitate Prussia's example by building up large efficient armies so that although the period from 1871 to 1914 was free of major wars, it can fairly be called the armed peace.

Further Reading

Anderson, M. S., *The Ascendancy of Europe*, Longmans, London, 1972.
—, *The Eastern Question*, Macmillan, London, 1966.
Howard, M., *The Franco–Prussian War*, Fontana, London, 1967.
Kohn, H., *Nationalism*, Anvil Books, London, 1965.
McManners, J., *Lectures in European History 1789–1914*, Blackwell, London, 1966.
Pflanze O., *Bismarck and the Development of Germany 1848–1871*, Princeton University Press, Princeton, 1963.
Seton-Watson, H., *The Russian Empire 1801–1917*, Clarendon Press, Oxford, 1967.
Smith, D. Mack., *Victor Emmanuel, Cavour and the Risorgimento*, Oxford University Press, London, 1971.
Taylor, A. J. P., *The Habsburg Empire 1809–1918*, Hamish Hamilton, London, 1960.
—, *The Struggle for Mastery in Europe 1848–1918*, Clarendon Press, Oxford, 1965.

Questions

1. What factors stimulated the growth of nationalism in nineteenth-century Europe?
2. Why did monarchical government survive so successfully in Europe before 1871?
3. Analyse the most important changes in warfare between 1815 and 1871.
4. Account for the successful unification of Italy and Germany by 1871.
5. Why may the Franco–Prussian War be regarded as a watershed in European history?

CHAPTER TWO

THE INDUSTRIAL SOCIETY AND THE CHALLENGE OF SOCIALISM

The Industrial Society

The Course of Technological Change

No revolution, asserts C. M. Cipolla, has been as dramatically revolutionary as the Industrial Revolution. It opened up a completely different world of new and untapped sources of energy such as coal, oil and electricity. Thus from a narrow technological point of view the Industrial Revolution can be defined as the process by which a society gained control of vast sources of inanimate energy. This process, which began in England in the eighteenth century, had by 1850 penetrated into Belgium, France, Germany and Switzerland, and by 1900 had extended to Sweden, Italy and Russia. The result was an amazing growth in output.

The year 1851 had marked the zenith of Britain's position as the workshop of the world. But already this model of industrial achievement was being copied as well as admired. In 1825 there were at least 2,000 British workers on the continent and from their teaching developed a generation of skilled workers, many of whom became entrepreneurs in their own right. The growing technical independence of the continent was also helped by the founding of technical schools by the state, for example the École Polytechnique in France. Improving transport and a growing home market resulting from the rapid rise in the population encouraged the use of new methods by the business community. Working capital was more easily available because of the development of joint-stock banking, state investment and the flow of funds from Britain.

In Britain industrial growth had been built on the cotton industry, which grew more rapidly than other branches of industry before 1800. On the continent, it was heavy industry—coal and iron—that was the leading sector and by the third quarter of the century continental industry had come of age. It was a period of unprecedentedly rapid growth in major sectors like the railways, coal and iron industries. These were the years of technological maturation. The power loom replaced the mule and the handloom, the iron industry used coal instead of charcoal, the steam engine triumphed over the waterwheel and a heavy chemicals industry was established. The use of power-driven machinery spread into many more areas of manufacture, from nail-making to tailoring. These were years of sustained creativity which saw the introduction of the Bessemer converter in steel manufacture, the industrial use of electricity, the manufacture of artificial dyes from coal tar and the Solvay ammonia process. These innovations did not come to fruition until the last third of the century and laid the foundations for a new long wave of expansion that some writers have called the Second Industrial Revolution. An important feature of this phase was the tendency of firms to increase in size.

According to David Landes, the technological advance in this period was encouraged by certain negative and creative stimuli. Among the negative stimuli one may cite the periodic commercial crises, such as that in 1857, which served as drastic purges of inefficient enterprises, and also the general lowering of tariffs which encouraged international trade and gave a powerful impetus to specialisation. There were four creative stimuli. First, the expansion of the railways was perhaps the most important; 50,000 miles of new line were built in Europe between 1850 and 1870. Second, new sources of energy and raw materials became available—for example, the use of deeper coal seams in Westphalia and the Northern field of France. Third, gold discoveries contributed to the increased supply of money and the issue of paper money also increased. This helped the rate of interest to fall to 3 per cent in France and the figure was only slightly higher in Germany. With the expansion of credit, three booms occurred, between 1852 and 1857, between 1861 and 1866, and between 1869 and 1873. Fourth, the expansion of credit was buttressed by important developments in banking. A banking revolution took place with a wider clientele for banking services and the rise of investment banks like the Crédit Mobilier in France in 1852, which was soon copied in Germany, Austria, Spain, Holland and Italy. The principal virtue of the investment banks lay in their ability to channel wealth into industry, which was of particular value as they often worked in areas where the supply of capital was limited. Investment banks made a greater contribution in Germany than in France, where the investor preferred government bonds, and family-based firms preferred to finance expansion out of profits.

By the late nineteenth century one important characteristic had become apparent: the protracted deflation caused by the fall in real costs, first in manufacturing and then, after the transport revolution, in food production. There were so many important innovations that, to quote Landes, 'the price decline of the nineteenth century is the consequence and barometer of European industrialisation'. Germany continued her high rate of growth and formerly underdeveloped countries embarked on their own industrial revolutions, notably Sweden and Russia.

By the last decades of the nineteenth century technical advance was proceeding on a broad front in many industries. The late nineteenth century was an Age of Steel. It replaced iron because it could combine strength, hardness and plasticity better than other metals like pig-iron, which was hard but also brittle because of its greater carbon content. The mass production of steel was made possible by the invention of the Bessemer converter, the Siemens–Martin process and the Gilchrist–Thomas process, the last-named being of great value to steel production in Germany and Austria–Hungary. These improvements drove down the real cost of crude steel some 80 or 90 per cent between the 1860s and the 1890s. In 1870 steel production in West Europe, including Britain, had been 385,000 tons; by 1913 it had reached 32 million tons, a gain of 83 times over the 43-year period. Germany overtook Britain in steel production in 1893 and was producing twice as much by 1914, by which time she was also a bigger exporter of steel than Britain.

In the chemicals industry vital developments occurred. The Solvay method of alkali manufacture replaced the more wasteful Leblanc method. Britain, which had a large investment in the Leblanc method, lagged behind the continent in the use of the new techniques. France led the way in the use of the Solvay method but Germany soon caught up and by 1900 had caught 90 per cent of the world market. David Landes admires this initiative. 'In technical virtuosity and aggressive enterprise, this leap to hegemony, almost to monopoly, has no parallel. It was Imperial Germany's greatest industrial achievement.' Only Switzerland succeeded in developing a vigorous dyestuffs industry in face of such stiff German competition. But artificial dyes were only one corner of a new world. There was a whole range of products derived from cellulose such as celluloid, the first modern plastic used for table-tennis balls, and artificial fibres such as viscose. Developments in the chemicals industry drove home two lessons. For technological progress to be maintained, full use must be made of science and therefore there was need for educational systems which would provide trained scientists.

New sources of energy and power were pioneered by 1914. The steam engine was improved for use on liners like the *Pacific* and *Orient*, but it now faced a rival, the internal combustion engine, which was more efficient in industrial processes as well as being cleaner and more labour-saving. Electricity made an immense contribution to industry because of its transmissibility and flexibility. Because it could move energy through space without serious loss, industry no longer had to be based near coalfields. As it was easily converted into other forms of energy—heat or light—it made power available to everyone. Once again Germany took the lead and her output of electrical products was twice that of Britain's by 1913.

The machines themselves had been improved in speed and durability through the use of hard steel alloys in machine tools, improvements in lubrication, the use of steel instead of wrought iron in the construction of machinery and the use of ball-bearings, first applied in the manufacture of bicycles. Two changes revolutionised work in the factory itself. Each job was broken down into a simple operation which was performed by a single-purpose machine run by unskilled labour. Also, methods of manufacture were devised that were so precise that assembly became routine—in other words, the production of interchangeable parts.

Attempts to improve the efficiency of the individual worker were not neglected. In the 1880s, in Midvale Steel Works in Pennsylvania, Frederick W. Taylor developed the system that came to be known as scientific management or time-and-motion study. The use of the methods of scientific management resulted, as Landes suggests, in 'the conversion of the operative into an automaton to match and keep pace with his equipment'. It foreshadowed the next stage of mechanisation, automation itself—the replacement of man by machines that think as well as do.

Demographic Developments

From 1850 to 1914, there was an unprecedented increase in the population of Europe from 266 million to more than 468 million. The population would have increased still further but for the exodus of many Europeans who from the mid-nineteenth century went to the new colonies and the United States. Despite emigration, the annual growth rate of the population was over 8 per cent in the years 1850 to 1900 and nearly 13 per cent in the years 1900 to 1913.

The towns drew heavily on the rural areas and the nineteenth century witnessed a great acceleration in the growth of the urban population, which by the late nineteenth century was beginning to outstrip the rural population. Agriculture ceased to be the most important activity in several West European countries and with the absolute or relative decline in the agricultural population came an expansion of the urban working classes and a spread of towns by the growth of suburbs. Suburban housing offered the advantage of lower costs and was facilitated by the improvements in transport.

The increase in the population was caused by an impressive fall in the death rate which can be explained by a number of factors. The majority of Europeans became better fed and more resistant to disease. The price of food dropped relative to manufactures after 1875 because of improved rail and marine transport, which caused a drop in freight charges, and because of new techniques like canning and refrigeration. Now Europeans could enjoy a wide range of products from overseas—cheap bread as a result of the massive flows of grain from North America and Russia, beef from the Argentine, tropical fruits and, with the use of vegetable oils, the poor man's substitute for butter, margarine. This competition forced European farmers to specialise on produce where the competition was less fierce and as a result vegetables, sugar beet and improved dairy produce were made available to the townsmen. In Denmark and the Low Countries rural cooperatives coordinated the efforts of the primary producers, while in Germany agricultural productivity was doubled by large capitalist farmers. By 1914 the people of the industrial cities were better fed than the mass of men had ever been before.

By 1871 notable advances had been made in medicine. The use of vaccination became widespread in the nineteenth century and smallpox began to disappear. Louis Pasteur's work resulted in new serums and vaccines which checked several major diseases like typhoid and diphtheria. Medicine was becoming for the first time truly scientific in its methods of diagnosis and in the development of anaesthetics to kill pain in operations.

From 1850 there was a marked acceleration in real incomes, even allowing for cyclical unemployment. In Germany, for example, real incomes rose by 64 per cent between 1871 and 1913. Even in Russia, where income per head was only half that of Germany, there was an increase in real incomes from about 1880. It is true that this steady rise in real incomes received a sharp check in the early years of the twentieth century but such estimates do not take into account other changes, such as the reduction in the average hours of work and efforts to improve the quality of life in the cities. The development of urban life had created grim factories, slag heaps and slum housing, termed by the Hammonds 'the barracks of industry'. Yet after 1870 some improvements were occurring through government insistence on minimum standards of hygiene and building. By the late nineteenth century the enlightened planning of cities had begun. It was seen in Haussmann's work in Paris, which Brussels and Vienna sought to emulate. The scientific organisation of urban living was to be seen in Germany in towns like Essen, with its Krupp housing estates, and in Dusseldorf, which became the 'garden city' of Germany. German cities adopted municipal socialism and brought in publicly owned gas and water works, tramways, theatres and symphony orchestras.

With the process of urbanisation consumer wants increased as millions had been introduced to a more expansive way of life. New methods of retail distribution contributed to a great rise in expectations. Department stores and chain stores developed with their devices for tempting the consumer—advertising, special 'sales' and catalogue orders. The technical advances after 1870 like cheap steel and electric power made available a whole new range of consumer durables—sewing machines, clocks and bicycles. With the extra degree of leisure allowed the workers, seaside holidays now became a possibility.

It must be stressed that these improvements applied mainly to Western Europe and even in the more advanced countries there remained a large minority of the working class which existed in abject poverty. Nevertheless, with the reduction in infant mortality there was an increase in life expectancy throughout Europe. In France it rose from 40 in the early nineteenth century to 50 in the early years of the twentieth century; in Italy it rose from 35 in 1874 to 44 in 1905. The fall in the mortality rate was accompanied by a slow fall in the birth rate for most of the nineteenth century, which led in time to an increase in the number of elderly and a decrease in the proportion of young people, particularly in France and Sweden. This transition from high birth and mortality rates to a reduction in both was so drastic that it may be called a demographic revolution.

The excess of births over deaths in most parts of Europe was one of the chief causes of mass migration. The motives for this phenomenon were complex but both the 'push' of adverse conditions at home and the 'pull' of better prospects overseas were major factors. Between 1841 and 1880, 13 million Europeans emigrated, mostly from Britain, Ireland and Germany. From 1871 to 1914 another 34 million Europeans left for the New World, the biggest contingents from 1885 coming from east and south Europe, from Spain, Portugal, Italy, Austria–Hungary and Russia. This European emigration, asserts Andre Armengaud, 'probably represents the greatest transfer of population in the history of mankind'. The results were immense. Emigration not only slowed down the population expansion of Europe but led to a considerable two-way movement of capital: money taken out by emigrants and money sent back to their dependants. Emigration also opened up new markets to the exporting nations because the emigrants continued to buy the products which they had used at home. It tended to bring about a general increase in wages by reducing the supply of labour and a lowering of land prices by reducing the demand for it. As emigrants were usually young adults, their exodus raised the average age of Europeans. Above all, emigration extended European civilisation across most of North America, Australia, Africa and even part of Asia, and was an important factor in ensuring the supremacy of Europe.

Before industrialisation, 60 to 80 per cent of European workers were employed in some form of agriculture. Then came a phase when industry replaced agriculture as the largest sector with the services sector also growing. The point at which the urban population outstripped the rural was reached at different dates in different countries—in Britain in 1851, in Germany in1891 and in France as late as 1931.

In the second phase, agriculture continued to decline, employing about 10 per cent of the active population, the rate of growth of industry slowed down, while the services sector grew substantially. Before industrialisation services had existed but were catered for by a small group of specialists or as a part-time activity. With industrialisation, a great expansion of the social overhead services like transport and education, and intermediate services like the retail and wholesale trades, was required. As cities grew rapidly, new services were created in crime prevention, public health and factory inspection. A new range of business professions, like accountancy, emerged. With the growth of state intervention, the numbers of the bureaucracy and its degree of specialisation increased. By 1900, comments R. M. Hartwell, a service revolution was under way over much of Europe. By the early years of the twentieth century the percentage employment of services in total employment was 30 to 35 per cent in Germany, Belgium, Holland and Norway and up to 25 per cent in France, Italy and Austria–Hungary.

Though all the various services contributed to industrialisation, particular importance has been attached to the role of transport. The development of railways, steam shipping, postal and telegraph services was quickly seen as essential, which is why they often came under government control. They were the spearheads of technical advance, large absorbers of capital and large creators of income. They contributed to the growth of a truly international economy. By 1913, half the world trade consisted of the imports and exports of the United Kingdom, France, Belgium, Germany, Holland, Switzerland and Denmark. These countries were interlocked with each other in trade and with the major primary producers of the world—the United States, Russia, India and China. From West Europe capital was exported for world-wide investment to the extent of £350 million a year. In spite of tariffs, international trade flowed freely and Asa Briggs calls the period from 1894 to 1914 'the golden age of economic specialisation and exchange'.

The Challenge of Socialism

Introduction

Socialism had its roots in the French Revolution, as it was in this period that the social problem was posed: the need for a rational reorganisation of society. The crucial years of early socialism were between 1830 and 1848 because, as George Lichtheim remarks, 'those were the years when socialism transformed itself from a doctrine into a movement'. It did so mainly in France through the work of St Simon, Fourier and Louis Blanc. Two major movements developed within socialism after 1848: Marxism and Anarchism.

Karl Marx

Karl Marx was born at Trier, in the Rhineland, of middle-class Jewish parents in 1818. Until 1843 he was a liberal but in that year he went to Paris, a city which Isaiah Berlin has referred to as rich in the international traffic of ideas. It was the home of exiles from central and eastern Europe. Here Marx met working-class socialists for the first time, including Engels, who in 1844 came from Manchester with the material for his book *The Economic Condition of the Working Classes in England in 1844*. The two men were a great contrast: Engels pleasure-loving with an Irish mistress in Salford, Marx morose and interested not in people but ideas. The time spent in Paris was a formative period in Marx's life for when he left the city in 1845 he was a dedicated socialist interested in economics and the nature of history. It was in Paris that he reached his interpretation of history which sees economic factors as the cause of all historical change. He was also sure that he was he only true socialist and wished with Engels to begin the organisation of an international socialist movement.

When the 1848 revolutions broke out, Marx was commissioned by the Communist League to write a manifesto which was published in England and Germany. In it Marx followed the line that all history is the history of class struggles, the theory of Historical Materialism. In his view there was a growing gulf between the middle-class owners of capital and the many workers who owned nothing but their labour. He believed that factories were filled with the exploited proletariat and thought that the capitalist system would be undermined by the terrible crises which would disorganise production and create unemployment and famine. These crises would become more severe and frequent and end in the inevitable overthrow of the capitalist system. 'What the bourgeoisie produces above all is its own gravediggers. Its fall and the victory of the proletariat are equally inevitable. . . . The proletarians have nothing to lose but their chains. They have a world to win. Workers of the world unite.'

Karl Marx was now at the age of thirty in the prime of life. Schurz, later to be an

American senator, has given us a clear idea of Marx's personality. 'What he said was weighty, logical and clear but never have I met a man of such offensive, insupportable arrogance.' Marx never respected another man's arguments if they differed from his. He was expelled from Germany in July 1849 and as he was not allowed to live in Paris he moved to London, where he stayed the rest of his life.

The 1850s were for Marx a wretched period. Only three out of seven children survived the years of poverty in Soho and only Engels remained his friend and helped him to have articles published. Yet the years of exile in London were important in two ways. Marx elaborated the theory behind the Communist Manifesto into his great work *Das Kapital*, of which the first volume was published in 1867. Secondly, he managed to impose his views on the European socialist movement.

After a decade of reaction in the 1850s came a democratic upsurge with the Polish Revolt and Lincoln's Emancipation Proclamation. In September 1864, the International Working Men's Association was founded in London with delegates from France, Switzerland, Italy, Germany and Britain. Marx for a change showed tact in gaining a dominant position by directing operations behind the scenes and in drawing up the rules. He took a strong dislike to the Proudhonists (Anarchists), who were in his opinion 'mere windbags'. There now developed a conflict between the two major movements in the International.

Anarchism and Marxism

Pierre Joseph Proudhon was born at Besançon in 1809. He was of working-class stock and was in large measure self-taught. His interests became social and political and in 1840 he published a pamphlet entitled *What is Property?* His answer was 'Property is theft', and it became one of the most famous revolutionary phrases of the nineteenth century. Proudhon asserted that property was a cancer at the heart of society, not a natural right. In its place should be complete equality of reward.

Proudhon also opposed traditional forms of government. In his opinion, centralised government was a tyranny which must be broken by the workers and the bourgeoisie by organising syndicates which they would control and manage. The syndicates would be the basis of a new society in which people would rule themselves in a system of non-government or anarchism. Thus Proudhon preached a doctrine of federation in which society would consist of small communities running their own affairs with little or no central administration. With the abolition of property and government, men would be free to develop the best part of their nature.

Proudhon's influence spread because of the impact of Michael Bakunin, the son of a Russian country gentleman. Lacking a cause to lead in Russia in his youth, Bakunin became a professional revolutionary and came to Paris in 1848, later suffering torture and exile in Siberia for four years. He wanted to destroy the Austrian Empire and create a free federation of Slav peoples. A giant of a man, passionate and generous, Bakunin saw the issues dividing Marx and Proudhon and took Proudhon's side. He declared war on all institutions—the state, capitalism, religion—which he believed hampered human growth, and founded a splinter group, the International Alliance for Social Democracy. Marx called its programme an empty rigmarole, fearing Bakunin's inspiring public presence and gift for galvanising a mass meeting. While Marx wanted an organisation to capture political power, Bakunin worked for a loose federal organisation to stimulate insurrections and thus dissolve authority. Marx saw no future except in the capture of the state and the setting up of the dictatorship of the proletariat after which he believed the State would wither away. Proudhon and Bakunin detested the centralised state, and aimed at extreme decentralisation and democracy. Bakunin ridiculed Marx as a 'state worshipper, triply so, as a Jew, a German and a Hegelian'.

He also conflicted with Marx over which classes were the right revolutionary material. He believed that true revolutionaries were those with nothing to lose; for example, the landless agricultural workers of Italy, Spain or Russia. Marx maintained that it was the industrial proletariat in advanced societies who would be the spearhead of the next revolution. Bakunin said that they were already enjoying the benefits of economic progress and therefore had a stake which they would not throw away. Marx believed that industrialisation and a middle-class revolution should precede the proletarian revolution, so that in certain countries of Europe such as Italy, Spain and Russia his ideas did not have much immediate impact as they seemed inappropriate in countries where industrialisation was still far behind several West European countries. In contrast Bakunin found much support in these countries, especially Spain, where his ideas dominated large sections of the Spanish workers such as the landless labourers of Andalusia and the textile workers of Catalonia.

Bakunin also went further than Marx in his belief of the need for violence to sweep away existing institutions, a violence which would regenerate ordinary people. This anarchy should be started by a group of young educated people who would inspire the people to acts of terrorism and revolution. This need for an élite is similar to Marx's, but it is the only point of contact between Marx and Bakunin. As well as disliking each other's ideas, they came to loathe each other, a development which was virtually inevitable when Marx refused to tolerate any rival in the international movement. He had been prepared to take Proudhon seriously but, as George Lichtheim comments, 'he seems to have regarded Bakunin's intervention as nothing more than a squalid nuisance'. In Marx's view, Bakunin lacked a proper theory or system, he was 'a Mahomet without a Koran', and therefore spread confusion in the movement. To the German Marx, Bakunin's support of pan-Slavism was also a detestable element.

The rift between the two factions in the international movement became clear at the Basle conference of 1869, and in 1872 Marx managed to expel Bakunin from the International. Yet this really represented Marx's failure to gain control of the whole international socialist movement and the first International virtually wound up its activities. Anarchism remained influential in France, Italy, Spain and Russia though by the 1870s it had become merely nihilistic with little of Proudhon's ideas remaining in it.

After his failure at the 1872 congress, Marx was never the same man again. His hopes of a German revolution had been dashed by Bismarck's victories and his health broke down through insomnia and a liver disease. Socialism was on the defensive in the 1870s and Marx sought to build up a stronger working-class party in Germany where he resented the influence of Lassalle. Lassalle wished to gain a broader franchise, which meant a degree of cooperation with Bismarck. Marx and Engels viewed such a policy as potentially demoralising. Therefore he sent his disciple Liebknecht to form an organisation which would split from Lassalle's party. In 1875, however, representatives of the two groups met at Gotha and merged into a single German Social Democratic Workers Union. Marx was furious as he believed Liebknecht should have settled for nothing less than total control, and he failed to see the real value of the union. Marx's final years were sad ones; he had to endure the death of his wife and his eldest daughter before he died in March 1883.

Marx's Importance

Engels made the funeral speech at Highgate cemetery. 'As Darwin discovered the law of evolution in organic matters, so Marx discovered the law of evolution in human history.' Marx's myth was based on the first volume of *Das Kapital*, published in Germany in 1867 and in Russia in 1872, later to be followed by two more volumes; but it was Engels who gave shape to orthodox Marxism and spread its ideas until his own death in 1895. It was he who made Marxism a rigid scientific doctrine, the doctrine of a casually determined process analogous to the scheme of Darwinian evolution; his linking of the two names of Marx and Darwin at Marx's graveside was quite deliberate.

Marx's influence on European thought was on many levels. His doctrine that all historical changes are to be explained in terms of economic causes has influenced methods of historical research and the social sciences. His doctrine of the class struggle and of the inevitable triumph of the working class made it immediately appealing to industrial workers. Marx inherited from Hegel the belief that history moved on a preordained course, but for Marx the change occurred through economic factors whereas Hegel believed that the key to change lay in the realm of ideas. At each stage of historical development, changes in the names of production caused a new class to take over. The feudal aristocracy made way for the bourgeoisie and in time the bourgeoisie would make way for the people. Once the proletariat had gained power, a new era of social justice would begin and the political authority of the state would die out, leaving Man free.

Marx believed that this process was inevitable because of certain features of the capitalist system. In his view, the labour force was being victimised by an organised system of robbery, for he believed in the labour theory of value—that is, the value of any commodity is measured by the labour expended on it. Therefore in a fair society the workers would receive in payment for its labour its equivalent in goods and services. This did not occur in the capitalist system as the employer kept hours long and wages low and therefore the workers created more goods than they received in wages, the surplus going to the employer as profit. As time went on, the workers would resent this more intensely.

Revolution approached inevitability because of another feature of the capitalist system. As industrialisation continued, small firms would be driven out as a process of concentration took place with control of the economic system vested in a few hands. This would make the issues of the class struggle crystal clear to the working classes, now swelled by the discontented lower middle class.

Thirdly, capitalism would be incapable of making the system work. Commercial crises would occur, each one worse than the last because of the effect of competition for profit. This would lead to economic anarchy with a period of boom being followed by a catastrophic slump. Therefore to Marx the end of the capitalist system lay in the logic of history.

The truth of the Marxian analysis has continued to be a matter of fierce debate. Surely in any issue, factors other than economic play a significant part—human talent or capacity for error, religious faith, geographical features and even sheer chance. 'The question of causation,' Gordon Craig remarked, 'is too complicated to permit us to claim that any single factor is always more important than others in determining the course of history.'

Marx also assumed that individuals would usually stay loyal to their own class, but in practice individuals and whole groups resolutely avoid conforming to a tidy Marxist pattern. The classic example is the attitude of the socialist parties on the outbreak of the First World War. Socialists in Germany, France, Russia and elsewhere found that their nationalism was far stronger than their desire for class solidarity.

Marx's ideas on economics can also be attacked. His theory of surplus value ignored hidden costs of production other than labour, such as administrative costs and interest payments which absorbed much of the profit that Marx asserted went to the employers. Nor did he appreciate the role of the entrepreneur as a risk-bearer and the role of profit as a reward for risk-taking. His belief that class warfare was inevitable was at best a half-truth. Already in Western Europe measures had been taken at government and factory level to improve the lot of the worker, even if much remained to be carried out.

Time has so far proved Marx wrong as the prophet of the inevitable proletarian revolution in Western Europe, where mixed economies—private enterprise and state socialism—have achieved considerable success. Proletarian revolutions have occurred in precisely those countries which Marx assumed would be least susceptible to revolution, like Russia and China, and no bourgeois industrialisation had taken place as the necessary prerequisite. The dictatorship of the proletariat in communist countries has not resulted in the withering away of the state, as Marx believed, but on the contrary it has led to the creation of new forms of totalitarian government.

That so many errors abound in the Marxian system has not detracted from its influence because Marxism has the messianic power and driving-force of a great religion. Behind the writings of Marx and Engels was the indignation at the squalor which Engels observed in Manchester and which Marx himself experienced in Soho. Marx's analysis of capitalism had a veneer of objectivity but in reality was a deep emotional response. In Schumpeter's phrase, it was 'preaching in the garb of analysis'. It became a substitute religion because working men could look forward to ultimate victory and a socialist millenium. As in Christianity, there is advance towards final salvation. George Lichtheim stresses the part Engels played in this development: 'Engel set the tone for a generation of Marxists and his interpretation of Marxism acquired canonical status.' He imported into Marxist thinking the cast-iron certainty that the stars in their courses were promoting the victory of the Socialist cause. It is small wonder that Marx's promise of sure salvation through social economy had tremendous appeal for the underprivileged and insecure.

Syndicalism

By 1900 an offshoot of anarchism threatened the position of orthodox socialism. Syndicalism, which took its name from the French word for labour union, *syndicat*, was a protest against the way in which European socialism was moving towards moderation, and represented a revival within socialism of the tendencies inherent in the 'libertarian' doctrine of Proudhon and his followers. Syndicalists argued that the emancipation of the workers would not be won by parliamentary action but by direct action to paralyse the economy through the use of sabotage and the strike. To this end, unions should eliminate activities such as the provision of friendly society benefits and organise on militant lines. Revolution would then become possible through the use of a general strike which would destroy the capitalist system.

The movement made headway in France through the work of Georges Sorel. That Sorel developed as a revolutionary after 1871 was determined by events in France. He saw decadence everywhere in the materialistic Third Republic and was converted to Marxism in 1893, but he came to believe that history was made by spontaneous movements which arose periodically in the masses. In 1898 he published *L'Avenir socialist des syndicats*, in which he affirmed that the syndicalist movement was for him the authentic manifestation of the revolutionary proletariat. Sorel also became involved in the Italian political and intellectual scene between 1903 and 1910, trying to demonstrate the need for catastrophic revolution through revolutionary syndicalism. For a time his views gained ground in a variety of groups. Arturo Labriola, the founder of Italian syndicalism and a professor of political economy in Milan, ran a workers' weekly paper, helping to foment a general strike in 1904. A strong anarcho-syndicalist group grew up under Filippo Corridoni and influenced Mussolini in the ways of applied violence.

But syndicalism gained more success in France. The *Confédération Générale du Travail* (CGT), founded by the anarchist Fernand Pelloutier, was syndicalist from the beginning, formally adopting a militant line in 1906. In Spain anarcho-syndicalism led to bitter and violent strikes. Here a federation of syndicalist unions, the *Confederación Nacional del Trabajo* (CNT), was founded in 1910 and by the post-war period had gained over one million members.

The Socialist Dilemma

Despite the growth of syndicalism, the main energies of most socialist movements in the late nineteenth century were spent in the political field, a major objective being that of strengthening their parliamentary position. Though Marxist in inspiration, as most of the socialist parties were, there were severe disputes over doctrine and tactics. The most serious was over revisionism. Many socialists became concerned at the continued progress of the capitalist system in spite of Marx's prediction of its imminent collapse. The German Social Democrat Edouard Bernstein wrote a book in 1899 called *Evolutionary Socialism*, in which he looked forward with confidence to greater prosperity and a more equitable distribution of wealth. He therefore engaged in a wholesale onslaught upon every aspect of the Marxist system. As the capitalist system was manifestly not on the point of collapse, said Bernstein, socialists should change tactics if not goals. Like the Fabians in England, they should attempt an evolutionary as opposed to a revolutionary course. In other words, socialists should work within the system using the democratic processes. This belief was shared by many socialists who saw that a policy of non-cooperation would condemn the movement to many years of futile opposition, whereas working within the system would at least bring useful, if piecemeal, reform.

The revisionist point of view was attacked by orthodox Marxists. V. I. Lenin, in *What is to be Done?* condemned the revisionists for their parliamentary tactics and insisted on the need for a revolutionary élite. The debate between the revolutionaries and the gradualists racked the socialist movement in almost every country down to 1914. In Germany, Bernstein was attacked by Bebel, Rosa Luxemburg and Kautsky. In France, Jean Jaurès, having turned to revisionism, was criticised by Guesde and in Russia Martov and Lenin broke over the nature of the party.

Marxism remained official policy of the continental socialist parties but it was sound and fury signifying nothing. In practice, they pursued revisionist tactics while condemning revisionist theory. They accepted working within the system while proclaiming a belief in the class struggle and the inevitability of revolution, a mistaken policy because it increased the hostility of the ruling class. 'In effect,' says G. D. H. Cole, 'West European socialism, whatever it called itself, was a reformist, not a revolutionary movement.'

Socialism and War

Despite this great dilemma over tactics, a new international organisation had been started in 1889, the Second International. It helped to forge links between the various socialist parties and in 1900 it set up a bureau in Brussels to coordinate policy. One issue on which it attempted to create a socialist public opinion was that of war. For years the International proclaimed its opposition to war and its determination to prevent it.

However, even the leaders were not entirely consistent in their opposition to war. Jaurès, like many other socialists, believed that in certain circumstances a war of national defence was justified, and in Germany Bebel spoke for many German socialists when he declared that war to defend Germany against tzarist Russia would be necessary. Thus when the International at its congress of 1907 tried to make a bold declaration against war, it was unable to give any clear idea of the means by which the outbreak of war might be prevented. When war broke out in 1914, socialists demonstrated national loyalty rather than class solidarity, with the exception of a small and courageous minority including Keir Hardie and Bernstein. The Second International did not survive the war.

Despite this failure, socialism through the spread of universal suffrage and the growth of the industrial proletariat was now a formidable mass movement, imposing enough to alarm governments. As it gained in strength, it provided the new proletariat with the hope that one day a more just and peaceful society would be created.

Further Reading

Cipolla, C. M. (ed.), *The Fontana Economic History of Europe* (Vols 3 and 4), Fontana, London, 1973.

Hampden-Jackson, J., *Marx, Proudhon and European Socialism*, English Universities Press, London, 1957.

Landes, D. S., *The Unbound Prometheus*, Cambridge UniversityPress, Cambridge, 1970.

Lichtheim, G., *Marxism*, Routledge and Kegan Paul, London, 1971.

Questions

1. Which factors stimulated technological advance in Europe in the nineteenth century?
2. Account for the improvement in living standards in Western Europe in the late nineteenth century.
3. What were the essential differences between Anarchism and Marxism?
4. What criticisms would you make of Marx's ideas?
5. What were the chief problems facing Socialism in the final decades of the nineteenth century?

CHAPTER THREE

SHAM-CONSTITUTIONALISM IN GERMANY 1871–1914

Bismarck as Imperial Chancellor

Otto von Bismarck was born in 1815 of a Junker family. His background made him despise the masses and democracy. Aided by diplomatic circumstances, he had been the chief architect of a united Germany, using a mixture of boldness and cunning. Now he faced the task of giving his new creation the security for which he craved and for which he was to strive for the next 20 years with mixed success.

On the surface, Bismarck was a typical burly Junker. He had been a keen sportsman and a man of animal appetites, proclaiming that his ambition was to smoke 100,000 cigars and to drink 5,000 bottles of champagne. This was a façade, however, and can partly be explained by his upbringing. A strong mother had given him brains but not love and therefore he copied his more earthy father. Underneath the solid image of Iron Chancellor, Bismarck was a neurotic, once admitting, 'I am all nerves; so much so that self-control has always been the greatest task of my life and still is'.

There was indeed a latent violence in Bismarck which was to be evident in his handling of domestic affairs in Germany after 1871. He was often vindictive and always dominating; he loathed the existence of any rival authority in German life. 'The single dominating impulse throughout his career,' writes W. N. Medlicott, 'was the exercise of power.' He was to ensure that other ministers remained subordinates in a very real sense. Before 1878 he insisted on signing every document in person. All contact between other ministers and the Kaiser was strictly prohibited 'without my express consent, unless that consent is self-evident'. If ministers were of independent mind, they were dismissed, and this, combined with his overwhelming influence over William I, gave Bismarck an unprecedented position of authority in Germany.

Bismarck's control of affairs after 1871 can be criticised for a lack of that restraint which he continued to demonstrate in foreign affairs. In part this was caused by overconfidence in the strength of his position, a confidence shown by his long absences from Berlin—for example, a six months' stay on his estates at Varzin after the War Scare of 1875. Another factor which made him violently irascible was poor health. He suffered from neuralgia, toothache and stomach troubles and he had a serious weight problem for he was 18 stones in 1881. His inability to sleep well, combined with the frustration caused by opposition, gave him a severe nervous twitch which he hid by growing a beard. For these reasons the Iron Chancellor conducted politics with little of his former tactical deftness but rather with a rough heavyhandedness.

The Constitution and Parliament

Bismarck's position of authority was safeguarded in the constitution of the new Empire. The Empire was a federal state, its powers and functions divided between the federal government and the 25 states which it comprised. While no longer sovereign or free to secede, the states preserved their own constitutions, rulers, parliaments and administrative systems. They were free to legislate for a wide variety of local matters, including raising their own taxation. But the federal government controlled the armed forces and was responsible for foreign policy, civil and criminal law, banking, press regulations and taxation for imperial purposes. Some of the federal rights were exercised by the monarch, who appointed the chancellor and was head of the army, others were shared with the Federal Council (the Upper House).

A summary of the constitution, however, disguises the extent of Prussian domination, a domination which was to last until 1933. Prussia possessed two thirds of German territory and three fifths of the population, whereas her closest rival, Bavaria, had only one quarter of her territory and one fifth of her population.

Constitutionally, Prussian dominance was secured in two ways: (a) the King of Prussia was to be hereditary head of the empire, controlling civil administration through the chancellor and the army through a military cabinet; (b) Prussia had sufficient voting power in the Federal Council to block any unwelcome constitutional amendment. She possessed 17 out of the 58 votes, as against Bavaria, the next highest, with 6. Since no less than 17 small states in this body possessed only one vote, Prussia could in practice usually secure a majority.

Bismarck, already Prussian Prime Minister and Foreign Minister and now Imperial Chancellor, exercised many of the powers ascribed to the Crown in the Constitution. He presided over the Federal Council, which was more a collection of state delegates than an upper chamber, regulated disputes between states, prepared legislation for the *Reichstag* (the Imperial Parliament), and possessed the right, with his monarch's consent, to dissolve that body.

The parliament was elected by universal manhood suffrage and had considerable powers. However, as a class, German politicians failed to exploit to the full the potentialities of the *Reichstag* as an instrument for political and social change. They could have withheld their consent to legislation or supplies in order to establish the supremacy of parliament through an imperial ministry responsible to parliament. The power to make federal law belonged to both the *Reichstag* and the Federal Council, yet in practice only Bismarck and the Federal Council drafted legislation and the *Reichstag* merely approved it.

The *Reichstag* also had the right to interpellate ministers or raise a debate on foreign and colonial issues, but as with the initiation of legislation, Bismarck found little in the way of opposition. Finally, the *Reichstag* had the right of voting supplies. The constitution provided that all federal income and expenditure must be proposed and presented to the *Reichstag* in an annual budget for approval, yet the *Reichstag's* financial powers became inadequate, with military expenditure, for example, being approved for seven-year periods in 1874, 1881 and 1887.

The nature of the Prussian state government also assisted authoritarianism. The king's position was buttressed by an entrenched ruling class which held an important share of the leadership in the civil service and army. The Junkers also dominated the Prussian parliament because of the three-class franchise which, by making an elector's voting strength dependent on the amount of taxes he paid, produced a permanent right-wing majority. The first class might consist of only 5 or 6 voters, the second class of between 50 and 60, the third class of between 500 or 600; as each class had equal weight, a wealthy man's vote might be worth a hundred times as much as the vote of an ordinary wage earner. Open voting permitted the use of intimidation. In time there was even more distortion of the Prussian state parliament as a reflection of public opinion because there was no redistribution of seats to take into account the shifts of population brought about by the growth of towns. The virtual disfranchisement of the propertyless majority in Prussia was inevitably a standing grievance on the Left and contributed to the growth of its more extreme policies.

The new German Empire has been described as a compromise between Prussian particularism and German nationalism, between absolutism and constitutionalism, with Bismarck giving a democratic franchise as a concession to the liberals; but the veneer of liberalism was very thin and in reality the constitution was tilted in favour of Prussian authoritarianism. For this reason Max Weber, Germany's leading sociologist, described the Bismarckian system as 'sham-constitutionalism'. German historians on the Left, like Arthur Rosenberg, have viewed this as the factor dooming the German Empire to ultimate failure. Nevertheless, it would be wrong to write off the *Reichstag* completely. Bismarck found it necessary to use parliamentary methods and win a majority in the *Reichstag* by close cooperation with one or more of the leading parties. He viewed the *Reichstag* as a safety valve and as a sounding-board for ideas and propaganda. Despite its failures, it was an indispensable link in the legislative process, debating, changing and sometimes defeating legislation.

The political parties in the *Reichstag* fell into six main groups:

(1) On the far right were the Conservatives, representing the Prussian landowners who were closely associated with the Lutheran Church. In foreign affairs they upheld the traditions of the Holy Alliance, which meant a policy of monarchical solidarity with Russia and Austria–Hungary against revolution.

(2) The Free Conservatives had landowning interests at heart like the Conservatives but there was also a significant big business element.

(3) The Centre Right was formed by the National Liberals, the party of big business supported by most of the Protestant middle classes. In practice they were more national than liberal. Only occasionally did they fight for parliamentary control of the executive because they had come to terms with Bismarck's authoritarian state in return for the blessings of unity, prosperity and national greatness. Many National Liberals were later to be members of the Pan-German League, advocating imperial expansion and the creation of a large navy.

(4) In the middle of the political spectrum, and after 1890 often holding the balance of power in the *Reichstag*, was the Centre Catholic party pledged to defend the interests of the Roman Catholic Church against the anti-clericalism of the liberals and the atheism of the Social Democrats. Socially it represented a cross-section of the population from the nobles of South Germany to the peasants of the Rhine and the miners of the Ruhr.

(5) Left of centre were the radicals, who had formed the Progressive party. Its unity was uncertain and though it opposed Bismarck on constitutional principles it was often drawn to support the government on specific issues like foreign policy. It drew its support from the middle-class intelligentsia, small businessmen and artisans.

(6) Further left was the Social Democratic party, drawn from the rapidly growing industrial working class. Its programme combined Marx's revolutionary ideology with a demand for comprehensive social reform. In foreign affairs it supported closer ties with the western liberal states and shared Marx's hatred of Russia. The Socialists subscribed to the international ideals of socialism as embodied in the First and Second Internationals. In the *Reichstag* they adopted a stand of permanent opposition on principle.

Bismarck's domestic policies have never enjoyed a high reputation because of the way his imperious temper, which he failed to bridle, sent him on a collision course with several of the main forces in German life. We shall examine four chief areas of his domestic work: (a) the struggle with the Roman Catholic Church (the *Kulturkampf*); (b) his reaction to the growth of socialism; (c) his treatment of national minorities; (d) colonies.

The Liberal Era and the *Kulturkampf*

In the early years after the founding of the Empire, Bismarck believed that because the strongest divisive forces were among the princes and state governments, the full use of the authority of the federal government was required. To this end he sought the cooperation of parliament, in which the National Liberals were dominant with 155 seats and could form a majority either with the Free Conservatives or the Progressives. Relations were never easy between the National Liberals and Bismarck but they did see eye to eye on economic measures up to 1879; for example, free trade and the founding of a central bank. The government and the liberal majority also worked together on the creation of a unified system of law. The two sides clashed whenever matters came under discussion which touched directly on the discretionary authority of the government. The liberals had to make major concessions, the most important of which was over the military budget. In 1874 the government presented a military law which laid down the figure of 401,659 men as the permanent strength of the army, which would be automatically financed by federal expenditure. This would have made the right of parliament to approve the budget practically meaningless, especially since four fifths of all federal expenditure was spent on the army. The National Liberals shrank from a conflict on the issue, which was all too similar to the great crisis which had brought Bismarck to power in Prussia in 1862. Furthermore, they knew that the army was immensely popular after its recent victories and that the government through its control of the press could influence public opinion on the matter. All that Bismarck would offer the liberals was a septennial law; federal military expenditure was to be presented to and approved by parliament once every seven years. This diminution of parliamentary power was serious. As Hajo Holborn stresses, 'The loss of the full right of budget approval blocked the growth of a parliamentary system in Germany.' The liberals mistakenly thought that time was on their side. William I's age seemed to make an early succession of the liberal Crown Prince Frederick likely and it was assumed that he would inaugurate a liberal era. Of course, William failed to oblige the liberals, living on until 1888!

In 1872 Bismarck and the liberals joined in a common fight against the Roman Catholic Church. From 1863 Pope Pius IX had been denouncing liberal principles and in 1870 the Vatican announced the dogma of papal infallibility; his *ex cathedra* decrees in matters of faith and morals were declared to be infallible. Both Bismarck and the liberals believed that the individual should give his undivided loyalty to the state and found it inconceivable that devout Catholics should accept the prior authority of a foreign ecclesiastical power. German Catholics now faced much enmity just at the time when, through the exclusion of Austria from the old German Confederation in 1866, they became a minority; there were now twice as many Protestants as Catholics in Germany. Therefore in 1870 German Catholics formed a new political party, the Centre Party, to defend the interests of the Catholic Church. They wanted a firm guarantee of the freedom of the Roman Catholic Church in the new German Empire. Bismarck was irritated by their demands and his fighting instincts were aroused by the appearance of a strong party which seemed to threaten his untrammelled leadership and to form the spearhead of a powerful opposition.

In 1871 the Centre Party won 57 seats, making it the second largest party. Its political weight was enhanced by its alliance with minority groups and it possessed in its leader, Ludwig Windthorst, the most brilliant politician with whom Bismarck had to deal in domestic politics.

In 1872 the Jesuit order was banned in Germany but the full attack on the Roman Catholic Church gained momentum in 1873. Adalbert Falk, Prussian Minister of Ecclesiastical Affairs, was the protagonist of an aggressive policy and between 1873 and 1875 he was responsible, with Bismarck's support, for the May Laws. The chief clauses were: (1) appointments of priests were now dependent on regular attendance at a German high school and university, the aim being to minimise all training by church schools so that the priests were sufficiently imbued with national ideals; (2) the state could veto unsuitable ecclesiastical appointments; (3) Papal jurisdiction over the Catholic Church in Prussia was ended and the state was to control matters of church discipline (a royal court was set up with powers to dismiss recalcitrant clergy); (4) there was to be lay inspection of schools; (5) civil marriage was made compulsory.

Catholic reaction was swift. The Pope denounced such legislation and German Catholics refused to recognise the validity of the May Laws because they had not even been consulted. Catholic opinion was solid too, with only 30 out of 10,000 priests submitting. Government reaction was severe with full enforcement of the laws. By 1876 all bishops in Prussia had been imprisoned or driven abroad. Of 4,600 Catholic parishes, 1,400 were without a priest by 1877, with the laws being enforced with particular harshness in Prussian Poland. The rebel group of 'Old Catholics', which was led by Dr Ignaz von Döllinger and rejected papal infallibility, failed to make any headway. In contrast, the Centre Party in the *Reichstag* grew from 58 to nearly 100 in the 1874 elections.

Bismarck's policy proved to be both futile and dangerous. On an international level it contributed to a deterioration in Franco–German relations and at home it created a deep and lasting mistrust of the government among German Catholics. Germany was divided along denominational lines again and, in particular areas like Alsace–Lorraine and Prussian Poland, existing aversion to Germany increased. Bismarckian persecution did not weaken the Church one whit; it experienced a new unity, deriving a new spiritual strength from its ordeal.

Bismarck had hoped that the *Kulturkampf* would put him at the head of a popular national Protestant crusade but he had exaggerated the dangers which the Catholics posed to the unity of the empire and his irritability created fresh sources of opposition; an opposition whose faith and strength he entirely failed to comprehend.The Roman Church, C. Grant Robertson once remarked, could not be beaten like a foreign army: 'Its capital was everywhere, planted in the consciences of millions of its communion.' The whole affair became an object lesson in the limitations of power. What is particularly inexcusable is that many of the objectives of the *Kulturkampf*, such as lay control of education, could have been won without a war against the Church, as was demonstrated in Austria–Hungary in the very same years.

Bismarck was soon made to realise what a hornets' nest he had stirred up. When a young Catholic cooper tried to murder him in 1874 the Iron Chancellor came to his senses. He saw the dangers of continuing the feud, especially as criticism of his policies had come not only from Catholics but from the Prussian Protestant Conservatives because his legislation had limited the influence of Protestant churches as well as that of the Catholic Church. He also wanted the Catholic Centre on his side against a potentially worse enemy, socialism. When, therefore, Pius IX died in 1878 and the more conciliatory Leo XIII became Pope, Bismarck welcomed the opportunity to change the direction of his policy. Falk was relieved of his post, ousted bishops were reinstated and all religious orders were allowed to function except the Jesuits. The Church was to have complete control of the education of its own priesthood. This process took ten years and finally all that remained of the May Laws were state supervision of schools, the anti-Jesuit law and obligatory civil marriage.

The Turning-point of 1879 and the Attack on Socialism

Bismarck's retreat over the *Kulturkampf* coincided with a change in his attitude to the National Liberals. In 1877 they had intimated to him that their future cooperation would be dependent upon concessions on his part in the form of ministerial appointments and a voice in policy determination. Bismarck offered their leader, Rudolf von Bennigsen, the post of Vice-Chancellor, but Bennigsen would only enter the government on condition that two more National Liberals, both on the left wing of the party, were appointed. Bismarck refused and in the next year his annoyance with the liberals increased when they voted against his anti-socialist legislation.

In 1879 Bismarck brutally ended the alliance with the liberals by bringing in protection. His motives for this move were various. First, no doubt he wished to free himself of all dependence on the liberals. Using the gutter press, Bismarck had them denounced as Jews and protectors of socialism. Second, he also approached the question of protection for financial reasons. Federal revenue was gathered partly from customs, partly from the contributions of the individual states. Bismarck disliked having to rely on the latter source of revenue as it gave the states more influence. An increase in tariffs would make him more independent of them. In any case, more revenue would be needed to cover increasing federal expenditure on defence and welfare. Third, there was considerable pressure on economic grounds for bringing in tariffs. By the late 1870s Russia, Austria and France had all set up highly protective tariffs and only Britain and the smaller European countries retained free trade. Agitation for protection had come from German industrialists who felt the pinch of competition from British iron and Alsatian textiles.

Of more influence was the change of attitude of the German landowners. While Germany was still an exporter of cereals they had supported free trade, but in the 1870s the German agrarian sector lost its markets in Britain and France because of the flood of cheap American wheat. Indeed, the home market itself was now invaded by imported grain from the United States, Russia and Hungary. Grain prices fell sharply after 1873 and now the landowning interest clamoured for protection along with big business.

Bismarck, a landowner himself and already anxious to broaden his support in the *Reichstag*, sought the opportunity to ingratiate himself with the landlords of the Conservative party and the industrialists in the Free Conservative party by bringing in tariffs. These two groups, combined with a more friendly Centre Party, would become his natural allies in the task of crushing socialism.

In 1869 a new socialist party was formed, the Social Democratic Party

(S.P.D.), which aimed at a radical change of the existing social order but through legal methods. In 1874 the party won 9 seats in the *Reichstag* and in 1877 12 seats, polling 9 per cent of the votes. The party was in no way a threat to the existing order but Bismarck's reaction to its growth was extreme. He was most apprehensive of revolution and socialism after the Paris Commune of 1871 and the rise of nihilism in Russia. He became convinced of the need to suppress the socialist movement in Germany and made cynical use of a pretext which occurred. In May 1878 a half-witted apprentice plumber with anarchist leanings, Max Hödel, made a vain attempt on the life of William I. He had no connection whatsoever with the S.P.D. but this did not prevent Bismarck from presenting a bill banning the party. The bill was defeated as only the Conservatives supported it but a few days later a demented individual, Dr Karl Nobiling, made a second attempt on the emperor's life, wounding him seriously. Although Nobiling, who committed suicide, had no connection with the S.P.D. either, Bismarck dissolved the *Reichstag* and in an anti-socialist election campaign socialism was presented as a real menace. The campaign succeeded and politics swung to the right. Together the Conservatives and Free Conservatives commanded 115 seats in the new *Reichstag* and could form a majority with either the Centre Party or the National Liberals, who had been compelled to promise an excited electorate an anti-socialist law.

The government was now able to introduce such a law; all socialist or communist associations, meetings and publications could be forbidden or dissolved. The government was empowered to restrict the right of assembly and to expel persons endangering public peace. The law took a heavy toll of the Social Democratic position. In the next twelve years 1,350 publications were suppressed, 900 people expelled and 1,500 imprisoned under the law, which inevitably aroused great bitterness. However, it failed in its objective of stamping out socialism. By 1890 the Socialist vote had trebled and by 1912 the S.P.D. was to become the biggest party in the *Reichstag* with four and a half million votes. Socialists found many ways of evading the law through secret meetings and if evicted from one area would agitate no less in the area to which they went, with the result that socialist propaganda was spread to places where it had not reached before. Exiled leaders continued to make a contribution from Switzerland, where party congresses were held. It was decided to erase the words 'with every legal means' from their statement of aims but this did not mean that the party now aimed at anarchy or revolution, merely a greater degree of agitation.

Bismarck had blundered. His policy had seriously retarded the integration of the growing working class in the new Empire and he had again been guilty of overestimating the danger of the opposition and underestimating its resilience. His repression contributed to a greater solidarity in the socialist movement. As with similar movements in other countries, the German S.P.D. faced the question of whether to follow a gradualist policy or resort to extremism. This socialist dilemma inevitably split the movement into factions. Bismarck's repression drove the two factions together because, as William Carr stresses, the anti-socialist law had the same traumatic effect on socialists as the May Laws were having on German Catholics. Socialism became a secular religion and the party experienced a new unity of purpose.

Bismarck was too shrewd a politician to rely on repression alone. He realised the legitimate grievances of the workers and tried to use state intervention to help them with the objective of killing socialism by kindness. Three laws were passed to protect workers against the main threats to their working capacity: sickness, accident, incapacity and old age. In 1883 a law introduced health insurance for many wage earners. The cost was divided between employers and workers, one third to be paid by employers and two thirds by workers. In 1884 a law on accident insurance was passed. Bismarck wanted to make a federal contribution to this insurance as a demonstration of government goodwill but the liberals opposed the move. The whole cost was borne by the employers. The third law, introducing old age and disability pensions, was not passed until 1889. Old age pensions were only paid after the seventieth year, an age which few people could expect to reach. This time the federal government did make a contribution as well as employers and employees.

Although a significant development, the practical value of these schemes was only to appear after a number of years and did not allay socialist hostility. Socialists believed that their interests would be better served by the return of trade union rights so that they could bargain freely for a living wage. Government intervention, they said, would be more useful improving working conditions in factories. On this issue Bismarck was adamant in his refusal and factory legislation only came in in 1891. The breach between the workers and other social classes continued to widen and for this Bismarck bears heavy responsibility.

The fact that Bismarck's state socialism failed in its political purpose should not, however, detract from its intrinsic merits. The system of social security that he built was the first of its kind in Europe and formed the foundations of the modern welfare state. W. N. Medlicott rightly praises Bismarck on this score: 'This programme is his greatest claim to statesmanship in the last decade of his career, for it offered a constructive and imaginative solution of an explosive situation.'

The Treatment of National Minorities

Little praise can accrue to Bismarck on the question of national minorities. The creation of a strong Prussia in the eighteenth century and a united Germany by Bismarck's three wars had resulted in the existence of several dispossessed minorities. In North Schleswig were the Danes. In the 1866 Treaty of Prague, Prussia had promised to hold a plebiscite in North Schleswig so that the population could decide whether to stay as part of Prussia or return to Denmark. This promise was never fulfilled and in 1879 Bismarck persuaded the Austro–Hungarian government to abrogate this particular clause. The result was strained relations with Denmark and the permanent opposition of the Danes of North Schleswig.

Bismarck felt a particular dislike for the Poles, especially as they were Roman Catholic and his opponents during the *Kulturkampf*. He tried to crush them by depriving them of their national leadership, which in his opinion was provided by the clergy and nobility. The primate of the Roman Catholic Church in Prussian Poland, Cardinal Ledochowski, was imprisoned and his see kept vacant for twelve years. German became the language of education, even in Polish village schools. Alarmed by the large Polish population increases, Bismarck in 1886 expelled 34,000 Poles who had filtered in from Russia and Austria. A fund was set up for the Prussian government to buy up the estates of Polish landowners when they fell under foreclosure and to transfer them to German ownership. The Poles, however, continued to be more prolific and kept back the German settlers by better agricultural techniques. Polish national feeling remained strong and was particularly vigorous among the growing middle class. The struggle, says Medlicott, 'further advertised the tendency to ultimate violence in Bismarck's policies.'

The most important minority problem was Alsace–Lorraine with its 1½ million population, three quarters of whom were Roman Catholic. It was not one of the federal states but merely a federal province under direct imperial rule. In 1874, the people of Alsace–Lorraine were given the right to elect deputies for the *Reichstag* but since there was no state government, Alsace–Lorraine had no representation on the Federal Council. This subordinate position created and made permanent among the people of Alsace–Lorraine the feeling that their land was merely a province of the empire. Emigration into France was heavy; between 1871 and 1914 more than 400,000 people left Alsace–Lorraine. Alsatian deputies protested at the annexation and opposed Bismarck in his contest with the Roman Catholic Church.

In 1879 a governor of Alsace–Lorraine was appointed to represent the emperor and a good choice was made in Field Marshal Edwin von Manteüffel, a humane and educated man who made great efforts to win over public opinion including the revival of Strasbourg University. This was not enough. Alsatians disliked the German monopoly of civil service posts and the garrisoning of large numbers of troops in the province. When Manteüffel died in 1885, Bismarck chose as governor the diplomatic Prince Chlodwig von Hohenlohe, but Alsatian opinion was not appeased. Alsace–Lorraine sent 15 deputies to the *Reichstag* and with the other national minorities formed a group holding nearly ten per cent of the seats. The group's attitude towards Bismarck was one of unrelenting hostility.

The Fall of Bismarck

Bismarck's position as actual ruler of Germany was based on the fact that William I gave him his full confidence. The emperor died in March 1888 at the age of 91. His successor, Frederick III, was already gravely ill with cancer of the throat and had lost his speech. Bismarck remained in full control until June, when the 29-year-old Prince William succeeded his father. William was not prepared to play second fiddle to Bismarck and his personal friends, who were very influential with him, were all hostile to Bismarck, notably Friedrich von Holstein and Count Philip Eulenburg. William would be acting within his constitutional rights in dismissing the chancellor and moreover such a move would win the support of large sections of public opinion. Bismarck had stayed in office only because of the support of three emperors, not because he consistently won fresh triumphs or pleased the majority of the electorate. So from his accession William had Bismarck's dismissal in mind. 'I will give the old man six months' breathing space, then I will rule myself,' he said.

William and Bismarck soon clashed over two issues: the treatment of the socialists and foreign policy. In 1890 the anti-socialist law was due for renewal. Bismarck wished to insert a clause for the expulsion of agitators with no time limit and to make the law permanent. In the *Reichstag* he clashed with the National Liberals and Free Conservatives over it. He refused to compromise, but William, who had already proposed a programme abolishing Sunday work, wished to be known as the poor man's emperor and disagreed with him. A stormy interview took place in March in which an altercation on foreign policy also occurred and Bismarck nearly threw an inkpot at William's head. William was opposed to the renewal of the Reinsurance Treaty which Bismarck desired and Bismarck enraged him by allowing him to see a letter from the Tzar in which he referred to William as 'un garçon mal élevé et de mauvaise foi'. The old chancellor resigned and spent his last years up to his death in 1898 bitterly criticising his successors.

By 1890 Bismarck's autocracy had become intolerable and his attempts to reduce the *Reichstag* to a talking-shop were much resented. He had been forced to use parliamentary methods but the general effect of his parliamentary strategy was to keep German parliamentary life incoherent. He wanted to preserve his own power, and to stay in office he played off the emperor against the *Reichstag*, bribed the press and prevented any one party becoming too strong, that is strong enough to direct policy. The electorate, therefore, had no choice between alternative governments, which is the essence of democracy. The alternative strategy of peaceful collaboration he never learned and his suspicion and combative outlook made it impossible to form relations of enduring trust with the party leaders. In short, he inhibited the growth of a workable system of responsible government.

Particularly damaging was his impact on the liberals. After the army reform crisis of 1862 he persuaded many of the Progressives to abandon the fight for parliamentary government and they accepted his constitutional authoritarianism, but a left-wing minority remained in opposition. Bismarck split the liberals for a second time when the National Liberals disagreed with Bismarck over the introduction of protection. A minority of the party seceded to join the Progressive party, which was soon in decline with the growth of socialism. In 1890 it held 76 seats, in 1912 only 42 seats. As Ryder indicates, 'the weakness of German liberalism left a significant gap in the country's political spectrum'.

Bismarck once commented thus on his relations with the national minorities: 'I regard them all as aliens and their treatment is a matter of war.' This suppressed violence was unfortunately part of his attitude to all groups in German life that did not conform to his wishes. His policies were essentially negative and divisive; his campaign against the Roman Catholic Church opened up new possibilities of denominational strife while his attack on socialism resulted in growing class divisions.

William II and the New Course

With the fall of Bismarck, William resolved to be his own chancellor but he was to demonstrate a lack of the application and patience needed for the continuous exercise of power. Germany entered a period of sporadic government punctuated by dramatic episodes when the emperor interfered directly. His personal rule was most evident up to 1908, at which point a humiliating *Daily Telegraph* interview caused his partial withdrawal from government, though not until the First World War did he withdraw virtually completely.

William had his good qualities. Full of energy, enthusiasm and good intentions, he possessed an inquiring mind but he was also an incurable dilettante, impulsive and easily persuaded by advisers to change his mind. He had become too accustomed to flattery, especially from his fellow officers during his period in the Potsdam guards, and, therefore, in A. J. Ryder's words, 'he combined the touchiness of a prima donna with the conceit of a spoilt child'. His authority was diminished by too many visits abroad and by too many ill-conceived speeches—for example, his call in the first three years for 'full steam ahead' on a new course after Bismarck's fall. Ministers had to spend a great deal of time trying to keep the emperor from committing blunders or, once they had happened, repairing the damage. William's biographer, Michael Balfour, emphasises William's verbosity. 'William's fluency in speaking meant that he approached all questions with an open mouth . . . he was constitutionally incapable of preventing himself from saying whatever came into his head, provided he imagined it would contribute to the effect which he was trying to make at that moment.' This theatrical, nervy individual was incapable of a sustained course of action and remained an amateur dabbling in matters whose significance he never really understood. Lacking a sense of reality he failed to see how his country's power could be effectively exerted. For all his gifts he remained a lightweight and was not up to the outsize job which destiny had assigned to him.

His pompous, nationalistic speeches aroused hostility abroad as the years wore on and were increasingly resented in Germany. Max Weber wrote in 1906: 'We are being isolated because this man governs us in this fashion and we tolerate and excuse it.' During his annual cruises rowdy parties were held in which practical jokes were considered high art. William amused himself by poking the ribs of elderly military men as they did physical jerks. One elderly general died of a heart attack after having to dress up as a ballerina to amuse the emperor.

William's eccentricities can be explained by his parentage. His father Frederick was overshadowed by his able wife Victoria, Queen Victoria's eldest daughter. She disliked Bismarck's Germany and Bismarck personally. William, brought up to be a Prussian patriot, admired Bismarck and resented his mother's attitude. His love-hate relationship with his parents extended to his mother's home country. He enjoyed visiting Queen Victoria in England and rushed to her bedside when she was dying but disliked his uncle, the future Edward VII. The two were in complete contrast, the nephew tense and assertive, the uncle relaxed and pleasure-loving but able to manage men. William was obsessively suspicious and jealous of Edward, who found his nephew insufferable.

Much of William's thinking was tinged with a brutal racialism and he regarded Houston Stuart Chamberlain as an ally, but the sufferings of his childhood explain this twisted part of his character. At his birth, a neck injury resulted in paralysis of the left arm and deafness in the left ear. The left side of his body remained weak and he had to be helped to dress by valets. There were certifiable lunatics among his ancestors on both sides of his family and the young prince, unable to use a knife at meals, faced psychological difficulties from the start. His mother grew exasperated with his infirmities even calling him 'cripple' to his face, sometimes in front of visitors. The military bearing which he was later to cultivate was merely a cover for an underlying lack of confidence which at critical moments became a complete loss of nerve.

With the fall of Bismarck, domestic politics in Germany became fluid and unpredictable. The complicated system of government created by Bismarck worked less smoothly under his successors, and a period of transition and extended crisis was ended only in 1897 with the establishment by William II of his 'personal rule' exercised through men of his own choice in key ministerial posts. (Tenniel's cartoon showing Bismarck as the dropped pilot was apt.) Germany now had a new pilot who was not sure where he intended to go but wanted to get there fast. The result was to highlight one of the main defects of the system, the reliance on the chancellor who needed to be exceptionally able. Bismarck's successors, lacking his prestige and talents, were unequal to the task. Nor was William the kind of ruler to allow the chancellor to govern without interference. In practice, German chancellors had too little real power and too many responsibilities. William listened to courtiers before them and they did not control the armed forces. When William's own blunders undermined his own prestige, no one knew where real authority lay in Germany. The classic case illustrating this was during the July crisis of 1914, when the Austrian foreign minister Berchtold received conflicting advice from the chancellor, Bethmann-Hollweg, and the army chief Moltke and was prompted to ask the historic question, 'What a joke! Who rules in Berlin, Bethmann or Moltke?'

The Chancellorship of Caprivi (1890–94)

William's first chancellor was General Leo von Caprivi who, although a man of commonsense and integrity, possessed limited experience in politics. He had to contend with the intrusion of others into his work, notably Bismarck in retirement and the grey eminence of the foreign minister, Baron Friedrich von Holstein. Norman Rich has shown that Holstein was neither so powerful nor so sinister as was once thought. He has been unfairly blamed for all the errors of foreign policy during his period of influence from 1890 to 1906, but he was responsible for the first vital mistake of these years, the non-renewal of the Reinsurance treaty with Russia.

The record of blunders in foreign policy was to some extent mitigated by the achievements of the New Course at home. Caprivi was more moderate than Bismarck and discontinued several of the Iron Chancellor's worst practices such as bribery of the press. A considerable measure of reform was introduced, including factory legislation, a reduction in tariffs and a progressive income tax. Caprivi resigned in 1894 after the rejection by the *Reichstag* of a stricter anti-socialist bill which had been brought in on William's insistence.

The Chancellorship of Hohenlohe and the Turning-point of 1897

Caprivi's successor was Chlodwig, Prince of Hohenlohe-Schillingsfürst. This liberal Catholic Bavarian magnate had had a long and distinguished career in government and was 75 years of age. He established an avuncular relationship with William and supported the policy of friendship with Russia, but he lacked energy and had no stomach for wrangling with the *Reichstag*. Although an obvious stopgap, Hohenlohe was retained until 1900 and his period as chancellor saw a further decline in the power of the office.

William immediately demonstrated his capacity for failing to learn by experience. He resumed his threatening attitude to the socialists, whom he dubbed 'fellows without a fatherland' and 'treasonable rabble' on account of their international ideals. An anti-strike bill was decisively rejected by the *Reichstag*, which proved its value as a guardian of popular liberties. William should have sought to reconcile the socialists to the Empire instead of trying to force a confrontation. With the S.P.D. becoming more moderate in the 1890s, an opportunity for reconciliation existed and was wasted.

According to J. G. Röhl it was in Hohenlohe's chancellorship that a decisive change occurred in the German government. William had worked uneasily with ministers after Bismarck's fall in 1890 and by early 1894 he had decided that it was his duty to restore unity to the government. Over the next three years he met with opposition from responsible statesmen but eventually he unseated the ringleaders of the opposition to his personal rule and replaced them with men of his own choice. By 1897 he had emerged as the decisive figure in the government and 'he dictated policy to an amazing extent in this period; all appointments, all bills, all diplomatic moves were made on his orders'. The keys to his victory were his control over appointments and the help of Eulenburg. Röhl sees 1897 as the decisive year in William's early reign. Only then did William achieve his aim of directing German policy as opposed to interfering in the schemes of men in office. Now with Tirpitz and Bulow he had advisers after his own heart. Tirpitz could construct a Grand Fleet and Bulow could pursue *Weltpolitik* (World policy). The road which Germany took in 1897 was in Röhl's view a fatal turning for it led to isolation, war, defeat and the collapse of the monarchy.

The growth of German global ambitions, the world policy, was indeed fateful for European peace. The new creeds of imperialism and racialism had become respectable in Germany with ideas borrowed from biology. The doctrine of the superiority of the Aryan race, of which the Germans were the élite, was borrowed from the writings of Houston Stuart Chamberlain and Heinrich von Treitschke. A new strident nationalism was developing which was preached by politicians, professors, journalists and various pressure groups. Three groups were of particular importance: the Colonial Society (founded in 1882), the Pan-German League (1890), and the Navy League (1898). The Pan-German League had the longest life and in the long run the most significance. By 1914 sixty members of the *Reichstag*, mostly National Liberals, belonged to the League. Its aims were to increase patriotism and to promote German culture and colonies abroad. It wanted a fair share of colonies for Germany, asserting that Britain and France had an unfair share. The activities of the League promoted distrust among other powers, especially when backed by the irresponsible remarks of Bulow and William. 'Germany demands her place in the sun,' stormed Bulow, while William, on the occasion of the 25th anniversary of the Empire, announced grandiloquently, 'Germany from a German Empire has become a World Empire.'

German ambitions were not solely outside Europe. The Pan-German League was most interested in the future of the German race in Europe, particularly the thirteen million Germans in the Habsburg monarchy. The League envisaged the inclusion in a united Germany of the German areas of Austria–Hungary—that is to say, Austria proper and Bohemia. It was hoped on the death of Francis-Joseph, 60 years old in 1890, that his Empire would break up and that the German provinces would then unite with Germany. The Pan-German League also followed the writer of the early nineteenth century, Ernst Moritz Arndt, in urging the incorporation into Germany of neighbouring peoples such as the Swiss, Belgians and Dutch.

The Navy League, with one million members and patronised by the government and Krupps, was most influential in a direct sense. It was an early example of a state-directed propaganda machine and was used to educate the German people to the idea of a new navy. Pressure for a large German navy had come from shipping and shipbuilding interests, liberals, economists and a new school of sociologists collected round Max Weber. It was a policy that captured the imagination of the emperor who exclaimed excitedly, 'The trident must be in our hands.' In 1897 he appointed Admiral Alfred von Tirpitz as Minister of Marine, who was to dominate naval policy from 1897 to 1917, supporting his plans with a ruthless clarity.

In March 1898, a new navy bill was passed for the creation of a large German navy. The building programme, which was to be completed by 1905, provided for 11 battleships, five large cruisers and 17 smaller ones. Tirpitz argued for a fleet not large enough to destroy the British fleet but able to do sufficient damage to it to make the British reluctant to accept battle. A second navy law was passed in 1900 for an even larger navy. It is difficult to exaggerate the importance of German naval development. Langer calls it one of the most dangerous of innovations. 'It helped tremendously to embitter Anglo-German relations and thereby to set the stage for the ultimate conflict.'

The Chancellorship of Bulow (1900–9)

Hohenlohe, tired of not being consulted at all on major issues like the expedition to China, resigned in 1900. Count Bernhard von Bulow, who succeeded him, had been foreign secretary since 1897. A cosmopolitan man, he was considered the ideal statesman to usher in modern world politics. His superficial brilliance hid a nature that loved bombast and drama as much as William himself. He was a courtier rather than a statesman, driven chiefly by his desire to enjoy the glamour of power and the company of the mighty. Bulow used any amount of flattery on William to safeguard his position. With William at his most assertive and Holstein still influential, it is small wonder that German government in this period committed many errors in foreign policy.

Bulow's career was ended by the fiasco of the *Daily Telegraph* interview. In October 1908 the *Daily Telegraph* published an account of an amazingly tactless interview with William II in which the emperor claimed that he was a good friend of England and had given the British staff the plan that had won the Boer War. The article aroused mild disdain in England and a storm of angry criticism in the German parliament and press. Bulow, who had actually seen the article prior to publication and should have stopped it, had to promise the *Reichstag* that he would guarantee more prudence on William's part in the future. William had to sign a declaration in which he promised to respect his constitutional responsibilities. The blow to his confidence was tantamount to a nervous breakdown and he now desperately craved revenge on 'that scoundrel Bulow'.

The opportunity soon occurred. Increased expenditure on the armed forces and social reforms had again exposed the federal weakness in finance. Bulow suggested an inheritance tax, the equivalent of British death duties. The Conservatives, Centre and the Polish parties combined to defeat the bill in June 1909, whereupon Bulow resigned fully aware that he no longer enjoyed the confidence of the emperor.

The Chancellorship of Bethmann-Hollwegg (1909–14)

William selected as his fourth chancellor the Minister of the Interior, Theobald von Bethmann-Hollwegg. Bethmann was an earnest, conscientious individual who knew little of foreign affairs, a sphere William treated as his own preserve. Bethmann was a persuasive mediator rather than a dominant personality. He was well aware of the limits of his power because of the situation in which he was the emperor's nominee yet still needed the cooperation of the *Reichstag*.

Bethmann undertook three major domestic tasks: the liberalisation of the Prussian franchise in 1910, the introduction of a new constitution for Alsace–Lorraine in 1911, and the reform of the federal budget in 1913. All three bills aroused considerable opposition and the reform of the Prussian franchise had to be abandoned.

Considering the pressure applied in these final years of peace by the *Reichstag*, its failure to make real constitutional gains indicates the impotence of German parliamentary life. No wonder the French socialist Jean Jaurès called the *Reichstag* a 'demi-parliament'. In practice, the old German ruling class still ruled, content to support a poseur like William II since they saw in an authoritarian monarchy the indispensable shield of their class privileges against the socialists.

For similar reasons the middle classes were equally convinced of the need for a strong monarchy. The growth of socialism did mean, of course, that a solution to this sham-constitutionalism could not be put off indefinitely. Yet though there was much political tension and frustration in Imperial Germany, so there was in other countries, and revolution was less likely here than elsewhere. It was to take four hard years of war to shake the deeply ingrained German respect for authority and make revolution possible.

The Influence of the Army

That Germany contrived to entangle herself in a major war is partly explained by the uneasy relationship between the civil and military authorities. The Head of the General Staff in practice ranked equally with the chancellor as adviser to the emperor. William on his accession detached the Naval High Command from the Imperial Admiralty and placed it directly under his command. The chief beneficiary of this naval reorganisation was Tirpitz, Chief of Staff to the Naval High Command, and soon to be Minister of Marine. Tirpitz played on his master's vanity on naval matters. 'Your Majesty can now be your own admiral.' William's policy of reducing civilian control of the armed forces widened the breach between the army and large sections of the public.

More seriously, the army pursued independence in matters of high policy. In 1891 Count Alfred von Schlieffen became Chief of the General Staff. Up to this point German plans for a war on two fronts had assigned the bulk of the army to the Russian front, where an offensive would be launched with defensive action against France. Schlieffen reversed these roles to concentrate in the West, believing that France could be knocked out of the war in a few weeks so that German forces could concentrate on the harder task of defeating Russia. The only way of defeating France quickly was by an outflanking movement through Belgium and Luxemburg, two countries guaranteed by the powers, including Germany. By 1897 the Schlieffen plan had been amended to take in these countries yet no politician objected to it despite the plan being, in Ritter's words, 'a daring, indeed an overdaring, gamble whose success depended on many lucky accidents.' Holstein himself remarked that German diplomacy should be adjusted to meet the needs of the General Staff in the matter. To quote Ritter again, 'to raise political objections to a strategic plan worked out by the General Staff would have appeared in the Germany of William II unwarranted interference in a foreign sphere.' Indeed, to Ritter the explanation of the German tragedy lay in the constitutional deformation which gave the Army a primacy in Germany. Germany became a state of soldiers and war rather than one of citizens and law. The army not only remained independent of any control other than that of the monarch himself. Through prolonged and universal military service it was able to influence the thinking of the greater part of the German nation. German society was one in which the upper classes were soaked in the ethos of the barrack square, in which social distinction was measured almost entirely by military rank. In such a society the military were allowed to interfere in diplomacy and subordinate the whole of national life to mobilisation timetables. The inability of the civilians to control the military was an important factor in the coming of the First World War.

Further Reading

Balfour, M., *The Kaiser and his Times*, Cresset Press, London, 1964.

Holborn, H., *A History of Modern Germany* (Vol. 3: 1840–1945), Eyre and Spottiswoode, London, 1965.
Medlicott, W. N., *Bismarck and Modern Germany*, English Universities Press, London, 1965.
Röhl, J. C. G., *Germany without Bismarck*, Batsford, London, 1967.
Ryder, A. J., *Twentieth Century Germany from Bismarck to Brandt*, Macmillan, London, 1973.

Questions

1. How was Prussian power safeguarded in the imperial constitution?
2. Account for the weakness of parliamentary life in Germany between 1871 and 1914.
3. Discuss Bismarck's handling of domestic affairs in Germany between 1871 and 1890.
4. 'Essentially a dabbler and an amateur.' Is this a fair assessment of William II?
5. Was 1897 a turning-point in German history?
6. Which pressure groups influenced the policies of the German Empire between 1871 and 1914?

CHAPTER FOUR

THE THIRD REPUBLIC IN FRANCE 1871–1914

Introduction

At first sight the Third Republic is one of the most confusing and paradoxical of political régimes. It was supposed to mark the advent of democracy, but in practice, as Theodore Zeldin notes, 'it gave power to an oligarchy of discredited professional politicians who maintained their dominance by placating the particularist interests of their more influential constituents and by closing their eyes to the corruption which surrounded them'. The long life of the régime is difficult to reconcile with its unprecedented instability. Since 1789, France had experienced virtually every possible form of government and this gave an unhealthy relativism to the French political process. In times of crisis there were always partisans of old régimes ready to call for radical change and this confirmed an impression of national instability. The impression was heightened by the endless succession of barely distinguishable ministries. Even when laws were enacted, as often as not they failed to be implemented.

Few Frenchmen in 1871 could have expected a life of 70 years for the new régime for it was born in the misery and humiliation of defeat and civil war.

The Siege of Paris and the Commune

The war which France so comprehensively lost in 1870 and early 1871 was especially bitter to the French because of the starving of Paris. After the defeat at Sedan on September 2, Prussian troops surrounded the city and gradually ground down resistance. To the injury of their bombardment of the city was added an appalling insult in January when the new German Empire was proclaimed in the Hall of Mirrors at Versailles. The combination of the two was to inject a special bitterness into Franco–German relations for the next 75 years. The efforts of Paris were of no avail. On January 27, 1871, an armistice was concluded with Bismarck. Worse was to come.

The uneasy truce between the extreme Republicans (called the Reds in moderate circles) and the government at the time of the proclamation of the Third Republic did not survive long. The extreme left started several newspapers which criticised the new government. Blanqui and Delescluze, two professional revolutionaries, represented proletarian opinion in Paris which was extremely belligerent. This left-wing patriotism, ardent and sincere, had a strongly particularist element to it. To the working classes Paris was France and had to be defended. The rest of the country, in their opinion, consisted of feudal landowners and reactionary peasants and clerics. Furthermore, the State had deprived Paris of self-governing institutions. It was administratively the most backward region in France in the sense that it had no mayor and no municipal independence. The prefect of police watched over it with an army of spies and agents. Yet Paris was the sacred city of revolution and, as memories were revived of the repelling of foreign invasion in 1792, demands were made for the rebirth of the Commune of Paris which, like its predecessor, would repeat the miracle.

As the Siege of Paris progressed, the gap between the bourgeoisie and the proletariat widened, for to the property-owning and commercial classes, the war as it dragged on was bound to be viewed as a waste of material assets. The left wing in Paris expected that the treacherous bourgeois would do a deal with the Prussians sooner or later. Clashes between the mob and bourgeois detachments of the National Guard took place in October and January during the Siege itself. The armistice arranged on January 27 was regarded as an act of treachery.

Proletarian anger increased in February, when elections for a new government were held. They resulted in a very conservative chamber which met at Bordeaux. More than 400 deputies were monarchists and there were only 150 genuine republicans. Republican Paris was outraged and felt betrayed by the provinces, especially as the head of the new government, Thiers, was known to have little sympathy for the workers. His first task was to conclude a peace treaty with Bismarck. The terms were harsh, as has been shown, but Paris was infuriated by the clause providing for a German triumphal march through the capital in return for the French retention of Belfort. When the new Assembly ratified the treaty, Paris again felt betrayed.

But the Assembly did not stop there. It passed two disastrous decrees which inflamed proletarian opinion even further. It decreed that all debts and rents on which a moratorium had been declared during the war were to be paid within 48 hours. Secondly, the pay of 1.50 francs a day to the National Guard was ended. The combined effect of the two decrees was to deal a heavy financial blow at hundreds of thousands of poor Parisians, including the lower middle-classes. On March 1, the Prussian troops marched through Paris. They were received by black flags, by silent streets and by a public day of mourning. When they left, bonfires were lit and the pavements scrubbed to purify the city. On March 10, the Assembly indicated its fear of the Paris population by deciding to reconvene at Versailles, not Paris.

The cumulative effect was to make the mood of Paris extremely ugly and the fact that the city was in one of its combatant moods was obvious. Thiers was concerned, as it was also heavily armed with 200 cannon. Feeling that it was necessary to show that the new government was master, he sent government troops into Paris on March 18 to recover the guns. The troops omitted to bring horses with which to tow the guns away. Huge crowds surrounded them and two generals, Lecomte and Thomas, were shot and mutilated as the regular troops deserted.

The incident made Thiers decide to evacuate all government troops from Paris and to make military preparations to retake it by force. This decision of Thiers has been strongly criticised by several historians. The Commune was not brought about by a real rebellion in Paris, writes Theodore Zeldin, it was brought about by the conservatives wishing to end the old problem of Parisian insubordination. Thiers 'determined not only to obtain the submission of the Parisians but to exterminate once and for all their intransigent radical opposition, the perpetual threat to all stability. It was this withdrawal of the government that created the Commune and made Paris autonomous for 73 days'. Left to themselves, the Parisians after their initial surprise elected a new municipal council, the Commune, on March 26.

The Commune of 1871 looked back to the Paris Commune of the 1790s which had helped to execute Louis XVI and set up the first French Republic. The Paris Commune was the real ruler of France during the Reign of Terror in 1793–94, and thus endeared itself to the Paris revolutionaries of 1871 to whom the ascendency of Paris over France was sacrosanct. The Commune of 1871 had no programme apart from asserting its own independence. This desire for independence combined with grievances against the Assembly and resentment of appalling social conditions to create a mood of revolt.

The Commune was composed of various groups. The biggest contingents were the Jacobins under Delescluze, who looked back to 1793, and the Socialists, under Blanqui, who wanted a society of small property owners. But there were many diverse groups and so from the first there was division. There were problems over leadership as Blanqui had been arrested and Delescluze, 62 years old, was ill after imprisonment on Devil's Island. Instead of using their temporary numerical superiority to attack Versailles, the Communards wasted time passing a flood of decrees. By early April Paris was under siege for a second time as government forces increased rapidly in number, helped by Bismarck's speedy return of 400,000 prisoners of war. Against trained troops the undisciplined Communards could only resort to their traditional method of setting up barricades.

The feature of the struggle that followed was its ferocity. The Communard Chief of Police, Rigault, was bitterly anticlerical and rounded up many priests, including the Archbishop of Paris. When government forces began to enter Paris in May all the prisoners were shot by the Communards, who also wreaked havoc on many of the city's most notable buildings, the Tuileries, the Hotel de Ville and out of spite, Thiers' own house. By May 25 they were leaderless, Delescluze, dressed as usual in top hat, frockcoat and cane, having died nobly on the barricades.

The government troops, who had begun to enter Paris proper on May 21, were really beginning mopping-up operations by May 26 as Communard resistance faded. The behaviour of the government forces was much worse than that of the Communards. Troops had orders to kill Communards who surrendered and any women carrying bottles were shot on sight as they were suspected of carrying petrol bombs. Atrocity piled on atrocity. Many Communards were burned alive in the streets of Paris and one Communard, Varlin, was beaten by rifle butts and half lynched by crowds. His face became a pulp and one eye was dangling out of its socket.

The Communards, knowing that no quarter would be given, fought desperately. Fifty hostages—gendarmes and priests—were massacred by them in drunken fury, one body receiving 70 bayonet thrusts. But in the main it was the Communards who were being massacred. In 'Bloody Week', May 21–28, over 3,000 were killed. Paris society wanted full revenge. Any slight evidence was enough for one to be shot; for example, a slight bruising on the right shoulder which might have been caused by a rifle butt. Many innocent people must have died and in all more than 20,000 Communards were killed during the fighting and executions. The trials of other Communards dragged on for five years and about 10,000 were imprisoned, many being transported.

Thiers, in Brogan's phrase, 'had tamed Paris. Never again did it decide the fate of France.' It is difficult to see the wisdom of such action. The Reign of Terror of 1793–94, with 2,500 executions over 15 months, seemed restrained by comparison with the Commune in which many more were killed than during the Prussian siege of Paris. Is there any justification for the harsh repression? David Thomson is more sympathetic to Thiers than most historians, seeing his aim as that of the preservation of political and constitutional unity as did his contemporary, Abraham Lincoln in America. 'Both had to fight a civil war in order to preserve union.' Paris, notes Thomson, was not the only revolt; unrest took place in other cities like Lyons and Marseilles.

The cost, however, seems high especially if one remembers the part which Thiers played in bringing about a confrontation. France's stock in the world was of course further lowered. To foreign nations the event appeared an outburst of primitive savagery. The French experienced the shame of having to fight a fresh war against their own countrymen under the disdainful eyes of the Prussians.

The Commune injected permanent rifts into French politics. The intense conservatism of French society was revealed by the savage repression of the Commune, which widened the breach between the middle classes and the masses. The Commune made the middle classes more conservative and less sympathetic to the workers than they would otherwise have been. It was difficult after all the slaughter for the socialists to be moderate. The growth of a moderate trade union movement in the 1860s was cut short and an opportunity given for more violent elements to come to the fore. Old socialist leaders like Louis Blanc had opposed the Commune and this created a breach among the socialists themselves. Denis Brogan asserts that the Commune was a folly. 'But the greatest crime of its authors (of whom Thiers was one) was in making final that alienation of the workers of Paris from the official organization of the French State which the days of June 1848 had begun. The "bloody week" of May 1871 was a wound that, if at times it seemed closed, was never really healed.' The class conflict was to be more bitter in France than in Germany or Britain.

The Survival of the Republic

Despite his part in provoking the Commune, Adolphe Thiers was the man who did as much as anyone to establish the Third Republic. He was not a republican but a believer in constitutional monarchy with a fine contempt for the masses. The effect of his tenure of power, argues Zeldin, was to stamp an indelible conservatism on the institutions of the régime. As chief of the executive power, he was called on to devise policy for a country shaken by recent events with the economy at a standstill. In two years he accomplished much.

Thiers realised the need to avoid the issue best calculated to cause new divisions: the question of a definitive form of government for France. He concentrated on the task of freeing France from the German occupation troops, who were authorised by treaty to remain in France until the war indemnity had been paid. Thiers paid off the entire sum by September 1873, six months before the final instalment was due, by floating two government bond issues to which the French eagerly subscribed.

The departure of German troops must have heartened the nation's morale. So did the restoration of French military power by a law of 1872. This adopted certain features of the Prussian system but Thiers insisted on a professional army rather than following the German model of a conscript army. As a result, the army became a bastion of conservatism. It was also Thiers who prevented the introduction of income tax and who insisted on the maintenance of France's centralised system of government through the power of the prefect to appoint the mayor in the larger towns. The self-confidence of Thiers reassured the French bourgeoisie that a republic could maintain order. As McManners phrased it, 'the rule of this sprightly septuagenarian proved it was not necessary to resort to kingship to preserve the conservative social order.'

The Royalist Threat

Yet the issue of whether France would really adopt a republican government appeared very much in doubt. In 1873 the royalist majority in the chamber combined to replace Thiers by Marshal MacMahon, the honest soldier who had been wounded at Sedan and had helped to crush the Commune. He seemed to be the right president to usher in a monarchy, but which one? There were three claimants: (1) the Count of Chambord, grandson of the Bourbon Charles X; (2) the Orleanist Count of Paris, grandson of Louis Philippe; and (3) the Prince Imperial, son of Napoleon III who had died in England in 1873.

A scheme was hatched whereby the Count of Chambord, who was childless, would become king with the Count of Paris as his heir. If Chambord had put forward his candidature, he would have been given the votes of most conservative deputies. This never happened because Chambord refused to abandon the old white flag of the Bourbons for the national flag, the tricolour, a decision to which he clung despite pressure from his supporters, including even the Pope who complained, 'Henry IV said Paris was worth a mass. Henry V finds France not worth a serviette.' Possibly the Pretender was taking an indirect way of evading the burden of kingship; possibly he was making a realistic objective test of the true loyalties of France. Whatever his motives, his attitude was fatal to the scheme for, as MacMahon said at the time, the repudiation of the flag that had waved over the fields of Marengo and Austerlitz would cause 'the chassepôts to go off by themselves'.

Yet the failure of the royalist cause was no accident. There was considerable division in the royalist ranks and many of his own supporters were at loggerheads with the Count of Chambord. He was now 53 years old and his able followers felt no respect for his dull and coarse personality. Too clearly the legitimist cause was that of the nobility and lacked any real programme that might have won over the bourgeoisie or the peasantry.

The royalist majority of 1871 was highly deceptive. The nation elected royalists because it wanted peace and the republicans wanted to carry on the war. The nation did not want a monarchical restoration; the peasants feared that such a restoration might mean the return of tithes and feudalism and hostility was even greater in the towns. Even if the royalists had succeeded in bringing about a restoration, civil war might well have followed. Henry V's refusal to abandon the white flag should not therefore be interpreted as a sudden caprice which ended a movement on the verge of success. His attachment to his flag had long been known. The reconciliation between Chambord and Paris was a transparent one; many Orleanists (supporters of the Count of Paris) preferred a republic to the rule of Chambord. Chambord's honesty, concludes Zeldin, 'spared France a second revolution of 1830'.

With the failure of the 1873 scheme, the Assembly could concentrate on its real work, the creation of new institutions. As Gambetta's paper *La République Française* put it, France entered the Republic backwards, the form of government that was to divide the nation the least.

The Constitution and the Nature of Politics

The executive office of President of the Republic was finally established by the Assembly in 1875 by a majority of one. There was to be manhood suffrage with the right to vote at the age of 20. A bicameral system would be set up with a Senate (the upper house) and a Chamber of Deputies (the lower house). The constitution was to last far longer than other French constitutions partly because it was vague and incomplete. No oath of loyalty was required, with the result that it excluded no one unnecessarily from the start. It was essentially a compromise, both monarchists and republicans gaining something from it. For example, the strong monarchist desire for a Senate was met, and so the constitution had few really implacable enemies. It had the merit of brevity as it was composed only of three laws which were more a guide to procedure than a proper constitution and contained a minimum to quarrel about. The Third Republic, writes Zeldin, was quite unique in coming near to having an unwritten constitution. This constitution also protected vested interests and the character of politics was unedifying.

Being a deputy became a profession. Parliament was not composed of a cross-section of the population. The lack of a two-party system meant that the political labels that a man used in order to get himself elected as a deputy were often no guide or guarantee of how he would behave in parliament. Scandals occurred regularly. They were simply the extension of common practices from a local to a national scale. There was no secret voting until 1914; votes could still be bought by cash or gifts at the appropriate moment. One Rothschild always had the village firemen measured for new uniforms at his expense on polling day. Corruption was general. When Rouvier was accused of dishonesty during the Panama Scandal of 1892 he protested, 'What I have done all politicians worthy of the name have done before me', and no one could deny it.

Real power lay with the deputies, who were able to restrict government activities in several ways. They had the right to interpellate or question government ministers and this right was much used to show constituents how busy they were on their behalf. Deputies could also initiate legislation. A deputy could rise in the middle of any debate to propose a bill on any subject he pleased. In the parliament of 1893 to 1898, 1,112 bills were proposed by deputies while the government presented 2,216 bills of its own. The effect of this appalling number was that most bills were passed into law without proper debate or discussion. Their effect depended on the goodwill of the civil service, for details of the law were left to the administration to work out.

The power of the deputies was often used irresponsibly. Whereas in England governments were overthrown only on major issues of policy, the French deputies did not hesitate to overthrow a government on points of detail. They could do so because, as we shall see, in practice the President lacked the power to dissolve parliament which always lasted its full term. When a ministry fell, it was often reconstituted with many of its old members and a few new members who quite often were those deputies whose actions had destroyed the old ministry. In the first 40 years of the Republic there were 50 changes of government.

Individual politicians could, however, remain in office for long periods by careful attention to the wishes of parliament. Though ministries fell, individuals stayed. Freycinet was prime minister nine times, Delcassé had a spell of 11 years in office and Poincaré did almost as well with a nine-year tenure of office. This factor did provide an underlying stability to the system.

The office of president was not unimportant. He appointed the prime minister and presided at meetings of the cabinet. Republicans were, however, keenly conscious of how Louis Napoleon had used his presidential powers to become an autocrat and were hostile to the idea of a responsible president elected by the people. The president was purposely made weak; he was elected by parliament so that he could have little authority over it. Parliament elected second-rate politicians to guarantee that they would not be faced by a rival. Outstanding characters like Clemenceau were refused the presidency whatever their services to the nation. The practice of appointing a politician meant that he was not above party bickering. The office rated the lowest salary of all the heads of state in Europe and royalists who were still socially influential viewed it with contempt.

Having formulated a constitution, the National Assembly dissolved itself in December 1875. The elections in 1876 produced a Chamber with a large republican majority which was highly embarrassing to the President, MacMahon, who had wished to restore the monarchy. He therefore dissolved the Chamber on May 16, 1877. This became known as the '*coup d'état*' of '*seize Mai*', though in fact MacMahon was strictly within his constitutional rights. He called the royalist Broglie to lead a new government with the express purpose of manipulating the next elections so as to return a royalist majority. The ruse was a total failure as the republicans won 326 seats, the right only 207. After this there was only one course for the President, resignation. He was the last President to use the power of dissolution. 'The election of 1877,' affirms Cobban, 'can be regarded as the real foundation of the Third Republic, not only as a political turning-point but also as a social revolution because rural France had repudiated the authority of the conservative and clerical nobility and upper bourgeoisie.'

The Triumph of the Republic

The years after 1877 witnessed the true establishment of a republican régime. It was fortunate that its birth coincided with a period of economic prosperity and France proclaimed her recovery to the world by holding a great exhibition in 1878. The republicans avoided too many radical measures and thus earned the description of Opportunists. In 1879 most of the Communards were amnestied. The 1880s saw three important developments which were chiefly influenced by Jules Ferry and Charles de Freycinet: (1) the attack on the Church; (2) colonialism; (3) economic reform.

The pattern of religious practice in France was complex but by the middle of the nineteenth century there were large areas of France where the hold of the Roman Catholic Church was weak and weakening with every year that passed, especially in Paris where the grim events of the Commune revealed the alienation of the Parisian working class from religion. But there were in rural France also large areas where the Church was treated with indifference. Anticlericals liked to explain this feature by pointing to the advent of railways, newspapers, education and the widening of peasant horizons. One recent writer has suggested that the Church's identification with political reaction made it unpopular, especially with the peasants, who feared the return of feudalism.

By 1870 anticlericalism was an established feature of French life. Its roots went back to the Middle Ages, an instinctive reaction to the existence of any organised priesthood. The Church's influence was resented, particularly its huge advantage of the right to set up its own schools. By 1870 Church schools were teaching about 40 per cent of the nation's children. The Church's lack of awareness of social problems meant that little contact with the workers was made. Its action in giving thanksgiving when the Commune had been destroyed was bound to alienate further the urban masses aroused by Gambetta's clarion call of 'Clericalism is the enemy'.

Republican propaganda in the 1870s proclaimed the Church as a real menace to liberty, but not until 1879 did the republicans control government. They intended to reduce the clergy to political impotence. As the educational establishments of the Church were a guarantee of its continued influence, republican policy aimed at the creation of lay education. Such an objective also served to unite republican supporters. Yet the republican programme was not conceived exclusively in terms of self-interest. Some of the republican leaders were inspired by a vision of a new educational order which would unite the nation.

Chief of these was Jules Ferry, a cold and intimidating man with a real talent for vigorous and clear argument. He saw education as being directed to creating a common morality by teachers of altruism, with the influence of the Church removed. Women should receive more education for no real democracy was possible while the Church still kept women in subjection. Ferry was minister of education for over four years, from 1879 to 1883, and his reforms touched every branch of education. Primary education was made both free and compulsory, the teaching of the catechism in schools was abolished and replaced by 'civil and moral' education given by teachers who were made lay state employees. This meant that a whole new race of lay schoolmistresses was required so that every department in France had to establish a training college for women primary teachers to replace the nuns. State help had to be provided for the provision of new schools. At secondary level, state schools were established for girls and the classical syllabus was reformed to allow more individual thinking. Gymnastics and military training were introduced. Catholic universities were suppressed. A ban on most Catholic teaching orders, the Jesuits in particular, was imposed and their members were forbidden to teach in the public schools. Ferry also attacked the Church by the institution of civil marriage and the reintroduction of divorce in France in 1884.

Far from establishing unity, the insistence on lay education divided the country profoundly. Ferry antagonised not only the Catholics but also the moderate republicans led by Jules Simon and the radicals led by Clemenceau, the former because they thought he was going too far and the latter because he was not doing enough. Both sides attributed far more influence to the schools than they proved to have. In the twentieth century it emerged that good Catholics could survive in lay schools, obtaining their faith from parents and priests. 'When the furore died down,' notes McManners, 'it gradually became evident that Ferry had succeeded in doing no more than levelling a few outworks of the fortress of Catholic education.' His new moral code was barely distinguishable from the old one and need not have alarmed traditionalists as much as it did. Nevertheless, the next fifty years were to be embittered.

Ferry was also associated with the development of French colonialism, but he was not originally responsible for the expansion which took place in these years. It was civil servants, explorers and soldiers who carried the French flag to new lands. But Ferry supported them in order to uphold the honour of France. Under his guidance, the French hold on Indo-China was tightened, Tunis was acquired in 1881, and at the Congress of Berlin in 1885 so were Madagascar and areas of Central Africa. He achieved what he did thanks to the encouragement of Bismarck, who was glad to turn France's energies away from Alsace. Ferry's realism in seeing that revenge on Germany had to be postponed won him many enemies in France and he was accused of treachery by supporters of 'revanche' like Clemenceau. A French defeat at Tonkin in 1885 was the immediate cause of Ferry's downfall but to some extent he had brought it on himself by adopting a highly irritating air of infallibility.

The wily Freycinet was not the man to make the same error. He had no gifts of oratory and no popular appeal but he became one of the most powerful men in the republic because he carried to perfection his role as a conciliator and manager. He was so self-effacing that he won the nickname of 'the white mouse', but this quality ensured that he made no enemies. He was the kind of minister who was most acceptable to parliament—a middle-of-the-road man who would serve rather than dominate, who would move reforms gradually rather than precipitately. As a result, Freycinet was prime minister four times and a member of nine other ministries.

Freycinet was particularly acceptable because he reflected the republican mentality in his keen sense of material interests. He saw that there were too many small railways in France and still insufficient network. Under his auspices the length of the railway network was doubled yet he avoided raising taxation to pay for this by a deal with the six largest railway companies in 1883. The companies were to raise the money to pay for the expansion of the railways and pay two thirds of their profits to the state but the state would guarantee dividends and interest on loans made to the companies by investors. The companies therefore could not lose, yet the politicians could claim that the state would get a railway network built without further taxation. The companies in fact had the better of the bargain as only one of the six made adequate profits because of insufficient traffic.

Freycinet had more success with his scheme for improvements in the French waterways. In 1879 a law brought in nationalisation of the waterways which was effective in several senses. The waterways were extended and between 1880 and 1906 enjoyed an increase in freight of ninety per cent.

Symptoms of Instability

By the mid-1880s republican confidence over the future of the Third Republic had grown. It seemed to have sufficient support but the régime had its limitations. It could be accused like the July Monarchy of being a joint-stock company to exploit the country for a small group of shareholders. A good deal of social discontent existed, much of it concentrated in Paris. In 1885 came an industrial slump which put a quarter of a million out of work and agriculture faced the severe problems of phylloxera and the competition of imported American wheat. Three outbreaks of excitement were to reveal the extent of opposition to the Third Republic: Boulangism, the Panama Scandal and the Dreyfus Affair.

Georges Boulanger had become a successful soldier during the Second Empire and in 1886 he became Minister of War, mainly through the support of Clemenceau who wanted an army purged of royalist elements. In 1887 he gained great popularity over the Schnaebele incident. The Germans arrested a French customs agent, Schnaebele, on German soil and accused him of espionage, later releasing him when they found that he had been invited in writing to meet his German colleagues. Boulanger, who had organised the spy system of which Schnaebele was part, made fighting speeches and the public assumed that Bismarck had backed down out of fear of Boulanger.

Moderates in government circles now turned against Boulanger because of his reckless behaviour and they left him out of the next government and packed him off to a provincial command in the Auvergne. When he left Paris, immense crowds tried to stop him leaving on the train. If Boulanger had wished to put himself at the head of a takeover bid at this juncture, he might well have succeeded but he was not ready for such drastic action.

Just when Boulanger appeared to be fading from public sight, corruption in high places was revealed when President Grévy's son-in-law, Wilson, was accused of selling decorations. Grévy himself was forced to resign in December 1887. The scandal crystallised support for the darling of society, Boulanger, who was courted by the Right and the Left. In six provincial by-elections he headed the poll in 1888 and in 1889 he was elected for Paris. There is little doubt that if he had attempted to overturn the republican régime, he would have received a lot of support, especially from Paul Déroulède's League of Patriots. This movement had been founded in 1882 and its objective was the revival of French nationalism by a mass appeal.

Boulanger was, however, a paper tiger. There was nothing heroic about him and he would not act illegally. He even lacked consistent interest in the acquisition of power, being rather too fond of going off for jaunts with his mistress. When the government began legal proceedings against Boulanger and he feared arrest, he fled to Brussels ignominiously and appropriately on April 1, 1889. When his mistress died of cancer in 1891, Boulanger shot himself.

The affair is significant because it was a challenge to the whole system. The massive support that united behind Boulanger showed how powerful were the forces which rejected the republic. The royalists put between six million and eight million francs into the campaign in his favour. Support came from contrasting sources—royalists, Jews, socialists, radicals and Bonapartists. Yet again much Republican support had remained steady among the rural classes, who preferred a pacific republic to a régime with warlike tendencies. The importance of the affair lay in its revelation of the republic's failure on social questions, for social discontent had given Boulanger much of his popular support.

Boulanger was scarcely in his grave when the system was again shaken. In 1879, at the age of 74, Ferdinand de Lesseps had floated the Panama Canal Company which ran into difficulties because of unrealistic engineering and natural difficulties in the area like incurable yellow fever. In 1888, the Assembly voted for the company to be helped by a large public loan. When the investors did not come forward in sufficient numbers, the company was forced into liquidation. In 1892 it was revealed that the company's interests had been promoted by dishonest finance and a system of bribery. As much as one third of its capital had been spent on bribing politicians and others who might have exposed the company's affairs to the investing public.

The scandal helped to increase anti-Semitism because two German Jews, Baron Jacques de Reinach and Cornelius Herz, had carried out much of the bribery. Herz blackmailed de Reinach who committed suicide. Among the incriminated deputies was Floquet, who had been prime minister during the Boulanger crisis. For the enemies of the republic the scandal merely proved that the régime was incurably corrupt. The anti-Semite Edouard Drumont, in his paper *La Libre Parole*, and the Boulangist deputy Paul Déroulède led the attack on republican politicians, chiefly Clemenceau. Clemenceau was hounded out of public life, de Lesseps and his son were given five years imprisonment, but Cornelius Herz escaped to Bournemouth.

Both Drumont and Déroulède demanded a new France purged of its internal weaknesses. Their position was not dissimilar to that of Catholics who saw their traditional France undermined by secularism nor to that of the socialists who charged the republic with capitalist decadence.

The economic recovery of the early 1890s and the conclusion of the Russian alliance in 1894 seemed to indicate the republic's recovery but the stability was superficial. The tensions in French society, exacerbated by the two recent crises, were unresolved and were now to break out with a new virulence in the Dreyfus Affair.

The father of Alfred Dreyfus was a rich textile manufacturer in Mulhouse, where Alfred was born in 1859. The family chose to remain in France after the loss of Alsace–Lorraine to Germany and Alfred entered the French army in 1880. He married the daughter of a rich diamond merchant and became the first Jew attached to the General Staff. In 1894 he was arrested and tried for communicating secrets to a foreign power (Germany). The *bordereau* on the strength of which Dreyfus had been arrested made reference to nothing of vital information: it was a sheet of paper listing a collection of documents but it was assumed that Dreyfus had communicated secrets of considerable importance as his handwriting was not dissimilar to that on the *bordereau*. He was found guilty and sent away to life imprisonment on Devil's Island. Only the family of Dreyfus was convinced of his innocence and set in motion a campaign to reverse the verdict which in the next three years drew in not only other Jews, notably Bernard Lazare, but important politicians like Clemenceau.

What really happened was that in September 1894 an officer serving in the Intelligence Bureau of the General Staff, Major Henry, was given an intercepted letter to the German military attaché in Paris, in which the writer said that he had information to sell from secret documents. The handwriting was that of Count Esterhazy, one of Henry's friends, so Henry tore up the letter. However, the secret agent who had contrived to get hold of the letter wanted the credit for it and made Henry piece it up and pass it on to his superiors.

As several pieces of information related to gunnery, Dreyfus, who was an artillery officer and also Jewish, became the scapegoat and was convicted on flimsy evidence. His trial was full of irregularities. Henry, for example, swore on oath that an unimpeachable source had confirmed to him that Dreyfus had engaged in treasonous correspondence, though his name could not be divulged! Mercier, the Minister of War, and Boisdeffre, Chief of the General Staff, had also introduced a secret dossier of papers to the judges without the knowledge of Dreyfus and his lawyers.

Much to the embarrassment of Mercier and Boisdeffre, the case was reopened because of Lieutenant-Colonel Picquart, who in July 1895 became Head of Intelligence. Picquart was not fond of Jews but he was a scrupulous Catholic. In March 1896 he learned that Esterhazy was in communication with the Germans and living beyond his means. His handwriting was identical to that of the *bordereau*. Picquart was also informed by a former German spy that the Germans were bewildered by the Dreyfus Case because they were only receiving information from a major in the infantry and Esterhazy was a major in the infantry. When Picquart tried to raise the question with his superiors he was sent away on a tour of inspection in Tunisia, but before he left he saw to it that his evidence reached republican deputies of known integrity like Scheurer-Kestner. Bernard Lazare, on behalf of the Dreyfus family, had also been informed by one of Esterhazy's creditors that it was Esterhazy's handwriting on the *bordereau*. As Dreyfus's brother made this information public, Esterhazy demanded a trial to clear his name. It was held in January 1898 and he was rapidly acquitted. Picquart, in contrast, was arrested the next day for calumniating Esterhazy's name.

But now two dramatic developments made the Affair one of violent national interest. Clemenceau's paper *L'Aurore* printed an open letter by Emile Zola under the arresting title of *J'accuse*. The article caused a sensation because of the extent of Zola's accusations against the army and the naming of individual officers. The government brought charges against Zola, who was forced to leave the country, but now those who had remained aloof from the Affair became involved. H. R. Kedward remarks, 'If the Affair was a catalyst, Zola's *J'accuse* is the prime catalysing force.' Many of the underlying tensions in French Society were brought to the surface. The anti-Dreyfusards stood for old monarchical, conservative France and believed that Dreyfus should be sacrificed to preserve the army's honour. The Dreyfusards stood for radicalism and the ideals of the French Revolution and they were now able to take the offensive.

The second dramatic development was the suicide of Colonel Henry. In 1898 a new Minister of War, Cavaignac, had Picquart's assertions investigated. It was discovered that one of the documents used against Dreyfus was a clumsy composite of two different types of paper. In August, Henry broke down under interrogation, was arrested, and cut his throat overnight. Realising the game was up, Esterhazy fled the country, and once safe in London confessed to writing the *bordereau*.

This should have been the end of the matter but the anti-Dreyfusards still resisted the truth. The country seemed on the verge of a new wave of violence. In February 1899, the anti-Dreyfusard President Faure died in the presence of his mistress and at his funeral Déroulède attempted to engineer a coup d'état. The new Dreyfusard President Loubet had his hat knocked off his head at the races by a nobleman. There was a patent need for a government that would govern and Loubet appointed the cool and authoritative Waldeck-Rousseau as prime minister. He formed a government with several strong men in it, including the socialist Millerand and General Gallifet as Minister of War to quell any unrest in the army. In June, another absurd travesty of justice occurred. Dreyfus, having been brought home weak and ill after four years' confinement, was again found guilty but with extenuating circumstances. The government then acted swiftly and in September Dreyfus received a full pardon, though not until 1906 was he fully reinstated. Picquart had already been freed and was to become a brigadier. After a sordid episode, justice did at least prevail in the end.

Yet this case showed the limitations of the French legal system, in which the odds were loaded against the accused. Dreyfus was a poor witness and could never refute the circumstantial evidence which made him a plausible culprit, particularly in the atmosphere of the time when spies were seen on every side. If the Affair was a legal failure, it was also a human failure. Once they had formed their opinion, people found it difficult to change it, partly because the evidence never seemed conclusive but mainly because passions and prejudices clouded the issues. The Affair obscured social problems for a decade and in this sense it was one of the great political failures of the republic. Existing tensions in French society were increased, especially anti-Semitism and anti-clericalism.

The Affair led to a purging of reactionary officers in the army. By 1900 the higher ranks in the army had become an almost solid conservative, monarchist and Catholic monopoly. Those who had figured prominently in the Affair were immediately purged. A more profound result was a change in the system of recruitment. In 1905 the republicans insisted on a reduction in the years of recruitment so as to diminish the control of the professional army officers over French youth, though the original three-year term of service was restored in 1913.

The Affair had even more profound implications for the Church. Before it occurred, as McManners notes, tolerance and compromise had been developing in relations between Church and State. The Affair created a new venom in anti-clericalism which to an extent was unfair. Many Catholics had stayed aloof, some like Picquart had even risked their careers and sided with revision, but the anti-clericals believed that the Church had been at the back of the Affair and wanted revenge.

In 1901 a law was brought in stating that religious orders were to apply for authorisation to parliament. If this was refused their corporate property would be auctioned and the members dispersed. Combes, who replaced Waldeck-Rousseau in 1902 was, in McManners' phrase, 'a man of inquisitional mentality' and he applied the new law severely, declaring all but five of the orders dissolved. In 1905 the Separation Law ended state support of the Church, which now had to pay its own clerical salaries. The way lay open for a more cordial relationship but it is a pity that it took so long. 'In this bitter conflict,' laments Brogan, 'France wasted for generations passion, faith, hate, thought that might have been better employed.'

One final consequence of the Dreyfus Affair was the stimulus which it gave to chauvinism in France. In 1899 a group was formed under Charles Maurras. The members believed that a strong government would not have allowed the humiliations which the Affair had heaped on France. Maurras was bitterly anti-Semitic and saw the restoration of the monarchy as the way to France's salvation; to him it was the only form of government that had consistently given France order. By 1905 the group was fully established as Action Française and by 1908 it had a paper of the same name. The movement stood for violent nationalism and educational establishments were founded to train the young. Action squads—the *Camelots du Roi*—were used in the streets supporting the pretender, the Duke of Orleans. If Maurras won more support from the right wing, nevertheless there were socialist elements in his doctrine.

Before 1914 Action Française was only of nuisance value but it did indicate the dangers to come.

The Rise of Socialism

The final years before 1914 saw the growth of a united socialist party in France. Its roots went back to the years of the Second Republic when many peasants of the backward centre and south-east of France became socialist. Thus the socialist party in France was able to become a major force in politics by 1900 while the country was still hardly industrialised.

Marxism was introduced into the movement in the 1870s, principally by the efforts of Jules Guesde. His bitter authoritarianism led to the nickname of the Red Jesuit but he spread Marxist ideas and won strong support in the textile towns. By the late nineteenth century he was in charge of the largest socialist group in France. Guesde made a contribution of lasting importance as he left behind a strong tradition of Marxist socialism which is one of the major strands in the party's history.

Guesde himself was too tactless to create a truly national party. That honour fell to Jean Jaurès, a spellbinding orator with the talent for reconciliation. He did not believe in the necessity of revolution but in parliamentary methods, supporting the bourgeoisie whenever they showed themselves willing to carry out reforms. He acquiesced to the socialists becoming a revolutionary party in 1905 when a united party was at last formed, yet he ingeniously reconciled the conflicting aims of the different socialist groups. Though the aims were revolutionary, with the use of insurrection and the general strike when the opportunity arose, the immediate method was working within the system.

In the elections of 1906 the united socialists won 54 seats and in the 1914 elections 103 seats. Yet the party membership of 90,000 in 1914 was trifling compared to that of the S.P.D. in Germany with over one million members. Once unification was achieved the old disputes broke out again with Jaurès and Guesde in opposition over the party's attitude to war, nationalisation and municipal socialism.

The socialist movement was further split by the cleavage between its political and industrial wings. The trade union organisation, the *Confédération Générale du Travail*, was suspicious of the political movement. Influenced by Georges Sorel, it advocated revolutionary syndicalism and believed in the myth of the General Strike. By 1909 the C.G.T.'s membership had risen to nearly a million and the organisation clashed with the government on several occasions during the final years of peace. Relations were particularly embittered by the use of troops against strikers in Clemenceau's premiership between 1906 and 1909.

Further Reading

Brogan, D. W., *The French Nation*, Hamish Hamilton, London, 1957.
Cobban, A., *A History of Modern France* (Vol. 3: 1871–1962), Penguin, London, 1972.
McManners, J., *Church and State in France 1870–1914*, S.P.C.K., London, 1972.
Zeldin, T., *France 1848–1945*, Clarendon Press, Oxford, 1973.

Questions

1. Assess the importance of the Commune in French history.
2. Account for the failure of royalism in France after 1871.
3. Why did the politics of the Third Republic appear so unstable?
4. Discuss the achievements of Ferry and Freycinet.
5. What were the chief consequences of the Dreyfus Affair?

CHAPTER FIVE

SPLENDOUR AND DECLINE THE AUSTRO–HUNGARIAN EMPIRE 1867–1914

The Emperor

If the Austro–Hungarian Empire experienced a long, slow decline in the late nineteenth century much responsibility must be laid on the emperor. An able ruler might have led a constructive attack on the problems of the realm; but, to quote the Austrian satirist Karl Kraus, Francis Joseph was an 'Un-Personality' and a 'Daemon of mediocrity'. He lacked ideas and imagination and these qualities would not be supplied by his ministers, for he avoided strong subordinates.

This failure of leadership meant that the most serious of the problems confronting the monarchy, the problem of the nationalities, was never really tackled. The Compromise of 1867, which created the Dual Monarchy by placing Hungary on an equal footing with Austria, was to remain unchanged until the end of the Empire. 'Once having taken the decision,' says C. A. Macartney, 'the emperor adhered to it with complete rigidity.' Any suggestion of changing the system was a sure way of earning a minister lasting disgrace. The result was the progressive alienation of the loyalty of the non-German and non-Magyar majority of the Habsburg peoples. The ruling class of the Empire made few efforts to avert this danger and in the last decade before the outbreak of the First World War, the emperor himself showed his lack of interest in real change by abandoning suffrage reform in Hungary. Foreign policy, anyway, was of more interest to him. By the turn of the century, Francis Joseph was 70 years of age and even less able to alter the mental outlook which he had acquired in his youth. As C. A. Macartney stresses, 'He simply did not appreciate the nature and the strength of the new forces which had grown larger since he was a younger man.'

The emperor's personal life was tragic. He came to the throne in 1848 with his lands in the throes of revolution. In 1854 he married the beautiful Elizabeth of Bavaria for love, the one irrational act in his life. The marriage soon went wrong, partly because of pressure of his public duties and also because of the interference of the emperor's mother, the Archduchess Sophie. A caricature of the bossy mother-in-law, she disapproved of Elizabeth's high spirits. Elizabeth reacted against the draconian discipline of the court and spent more time with her horses and Hungarian friends than with her husband. She led a more and more separate life until 1898, when she was assassinated by an Italian anarchist on the shores of Lake Geneva. Their only son, Crown Prince Rudolf, married Princess Stephanie of Belgium. He was highly critical of the way in which the emperor ruled. After a tragic love affair with Baroness Marie Vetsera, the two committed suicide at the Mayerling hunting lodge in 1889.

Earlier, Francis Joseph's younger brother, Maximilian, had died miserably in Mexico in 1867. Placed on the throne of Mexico through the help of Napoleon III in 1864, he was captured and shot by republicans in 1867. Finally came the murder of the Emperor's nephew and heir Franz Ferdinand at Sarajevo in June 1914. Francis Joseph had good reason to say, 'I have been spared nothing.'

Francis Joseph inspired loyalty, even veneration, among his subjects. It was he, not the institutional machinery of state, who truly embodied the political unity that existed within the empire. Over the years Francis Joseph developed an impressive patriarchal personality. He possessed a certain austere and often humourless dignity, always preserving a distant formality even with his closest advisers. He was not overfond of ostentatious ceremonial but no private or public tragedy ever disrupted his well-organised life. A. J. May likens him to a stoical Spartan. He began work at 5 a.m. and his long hours of work were consumed by the petty details of government. He always attended his audiences and ceremonies—for example, the Maundy Thursday ceremony when he washed the feet of old men from the almshouse. His high sense of duty made him regard the Habsburg Empire as a God-given responsibility. He was a devout man and a pillar of the Roman Church. His recreation was sought in two ways; in hunting and in a number of extramarital affairs when his wife was absent.

The Liberal Phase in Austria (1867–79)

The government of the Empire after 1867 was conducted on three separate levels: the intergovernmental, the Austrian and the Hungarian. Certain matters of common concern such as foreign policy were conducted by a joint ministry appointed by the monarch and supervised in a vague way by Austrian and Hungarian delegates. The internal affairs of Austria and Hungary were handled by two separate governments.

The 17 provinces that made up Austria possessed individual diets that administered local affairs and were represented in the Imperial parliament that met in Vienna. The parliament had two chambers: an upper one composed of leading aristocrats, churchmen and other men of importance appointed by the emperor; and a lower house whose members were elected by an indirect system of voting which gave preference to men of property and education. Parliament as a whole had the right to approve or reject important items of state business such as the budget. Ministers were appointed by the emperor and in practice depended on the monarch rather than on parliament for continuance in office. The emperor also had the right to dissolve parliament and to issue decrees that had the full force of law when parliament was not in session. These powers made it possible for the emperor to impose his will on an awkward parliament, though he preferred cooperation with ministers who could command parliamentary majorities.

As in Germany, there was the growth of a strong Liberal party which represented the German middle class created by the industrialisation of Austria and Bohemia. The party favoured constitutional government and an efficient centralised administration in the interests of commercial progress. It also shared the usual Liberal dislike of any clerical influences. In the 1870s, Francis Joseph found it necessary to rely on the Liberals for parliamentary support as he tried to solve the problems created by the reorganization of the monarchy after 1867. Another major difficulty was economic. The war of 1866 had ushered in a period of boom but in 1873 came a severe financial crash and many Liberal politicians were compromised because of the subsequent revelation of their business interests.

Nevertheless, the Liberals won a number of concessions—a freer press, more rights for Jews, the removal of schools from the control of the Church, voluntary religious education, and the authorization of civil marriage. A law of 1869 made elementary education free and compulsory for all children but this was not implemented in the 1870s. The amount of legislation looked impressive to foreign observers but the only concession made to the subject nationalities was more autonomy for the Poles in Galicia, which made them the most loyal supporters of the monarchy.

The Liberal era ended abruptly in 1879. The emperor was annoyed by Liberal criticism of the results of the Congress of Berlin and the assumption by Austria of administrative control of Bosnia and Herzegovina which, the Liberals believed, would prove burdensome. He had, in any case, disliked Liberal rule from the start. Liberal ministers were pedantic, middle-class lawyers with anti-clerical views and the parliament in Vienna annoyed the emperor by its very proximity. At heart he was authoritarian and 'for popular participation in government this arch-conservative had positive detestation' (A. J. May). He suspected the Liberals, moreover, of aiming at a further reduction in his power. A. J. P. Taylor points out that a further reason for dropping the Liberals was the old Habsburg policy of 'divide and rule', of playing off the nationalities of Austria against each other, especially the Czechs and the Germans. The German Liberals deserved Czech hostility for they consistently regarded Bohemia as a German protectorate despite the large Czech majority in the population.

The Czech problem had indeed become serious. Like the Serbs and Slovenes in the south, they resented German domination and the Empire's failure to solve the Czech problem was to be one of the most important reasons for its collapse. On only one occasion did Francis Joseph try to deal with it. In 1871 he promised to elevate Bohemia into the same position as Austria and Hungary—to turn the Dual Monarchy into a Triple Monarchy—but the plan was blocked by the Austrian Germans, who feared the loss of their predominance, and by the Magyars of Hungary, who feared that Czech liberation would result in demands for similar rights on the part of their own subject nationalities. The emperor gave way in the face of German and Hungarian objections. The Czechs never forgave him for this surrender and boycotted parliamentary life after 1871.

Taaffe's Iron Ring (1879–93)

When in 1879 Francis Joseph broke with the Liberals, he wished to appease the Czechs and the other subject nationalities through an alliance with the conservatives. The man he chose to do this was a friend of his youth, Count Taaffe, whose political talent enabled him to be the emperor's chief minister from 1879 to 1893. The other reason for his long tenure of office was his subservience to the emperor. A. J. P. Taylor calls him a true Emperor's man and Taaffe himself admitted, 'The will of the Emperor must, and will, be decisive for me.' An aristocrat of Irish origin, he was tactful and relied on time rather than energy to provide solutions.

The political combination which he chose to replace the Liberals was known as the 'Iron Ring'. In essence Taaffe was appealing for loyalty to the emperor and he managed to win over great landowners, the Poles, the German Catholic peasantry and even the Czechs and the Slovenes. The partners were kept together by concessions to their special interests. In Galicia the Poles won privileges over the Ruthenes—for example, in the use of the Polish language on the railways. The Czechs were granted a new electoral law in 1882 which gave them a majority in the Bohemian diet as well as stronger representation in the Imperial parliament; in 1882 also the University of Prague was divided into two universities, one of which was Czech. A new law of 1879 required all civil servants in Bohemia and Moravia to give judgments in the language of the petitioner and to conduct trials in the language of the accused. This law dethroned German as the sole official language in Bohemia. German officials now had to learn Czech and the number of Czechs in the civil service increased. In return for these concessions the Czechs ended their boycott of parliamentary life.

Historians appear to view Taaffe's career in an ambivalent way. He once described his aim as one of keeping all the nationalities in a balanced state of mild dissatisfaction, but, as A. J. P. Taylor emphasises, 'Taaffe's system of "muddling along" gave Austria a stability and calm such as she had not enjoyed since the days of Francis I. For a decade bitterness went out of public life.' A. J. May praises Taaffe's handling of other politicians and his dedication. Under a flippant exterior, he was a 'deadly earnest man'.

Yet the same historians note the long-term futility of Taaffe's policy of appeasement. By 1890 mild dissatisfaction had turned into violent dissatisfaction and Francis Joseph dismissed Taaffe with scant gratitude in 1893. 'Taaffe had given Austria a breathing space of fourteen years; it had not been used to good purpose. Within a few years everyone would regret the easy days of the "iron ring" and Taaffe's "muddling along".' (Taylor). In fact he had avoided fundamental and necessary change, while his tinkering with the nationalities problem stimulated the appetite of the subject nationalities for more concessions and aroused the fury of the Germans. In the long run this was to make a solution to the problems even harder to find. The Czechs, for example, were not satisfied with the concessions granted for they demanded an autonomous Bohemian kingdom. Other Slav peoples also grew more outspoken and the idea of a federation of Slav peoples free from Austro–Hungarian control gained ground. Thus C. A. Macartney, who also praises Taaffe's adroitness, sees his impact as essentially negative. 'Taaffe not only did not produce an answer to the riddle of the monarchy, he did not even look for one.' In defence of Taaffe it must be pointed out that he was not solely responsible for the outburst of discontent after 1890. He was the prisoner of an emperor who refused to alter the constitution of the Dual Monarchy.

Taaffe's policies had aroused the Germans in Bohemia who opposed any concessions whatever to the Czechs. Such disorders occurred that the government was forced to place Prague under martial law and it was over this issue that Francis Joseph dismissed his faithful minister. The virulence of German feeling was reflected in the rise of a new Pan-German movement led by Georg von Schönerer which preached the racial superiority of the Germans over the Slavs and called for the union of Austria's German provinces with the German Empire. A violent man, Schönerer quarrelled with all his political associates and was imprisoned for assault on one of his many opponents. He attacked the Roman Catholic Church, Jews and Slavs.

Taaffe's system had worked for so long that no one knew what could take its place. Owing to this bankruptcy of policy, the period 1893 to 1897 was one of confusion. In the end the emperor turned to the former Governor of Galicia, Badeni, in the hope that he would prove a strong minister. When Badeni attempted to increase the use of the Czech language in 1897, Schönerer's German nationalists brought parliamentary life to a standstill and great demonstrations took place in the main cities. Francis Joseph was forced to dismiss Badeni, a development which had no precedent since 1848 when revolution forced the flight of Metternich. The emperor deserved this defeat for employing a Polish noble without constitutional experience. Badeni's ordinance was withdrawn; it was the last real attempt to break the deadlock of national conflicts in Austria.

The Growth of New Parties

Throughout the Taaffe period, opposition to his coalition had come mainly from the old Liberal party, still the strongest party in Austria. However, they never recovered the influence which they had enjoyed before 1879 and they entered a period of decline. Their strength was sapped by the extension of universal manhood suffrage in Austria by 1907 and by the growth of a large proletariat. These factors led to the emergence of two parties which replaced liberalism.

The first of these was the Christian Socialist party, which combined within its membership some of the most progressive and some of the most prejudiced elements in Austria. It was a Catholic party which also emphasised democracy, social reform and a progressive attitude towards the nationalities problem. Their greatest leader was Karl Lueger, Mayor of Vienna between 1897 and 1907. He was born into a lower-middle-class Viennese family and remained true to his origins throughout his political career. He abandoned his alliance with Schönerer who directed his appeal mainly at middle and upper class audiences. Lueger appealed to the lower middle classes and the working classes. His handsome appearance and homely humour made him immensely popular.

Under Lueger, the Christian Socialists supported the successful movements to legalise trade unions and to grant accident and sickness insurance to workers. In Vienna was carried through a programme of municipal socialism similar to Chamberlain's in Birmingham.

But an important factor in attracting mass support to the Christian Socialist party was anti-Semitism. Industrialism in Austria had brought economic dislocation as well as profit. Many of the petty bourgeoisie had been ruined and it was all too easy to fix blame on the Jews for their troubles. By 1890 the Jews made up 12 per cent of the total population of Vienna and were therefore a sufficiently large minority to be a credible target. They were prominent in finance, medicine, law, journalism, university teaching and cultural life in general. Lueger used an anti-Semitic platform because he knew it had such an appeal, especially as he blamed the Jews for corruption in political life. Both Lueger and Schönerer were admired by Hitler.

After the suffrage reform of 1907, the Christian Socialist movement turned to the Right, merging with the Conservatives. Meanwhile, the spread of the vote to the working classes helped the growth of a Social Democratic party, organised by Viktor Adler, though it had already built up a mass party before 1907. It had been formally organised in 1888 and in 1897 won 14 seats in the *Reichsrat* with the help of the trade union movement.

Adler himself was an attractive figure. He was born in Prague in 1852 of a wealthy Jewish family. He became politically active when he studied medicine, for as a doctor he came into contact with real poverty. In 1883 he came to England to study social legislation and formed a firm friendship with Friedrich Engels. He had a warm compassionate personality and was liked and admired in the Socialist movement. In 1886 he used money which he inherited to start a party newspaper, the *Arbeiterzeitung*, which he edited until his death in 1918.

In time, the Socialists gained more control in Vienna from the Christian Socialists whose strength lay more in rural Austria. Marxist in inspiration, the Socialist party maintained close links with Socialist parties in other countries. The Austrian Socialists became more moderate, advocating gradual social change by parliamentary methods, the support of the Imperial tie and a liberal policy of concessions to the nationalities. In 1906 the outstanding socialist Karl Renner wrote persuasively in favour of a scheme of democratic federalism to help the survival of the Empire. Only by giving of national rights under such a scheme, argued Renner, would the perpetual national conflicts in the Empire be mitigated.

The bitterness in parliamentary life in Austria in the years before the war appeared to demonstrate the common sense of Renner's views. National groups increased their agitation and the government was forced to rely on a frequent resort to emergency powers.

Magyarisation in Hungary (1867–1914)

In Hungary, as in Austria, a bicameral system existed, yet the lower house—the House of Deputies—was in no sense a popular assembly for the franchise was restricted to 25 per cent of the male population. The consistent factor in the history of Hungary after 1867 was the ruthless policy pursued by the Magyars of making their race absolutely dominant in the kingdom.

Out of Hungary's 15 million population, the Magyars constituted less than half but they held a monopoly of political power. By the early years of the twentieth century a quarter of a million Magyar gentry had found employment in the bureaucracy: 95 per cent of state officials and 90 per cent of the judges were Magyar; 80 per cent of newspapers were in the Magyar language. Only one race, the Croats, avoided complete domination because they had helped the Emperor during the 1848 revolutions and their services were not forgotten. They were allowed their own diet, courts, schools and police and to send a separate bloc of 40 deputies to the House of Deputies. Other nationalities—for example, Rumanians, Serbs and Slovaks—were forced to endure a policy of Magyarisation. The government tried to wipe out national differences by suppressing newspapers, schools and other institutions which might keep the languages, arts and customs of the other nationalities alive. The Magyar language was made compulsory in parliament, government service, courts and even on the railways. Teachers were liable to dismissal if the pupils did not know Magyar.

This ruthless subjugation of the subject nationalities was implicit in the Compromise of 1867 and was the price paid to the Magyars by the emperor for their continued support. In the short run this policy paid off. Under Koloman Tisza, Hungarian prime minister from 1875 to 1890, the Magyars did support the Habsburg monarchy, for they saw that the Habsburg connection was vital for the maintenance of Hungary as a great state.

A more chauvinistic element grew up in Hungary as the years passed. Francis Kossuth, son of the Magyar hero of 1848, formed an Independence Party and demanded that Hungary be able to direct her own tariff and foreign policies and that Magyar should become the language used in the Hungarian regiments in the Imperial army.

This would have threatened the effectiveness of the army and Francis Joseph, who regarded the army as the real prop of his régime, reacted swiftly. A confrontation arose in 1905 when Kossuth's coalition won a victory in the parliamentary elections and seemed capable of implementing its plans. At this point the emperor appointed an emergency government which threatened to introduce manhood suffrage in place of the limited franchise which assisted the Magyar monopoly of political power. Had this extension of the suffrage been carried through, the subject nationalities might well have become more content, but in 1906 the coalition leaders, appalled by the prospect of manhood suffrage, agreed to drop their plans for army reform. In return, the emperor agreed to drop the plan for extending the vote and Hungarian politics became more tranquil with the elections of 1910. A new party founded by Stephen Tisza, son of Koloman Tisza, was resolved to maintain the Compromise of 1867. The movement led by Kossuth declined and Tisza ran Hungarian politics until 1917. He checked attacks on the emperor's position and intensified the policy of Magyarisation. Now even the Croats felt the full force of Magyar exclusiveness. Their newspapers were closed down and their constitution suspended in 1912.

The abandonment by the emperor of the subject nationalities in Hungary was a fatal error. The issue of suffrage reform in 1905–6 was, perhaps, the government's last opportunity of breaking the power of the Magyar oligarchy and it had been thrown away. The loyalty of the subject nationalities to the crown was thus eroded and the dissolution of the empire became more likely.

Appearance and Reality

The grave problems of the realm were to an extent hidden by the superficial splendour of the empire in the decades before the war. The capital, Vienna, was the easy-going city of Strauss waltzes; it was full of the pomp and majesty of court ceremony, but it was also an immensely stimulating city. Robert Musil, who set his novel *The Man Without Qualities* in Vienna just before the war, called Vienna a home for genius.

There was indeed a flowering of its culture in the last years of peace. Freud analysed the motive forces of human behaviour and published *The Interpretation of Dreams* in 1900. His psychoanalytic methods influenced writers like Arthur Snitzler, whose sad comedies of seduction pointed to the incompatibility of men and women. The bold innovations which occurred in painting were found chiefly in the work of Oskar Kokoschka, while Gustav Mahler and Arnold Schönberg were major contributors to modern music.

The city of Vienna itself altered radically in the period. Its population grew from 500,000 in 1840 to over 2 million in 1910. From the 1860s its beauty was enhanced by the razing of the medieval walls around the city and the construction of the *Ringstrasse*, one of the most beautiful avenues in the world. There were many architectural triumphs such as the new opera house.

Vienna was so stimulating because it was a very cosmopolitan city, a fitting symbol of the Empire, where Germans, Czechs, Jews, Poles and Magyars contrived to live together with a measure of harmony. The material and artistic success that they achieved can be taken as proof of the vitality still possessed by the Habsburg Empire.

Yet the fundamental problems still existed and the decline continued. There were few prospects of Habsburg rule becoming more enlightened in time. Francis Joseph did not acquire wisdom with age. Nor was there any evidence that government would improve after his death. When Rudolf died in 1889, the emperor's nephew Franz Ferdinand became the heir apparent. He once had a reputation as a liberal, interested in the problems of the subject races, but this is a gross distortion of the truth. Indeed, he appears as one of the most unpleasant of all the Habsburg family. Taylor calls him one of the worst products of the Habsburg house, violent, reactionary and autocratic. His only saving grace was his love for Countess Sophie Chotek with whom he concluded a morganatic marriage in 1900, thereby losing the favour of Francis Joseph. In reality, Franz Ferdinand disliked all the national movements especially when they strove for more democracy. His scheme to restore the Kingdom of Croatia arose not out of sympathy for the South Slavs but from a desire to increase monarchical power by weakening Hungary. His ideal was a restoration of monarchical absolutism based on the army. Even if he had escaped death at Sarajevo in 1914, it is unlikely that this mean and morose individual could have checked the dissolution of the empire; it is much more likely that he would have accelerated the process.

Nor were the other forces holding the empire together—the centripetal forces, as Jaszi terms them—as strong as they appeared. Social order was founded on the ownership of land and on state control and was supported by the aristocracy, the Church, the army and the civil service. The system came under increasingly severe strain in the nineteenth century.

The army was the force on which the government would rely in the last resort. It had gained too much influence over policy, especially after 1906 when Conrad von Hotzendorff was chief of staff. He openly advocated war against Serbia as a solution to the South Slav problem. Army unity itself was weakened by the long dispute over the proposed use of the Magyar language in the Hungarian regiments and doubts were felt about the loyalty of some of the national contingents in time of war, doubts that proved to be well-founded. The scandal of May 1913 seriously weakened morale in the army. The newspapers revealed that Colonel Alfred Redl, former deputy chief of the army's Intelligence Bureau, had been serving as a spy for Russia for more than ten years.

Another pillar of the Habsburg state, the aristocracy, still appeared to retain its economic power and political influence. The great landowners still led very luxurious lives, Prince Liechtenstein for example employing 1,100 gamekeepers and foresters on his Bohemian estates. The aristocracy was an exclusive caste with unbending views on the social proprieties. When Sarah, Countess of Jersey, came to Vienna in the early 1890s, she was cold-shouldered by the local aristocracy, not because of her supposed liaison with the Prince of Wales (later Edward VII) but on account of her partnership in Coutts Bank in London.

The aristocracy continued to retain a firm foothold in the diplomatic service but the introduction in 1866 of compulsory military service, as well as a stiff civil service examination, reduced the number of nobly-born entrants in the civil service and the army. The officer corps of the army was drawn more and more from the middle classes. The emperor came to prefer men of humbler origins because they were frequently more able and more reliable—in Francis Joseph's words, 'patriots for me'. The indifference of many of the nobles to finance and the declining value of land were other factors undermining the entrenched power of the aristocracy in the period, though the last factor should not be overestimated. Many large landowners modernised their estates, bringing in mechanisation and going over to industrial crops such as sugar-beet.

The civil service of Austria–Hungary was the inheritance of the reforms introduced by Joseph II at the end of the eighteenth century. It still was composed of honest educated personnel. But by the late nineteenth century it had become authoritarian and, like the aristocracy, a caste apart. It preferred the routine of administration to the responsibility of decision-making. Stiff competition between the various nationalities of the Empire for posts in the bureaucratic hierarchy divided the civil service and so mirrored the growing national divisions.

If certain of the centripetal forces were weakening, there was no consolation for the monarchy in any great increase in prosperity. On the contrary, the 1870s and 1880s saw a steady decline in the position of the peasantry in Austria. Agriculture felt the blast of imported Hungarian grain and peasants were often forced to borrow at high rates of interest. Many peasants, unable to meet their obligations, were evicted from their land. Between 1875 and 1879 alone 37,500 holdings came under the hammer. The number of emigrants, negligible before 1880, increased to 103,000 a year by 1903. The rise of the population to over 26 million was an important factor in addition to competition, as it led to rural overpopulation and land hunger in areas like Galicia.

The years after 1870 saw the growth of a large industrial proletariat. Little was done at government level to protect this new class from the worst evils of industrialism—low wages, overcrowded and insanitary housing and long hours. Violence in Vienna increased so alarmingly that in 1884 a state of emergency was proclaimed and 300 workers were expelled.

The Balkans Problem

All the internal problems of the Austro–Hungarian monarchy were aggravated by its relations with the lesser states of south-eastern Europe, with the Turkish Empire and Russia. The Habsburgs were drawn into the Balkans by strategic and economic factors affecting the security of the whole Empire.

The Danube was regarded by the monarchy as a vital artery of trade and this consideration involved the Habsburgs in the politics of Serbia, Bulgaria and Rumania. Also, the Empire's access to the sea depended upon its continued possession of the Istrian Peninsula at the head of the Adriatic, and the Dalmatian coast. These areas, as well as the provinces of Bosnia and Herzegovina, which had been under Austrian administration since 1878, were coveted by Serbia in its desire for an outlet to the Adriatic. The monarchy came to regard Serbia as a serious threat, particularly after 1903, when the pro-Austrian King Alexander was replaced by the pro-Russian Peter Karageorge in Serbia after a palace revolution.

Until then one school of thought in Austria had believed that all the South Slavs could be united in one Slav state within the Empire holding the same status as Austria and Hungary. This was 'trialism'. Its supporters believed that it would please the discontented Serbs and Croats and give Austria dominance in the West Balkans. The plan was, of course, opposed by the Magyars and this was enough to destroy its chances of success. Serb intrigues in Bosnia convinced the Austrians that the destruction of Serbia was necessary for the survival of the monarchy. The pursuit of this policy brought about a confrontation with Russia in 1908 and set in train the events that were to lead to the First World War. That Serbia should be regarded as a real threat was proof of Austria–Hungary's decline as a great power.

There is no doubt that much Serbian provocation took place in the years before 1914, but it was grossly exaggerated and to some extent created by the Habsburg government itself. By 1907 Serbia was being called the 'Piedmont of the South Slavs'. The Habsburg monarchy, therefore, feared defeats similar to those of 1859 and, as Taylor stresses, followed a mistaken policy because of this false analogy between the Italian and South Slav nationalism. Force seemed the only remedy. Yet the vast majority of Croats and even most of the Serbs within the monarchy desired its maintenance if they could obtain fair treatment. Indeed, the Croats opposed political union with the Serbs because they realised that they would be dominated by the Serbs and this thought was intolerable to them. The real stumbling block was not South Slav nationalism but the ruthless policy of Magyarisation in Hungary which might have been checked by Francis Joseph in 1906. He preferred instead to demonstrate the strength of the Habsburg state by an aggressive foreign policy against Serbia. It was Aerenthal's annexation of Bosnia–Herzegovina in 1908 which raised the South Slav problem to a new dimension. Serbia became convinced of Austrian hostility and became anti-Austrian in earnest.

In attempting to expose Serbian agitation, the Habsburg monarchy on two occasions suffered loss of face. Both occurred in 1909. In Croatia, the Zagreb trial involving 53 Serbs opened in January. They had all been arrested on charges of agitation on Serbia's behalf. The principal defendants received sentences of up to eight years, but the sentences could not be enforced. A similar scandal took place in Austria, where the leading members of the Serbo–Croat Coalition were accused of receiving money and of acting in collusion with the Serbian government. Again the case against the defendants broke down and they were able to sue for libel. The trials were hastily prepared and both relied on forged evidence. They demonstrate the unreasoning hostility of the Austro–Hungarian authorities towards the South Slavs. The two cases reduced the credibility of the Viennese government and in Taylor's words 'involved the moral ruin of the Habsburg monarchy'.

Habsburg policy almost certainly helped to create what it most wished to avoid. Contacts between Serbia and the South Slavs increased. Serbian schools and universities were thrown open to students from Austria–Hungary. Serbia even supplied schools and universities in Austria–Hungary with propaganda material and textbooks. From Serbia was organised terrorism which negated any constructive moves by the Imperial government.

It is important to note that the Austrian authorities were as concerned with the growth of agitation in other areas of the empire as with Serb propaganda in the Balkans. In Galicia the domination of Polish landlords provoked the growth of extremism among the Ruthene (Little Russian) peasantry. Opposition to the monarchy was growing among the Czechs of Bohemia and both the Czech and Ruthene nationalists were given more than tacit support by Russia.

Conclusion

With the Empire facing so many problems it is tempting to recall Francis I's reference to his realm as a worm-eaten house and therefore regard the early dissolution of the Habsburg monarchy as inevitable even without the advent of war. In an epoch of emergent nationalism, it seems hard to believe that the multinational Habsburg state could have survived for much longer. Yet nothing is inevitable until it happens, and, as A. J. May points out, it took four years of terrible war and defeat, involving cruel human suffering, before the Habsburg realm finally collapsed. He therefore concludes that it still possessed elements of toughness and vitality, a view very different to Taylor's and Jaszi's.

In the Austrian half of the monarchy, the interests of the national minorities were given some consideration and the monarchy could still be regarded as fulfilling an historic role as protector. Most Habsburg citizens also benefited from living in the largest free-trade area outside of Russia. The two halves of the monarchy were complementary, Hungary supplying grain for the industrialised areas of Austria. The realm was bound together by the great natural highway for trade, the Danube. The Crown itself, supported by the Church, the army and bureaucracy, was still a focus of loyalty against which the discontented national elements were rarely able to unite. As we have seen, they were more generally at odds with one another than capable of cooperation against the monarchy. Among many of the rural population, anyway, national consciousness was still weak.

Given a period of peace, it is conceivable that the Austro–Hungarian Empire, having existed for a century as a state apparently on the verge of dissolution, might have survived for some while longer.

Further Reading

Macartney, C. A., *The Habsburg Empire 1790–1918*, Weidenfeld and Nicolson, London, 1971.

May, A. J., *The Habsburg Monarchy 1867–1914*, Harvard University Press, Harvard, 1965.

Taylor, A. J. P., *The Habsburg Empire 1809–1918*, Hamilton, London, 1960.

Zeman, Z. A. B., *Twilight of the Habsburgs*, Macdonald, London, 1971.

Questions

1. Was the Compromise of 1867 a reprieve or a death-warrant?
2. How far may Francis Joseph be blamed for the decline of the Habsburg Empire?
3. What can be said for and against the policies of Taaffe?
4. 'Ruthless Magyarisation': is this view of Magyar rule in Hungary between 1867 and 1914 justified?
5. In what ways were the final decades before 1914 a 'golden age' in Austria-Hungary?

CHAPTER SIX

REFORM AND REACTION IN RUSSIA 1871–1914

The Attitude of Alexander II

By the late nineteenth century three major problems confronted the Russian government: (1) the agrarian question, (2) industrialisation and (3) political reform. For Russia to be transformed into a modern state, all three problems required urgent attention but after 1866 Alexander II became more reactionary. The only important reform in the second half of his reign concerned the army, which was transformed by the zeal of the minister of war Milyutin.

Alexander would not countenance further change. Indeed, after 1866 police restrictions grew again in Russia. The Tzar was jealous of the success of the *zemstvos* and obstructed their work by limiting the amount of money which they could raise by taxation. The liberals in their turn clamoured for some kind of national assembly as a logical development from the local assemblies. This smacked too much of parliamentary power for Alexander's liking and throughout the late 1860s and 1870s he set his face firmly against the demands of the liberals as encroaching on his autocratic power.

The Rising Tide of Violence

Hugh Seton-Watson views Alexander's refusal to introduce a national assembly in the 1860s as a turning-point in Russia's history. Such a creation could have played a useful role even if only with consultative powers and recruited from only a minority of the Russian people. The gentry and the rising business and professional classes could have gained political experience and in the course of time the franchise could have been extended peacefully. Alexander's attitude on this question was one factor in the development of a more violent revolutionary movement in Russia from the 1860s. The foremost current in the revolutionary movement was Populism. The Populists (*narodniki*) derived their rather vague political philosophy from both the Westerners and Slavophils. From the Westerners they inherited a belief in progress and parliamentary institutions. From the Slavophils they inherited a belief in the *mir* (village commune). As they believed that the state would try and destroy the *mir* by the development of capitalism, they believed that an early seizure of power was vital. Their ultimate objective was a state composed of a free federation of peasant communes. Leaders like P. L. Lavrov believed that the liberation of the people should be the work not of a vanguard of professional revolutionaries but of the people itself.

In 1873 the Populists tried to initiate a mass movement, known as 'going to the people'. The expression was derived from an earlier appeal to Russian youth by Herzen who had written *To the people!* From the slogan was derived the name of the whole revolutionary movement. In 1873, and still more in 1874, about 2,000 young people went into the villages to arouse the interest of the peasants in revolution. Most peasants were hostile or merely uncomprehending and no results were achieved. The preachers were very conspicuous, and about 1,600 were easily rounded up by the police. The public trials which took place in 1877 and 1878 did give the accused a great opportunity to publicise their views. In January 1878, the day after the conclusion of the trial of 193 people, a young woman named Vera Zasulich shot the St. Petersburg police chief, General Trepov. He recovered from the wound but when Zasulich was brought to trial she was acquitted. When the police tried to rearrest her outside the court the crowd helped her to escape and flee abroad.

Vera Zasulich's attempt on Trepov marked the beginning of a series of assassinations which the revolutionaries believed were the only means of action against brutal authority. In 1876 the first revolutionary party proper, 'Land and Liberty', was started. A number of eminent government officials were killed and by 1879 it was decided that the Tzar himself should be assassinated. This extent of terrorism created a split in 'Land and Liberty'. G. V. Plekhanov and P. B. Akselrod formed a separate group called 'Black Partition' which rejected terrorism and believed that the primary concern should be with the peasants rather than the urban workers. The terrorists took the name 'People's Will' and made the assassination of the Tzar their main aim. Several attempts on his life failed but on March 1, 1881, a bomb was thrown at the Tzar's carriage as he returned from a military parade. Alexander was unscathed but got out to enquire after the welfare of those injured. A second bomb was thrown which shattered both his legs and caused fearful mutilation of the face and body.

Both the event and its timing have a tragic irony, as General M. T. Loris-Melikov had been appointed head of a commission which investigated the causes of unrest and the means of alleviating them. Loris-Melikov proposed that an assembly of elected representatives from the *zemstvos* and town councils should be convened to advise the government in the preparation of new legislation. The liberals had welcomed this as a step towards constitutional reform. Alexander had given formal approval to Loris-Melikov's proposals on the very morning of his assassination. The proposals were very much less than a constitution, which they have sometimes been called, but they were a step in the right direction. For once a Russian government was more intelligent than its people. It would now be replaced by a government of tyrannical reaction which would hunt down the assassins. In Donald Treadgold's words, 'There have been few more grotesque tragedies than that of the execution or imprisonment of the deeply moral and humanitarian boys and girls who had in their zeal murdered the ruler who perhaps had done more to improve the lot of the Russian people than any other single person in their history.'

Alexander did indeed deserve a kinder fate. Like Peter the Great before him, he had launched Russia on the road to modernisation. The emancipation of the serfs, the creation of *zemstvos* and the new legal system were of profound importance. Of course, there were shortcomings in his work. He was a conservative and the phrase 'Tzar-Liberator' which has been applied to him should be used with reservations only. That the real theme of his reign is that of tragic failure rings true especially if one compares Russia with Japan which, having experienced a genuine political revolution in 1868, embarked on a process of rapid and deliberate modernisation with great success.

The Reign of Alexander III (1881–94)

The new tzar was an impressive figure of a man, tall, heavily built and so strong that he could bend an iron bar with his bare hands. He did not possess great intellect but at times he chose able ministers like Witte. He was a natural autocrat who expected to be, and was, obeyed. His father's death made a deep impression on him and he saw in it a vivid demonstration of the evil of liberal and revolutionary ideas. Public opinion was of the same mind, for the murder of Alexander II sent a wave of horror through the country. The mood of the majority of the Russian people was thus conducive to the black reaction, the chauvinism and the bigotry which were to characterise the reign of Alexander III. Only in his favouring of industrial development, to be treated separately, did the Tzar show himself as a man of the modern age.

The dominant influence behind the throne was Constantine Pobedonostsev. As Over-Procuror of the Holy Synod from 1880 to 1905, he exercised a decisive voice in government. His efforts to preserve autocracy made him hated by liberal opinion as 'the pacesetter of reaction'. He wrote to Alexander in 1876, 'The whole secret of Russian order and prosperity is in the top, in the person of the supreme authority.' He once referred to parliamentary government as 'the greatest lie of our times'. Now he became autocracy's watchdog and his nominees were made Ministers of the Interior and Education. With the same rigid fanaticism he upheld the claims of the Orthodox Church against other denominations.

Deluding himself that his policies were popular with all but a handful of misguided persons, Pobedonostsev constantly interfered in all matters of government business. Now in government, in Seton-Watson's words, the main characteristics were 'an overall attitude of nostalgia, obscurantist and narrowly bureaucratic paternalism.' This was inevitable; Pobedonostsev had a sombre view of human nature. In his view men were incapable of goodness or rationality. They had to be led!

The most urgent task was the crushing of political opposition. The police rounded up those involved in the assassination of Alexander II and five were hanged. Governors and police were given special powers and could declare a state of emergency. Censorship, which became more repressive, was one of Pobedonostsev's obsessions and he was a member of a new committee which had power to close any offending publication and ban the editor from any future activity.

Restrictive policies governed education. The Minister of Education was the reactionary Delyanov, who combined harsh treatment of the students with social exclusiveness. Universities were deprived of their independence and all student organisations were suppressed. Delyanov was determined to keep persons of humble origins out of the universities. To this end he sought to make their entry into secondary schools more difficult. Fees were raised in 1887 and the number of pupils actually fell in the reign, though there was a rise in the number of elementary school pupils because Pobedonostsev did not object to elementary education for the lower classes so long as it was controlled by the Orthodox Church. In 1904 only 27 per cent of children of school age were actually at school and in the 1897 census it was found that only 21 per cent of the population could read and write. This failure in educational development in Russia is in stark contrast with Japan, where 93 per cent of all boys and girls of school age were attending school by 1903. Russia was spending on education less than one tenth of the sum spent on defence.

As the régime depended on the support of the landowning nobility, steps were taken to strengthen its political and economic position. In 1885 the Nobles' State Bank was established to provide credit on favourable terms though this did not prevent many large estates from being broken up. A statute of 1890 reduced peasant representation in the *zemstvo* assemblies and meant that the nobles would in future have a 57 per cent majority of delegates. The state governor was given power to veto any *zemstvo* measure of which he disapproved. Given the government hostility towards the *zemstvos*, it is to their credit that they still achieved much in the way of local improvements.

The peasants were brought more closely under the supervision of the nobility by the appointment of land captains chosen from the nobility in each locality. The land captain possessed almost dictatorial powers over the communal life of the peasant. He could cancel the decisions of the village assemblies, add items of his choice to the agenda of their meetings and remove unreliable village elders from their posts. He could suspend the verdicts of the village courts. Many land captains no doubt were just, but the institution itself was created as part of a deliberately reactionary policy designed to maintain peasants in a condition of tutelage and to make it more difficult for them to acquire the practice in self-government so necessary to the process of transforming former serfs into citizens of a modern state. As R. D. Charques rightly remarks, 'No single act of government in the reign of Alexander III stirred the Russian peasant to more bitter resentment; it brought back the breath and being of serf law.'

The repressive policies which Alexander imposed on his own people were matched by the chauvinism and bigotry of his persecuting rule over the minorities. It was in his reign that russification became an official policy. Russification may be defined as a policy in which the Russian people and the Russian language should have first place in the empire. Other peoples would be made into Russians in the interests of the Empire, regardless of their wishes. Pobedonostsev exercised a baneful influence here as he was intensely hostile to Jews, Poles and dissenters. His supporters in the implementing of the new ideology were bureaucrats and soldiers, who insisted that special precautions must be taken to strengthen security in border regions like the Baltic coast, and Orthodox priests anxious to convert Catholics and Moslems. Russification was enforced with special severity in Russian Poland. All teaching in Polish schools had to be carried on in Russian and Polish Catholics could not hold any office. But the Finns, the Baltic Germans and the people of Central Asia were subjected to similar regulations, yet they had hitherto served the Empire with unquestioning loyalty. The result of the policy of russification was to strengthen the determination of the nationalist intelligentsia and to awaken national consciousness in other classes in which it had previously been dormant if indeed it had existed at all.

Anti-Semitism, which had long been widespread, became an active policy under Alexander III especially as many Russians blamed Jewish revolutionaries for the murder of Alexander II. It is possible to distinguish two types of anti-Semitism in Russia in this period. In government circles it was a natural attitude of dignitaries of the Orthodox Church who viewed the Jews as killers of Christ. This attitude was encouraged by Pobedonostsev and shared to some extent by Alexander III and his successor Nicholas II. The other type of anti-Semitism was found in the illiterate masses and petty officials in regions with a large Jewish population. It was a crude class hatred of a minority which concerned itself with finance and into whose pockets the small savings of many peasants disappeared.

May 1881 saw the start of the pogroms—that is to say, the destruction of Jewish property and the murder of Jews. A total of 215 pogroms took place and though the government officially condemned the excesses, it showed little sense of urgency in stopping them until Tolstoy, who disliked disorder, became Minister of Interior; but he also disliked Jews and brought into law further restriction of

Jewish rights. Jews were forbidden to live or acquire property outside the towns or large villages, thus concentrating their growing numbers into a small area and forcing them into those professions which they were denounced for monopolising. In 1882, the war ministry limited the number of Jews in the medical corps to five per cent of the personnel, also asserting that Jews lowered the standards of sanitation. In 1887, quotas kept to a minimum the number of Jewish children who could obtain university or secondary education. All Jews were from 1889 barred from practising law and in 1890 were denied a vote in the *zemstvo* assembly elections though they still had to pay *zemstvo* taxes. In 1894, Jews were refused licences to sell spirits, a law which removed one of the few jobs open to them. With this kind of treatment it was inevitable that Jews were especially susceptible to revolutionary ideas and they were an important element in both the Populist and Marxist movements.

In 1894 Alexander III began to suffer from migraine, insomnia and weakness in the legs. It seemed inconceivable that a man of such strength could fade away but in October he died of nephritis.

Nicholas II

The man who was to allow the autocratic regime to collapse about him and was to be responsible for the extinction of his dynasty was too shy and gentle to be an autocrat. He had more intelligence and sensitivity than his father and exceptional personal charm but too often he gave an impression of weakness, appearing to agree with the last person to whom he had talked, and no one could tell what he would do next. He was a little man lost in the immensity of his realm and he knew it. He felt that he would never be able to measure up to his father's standards yet Pobedonostsev had instilled into him a blind faith in autocracy and Orthodoxy. At the age of 13 he had been led into the presence of his dying grandfather to take leave of him and that grim event had left an indelible impression. Indeed, so many of his predecessors had died by violence that there was a strong fatalism in the last tzar's make-up. His father had done nothing to prepare him for the throne by giving him experience of government work.

In 1894 he married Princess Alice of Hesse-Darmstadt, a granddaughter of Queen Victoria who became Alexandra Fedorovna. They remained a deeply attached couple but their union was to give rise to tragedy as in time she became the dominant influence in his life. Her devoted but misguided interference in matters of government was to be a major factor in the downfall of the monarchy. Nicholas disliked the whole business of government and was happiest when living the life of a country squire with his family at one of the Imperial estates. He was a good family man, an ardent bicyclist and a devotee of amateur photography. He kept a diary assiduously. This life, asserts Donald Treadgold, resulted in an utter lack of comprehension of the world outside and made him densely self-assured. On the day that the Russian fleet went to its destruction at Tsushima in May 1905, the home-loving tzar entered in his diary, 'Had a very nice picnic'. With Nicholas as tzar, the political climate changed. People were no longer intimidated by the figure of the new ruler as they had been by that of Alexander III. The pressure for change began to build up as it had after the Crimean War.

Nicholas, however, soon destroyed hopes that his accession would bring any new style to Russian government. In January 1895 he delivered a speech to an assembly of *zemstvo* delegates which had been drafted by Pobedonostsev. 'I shall defend the principle of autocracy as unswervingly as my deceased father,' he said, and went on to describe the hopes of the liberals for participation in government as 'senseless dreams'.

Liberalism, Marxism and the Social Revolutionary Movement

Though there was increasing prosperity, real discontents remained. Indeed, the new prosperity, by making the struggle for existence a little easier, enabled the revolutionaries to think more about politics and thus on balance increased political opposition to the regime. Despite government action, conditions of work were often vile. Accidents in factories were astonishingly frequent. In one year alone, 1904, some 11 per cent of labour in metallurgical factories suffered death or injury. The influx of peasants into the cities in search of jobs created a huge demand for housing. Many workers were forced to live in filthy hovels and still faced rising rents. The Russian urban poor suffered not only material exploitation but emotional deprivation, the result of being uprooted from the village, where they had belonged, and being faced with a strange and hostile environment. They were ready supporters of revolutionary movements. The leaders of those movements came not from the most deprived sectors but from the better-paid and more skilled such as printers and metal-workers who were interested in politics and prepared to give time and energy to the task of organisation.

During the decade from the accession of Nicholas II to the crisis of 1905, three political movements developed. They were Liberalism, Marxism and a revived form of Populism. In the years after Alexander II's reforms the gentry had been the major strength in Russian liberalism and their talents had been concentrated in the new self-government. In time, Russian liberalism broadened its base, gaining adherents from the professions—professors, students, doctors, lawyers and journalists. Work in the *zemstvos* gained the professional personnel the name of the 'third element' from a chance remark of Saratov's in 1899, by which time they comprised 65,000 of the *zemstvo* employees. The third element made the *zemstvos* more democratic because of their influence on the gentry. While the gentry aimed, in Fischer's phrase, at 'small deeds' in the sense of piecemeal local reform, the intelligentsia aimed at 'senseless dreams', the achievement of a democratic constitution. This was senseless, says Fischer, because the liberal movement was too new and weak to be politically important. It lacked any national organisation, an uncensored journal, a clear-cut programme or an identifiable group of spokesmen. The liberal intelligentsia continued to need the gentry class; which had more influence in government circles, and this led to years of compromise and tactical wavering.

By the 1890s two lines of action were open to the Russian liberals and both were used. One was to press the government for more participation in government, and this the liberals continued to do against a government which was uncooperative. The alternative policy was to set up an illegal political organisation and to campaign for more liberties. The attitude of the government strengthened the arguments of those who favoured this line. In 1901, P. B. Struve became the editor of a radical paper *Liberation* and an illegal opposition party, the Union of Liberation, was founded to work towards ending autocracy and creating constitutional government. It did not advocate revolutionary violence but it was too radical for the more conservative *zemstvo* leaders. It was the Union of Liberation that held public banquets in November 1904 to rally support for a constitution, as did also a congress of *zemstvo* representatives.

Marxist ideas were propagated in Russia from the mid-1880s by Plekhanov.

Once a follower of Black Partition, he abandoned Populism and embraced Marxism in 1883. In that year he founded a Liberation of Labour group in Switzerland with Vera Zasulich and P. B. Akselrod and formulated the Marxist case against Populism. He maintained that capitalism was bound to come to Russia and that only after it had worked its changes on Russian society would conditions be appropriate for socialism.

By the end of the 1880s Marxist ideas were popular with university students and members of the intelligentsia. The specific, concrete and scientific approach to social questions stressed by the Marxists compared favourably with the vague and old-fashioned Populist slogans. Marxist groups were also formed among the workers of some St. Petersburg factories who wished not only for political education but education in a wider sense as a means of escape from factory conditions. Lenin joined one of the intellectual groups in 1893 and soon became close friends with Julius Martov. They were arrested in 1895 and were given a sentence of three years' exile in Siberia. Despite the arrest of many of the Marxist intellectuals in St. Petersburg, in 1898 a secret congress was held in Minsk and a Marxist party was formed, the Russian Social Democratic Labour Party. It was soon broken up by the arrest of most of the delegates in 1899 for the police found such groups easy to infiltrate.

This failure caused bitter disputes among Russian Marxists, particularly on the nature of the party. Some Marxists believed that the political struggle should be conducted by the workers themselves in a mass movement, not by an élite of intellectuals. Lenin opposed this, not merely because the growth of a mass movement was impossible under an autocratic régime but because he opposed the idea of a democratic mass movement under any circumstances and insisted on an elitist organisation. Lenin and Martov founded a new paper *Iskra* (*The Spark*) in Germany in 1900, and in 1901 Lenin wrote a book, taking Chernyshevsky's title, *What is to be Done?* It was a blueprint for his future Bolshevik party. The party, said Lenin, must be based on a thorough understanding of Marxist theory and on firm internal discipline. Intellectuals were to have a decisive role to play as leaders of the working class. They would form the élite of a party which must be composed of professional revolutionaries, 'dedicating their whole lives to the revolution, not just a free evening'. Lenin also learned from the Populists that the peasantry would play a large role in the coming revolution.

In 1903 these disputes came to a head at the second party congress and a split in the party took place. Martov opposed Lenin on the nature of the party as he wanted a broader definition of party membership than had been envisaged. On this issue Lenin was outvoted. At a later stage in the congress, a vote took place on the composition of the editorial board of *Iskra* and this time Lenin's supporters were in the majority. It was from the voting on this issue that the names were derived which were later attached to the two sections into which the party had split. Lenin called his group the majority (*bolsheviki*) and his opponents the minority (*mensheviki*). The groups differed not only on the nature of the party but also on their attitude to the peasantry and the bourgeoisie. Lenin wanted an alliance with the peasantry, while the Mensheviks were dubious of the value of such a policy. They believed in the necessity of cooperation with the bourgeoisie, a course which Lenin opposed inflexibly. Thus when the revolutionary crisis came in Russia there were two Marxist parties.

There were still various Populist groups in Russia in the early 1890s and from them emerged a new important political force, the Social Revolutionary movement led by Victor Chernov. He recognised the arrival of capitalism in Russia which Populists had so far denied. The great famine of 1891 revived the interest of the Social Revolutionaries in the peasantry. Chernov laid down a policy of immediate revolution without waiting for power to devolve to the bourgeoisie, which had been the Marxist line. After the revolution land would be distributed to the peasantry. Thus the Social Revolutionaries were extremists but they were also democratic, favouring universal suffrage and therefore having some common ground with the *zemstvo* liberals.

At the end of 1901 a united Social Revolutionary Party was formed. It was never as tightly disciplined a party as the Social Democrats but it was a significant force that could goad the peasants into action, as in 1902, when large-scale riots occurred which demonstrated that the peasants were not the apathetic reactionary force as was sometimes assumed. The Social Revolutionaries were more feared by the authorities than the Marxists because they set up a Battle Organisation to assassinate key figures whereas the Marxists opposed terrorism, which they considered historically useless, and seemed only interested in talking and writing.

The Revolution of 1905

Though the Tzar did support Witte's reforms for nine years, his usual choice of ministers to deal with the mounting unrest was unwise. A particularly unfortunate appointment as Minister of the Interior was Vyacheslav Plehve. He was a narrow police bureaucrat who had won recognition by bringing to justice the murderers of Alexander II. Plehve was virulently anti-Semitic and in his ministry were forged the *Protocols of the Elders of Zion*, purporting to be plans drawn up by the Zionist Congress of 1897 for the domination of the world by the Jews. Other minorities, especially the Finns, Poles and Armenians, also suffered increased persecution. Plehve was most active in promoting police activity and his agents infiltrated every political group in Russia. In July 1904 he was killed by a Social Revolutionary bomb, an event which made a tremendous impression on the public. Plehve had aggravated more unrest by his policies and it was partly through his advice that Nicholas allowed himself to be drawn into the war with Japan that broke out in 1904, though the Tzar himself believed that Russia had a great mission to perform in Asia, an idea derived from a journey made in his youth. Plehve had argued that 'a small victorious war would stop the revolutionary tide'. Instead the war proved to be an unnecessary, large and humiliating disaster.

By January 1905, public anger over the defeats in the Far East was mounting when a calamity occurred in St. Petersburg which fundamentally undermined the Tzar's prestige. The head of the defence section of the police in Moscow, Colonel Zubatov, had set up workers' organisations in 1902 in order to steer their discontent away from the government and towards their employers. The policy rebounded on the government in 1905, when a strike in the Putilov armaments works spread and involved all the workers in the capital. Their leader was Father Georgii Gapon, who had helped to organise the new unions and was a police agent. In January, probably with genuine motives, he urged the workers to march to the Winter Palace and present a petition to the Tzar setting out their demands. On Sunday, January 22, the workers with their wives and children joined him in an orderly march, singing hymns and carrying the Tzar's portrait as an emblem of loyalty. In the approaches to the palace the police and military ordered the marchers to halt but with the momentum of their numbers they continued to move forward. The troops and police lost their heads and began firing into the crowd, wounding several hundred and killing over one hundred people. It was believed that the Tzar had given the order to shoot, though Nicholas was not in the Winter Palace at the time. Father Gapon summed up the universal disillusionment after Bloody Sunday in the phrase 'Nicholas Romanov, formerly Tzar and now destroyer of souls.' No longer could the Tzar be regarded as the 'Little Father' of his people. 'This event,' says Hugh Seton-Watson, 'one of the landmarks of Russian history, started off the process which has become known as the Revolution of 1905.'

Nicholas had appointed as successor to Plehve, Prince Svyatopolk Mirsky, a man of integrity and a liberal. This appointment opened a new period known as the 'Russian spring'. A conference of *zemstvo* representatives had met in St. Petersburg in November 1904 and called for new developments in government, including an increase in electoral rights and abolition of the police state. The illegal Union of Liberation also took action in November. It held a series of public banquets to rally public opinion to press for a constitution. The organisers had in mind the banquets which preceded the downfall of Louis Philippe in France in 1848. The massacre of Bloody Sunday and the news of the surrender of Port Arthur in January caused a fresh eruption of violence, including the murder of Grand Duke Sergei in the Kremlin in broad daylight. During February peasant revolts broke out in Kursk province and spread extensively. In June, the crew of the battleship *Potemkin* mutinied and took the ship to a Rumanian port. All this time the liberals were active in pressing for radical change and in August the opposition to the Tzar was strengthened by a grant of autonomy to the universities which allowed the students to use lecture-halls for political meetings.

In this period of crisis the government had shown itself both weak and shortsighted. Though it could not assert its will by force it still refused to make any concessions, even to the moderate liberals. In September spontaneous strikes spread from the printers and railway workers to the professions until the whole country was at a standstill. In desperation Nicholas, who had still been hoping for a military dictatorship, turned for help to Witte who had just negotiated the peace treaty with Japan. Witte strongly advised Nicholas to give a constitution and in October an Imperial manifesto proclaimed a grant of civil rights, the institution of a *Duma* (parliament) in the election of which all classes would participate and a guarantee that all laws including decrees of the Tzar would be enacted only with the consent of the Duma. This went a long way towards democratic government. It received a jubilant welcome from many quarters though it still fell far short of establishing the supremacy of parliament.

The part played by the industrial working class in the Revolution of 1905 was crucial, even though it was only a small minority of the population. The political consciousness of the workers had been developing rapidly, influenced by the propaganda of the socialist parties and their own experience. Sympathetic strikes in January 1905, affecting over 400,000, were evidence of real solidarity. The culmination of the workers' movement of 1905 was the establishment of the St. Petersburg *Soviet* (workers' council). This council was not created by order of the political parties but by the initiative of the workers themselves. The socialists realised the importance of the Soviet as a workers' parliament and the workers were glad to let them play a leading part on the executive committee. By October the Soviet had more power in St. Petersburg than the government. The Marxists, with the exception of Trotsky, played little part in the crisis as many were in exile and engaged in factional rivalry though Lenin realised that in any future uprising the Soviets would be a crucial factor.

With the granting of the October Manifesto, Nicholas now had an opportunity to rally support to his cause by fulfilling the role of a constitutional monarch. He failed to grasp the opportunity partly because of his own stupidity and partly because of his wife's instability, which became worse after the birth of her son Alexei in 1904. It was found that Alexei suffered from the incurable disease of haemophilia. Alexandra herself had introduced it into the Russian family as she was a carrier of the disease through her grandmother, Queen Victoria. The blow made Alexandra willing to seek help from any crank or charlatan who might save her son. In 1905 the family fell under the sway of a monk, Gregory Rasputin (meaning 'debauched'). He was a peculiar mixture of cruelty and kindness, viciousness and piety. He was a malodorous drunkard and a sensualist but he had powers of healing and was able to give the Tzarevich relief from pain when he lay in agony from internal haemorrhages. Yet his drunken orgies and predilection for raping ladies of the nobility gave rise to terrible scandals. Nicholas and Alexandra refused to believe any accusations against Rasputin and the Tzar condoned the monk's powerful influence over his wife as Alexandra believed that while Rasputin lived the Tzarevich could not die.

The Dumas

Even before the first Duma opened, the political atmosphere had been soured by government violence. Troops suppressed a general strike in Moscow in December and more than 1,000 people were killed, many being executed after being taken prisoner. Special punitive contingents of reliable troops were sent to rebellious areas like the Baltic and Georgia. Counter-revolutionary groups, the 'black hundreds', caused havoc; claiming to defend order, they carried out pogroms of Jewish property.

Five days before the first Duma opened in May 1906, Nicholas, at the prompting of two reactionaries Durnov and Trepov, dismissed Witte who was one of the few men who might have saved the dynasty. Nicholas and Alexandra had come to hate the man who had counselled concession. 'I have never seen such a chameleon of a man,' remarked Nicholas. Witte, of course, owed his position only to the Tzar's goodwill and not to the Duma. The Tzar still retained wide powers, including the right to suspend the Duma, proclaim a state of emergency and thus suspend the constitution, and he held sole command of the armed forces. The Duma could not even initiate constitutional amendments. In this sense the Revolution of 1905 did not represent much progress.

The Tzar now appointed I. L. Goremykin as Prime Minister, a bureaucrat who hated change and regarded the Tzar as an autocrat. The Duma was dominated by a liberal party, the Constitutional Democrats, who became known as the Cadets. It clashed immediately with the government over the question of land for the peasants and religious and national rights for the minorities. In July, Nicholas dissolved the Duma but the elections still did not result in a new Duma conservative enough for the government, and the second Duma was dissolved in June 1907. Peter Stolypin now introduced a new electoral law, enormously restricting the franchise, a clear violation of the Tzar's promises. The restrictive franchise under which the third Duma was elected increased the representation of both the extreme right and the right centre at the expense of the parties of the left. The largest group in the new Duma were the Octobrists, under A. I. Guchkov, who were moderate conservatives.

The fact that the Duma was conservative did not mean that the régime had restored its old autocratic power. The organisation of political parties and a milder censorship were important developments. Nor was the third Duma servile. The Octobrists were enlightened gentry who could criticise the government keenly and support liberal measures. Guchkov, for example, condemned government handling of the army during the war and called on the Grand Dukes to resign their commands. Such independence of spirit impressed the public, while the Duma's restraint won a certain grudging respect from the government. The third Duma was able, therefore, to last for five years and contribute to many improvements in the period.

Most of these advances were won in cooperation with Peter Stolypin, who remains a controversial figure. He was hated by the left as the man who had dissolved two dumas and changed the electoral law. He could be ruthless. When he was appointed Prime Minister in July 1906 he took stern measures to quell disorder. Courts-martial between September 1906 and May 1907 executed 1,144 people. The harshness seemed justified in one sense because the number of people killed or wounded by terrorists fell sharply after 1907.

The extreme right hated him because he was willing to play the part of Prime Minister and believed in economic policies designed to modernise Russia, yet he was also a narrow Russian nationalist. He was devoted to the peasants and he was resolved at all costs to institute private peasant ownership in Russia. He was in favour of cooperating with the Duma though at heart he remained a conservative authoritarian capable of political sharp practice. When in 1911 he met opposition from the Duma over a *zemstvo* reform for Russian Poland, he had the Tzar prorogue the two chambers for three days and passed his measure as an emergency decree, a move that alienated the moderate majority in the Duma. He is thus difficult to label and can almost be described as an enlightened despot.

From the first, Stolypin was a hunted man but faced this unpleasant situation with courage. Until 1911 he above all other politicians could handle the Duma, especially as he and Alexander Guchkov respected each other. The years 1907 to 1911 saw land reform and changes in education, the law and health insurance implemented in a period of greater calm and prosperity. But intrigues by reactionaries against him made it likely that Stolypin would eventually be dismissed. Nicholas was spared the need to do this. In September 1911, Stolypin was shot dead at the opera by a Social Revolutionary who was also a police agent. He had unfortunately offended both Nicholas and Alexandra. He had offended the Tzar by requesting written confirmation of the sovereign's assent to the proroguing of the Duma, a sign of distrust. Alexandra he had offended by ordering Rasputin to leave St. Petersburg. Stolypin's death was a grave blow to the dynasty for all that.

In 1913, the tercentenary of the Romanov dynasty was celebrated and Nicholas and Alexandra were cheered by huge crowds as they attended a thanksgiving service in Kazan Cathedral. Demonstrations of loyalty were evident when they travelled downriver to Moscow; similar demonstrations were evident on the outbreak of war in 1914 and a fund of popular support for the dynasty still existed. The experience merely confirmed Alexandra's belief in autocracy and she waged a tireless war against reform, urging Nicholas to dissolve the Duma and repudiate the 1905 constitution.

Imperial Expansion

It is sometimes overlooked that Russia has been an Imperialist state just as much as western states because her menace in Europe has obscured her expansion in Asia. Indeed the colonisation of the steppes may be regarded as the central thread in her whole development. Kliuchevsky asserted, 'Russia's history, throughout, is the history of a country undergoing colonisation. . . . Migration and colonisation constituted the basic factor of our history to which all other factors were more or less related.' The nature of the régime itself stimulated individuals to escape to freedom but more fundamental was the pressure of population growth. The Russian population, which was 36 million in 1791, had reached 170 million by 1914 and these people had to live somewhere. Millions of peasants migrated illegally or legally to the southern and eastern frontiers in the nineteenth and early twentieth centuries. In this period Russia experienced a moving frontier in the same manner as did the United States with the exception that Russia's moving frontier did not stop in the early 1890s. The main areas of expansion were Siberia, Central Asia and Manchuria.

The Russian Economy and the Achievements of Witte

In the period from 1870 to the mid-1880s Russian industry grew slowly but from the mid-1880s a significant upturn in the rate of growth occurred. Three factors explain this improvement: (1) the expansion of the railways; (2) the help of foreign experts like the Nobels in the oil industry; and (3) the more active role played by the state in protecting industry. Government policy conditioned the industrial structure that emerged in Russia, particularly the emphasis on capital goods industries rather than consumer goods industries and also the use of foreign capital.

The industrial boom of the 1890s was closely linked with the policies of the powerful and able Minister of Finance, Sergei Witte, whose tenure at the ministry lasted from 1893 to 1903. He was disliked by many in government and court circles, where he was regarded as an upstart, especially as he was married to a Jewish divorcee. His policies were attacked as being extravagant and he was accused of selling out Russia to foreign capitalists. Yet Witte was one of the outstanding statesmen of the nineteenth century. He is described by Hugh Seton-Watson as 'both a brilliant organiser and a man of broad ideas. . . . He was determined to bring Russia into the modern world and the motive of his economic policy may be described as essentially non-economic; his aim was the greatness of the Russian state.' Witte realised that Russia was the most backward of the great powers and that her international position was precarious with the decline of Russo–German relations after 1878. As von Laue has shown, Witte made the industrialisation of Russia a prime objective; for him it was a race against time. Economic strength had to be built up rapidly for Russia to maintain her position as a great power. The basis of industrial strength was to be the rapid development of railways and heavy industry. The means by which this objective was achieved have been called the Witte system; it incorporated tariff protection, monetary stability, heavy taxation and the encouragement of foreign investment.

Witte preserved the favourable balance of trade, already secured in the 1880s, by continuing a highly protective tariff policy. Russian industry was encouraged by state contracts and the regulation of railway freight charges so that it could supply the needs of the home market. The production of pig-iron, which in the

1870s had satisfied only two fifths of domestic consumption, provided three quarters of domestic consumption by the 1890s. The state also took measures to stimulate agricultural exports in the interests of the balance of trade. The construction of railways in regions supplying grain for export helped the expansion of foreign sales. Von Laue suggests that heavy taxation of the peasantry forced them to sell more of their agricultural produce. Taxation therefore served a dual purpose; it provided funds for state investment and fostered exports by squeezing an agricultural surplus from the Russian peasant. Yet high taxation limited the growth of a large domestic market in Russia.

It is important not to exaggerate the novelty of Witte's work. Most of the features of his system were used by earlier Ministers of Finance like Vishnegradski, who had already taken action to stabilise the rouble and encourage foreign capital. Nevertheless, Witte made a unique contribution because of his single-minded vigour and his success was great. The annual rate of industrial growth was more than eight per cent; its basis was the expansion of heavy industry in the Ukraine stimulated by railway construction. Between 1890 and 1900 the length of track expanded from 30,000 to 53,000 kilometres. The state played a major part in this burst of construction, investing 3,500 million roubles in the railways in the decade. The railway network of European Russia was enlarged and important new lines were built in the Urals, the Lower Volga region and the Caucasus. The most ambitious undertakings were in Asia, above all the Trans-Siberian railway begun in 1891. It linked Moscow and St. Petersburg with Vladivostock on the Pacific coast. The exploitation of new areas was now feasible and large-scale emigration to western Siberia developed. Cotton growing in Turkestan was now a viable proposition and by 1913 over half of the cotton consumed by Russian industry was produced at home. In 1890 Russia had ranked fifth among the nations in terms of length of railway network. By 1900 she was in second place behind the United States. Railway construction stimulated home industry by its demand for capital equipment, taking more than one third of Russia's iron output directly and also stimulating the establishment of large locomotive works and coalmining.

The weight of heavy industry in the economy increased considerably. In the 1890s coal production nearly trebled and pig-iron output grew three and a half fold with a tendency towards concentration into larger units of production. In the Ivanovo textile region, factories employing more than 1,000 workers were producing 82 per cent of the region's output by 1913. In the Ukraine metallurgical industries the average number of workers per factory was 4,600 by 1900, a feature soon to be of immense political significance as it facilitated the growth of working-class organisations. This size of plant was often an indication of technological backwardness because labour productivity was so low that a large work force was necessary.

Foreign capital was attracted to Russia in such amounts that by 1914 Russia was Europe's largest debtor nation. In the 1890s foreign investment in Russia rose more than fourfold to 911 million roubles and more than doubled again by 1914 to some 2,000 million roubles. Much of it went into heavy industry. Half of it went into the mining and metallurgical industries and foreign capital accounted for nearly 90 per cent of total capital investment in this sector by 1900. After 1890 the bulk of the foreign investment was provided by France and Belgium. These countries invested 521 million roubles in Russia in the decade, though British capital remained important in the oil and cotton industries. Russia was an attractive area in which to invest for several reasons. High profits seemed likely because of the high tariffs protecting Russian industry, and the many government contracts to industry. Witte also took steps to stabilise the paper rouble by going on the Gold Standard and checking speculation on paper roubles. He enjoyed good fortune in that low international interest rates prevailed in the period which made it easier to attract foreign capital to Russia.

There were, however, adverse effects in the Witte system. Some government policies may have exercised a retarding influence on the economy. Heavy taxation prevented Russian peasants from adopting new techniques and raising their productivity. It also kept domestic demand for industrial products low, though as von Laue has pointed out, industrial side-earnings in time helped more and more to sustain the peasant's standard of living. Railways were often built more for strategic requirements than to serve industry. Tariff policies, by raising the price of imported foods like tea and salt, further reduced the purchasing power of the mass of the population. Duties on imported raw materials and capital goods raised manufacturing costs considerably.

Stagnation, Boom and the Reforms of Stolypin (1900–13)

After 1900 came an industrial crisis with numerous bankruptcies and falling production in the heavy industry sector. The immediate cause of the recession was a tightening of the world money market in 1899, a product of several factors including the outbreak of the Boer War. The consequent rise in world interest rates hit Russian industry. More fundamental was Russia's agrarian problem. The living standards of the peasantry fell in the 1890s as a result of high taxation and a run of poor harvests. This important source of government revenue declined and as a result government orders to heavy industry were reduced by 10 per cent in 1900.

After 1906 came a period of recovery with an overall growth rate of over six per cent. Gerschenkron points out that it was a boom of a different kind from that of the 1890s. The government left private enterprise to play a greater role in fostering industry. Unlike in the 1890s, the peasants experienced improving conditions, enabling them to provide a greater market for industrial products. The reduction in the importance of the village commune stimulated the growth of an industrial labour force.

One factor contributing to greater peasant prosperity was an improvement in the terms of trade for agricultural producers. Grain prices rose relative to the prices of industrial goods both on the domestic and the world markets. The overall general price level in Russia increased by some 29 per cent between 1900 and 1913 while the price of agricultural products rose by 41 per cent.

Legislation did much to improve the lot of the peasants. In 1905 redemption payments on land being purchased by the peasants were abolished. In 1906 and 1910 came the famous Stolypin land reforms. Stolypin recognised the deep-seated aspirations of the Russian peasant to own and manage his own land, and saw that peasant discontent had been a major factor in the abortive revolution of 1905. His reforms therefore aimed at creating a prosperous class of peasants which would provide a firm basis of political support for tzarist governments. Thus he set out to break the hold of the *mir* over the individual peasant and by the end of 1906 decrees had been issued allowing the peasant to leave the *mir* when he wished or, if he remained, to consolidate his strips of land in one place and to hold them permanently. Communal responsibility for taxation was ended.

The best compliment on the effectiveness of the land reforms is that Lenin feared their effect, for the creation of a strong class of peasant farmers would have been a bulwark against revolution. In European Russia between 1907 and 1916 at least 2½ million households left the communes and acquired land so that about half the peasants owned their own land. As a class, the peasantry owned four times as much land as the nobility by 1914. Agricultural techniques were now improving.

The state had already taken steps to improve agriculture by founding the Peasant Land Bank in 1885 to buy land from the gentry and resell it to the peasants. Between 1906 and 1914 it sold four times as much land to the peasants as it had in the previous decade. The government also encouraged the migration of the peasants to West Siberia after 1905. The peak years of migration—1907 to 1909—saw more than two million peasants arrive there and the region became important for dairy produce and grain.

By 1913 the boom in Russia was based on more secure foundations than that of the 1890s though inadequate data make a final judgment impossible. There were, of course, disquieting social and economic features—for example, the continued low level of agricultural productivity which was rising at only one per cent a year—but it is legitimate to speculate that if a prolonged exhausting war culminating in revolution and civil war had not intervened, agricultural and industrial improvements would have continued. A bulwark against revolution would have been created in the form of a class of independent farmers, and industrial modernisation on western lines would have created a more prosperous proletariat. Revolutionary violence was still a formidable factor in 1914 but the labour movement was turning to revision and trades union organisation. The third Duma had begun to make a significant contribution to government, passing measures for universal education.

The war, however, arrived at a particularly unfortunate time for Russia. It caught the country in the process of radical internal reorganisation. The constitutional experiment was less than a decade old; the land reforms of Stolypin had been in operation only a few years and the scheme for universal education was only just being implemented. Under such conditions war was bound to cause grave dislocation which made revolution more likely. Human folly was to make it almost inevitable.

Further Reading

Falkus, M. E., *The Industrialization of Russia 1700–1914*, Macmillan, London, 1972.

Mosse, W. E., *Alexander II and the Modernization of Russia*, English Universities Press, London, 1958.

Seton-Watson, H., *The Russian Empire 1801–1917*, Clarendon Press, Oxford, 1967.

Questions

1. 'The tzar-liberator'. How far do you agree with this view of Alexander II?
2. 'Black reaction'. Is this a fair comment on the reign of Alexander III?
3. Examine the rise of opposition to tzarism in Russia between 1871 and 1914.
4. Account for the outbreak of the Revolution of 1905 in Russia.
5. To what extent had tzarist Russia transformed its economy and political institutions by 1914?

CHAPTER SEVEN

INTERNATIONAL AFFAIRS 1871–1914

Bismarck's Foreign Policy (1871–90)

Bismarck's Aims

The three wars by which German unification was achieved between 1864 and 1871 introduced a new degree of insecurity into European affairs which was to be a permanent feature until the outbreak of war in 1914. France, of course, was to regard the new Germany with fear and jealousy but feelings of disquiet were also voiced in Britain. When Disraeli spoke of the balance of power being entirely destroyed, he felt that it was Britain which would suffer from the change. Gorchakov, the Russian Foreign Secretary, was envious of Bismarck's success and was determined that Russia should not be ignored in Europe in any new crisis. The Austro–Hungarian government was afraid that Bismarck still had certain territorial objectives, in particular the acquisition of Austria's German provinces. It was clear that the other great powers would be unlikely to stand aside in the event of a new Franco–German war.

Yet Bismarck possessed a strong hand. He enjoyed more unchallenged control in the handling of diplomatic affairs than in domestic matters. Germany was the greatest military power in Europe and her alliance was eagerly sought. She was also a sated power; Bismarck had no more territorial acquisitions to make and his main aim after 1871 was the preservation of the status quo. He felt that he could safely ignore Britain because Gladstone's government was firmly pacific, while in Austria the Hungarian Count Andrassy had become Foreign Secretary and he was anti-Russian. Moreover, Bismarck's support for the establishment of a republic in France was to bear fruit as it would help to keep France isolated in a Europe of monarchical states. His moderation was to prevent the growth of any coalition against Germany; he avoided unnecessary disputes with other powers and sought to provide outlets for their ambitions. Only late did he try to gain colonies for Germany; until then he encouraged the expansion of the French empire—for example in Tunis—in the interests of a genuine rapprochement which would make the loss of Alsace–Lorraine easier to forget. He also realised that French expansion would cause quarrels between France and other colonial powers.

In practice, Bismarck's main task was to remain on good terms with both Austria–Hungary and Russia. In May 1873, the League of the Three Emperors was formed between Germany, Austria–Hungary and Russia. The three proclaimed their monarchical solidarity and common stand against revolution. They agreed to work together to maintain peace and to conclude military alliances if necessary. Nothing was said about specific political problems—for example, the Balkans, where Russia and Austria were rivals—for the simple reason that this would immediately demonstrate the fragility of the League. 'Suspicion between Vienna and St. Petersburg was the essential flaw in the League of the Three Emperors,' says A. J. P. Taylor, who rightly describes it as a fair-weather system.

The war scare of 1875 showed the limitations of the League. It was well known that Bismarck was angered by the swift recovery of France after 1871 and rumours spread in international circles in 1875 that he was planning a preventive war on the French. The British expressed their alarm through normal diplomatic channels while Gorchakov, always glad of an opportunity to score off Bismarck, accompanied the tzar on a visit to Berlin to warn off the Germans. Bismarck proclaimed his peaceful intentions and waxed sarcastic about Gorchakov, France's 'guardian angel'. The incident, trivial in its way, was a rebuff for Bismarck and a demonstration of goodwill for France.

The Balkan Crisis (1875–78)

Bismarck was in a sense fortunate that attention was drawn away from Europe to the Balkans by a revival of the Eastern Question. The essence of the Eastern Question was the decline of the Turkish Empire from the late seventeenth century. The decadent rule of its sultans meant that effective control of the huge empire, with its mixture of different traditions, languages, races, laws and religions could no longer be maintained. But who would fill the vacuum left by the Turkish withdrawal? The state likely to gain most appeared to be Russia, which not only possessed military power but shared the Orthodox religion with many of the subject peoples in Balkan Turkey. To Russian encroachment Austria–Hungary and Britain were sternly opposed. Both states had supported the maintenance of the Turkish Empire, the British fearing the Russian threat to their naval supremacy in the eastern Mediterranean and the security of their routes to India. Austria–Hungary's motives for supporting Turkey were clearly expressed by Andrassy in January 1875: 'Turkey possesses a utility almost providential for Austria–Hungary. For Turkey maintains the "status quo" of the small Balkan states and impedes their aspirations. If it were not for Turkey, all these aspirations would fall down on our heads . . . if Bosnia–Herzegovina should go to Serbia or Montenegro, or if a new state should be formed there which we cannot prevent, then we should be ruined and should ourselves assume the role of the "Sick Man".'

Despite the attitude of Britain and Austria–Hungary, Turkish decline had continued steadily throughout the nineteenth century. Greece and Rumania had won independence and a number of other provinces like Serbia had won practical autonomy. In August 1875, a revolt broke out against Turkish rule in Bosnia and Herzegovina, an area lying to the north-west of Serbia, and it soon spread to other parts of the empire, particularly Bulgaria. All the old problems implicit in the Eastern Question came to the fore again, with the other powers fearing that Russia would seek to take advantage of the situation.

Russian policy in the crisis was weakened by division. Tzar Alexander realised the delicacy of the situation and so did Gorchakov. The foreign secretary, now nearly 80, was a professional diplomat, a man of caution, who preferred international discussion of any given problem. The Russian government, however, was under pressure from the development of Pan-Slav ideas in Russia. Pan-Slavism aimed at the cultural and linguistic union of all Slav peoples and as such appealed to the Russian public. While official Russian policy was caution, certain Pan-Slav members of the government—for example, Ignatiev, the Russian ambassador to Turkey—worked for unilateral Russian intervention in the Balkans, a move desired by a Russian public which sympathised with the rebels.

International attempts at mediation were unsuccessful and by mid-1876 Turkey seemed near collapse. In June, Serbia and Montenegro declared war and the extravagant sultan, Abdul Aziz, was murdered. By the autumn, however, Turkey had recovered. The Bulgarian revolt was brutally crushed with the massacre of over 12,000 Bulgars by Turkish irregulars, the Bashi-Bazouks. These atrocities brought Gladstone out of retirement to write a famous pamphlet on the question which helped to make the British public anti-Turkish and Disraeli's policy of helping Turkey more difficult. The revival of Turkish arms continued with the rout of the Serbian and Montenegrin armies.

This revival swung Alexander round to the Pan-Slav view that Russia should take direct military action against Turkey. The tzar knew that this would anger the Austro–Hungarian government and he turned for assurance of support to Bismarck. Bismarck for his part wished to keep Germany out of the dispute and to avoid firm commitments. 'The whole of the Balkans is not worth the healthy bones of a single Pomeranian musketeer,' he remarked in the *Reichstag*. He did not dominate events during the eastern crisis and he hoped to avoid choosing between Austria–Hungary and Russia in the dispute. Therefore when in December 1876 the tzar asked for an assurance of German neutrality in the event of an Austro–Russian war, Bismarck was evasive, replying that he would not wish to see either power seriously defeated. He similarly refused Andrassy's offer of an Austro–German alliance against Russia. 'Balance between the two, not the victory of either, was his objective,' says W. Carr. The Russians felt that Bismarck was showing scant gratitude for their promise made before the Franco–Prussian war to concentrate troops on the Austrian border if Austria–Hungary showed any signs of intervening on behalf of France.

Events now moved swiftly. In January 1877, the Russians managed to buy Austro–Hungarian neutrality in the forthcoming war by a secret treaty whereby Austria–Hungary would receive Bosnia–Herzegovina and no large Slav state would be set up in the Balkans. The Turkish refusal to consider reform exhausted Russian patience and in April war was declared. At first Russian troops made rapid progress towards Constantinople with every prospect of taking it within a month, but in the middle of July they were held up at Plevna by heroic Turkish resistance under Osman Pasha. By the time Plevna had been taken in December, the likelihood of European interference in the war had greatly increased. Despite taking Adrianople in January 1878, the Russian forces were exhausted and an armistice was signed.

The Peace of San Stefano in March concluded the Russo–Turkish war. It was a grave error of the Russian government to allow Ignatiev to negotiate the treaty, for the terms were bound to increase the opposition of Britain and Austria–Hungary. To Russia was ceded Kars and Batum on the eastern shores of the Black Sea, as well as southern Bessarabia. More significantly, a large Bulgarian state would be created and occupied by Russian troops for two years. Serbia, Montenegro and Rumania were to be independent of Turkey and were to extend their frontiers. There was no mention of Austria–Hungary's right to annex Bosnia–Herzegovina and this insult ended the Austro–Russian entente.

During the next three months anxious negotiations between Andrassy and Ignatiev came to nothing. Meanwhile, Lord Salisbury, the new British Foreign Secretary, brought a new consistency to British policy. Seven thousand Indian troops were brought to Malta, the fleet having already proceeded to the Dardanelles Straits before the signing of the peace treaty. The British government now had the support of a belligerent public which regarded the Turks as heroes. Salisbury was able to exploit the fact that Russia was in no fit state for another war and in any case Alexander II and Gorchakov, furious with Ignatiev, were prepared to make considerable changes in the San Stefano treaty. Bismarck offered Berlin for an international congress to draw up a general settlement for the Middle East though a number of secret agreements were made between the powers before the congress met in June.

The Congress of Berlin

The congress was the last of the old-style congresses run by a small group of the great powers. Though a number of decisions had been reached before it met, there were still difficult negotiations, particularly over Bulgaria and Bosnia–Herzegovina. Britain and Russia nearly split over the Bulgarian question, and Disraeli was forced to use bluff by ordering a train home. However, with only a few states having any effective say in the proceedings and with Bismarck's skilful control, the main issues were settled fairly quickly.

The 'big' Bulgaria of the Treaty of San Stefano was cut into three parts: a small independent Bulgaria; Easter Rumelia, semi-independent of Turkey; and Macedonia, which remained an integral part of Turkey. Austria was to be allowed to occupy (not annex) Bosnia and Herzegovina and to garrison the Sanjak of the Novibazar which separated the frontiers of Serbia and Montenegro (see Map 2, Appendix). Russia retained southern Bessarabia, Kars and Batum. Britain gained Cyprus, guaranteed Turkey's Asiatic frontiers and declared her freedom to send a fleet through the Straits when she wished.

Disraeli and Salisbury returned home from the congress proclaiming the acquisition of 'peace with honour'. The British triumph seemed complete. A firm stand had checked Russia, and the League of the Three Emperors which threatened to leave Britain isolated had been broken. With the gain of Cyprus, as well as her share in the Suez Canal and her rights at the Straits, British control of the Mediterranean was again effective. But perhaps, as A. J. P. Taylor suggests, the bloodless triumph was too easy and weakened the effectiveness of British policy in the long run. The British came to believe that they could play a great role without much expense or exertion and failed in the next twenty years to reform the navy, to create a large army or to gain allies.

Russia had received a humiliating diplomatic defeat. The Russian government did in fact gain more than it aimed at before the war, but the climb-down over Bulgaria was a slap in the face for Pan-Slav sentiment. The Russians felt less secure after the war than before despite the territorial gains because the British fleet could enter the Black Sea with ease. It was particularly galling that Russia had fought a war that ultimately benefited both Austria–Hungary and Britain.

For Austria, too, the congress was in reality a defeat. Andrassy had wished to preserve the Turkish Empire but the settlement amounted to a dismemberment of Turkey. The gain of Bosnia–Herzegovina contained the seeds of future disaster. Its population was to be a turbulent addition to the multi-racial empire and open revolt occurred in 1882; it was also over Bosnia that crises were provoked in 1908 and in 1914, the second precipitating a war which ended the Habsburg monarchy.

For Bismarck the congress was a mixed blessing. That it met in Berlin demonstrated how European affairs now centred on Germany, and Bismarck as 'honest broker' had refused to ask for any gains. His main desire, that of keeping the peace, had been achieved. Yet the Russians blamed their disappointing results at the congress on Bismarck's failure to give them more support and Russo–German relations deteriorated. He now feared that the Russians would try for a rapprochement with the French.

The treaty has been defended on the grounds that no major war occurred for 36 years and that it had avoided war between the great powers in a very complex area of Europe that has presented baffling problems in the twentieth century. But if Disraeli claimed peace with honour there is some truth in the reply that the treaty of 1878 was 'the peace that passeth all understanding and the honour that is common among thieves'. As we have seen, it had grave consequences for the great powers directly; it also disappointed the hopes of the Balkan nationalities—the Serbs, soon to be bitter rivals of Austria, the Rumanians who had lost southern Bessarabia to Russia, the Bulgars who had expected a larger state, and the Greeks who had hoped for Crete. These disappointments were inevitable because the settlement was designed to suit the convenience of the great powers; but it was essentially a fragile settlement because almost every territorial arrangement in the treaty disappointed one or more states and contained the seeds of future Balkan wars.

The Berlin settlement was a turning-point in European politics for another reason. Before the crisis of 1875 to 1878, great power relations had been fluid; there were no fixed alliances or groupings. The crisis revealed tensions between the powers which led to the formation of formal alliances such as the Austro–German alliance of 1879. 'International relations were now more rigid than for two generations,' says M. S. Anderson. 'It was the events of 1875 to 1878 which had set this dangerous alliance-making process in motion.'

The Formation of the Bismarckian 'System' (1879–82)

Russian suspicion of Bismarck continued to deepen after the end of the congress. In February 1879 came news of an Austro–German agreement to abrogate Article 5 of the Treaty of Prague of 1866, which had promised that a plebiscite would be held in North Schleswig to decide whether the population wished the area to be returned to Denmark. The Russian government wondered what Bismarck had promised in return for this Austrian concession. For his part, Bismarck found the attitude of the Russians threatening and in August he met Andrassy with the purpose of concluding a formal alliance with Austria–Hungary—the Dual Alliance.

Bismarck had hoped to make this a general treaty calling for mutual assistance if either partner were attacked by a third power because William I valued his good relations with the tzar. Andrassy, perceiving Bismarck's sense of insecurity, pointed out that this might be construed as anti-French and insisted that in the new treaty Russia should be explicitly named. Bismarck gave way and the treaty called for mutual assistance if either partner were attacked by Russia and for benevolent neutrality if either were attacked by another power. Because of the long tradition of Russo–Prussian friendship, Bismarck had to threaten resignation to force grudging agreement to the treaty from his emperor.

Why did Bismarck choose a firm alliance with Austria–Hungary rather than Russia? Several motives can be put forward though it is difficult to decide which was the most important. Perhaps Bismarck believed that she was a less adventurous power than Russia and therefore less likely to drag Germany into Balkan politics; time was to prove him wrong. Of course, an alliance with a fellow German power would be more popular in Germany, especially as Austro–Hungary was weaker than Russia and could, theoretically anyway, be more easily controlled by Germany. Bismarck also believed that Russia was nearer revolution than

Austria–Hungary and the personal factor must not be discounted—Bismarck's desire to score off his old enemy Gorchakov. Probably the 1879 alliance was a temporary expedient to compel a more friendly Russian attitude towards Austria–Hungary as well as Germany, and was not a final choice between them. Langer, who is very favourable to Bismarck, praises the alliance as the mainspring of Bismarck's system and as a factor which helped to keep the peace of Europe for many years. In fact, the alliance was to have its drawbacks; in time it drove Russia towards an alliance with France and it also encouraged Austria–Hungary to embark on a more venturesome policy in the Balkans, eventually dragging Germany into the war of 1914.

With the long-term results, however, Bismarck was not concerned. He had sought the Austrian treaty for immediate security against a Russia which had troop concentrations in Russian Poland. It had the effect, in the short term at least, of making the Russians anxious to seek a new agreement with Germany rather than one with France. Even before the Austro–German alliance was signed, Saburov, an influential Russian diplomat, came to Berlin wanting a defensive alliance with Germany and he renewed his advances in 1880. The negotiations were interrupted by the untimely death of Alexander II in March 1881 but in June the League of the Three Emperors was renewed; but whereas the agreement of 1873 was merely a gesture of conservative solidarity, the treaty of 1881 was a practical agreement on the problems of the Middle East. If one of the three partners was at war with a fourth power, the other two partners would observe a friendly neutrality. Austria–Hungary was to be allowed to annex Bosnia–Herzegovina whenever she chose to do so. In return the Austrians promised not to oppose the union of Eastern Rumelia and Bulgaria. The three powers recognised the importance of the Straits and would insist that Turkey enforced her rule there; in other words, the British would not be free to use the Straits whenever they wished. Thus the Russians would be free of the threat of a British expedition to the Black Sea.

For Bismarck the importance of the treaty lay in the fact that it spared him the worry of having to choose between Russia and Austria–Hungary and gave him hope that the two might cooperate in the Balkans. More generally, the treaty gave him a mastery of European diplomacy, for the alliance of 1881 effectively isolated France. 'All politics reduce themselves to this formula,' he once said, 'Try to be one of three, so long as the world is governed by an unstable equilibrium of five great powers.'

The web of treaties of which Berlin was the central point expanded the next year with the formation in May of the Triple Alliance between Germany, Austria–Hungary and Italy. At the Congress of Berlin, Salisbury and Bismarck had secretly offered France a free hand in Tunis. The French, suspicious of Bismarck's motives, delayed their seizure of Tunis until 1881, when they acted quickly to forestall any Italian move there. The Italian public was furious for Italy had a special interest in Tunis where 20,000 Italians lived. There was a clamour in Italy for a reorientation of foreign policy. Previously good relations with France had been the cornerstone of Italian foreign policy, combined with hostility towards Austria–Hungary. Now the Italians sought an agreement with the Central Powers.

Bismarck suddenly took an interest in the idea of an Italian alliance in 1882. Again it was caused by the need to meet an immediate emergency. In 1881, the great radical Gambetta had become Prime Minister in France; it was widely believed that this would mean a more active French policy in pursuit of the lost lands. Bismarck also knew that Pan-Slavs and conservatives in the Russian government would welcome an alliance with France and in January 1882, when General Skobelev, the hero of the Russo–Turkish war, visited Paris, Bismarck's worst fears were aroused, especially when the general spoke of the coming struggle between the Teutons and the Slavs! In the new treaty Austria–Hungary and Germany promised to assist Italy against a French attack. Italy, but not Austria, made the same promise to Germany. Each of the three would assist the others if one or both became involved in war with two other great powers and would remain neutral in case of war with one. In no case would Italy be required to fight Britain. The treaty lasted until 1915 but was not all that important. Germany certainly gained little. She promised to support Italy against France, and since Italian help was worthless, received little in return, except that one more potential ally of France was eliminated. The Italian gains from the treaty were also illusory; the alliance carried some prestige, no doubt, in the recognition of Italy as a great power; but there was no backing for Italy in the treaty for her Imperial hopes in the Mediterranean, and French resentment at Italy's association with Germany took the form of a tariff war which had ruinous effects in Italy. All Italy gained was a promise of support if France attacked her, which was an unlikely eventuality, while her hopes of recovering 'unredeemed' Italy from Austria–Hungary had to be shelved.

Two other alliances completed Bismarck's system. In June 1881, Austria–Hungary made a secret treaty with Serbia making her virtually a protectorate. In October 1883, Austria–Hungary and Germany undertook to defend Rumania while Rumania undertook to fight if Russia attacked Austria–Hungary. The treaty demonstrated how Russo–Rumanian relations had been soured by Rumania's loss of Southern Bessarabia. It was also incompatible with the promises made by Bismarck to the Russians that he was committed only to the defence of Austria–Hungary. Perhaps there were even more serious contradictions in Bismarck's system. His two great creations, the League of the Three Emperors and the Triple Alliance appear contradictory for while the League was based on Austro–Russian cooperation, the Alliance envisaged an Austro–Russian war. And while Bismarck aimed to preserve the status quo, he had in the Triple Alliance associated Germany with two of the more disruptive powers in Europe.

For a period the system worked, and the zenith of Bismarck's diplomacy was reached in 1884 with the renewal of the League of the Three Emperors and a period of Franco–German friendship. Bismarck, as we have seen, embarked on a colonial policy for domestic reasons but also because colonies fitted in with the general objectives of his foreign policy. As he watched Anglo–French colonial rivalry growing in Africa, particularly over Egypt, he saw that it might be turned to Germany's advantage by the creation of a lasting reconciliation with France. Therefore he picked quarrels with Britain over German colonial claims in South-West Africa and the Pacific and sided with France in opposition to British plans for financial reform in Egypt. The Franco–German entente reached its high-water mark at the Berlin Conference of 1884–85, called to regulate the affairs of Central Africa. The entente, however, was shortlived. It survived while Ferry was in power in France but a French defeat in Indo-China caused his fall in March 1885 and Franco–German relations deteriorated when the revanchist Boulanger became Minister of War in France in 1886. By then Bismarck's security system was already strained by a recurrence of trouble in the Balkans.

The Bulgarian Crisis

Langer has praised the League of the Three Emperors in 1881 as an achievement of real statesmanship and an important step in the evolution of the Bismarckian system; but it did not remove Austro–Russian rivalry in the Balkans, and Bismarck himself admitted that only mitigation of the rivalry was possible. This became evident in 1885 when new complications arose in Bulgaria which tested Bismarck's diplomatic expertise to the utmost.

The institutions of the new state of Bulgaria created by the Berlin settlement were very much under Russian control after 1878, particularly the army. This was resented by the nationalistic Bulgarians, whose ruler was Prince Alexander of Battenberg, a nephew of the tzar, who had been elected to the Bulgarian throne in 1879 with Russian approval. Energetic but unstable, Alexander in fact despised the Russians and gave preference to Austrian financial interests in railway construction in Bulgaria. The tzar now disliked the idea of Bulgaria acquiring Eastern Rumelia as promised in the 1881 treaty, but in 1885 a successful revolt for union with Bulgaria broke out in Eastern Rumelia. Alexander accepted the crown of Eastern Rumelia to the disgust of the tzar, who recalled Russian officers serving in the Bulgarian army. The tzar was even more displeased when Milan of Serbia demanded compensation for the Bulgarian gains and, after attacking Bulgaria in November 1885, was soundly defeated.

Afraid of losing control of Bulgaria altogether, the Russians instigated a conspiracy in the Bulgarian army in August 1886 and Alexander was kidnapped. When he returned in September the tzar ordered him to abdicate and Alexander, his nerve gone, complied. The Bulgarian assembly, led by Stambulov, was not so easily quelled. Angry at the overbearing attitude of the Russians over the choice of a new ruler, Bulgaria broke off diplomatic relations in November.

One factor promoting Bulgarian resistance was confidence of support from Britain and Austria–Hungary. Both powers now saw a strong independent Bulgaria as an effective barrier against Russia. Kalnoky, the Austrian Foreign Secretary, fearing a Russian invasion of Bulgaria, asked Bismarck for support if this occurred. Bismarck refused, insisting as usual that the Austro–German alliance was defensive; yet he felt compelled to warn the Russians that he could not abandon Austria. The League of the Three Emperors was killed stone dead.

The Bulgarian question was only one side of Bismarck's problem. He was convinced that if a Russo–German war occurred, then the French would take advantage of the situation to attack Germany. Nationalistic feeling had been whipped up in France by Déroulède's League of Patriots, which aimed at revenge on Germany, and the patriotic revival had found a symbol in General Boulanger. The nightmare of coalitions and a war on two fronts seemed too close for comfort.

To meet the French threat, Bismarck called for an increase in the German army of 40,000 men, dissolving the *Reichstag* when it refused to approve the measure in November 1886. During the elections the German press was most inflammatory, the *Berlin Post* printing an article *On the razor's edge* in January 1887 which declared that the French were planning a war of aggression. This campaign brought home to the sober politicians of the Third Republic that Bismarck meant business. So did the news in February 1887 that Germany had renewed the Triple Alliance with Italy and Austria–Hungary.

Bismarck now encouraged a new diplomatic development which might restrain the Russians in the Balkans. When he heard that Italy disliked the idea of Russian domination there, he suggested that Italy should align herself with Britain and Austria–Hungary on the matter. In March 1887, a Mediterranean Agreement was signed between the three powers. They agreed to maintain the status quo in the Middle East and to give mutual support in case of differences with a fourth power; as Tripoli and Egypt were mentioned, this might be France or Russia; but in December 1887 a second Mediterranean agreement between the three powers was directed solely against Russia.

The Schnaebele incident of April 1887 (see Chapter Four) kept Bismarck aware of the need for a new agreement with Russia and in June he negotiated a new alliance with Shuvalov. The Reinsurance Treaty pledged each of the partners to benevolent neutrality if the other were attacked by a third power but this agreement would not apply if Germany attacked France or if Russia attacked Austria–Hungary. The treaty was not strictly a contravention of the Dual Alliance, which was purely defensive, but it was a dubious transaction which depended on Germany deciding whether Russia or Austria–Hungary was the aggressor if war did break out between them. But Bismarck hoped that the treaty would discourage aggressive action by Russia against Austria–Hungary and renewed his promises of diplomatic support for Russia in Bulgaria. In reality the importance of the Reinsurance Treaty has been exaggerated. It certainly was not the 'very keystone of the Bismarckian structure' as Langer asserts. Bismarck himself attached little importance to it, for it was merely another temporary expedient to keep Russia quiet. It was a very limited agreement for it did not exclude a Franco–Russian agreement to resist Austrian or German aggression and therefore the element of 'reinsurance' was slight. Nor did Russo–German relations become easier after it was signed.

Hardly had the treaty been made when in July the Bulgarians elected Ferdinand of Saxe-Coburg as prince in defiance of Russian wishes, and the moment for Russian intervention seemed to have arrived. Bismarck reacted with a blend of firmness and conciliation. In February 1888 he called for more troop increases, declaring in the *Reichstag* that 'We Germans fear God and nothing else in the world'. But he also published the text of the Austro–German alliance to prove to Russia that it was purely defensive and in the same speech he approved of Russian policy in Bulgaria, affirming his trust in the good faith of the tzar. In fact, Ferdinand remained as ruler in Bulgaria; the crisis fizzled out, less through Bismarck's influence than through Russia's growing interest in Central Asia and the Far East. Relative peace descended on the Balkans.

Conclusion

Whether Bismarck could have retained Russia's friendship for much longer if he had stayed in power has always been a matter of debate among historians. He had himself contributed to strained Russo–German relations when he forbade the *Reichsbank* to accept Russian securities as collateral for loans in December 1887; instead the French supplied the loans that financed Russian industrialisation. Yet difficulties between states do not necessarily lead to enmity and it is worth remembering that in 1890 the Russians were eager to renew the Reinsurance Treaty and still reluctant to come to any alliance with France. It is therefore nonsense to talk about Bismarck's foreign policy as being in ruins in 1890 as some historians have done. It was not even inevitable that Austro–Russian relations should deteriorate over the Balkans. The Russians were looking more to Central Asia and the Far East, and Balkan problems were shelved until 1908 when Aerenthal by an act of criminal folly resurrected the quarrel.

Bismarck's 'system' was workable and he left Germany in a powerful position. His moderation and skill had contributed, with other factors such as colonial expansion, to a period of European peace. Shortsighted successors threw away his legacy. Unlike him, they failed to limit and control the ambitions of Germany's chief ally, Austria–Hungary. He also was more successful in diverting French ambitions to Imperial expansion whereas William II and his advisers in their vainglorious seeking after prestige and world influence challenged French activities in Africa. Finally, Bismarck never raised the issue of sea power, which perhaps as much as any factor was to overthrow Imperial Germany.

The New Imperialism

The Extent of Expansion

During the first three quarters of the nineteenth century, the interest of European states in overseas expansion reached its lowest point in several centuries. By 1800 France had lost most of her old empire, Great Britain had lost the 13 American colonies and early in the nineteenth century Spain and Portugal lost their possessions in South America. Only France of the great powers undertook serious colonisation in the 50 years after 1815, acquiring Cochin China, Algeria and Tahiti. Great Britain also acquired large territories—for example, New Zealand and Australia—but only with reluctance when intrepid settlers made it inevitable. British governments regarded the growing empire as an encumbrance, and their attitude has been well summed up by Disraeli. 'These wretched colonies,' he wrote in 1852, 'will all be independent in a few years and are millstones round our necks.' Only India was accepted as a predestined duty but elsewhere effective access was preferred to formal control because of the expense of direct rule.

But between 1870 and 1900 the states of Europe began to extend their control over vast areas of the world. About 10 million square miles and 150 million people were brought under imperial rule, usually by the waging of aggressive wars in one-sided conflicts which Bismarck sardonically called 'sporting wars'. Any territory overseas, whether desert or swamp, was considered worthy of annexation. 'Expansion is everything,' said Cecil Rhodes. 'I would annex the planets if I could.' What was strikingly novel about the new imperialism was its concentration upon two continents, Africa and eastern Asia, the only two important areas of the globe uninfluenced by Europe before 1870. Africa and Asia were opened up more than ever before to the benefits as well as to the evils of European civilisation.

In 1875, less than one tenth of Africa had been annexed by European states, yet by 1895 only one tenth remained unappropriated. Between 1871 and 1900, Britain added $4\frac{1}{4}$ million square miles and 66 million people to her empire, France added $3\frac{1}{2}$ million square miles and 26 million people, Russia $\frac{1}{2}$ million square miles and $6\frac{1}{2}$ million people. Germany acquired a new empire of 1 million square miles and 13 million people and Belgium and Italy also gained considerable territory in Africa. By the end of the nineteenth century much of the international tension was caused by questions of empire; undoubtedly a phenomenon of the greatest importance had taken place.

The Motives Behind Imperialism

The most comprehensive explanation of imperialism is that which concentrates on economic factors. This thesis was first developed by J. A. Hobson in 1902 and later by Lenin. Hobson's interest in imperialism stemmed from a visit made to South Africa as a correspondent of the *Manchester Guardian* just before the Boer War, and he became a severe critic of British policy there. In his view the 'disastrous folly' of imperial wars was partly on account of certain sectional interests—the armament firms, manufacturers relying on exports, the shipping trade, the armed forces and the professions generally. They all benefited from imperialism because it was a creator of job opportunities and so Hobson quotes James Mill's description of colonies as 'a vast system of outdoor relief for the upper classes'.

But to Hobson the most important factor in imperialism was investment. British capital invested abroad in 1893 represented about 15 per cent of the total wealth of the United Kingdom and in his view this profoundly influenced the actions of government, and he claimed that 'the modern foreign policy of Great Britain is primarily a struggle for profitable markets of investment'. Imperialists in European countries as well as the United States justified imperialism as a necessity because large savings of capital were made which could not find profitable use in the mother country and colonies were required as fields of investment. This need for investment, says Hobson, is the 'economic taproot of imperialism'. He saw imperialism as motivated only by selfish forces which would manipulate the idealism of missionaries and politicians.

Lenin's views on imperialism were contained in a pamphlet written in 1916 called *Imperialism, the Highest Stage of Capitalism.* He saw imperialism arising out of modern capitalism, which had become dominated by monopolistic combines. These combines found difficulty in investing at home because the European market was saturated and they were also anxious to control all sources of raw materials. The direct acquisition of colonies was the solution, for 'colonial possession alone gives complete guarantee of success to the monopolies against all the risks of the struggle with competitors'. Free markets would become a thing of the past under imperialism, which was 'the monopoly stage of capitalism'. In Lenin's view, the action of European powers in dividing the world between them to safeguard investments increased tension and inevitably led to war.

The Marxist thesis is very one-sided and can be refuted when the actual evidence is analysed. The export of capital in fact seems to have had little connection with imperial expansion. There was much British investment abroad before 1875, when imperialism was out of vogue, and the rate of growth in foreign investment fell away in the period between 1875 and 1895 when imperial aggrandisement was at its height. Nor did a large proportion of this investment go into the new colonies. In 1913 Britain had more money invested in the United States than in any colony; less than half the total export of capital was to her empire and most of this was in the old white dominions like Canada, New Zealand and Australia, not in the new acquisitions in Africa or Asia. France sent most of her capital to Russia and other European countries, investing less than seven per cent of her foreign capital in her colonies. Germany in 1913 had only three per cent of her foreign investment in Africa and Asia and only a small proportion of this amount was invested in her own colonies. Three of the most important imperial nations—Russia, Italy and Japan—had too little capital for domestic requirements to send any significant amount abroad, Russia in particular borrowing heavily from France.

Nor can the urge for colonial markets and raw materials have been a crucial factor in imperialism. The great industrial countries obtained only a fraction of their raw materials from the colonies and the colonial trade in general played a relatively unimportant part in the total foreign commerce of the industrial nations because of the low purchasing power of the colonial natives. The industrial nations were each other's best customers despite the international rivalry, whereas trade and investment in Africa and Asia had a high risk content which made them unattractive.

Lenin's view of European industry under the domination of huge combines also fails to square with reality. Only in Germany had the trust movement made much headway by 1914; it came much later in other countries—even in England, the state which controlled the largest empire. The combines that did exist did not support their country's foreign policy as one might expect. During the Bosnian crisis of 1908, when France should have been supporting Russia, Franco–German talks were held over Moroccan mining rights. The talks were inspired by the two great combines Schneider–Creusot and Krupps, and are proof that international capitalism could combine as well as compete. If big business had controlled government, it would have stopped the coming of war in 1914 because it resulted in the destruction of its best customers and sources of supply. Schumpeter went as far as asserting that capitalism was anti-imperialist because it regarded imperial adventures as a distraction from the realities of economic activity.

In fact, it was the politicians who were the prophets of imperial expansion and the new imperialism was a nationalistic, not an economic, phenomenon. It grew out of the diplomatic situation in Europe after the Franco–Prussian war when the French government sought prestige abroad as consolation for the loss of Alsace–Lorraine. This Bismarck encouraged in the interests of Franco–German friendship, giving France a free hand in Tunis. He also had in mind the hope that England and Italy would be alienated, as indeed they were. Britain, already in possession of a great empire, was now apprehensive of the growing interest of other countries in imperialism and sought to take measures to safeguard it. Her concern for the security of the routes to India led to her occupying Egypt. To other powers envious of the British Empire, British action did not seem to aim at security only but at ever greater empire. France and Russia were particularly hostile to consolidation of the British position in the eastern Mediterranean. The scramble for Africa was under way.

Once the imperial movement had started, it generated its own momentum. Often territories were absorbed not for their present value but as an insurance against the future. Baumont described this process as 'taking as much as possible without knowing what to do with it, taking what others want because they want it and to prevent them getting it'. Lord Rosebery in 1893 told the Colonial Institute that the government was pegging out claims for the future, implying that otherwise Britain would be left out of the partition of the rest of the world. Many like him admitted that the colonies were not worth much at present but dwelt on the future commercial advantages because these were easier to justify than the real strategic and political motives.

Considerations of national prestige played a large part in the imperial saga. Governments accepted, often uncritically, the words of Gambetta that 'to remain a great nation or to become one, you must colonise.' When he became head of the French government in 1881, Jules Ferry remarked, 'It is a question of fifty or a hundred years' time . . . of the future heritage of our children.' The imperial scramble was more than a vogue; it became a mania, a process which possessed, says

Hannah Arendt, its own 'inherent insanity'.

Another vital political factor was the relationship between imperialism and democracy in Western Europe. The industrial and white-collar classes were gradually being enfranchised in the late nineteenth century. Politicians could no longer ignore their opinions and if colonial adventures satisfied the craving of the masses for excitement, then it was political wisdom to follow a 'forward' policy in imperial affairs. Gladstone's Liberal party was out of office for most of the period from 1885 to 1905 because its policy of Home Rule for Ireland was against the spirit of the times, while the Conservative party, which supported imperialism, enjoyed a secure period of power. Thus C. J. H. Hayes concludes that in the last analysis it was the nationalistic masses who made imperialism possible and who most vociferously applauded and most constantly backed it. It possessed inherent attractions and Marxists have given insufficient attention to the psychological ingredients in imperialism. Imperial adventure was exciting and a change from dull routine for workers confined to ugly cities. They could identify with the nation's colonial victories and prestige, and feel a share in them. When Mafeking was relieved during the Boer War, the London public went wild. Feeling was as intense in other countries. The Italian public fervently supported its government's imperial adventures in Africa because, as Christopher Seton-Watson phrases it, they brought back the poetry to national life and were a vivid contrast to the humdrum prose of parliamentary life. Critics of imperialism like G. P. Gooch condemned it as the equivalent of bread and circuses in Roman times.

Whatever the psychological factors, imperialism became a great theme on which pressure groups, the press, men of letters and even the song-writers went into eulogies. Politicians could not remain immune to the pressure of patriots, whether those of the Primrose League in Britain or the Colonial Society in Germany. Even the revisionist socialists gave guarded support for imperialism. Eduard Bernstein stressed its humanitarian aspects and saw material benefits in it for the working classes. 'A certain tutelage of the civilised peoples over the uncivilised is a necessity,' he asserted.

The imperialism of the period was one aspect of a revolution which was challenging the ideas of earlier generations. Relations between states were now based on fresh assumptions about the nature of men and society. These assumptions included the belief in the duty of the advanced peoples to bring civilisation to the backward ones. This need for idealistic devotion to duty was enshrined in Kipling's *The White Man's Burden.* Obviously, at times such thoughts were hypocritical but imperial administration furnished many examples of dedicated governors sincerely desirous of bringing benefits to their colonies—for example, Cromer in Egypt, Karl Peters in German East Africa and Marshal Lyautey in Morocco.

The most profound of the ideas underlying imperialism was Social Darwinism, which took Charles Darwin's ideas on evolution and applied them to international relations. It reviewed relations between states as a perpetual struggle for existence in which only the strongest survived. Living meant fighting for the international scene was like nature itself, a vast field of carnage. In practice, it encouraged the naked use of force and a glorification of the military life. It also led to a belief that states must expand or decline; they must increase their empires or be overtaken by others. Joseph Chamberlain said in 1902, 'The future is with the great Empires and there is no greater Empire than the British Empire.' The law of the survival of the fittest came to be seen almost as a revelation of the Divine Will on earth, and the act of obstructing the growth of the nation's empire was disobedience to the will of God! Perhaps the definition of imperialism given by John McManners is the most appropriate; it was not the highest stage of capitalism but the highest stage of nationalism.

In addition to international tensions, two other factors decided the timing of imperialism: exploration and technology. The work of explorers like Peters, Livingstone and Stanley opened up the hitherto dark continent of Africa, Livingstone crossing the Kalahari Desert, exploring the River Zambesi and penetrating into what became Nyasaland and Tanganyika. After Livingstone's death in 1873, Stanley explored the area around Lake Victoria and reached the River Congo. The continent could be exploited by this period through the development of railways and the steamship. The indigenous population could not prevent this because of the vast superiority in weaponry possessed by the Europeans, so that in Africa and Asia a handful of European soldiers could control vast territories. The reason was wittily summed up in Hillaire Belloc's couplet:

'Thank the Lord that we have got
The Gatling gun and they have not.'

This superiority in weaponry encourages K. R. Minogue to suggest a technological theory of imperialism. Europe expanded when the use of force was easy but imperialism ceased when the natives acquired guns, for the game now cost more than it was worth.

These considerations—the political rivalries, the popularity of imperialism with the masses, its Social Darwinism and its technological aspects—all demonstrate that the Marxist interpretation is an over-simplification. Yet it would be unwise to attempt to eliminate the economic factor altogether. Profits were made out of imperial development by munitions manufacturers and traders in raw materials from the colonies like ivory and rubber. There were examples of gross exploitation, possibly the worst example being the activities of Leopold, King of the Belgians, in the Congo. Imperial expansion provided jobs for soldiers and administrators and economic pressure groups at times played a considerable part in persuading the governments of Europe to embark on colonial expansion, as in Germany.

Yet if one thinks in terms of pressure groups, it is equally fair to say that missionary societies played as important a role as financial interests. In both France and Britain the anti-slavery movement campaigned for government intervention in Africa; it was an impressive campaign, too, dramatised by the work of Livingstone and publicised by church leaders like Cardinal Lavigerie. Indeed, the late nineteenth century was perhaps the greatest period of missionary work in the history of the Christian Church. About 40,000 Roman Catholic and 20,000 Protestant missionaries went to Asia and Africa, making the conversion of the whole world seem, for a short time anyway, a real possibility. The activities of the Church facilitated a political take-over later. Lavigerie's Society of African Missionaries extended their work from Algeria into Tunisia in 1875, easing the task of the French government in taking over Tunis in 1881. Gambetta said of Lavigerie, 'His presence in Tunisia is worth an army for France.' The presence of the Church could also furnish pretexts for government intervention. It was the murder of two German missionaries in China in 1897 which gave the German government the excuse to seize the port of Kiao-Chow.

Enthusiasm for imperial adventures began to decline from 1905 after a series of crises. Spain suffered losses in the war of 1898 with the United States, ceding Cuba and the Philippines. The British, victorious in the Sudan at the Battle of Omdurman in 1898, were soon to be deflated by the outbreak of the costly Boer War in 1899. Faith in imperial invincibility was shaken by two other clashes which showed that it was not inevitable that Asians and Africans must always be defeated in any encounter with the West. In 1896 the defeat of the Italian army at Adowa in Abyssinia caused the fall of the Italian prime minister Crispi. Even more astonishing were the setbacks on land and sea which befell the Russians during the Russo–Japanese war of 1904–5 which precipitated the 1905 revolution. The great age of imperialism was drawing to a close.

There were few more acquisitions to be made and the expense of empire was beginning to appear disproportionate to the gains. Already demands for political rights and independence were being made in the colonies, for as K. R. Minogue points out, 'modern Europeans carried with them the boot that would eventually send them packing—the nationalistic belief that anything else but self-government is a kind of slavery.'

The Road to War (1890–1914)

The Franco–Russian Entente

The fall of Bismarck in March 1890 was a great turning-point in European diplomacy. Ever since 1871 he had followed a policy of restraint and he bequeathed to Germany a strong international position. Given astute handling, his system was workable but it was doomed once William II ascended the throne. By 1907 Germany's diplomatic position was no longer secure; a coalition had drawn together against her, forged more by a series of German blunders rather than by any sinister designs in German policy.

The first blunder was not long in coming. William was much influenced by Holstein, who was anti-Russian. German foreign policy now aimed at friendship with Britain as well as with Austria–Hungary and because William disliked the complexity of Bismarck's alliances a more open style of diplomacy was attempted. Accordingly, when Shuvalov in March 1890 proposed the renewal of the Reinsurance Treaty for six years, he was astonished at German rejection of the proposal on the grounds that it would offend Britain and German public opinion. The non-renewal of the treaty restored to Russia a freedom of action which at the time was not desired. Russian suspicion of German aims was further aroused in July by the Anglo–German colonial agreement, by which Germany gained Heligoland in return for giving up her rights at Zanzibar and limiting her rights in East Africa. Good in itself, the agreement made both the Russians and the French believe that a virtual Anglo–German alliance had come into existence.

Fear of isolation gradually drew Russia and France together, yet the process was slow and certainly not inevitable. The reactionary Alexander III was reluctant to make any firm alliance with a republican government and it was left to the French to press hard for negotiations, alarmed at the renewal of the Triple Alliance in May 1891 and the erratic personality of William II. Yet Alexander himself resented the drawing together of Britain and the Triple Alliance and was acutely aware of his country's need for French loans which might be withheld if he refused an alliance with France. Therefore in July 1891, a French squadron visited Kronstadt and the tzar even stood bare-headed to listen to the Marseillaise. Serious negotiations now began, a major difficulty being that whereas France wanted an alliance directed mainly against Germany, the Russians wanted an alliance directed mainly against Britain. The Russians still had feelings of reservation at the idea of an alliance and wanted a general agreement which would in practice leave them with freedom of action. In contrast, the French wanted specific guarantees of Russian help if they were embroiled in a conflict with the Triple Alliance powers or Britain. In August, the two powers agreed to consult on necessary measures if one of the parties were menaced by aggression. Though it was a vague arrangement, this new entente was a turning-point in the history of Europe and it was soon given military teeth. In December 1893, a military convention was signed whereby the two partners pledged themselves to give each other assistance in the event of any attack by Germany. The general staffs of the two countries were to hold talks and mobilisation would take place if any of the Triple Alliance powers mobilised, the French supplying 1,300,000 troops and the Russians not less than 700,000. The alliance was now a reality. Its aim was to keep Germany neutral while the two partners pursued their ambitions overseas. In most crises diplomatic support was all that the new allies were to give each other and it was a passive alliance as late as the Russo–Japanese war of 1904–5. 'All the same,' remarks A. J. P. Taylor, 'it was a weapon loaded only against Germany.'

The Germans at the time did not take this new development very seriously. Indeed, they believed that it might improve their position by forcing Britain into the Triple Alliance. The new alliance did have an anti-British aspect for both powers would be better placed to defeat Britain when there was a collision of colonial interests as in Egypt or the Far East.

The British Position

The British reaction to the new alliance was one of apprehension. In a Europe divided into two blocs, at a time when European interests had become global, Britain came to feel more and more isolated, especially in view of the tone of German diplomacy. The Germans aimed at bringing Britain into the Triple Alliance but mistakenly believed that they would achieve this by blackmail and threats. The peremptory tone of German diplomats irritated British statesmen as the German historian, Brandenburg, admits: 'The way in which German policy invariably opened fire at once with its biggest guns was extremely antipathetic to English statesmen who were more tranquil and tolerant, and very sensitive to threat.'

The weakness of the British position became clear from 1895, when a series of diplomatic crises occurred which forced the British to seek allies. Their isolation became very evident in the Far East, now assuming great importance in European diplomacy. Britain had long been accustomed to a dominant position in China, but this state of affairs was now threatened by other European powers, especially Russia. But a new power had arisen in the Far East itself. Japan, from being a medieval state earlier in the nineteenth century, was by the 1890s in the course of being transformed into a modern industrial state and the Japanese were determined to make their country a great power. They particularly coveted Korea and were fearful of being forestalled there by the Russians. In September 1894 they waged a successful war against China and the Chinese government was forced to sign the Treaty of Shimoneseki in April 1895. By this treaty Korea became independent and Japan gained Port Arthur and the Liaotung Peninsula, the keys to Manchuria and north China. The Russians were furious at the Japanese success and organised a protest, being joined by Germany and France. The Japanese government was forced to 'bear the unbearable' and return its gains to China. It was a cynical move by the European powers for they were soon to extract concessions from China themselves. For Britain the affair was novel and humiliating. The other powers had simply elbowed her aside in an area which had formerly been a British preserve.

Further British embarrassment occurred in South Africa. The existence there of independent Boer republics, especially the Transvaal, hampered the British objective of a united South Africa which would give security at the Cape. In December 1895, Dr Jameson, an agent of Cecil Rhodes, Prime Minister of Cape Colony, launched an abortive raid into the Transvaal in the hope of provoking an uprising of the Uitlanders (white non-Boers). The raid, in which Joseph Chamberlain was implicated, was a fiasco and gave an opportunity to the Germans to thrust themselves forward as champions of Boer independence. In January 1896, William II sent a telegram to Kruger, the Boer president, congratulating him on having preserved the independence of his country 'without appealing to the help of friendly powers'. This was a gross miscalculation; the British responded strongly by organising a 'flying squadron', a powerful and fast naval force, which made it ridiculous for the Germans to imply that they could defend the Transvaal. Langer is right to refer to William's diplomacy as 'amateurish jockeyings' and calls the telegram one of the greatest blunders in the history of modern diplomacy. The kaiser later sent Queen Victoria a letter, explaining rather lamely that the telegram was sent in the name of peace. It had, however, crystallised British resentment of German economic rivalry and aroused similar feelings against Britain in Germany, where pressure for the development of a strong navy grew. Unfortunately, William did not learn from the affair; he was to make similar errors in the future.

African affairs continued to trouble the British. In 1898 they clashed with France over control of the Sudan. The French had no alternative but to give way because the Dreyfus Affair was pulling France towards civil war and in any case the British possessed a superior navy, and already had an army in the disputed area. The quarrel aroused the furious anglophobia of the French public but paradoxically the affair encouraged Delcassé, the French Foreign Minister, to aim at a reconciliation with Britain.

British self-satisfaction over the result of the Sudan incident was short-lived. In October 1899 came the outbreak of the Boer War, which proved to be a much tougher campaign that the British expected, 300,000 troops being required to crush the resistance of 60,000 Boers. The war was an uncomfortable demonstration of Britain's lack of allies as well as proof of the limitations of the British army. On the continent, public opinion strongly favoured the Boers and there was much talk of a continental league against Britain though this necessarily remained talk because the decisive factor in the situation was the British navy; but if British security at home was never in doubt Britain's interests elsewhere certainly were in question because both the armed forces were fully extended by the war.

German World Policy

In the late 1890s the opportunities for peace in Europe were considerable, for in April 1897 came an Austro–Russian agreement to maintain the 'status quo' in the Middle East. For the next decade the Balkans were relatively quiet and in 1897 no burning issue in Europe threatened peace. It was singularly unfortunate, therefore, that 1897 marked a distinct change of course in German policy: the promotion of a thrusting, forward attitude in world affairs. It was motivated by a craving for prestige, a 'place in the sun' as befitted a nation of Germany's rank, but it was also a ruse to divert public attention away from difficulties at home. The flaw in the policy was that Germany could not play a world role; she was a European power with two hostile neighbours, and the clumsiness of her diplomacy was to add Britain to the number of her potential enemies.

The German government came to feel that for purposes of world greatness a strong navy must be developed. William, influenced by Tirpitz, became enthusiastic at the idea of Germany possessing a formidable battle fleet and in March 1898 the German Navy Code was enacted. Behind German thinking was the belief that the possession of a strong navy would force Britain into an alliance with Germany and at the same time break Britain's world-wide predominance. It was dangerously like blackmail and the British resented it. The Germans failed to comprehend the British feeling that such a development undermined their security as an island state with a scattered empire. As Winston Churchill put it, the British fleet was a necessity and the German fleet was a luxury. Germany was already the most powerful military state; against whom would she wish to use a powerful navy? The answer to the British could only be: the greatest naval power. The German attitude to these fears was unsympathetic, as E. L. Woodward has demonstrated: 'In public discussions and in official negotiations, the German people and their rulers took little account of English susceptibilities and fears. They were inclined to complain of exaggerated suspicions and unreasonable anxiety. They did not pay enough attention to the fair and logical deductions which might be made not merely from their words but from the steady increase in the number of their ships.'

At first the German challenge did not appear very serious, for despite a further increase in the German fleet in 1900 the British lead appeared unassailable. In 1906, however, the British Admiralty launched the *Dreadnought*, the first all big-gun ship, which made all existing battleships obsolete. The British now had to reconstruct their lead and an expensive naval arms race began. British suggestions that the naval programmes be cut in 1908 were turned down by the Germans. Public opinion in Britain now backed the government in its naval development. 'We want eight and we won't wait,' was the cry of the public in 1909 when the Germans were thought to be catching up with the British. German naval policy gradually estranged Britain while serving no important national interest whatsoever. If the Germans had abandoned their unnecessary naval programme they might well have won British neutrality in the war and, with the extra resources available, have won it as well. When war did come the German fleet, despite its quality, proved to be a white elephant, fighting only one major engagement. The naval rivalry pushed Britain and France towards an informal alliance which Grey, Foreign Secretary from 1906, came to regard as a morally binding commitment, so that in the event of war it would be difficult for Britain to keep out.

The second aspect of German world policy was the new willingness of the German government to make unexpected incursions into any international issue. By 1897 the issue that overshadowed all others was the Far East. In Taylor's phrase, China had taken the place of Turkey as the 'pre-eminent Sick Man', and between 1897 and 1905 the future of China determined the relations of the great powers. The Germans helped to provoke a period of crisis in the Far Eastern affairs by seizing Kiao-Chow in November, 1897, thus precipitating the seizure of Chinese territory by other powers. The Russians took over Port Arthur and the British gained Wei-hai-wei, and insufficient sop to the British public, which termed it 'Woe-Woe-Woe'. This degree of foreign aggression stimulated the growth of a nationalistic Chinese organisation called the Society of the Harmonious Fists (the

Boxers). In June 1900 came the Boxer Rising, which led to the siege of the European legations in China. Though the legations were saved by a joint European military expedition, the troubles gave Russia a pretext for invading Manchuria and British interests in the Far East appeared even more precarious.

The Creation of New Alliances (1902–7)

The conclusion of the Franco–Russian alliance, German pressure, and the strain of her global commitments made Britain seek closer relations with several powers after 1894. In January 1898, the British sought some deal over the Far East with Russia but the Russians broke off negotiations and seized Port Arthur as a base to exploit Manchuria and challenge British trade in China. The British therefore turned to Germany and three main attempts were made in 1898, 1899 and 1901 to form an alliance. The attempts failed because of lack of common interests. The British would not join the Triple Alliance (as the Germans suggested) for such a move might involve a war against France for the sake of German security in Europe. The Germans, who wished to remain on good terms with Russia, would not join in an anti-Russian alliance (as the British suggested) for the sake of British interests in China.

The course of events was now influenced by Japan. The Japanese had viewed the European gains in China in 1897 and 1898 with impotent rage and felt that their stake in Korea was being increasingly threatened by Russia. In 1901 they sought desperately for an alliance with either Russia or Britain. The Russians would not compromise over the Korean question but the British, involved in the Boer War and anxious to safeguard their Far Eastern interests, came to an agreement with Japan in January 1902. The treaty recognised Korea as Japan's special sphere of influence and provided for intervention by one partner if the other partner were involved in a war with two powers. Now Japan could go to war with Russia confident that Britain would keep France neutral, while Britain could afford to concentrate more of the fleet in home waters with an ally in the Far East to protect her interests there. In a European context, the alliance confirmed rather than ended Britain's isolation, for she could now stay aloof of European powers, especially with the recent improvement in her naval strength.

Nevertheless, Britain's relations with France since the Sudan quarrel had started to improve while Anglo–German relations had continued to deteriorate. The British refused to contribute capital required by German entrepreneurs for the construction of the Berlin to Baghdad railway, thus delaying its completion until 1914. Meanwhile, an Anglo–French rapprochement was worked at by Delcassé. The influence of Edward VII was useful in promoting a more cordial relationship between the two countries, and in 1903 he visited Paris for the first time as king. Hard negotiations between Delcassé and Lansdowne came to fruition in April 1904 with the signing of the Anglo–French entente. It settled minor disputes over Siam and Newfoundland fishing rights but the main issues were Egypt and Morocco. Britain agreed that Morocco was a French sphere of influence while the French in their turn admitted British supremacy in Egypt. The two powers agreed to give each other support in the event of any modification in the 'status quo' in those two areas.

At the time it was the French who appeared to have conceded most; they renounced in Egypt an area of proven worth while Morocco's value, great in the future, was an unknown quantity in 1904. The French hand was to some extent forced by the outbreak of the Russo–Japanese war in February, which made them anxious to limit the area of conflict to the Far East. In the long run they were aiming at more than a mere settling of colonial disputes; they wanted a firm alliance with Britain as further protection against Germany. Perhaps the British did not quite realise this as they wished to live in peace with other countries and did not foresee how the entente would become a more binding commitment. The German government was sure that Britain had taken a firm stand with France against the Triple Alliance and was soon to put pressure on the new entente.

German opportunities to do so were created by the developments in the Far East. The Russian refusal to compromise over Korea finally exhausted Japanese patience. In February 1904, Japan precipitated war by a surprise attack on Port Arthur. The war had an epic quality with clear-cut victories in major engagements for the Japanese and chivalry shown on both sides. Port Arthur, after siege by land and sea, fell in January 1905 and on the other major front the Japanese won the Battle of Mukden in March. The Russians in desperation sent their Baltic fleet round the world to the Far East and on the way it caused a row with Britain by firing in panic on British fishing boats on the Dogger Bank in October. The Japanese admiral, Togo, worked out the course which the Russian fleet would take and was able to annihilate it at Tsushima in May, only two out of forty ships escaping destruction. The Japanese victories were gained by superior command and organisation, by the advantage of shorter supply lines and fervent public support for the war. After such defeats the Russian government, with a revolution at home, was forced to sue for peace and it found Japan willing to negotiate, for the war had strained Japanese resources as well. Therefore in September 1905 the Treaty of Portsmouth was signed, the Russians recognising Korea as a Japanese sphere of influence and ceding the Liaotung Peninsula and the southern half of Sakhalin.

In the long run the war was to alter the course of history, and as the French Ambassador to Britain, Paul Cambon, remarked, it was to 'weigh upon the whole century'. Japan was now a great power in the Far East and it was significant that in 1905 her alliance with Britain was modified so that in the future one partner would help the other in the event of attack by one or more powers. Japan was now on the road to confrontation with the United States and she had destroyed the myth of the White Man's invincibility, thus stimulating the growth of Asian nationalism.

Russia for a period no longer counted as a great power until the military reforms after 1905 began to take effect. Her relations with Japan now improved and further agreements on spheres of influence took place in 1907 and 1910. Russia, in fact, kept control of Manchuria and the emphasis of her foreign policy after defeat in the Far East shifted back to the Balkans with fateful consequences for European peace.

The destruction of Russian power presented the Germans with a unique opportunity to change the European balance of power in their favour. They had two alternative lines of action. They could maintain friendly neutrality in the war to win Russian support or they could attack France while her major ally was helpless. In fact, the Germans muddled along, trying to do both. During the war a series of telegrams passed between the tzar and the kaiser known as the 'Willy-Nicky' correspondence. William tried to persuade the tzar that British neutrality in the war was really anti-Russian. In July 1905 he met Nicholas II on a Baltic yachting cruise and they signed the Treaty of Bjorko, a defensive alliance against attack by a European power in Europe. William hoped that the French would have to join the alliance and would thus be separated from their new partner, Britain. In practice the treaty became a dead letter almost immediately. The Russians soon realised that the alliance would be of no military value in the Far East. Nor would it even keep Britain neutral in the event of a second Russo–Japanese war, for Britain in August pledged herself to help Japan if war broke out. The alliance also offended the French and threatened the supply of French loans which were so necessary for Russian recovery.

The second German move during the Russo–Japanese war was interference in the affairs of Morocco to show the world that Germany could not be ignored in any international issue and perhaps to shake the Anglo–French entente. In March 1905, William was induced by Holstein and Bulow to break his Mediterranean cruise by landing at Tangier. He assured the Sultan of Morocco that he regarded him as a free and independent sovereign, thus repudiating the Anglo–French agreement on Morocco. The Germans next demanded a conference on the question and won the first round of the dispute because Delcassé, who opposed surrender to the German demand, found the rest of the French cabinet against him and resigned. The conference met at Algeciras in January 1906 and went very differently from German expectations. At the conference not only Britain supported French claims in Morocco but also Russia, Spain, Italy and the United States. Imperial Germany was unaccustomed to such a rebuff, which ended Holstein's career. The Germans had not been aiming at war and they had a good case on the Moroccan question over which they had never been consulted. But the brusque stupidity of their diplomacy ruined their case and strengthened, rather than weakened, the Anglo–French entente. Grey, the new British Foreign Secretary, authorised conversations between the British and French general staffs.

The Moroccan crisis also contributed to a reconciliation between Britain and Russia. The British for years had wanted to settle various questions which kept them at loggerheads with the Russians. After their defeat by Japan, the Russians were more willing to negotiate. Izvolsky, who became Russian Foreign Minister in 1906, favoured a rapprochement with Britain and in August 1907 the main areas of friction were settled. Tibet was made a buffer state and the Russians renounced direct contact with Afghanistan so that India's north-west frontier became more secure. The main question was Persia, which was to be divided into three zones, the north becoming a Russian sphere of interest, the south-east adjacent to India a British sphere of interest, with a neutral zone in the centre.

As with the Anglo–French entente, the agreement was an elimination of differences, not an alliance. Relations between the two countries remained uneasy because of continued Russian advances in Persia and the hostility of liberal opinion in Britain towards agreement with autocratic Russia. 'If the Germans had kept quiet,' notes A. J. P. Taylor, 'the triple entente might soon have dissolved; instead their actions turned it into a reality.' The Germans came to believe that Britain was following a deliberate policy of encircling Germany, when in fact the British moves were purely precautionary. After 1907, fear of encirclement undermined any remaining common-sense in German policy that might have checked the drift to war.

The Growth of Tension (1908–14)

The Austro–Russian agreement of 1897 had, in Taylor's phrase, put the Balkans 'on ice' for a decade though it still remained a problem area. The years after 1897 saw a sharp decline in Austro–Serb relations. Austro–Hungarian treatment of Slavs inside the Empire angered the Serbs who dreamt of a Great

Yugoslavia. In 1903 the pro-Austrian Alexander of Serbia was murdered and Peter Karageorge, who favoured closer relations with Russia, became king. The Serbian Prime Minister, Pasich, tried to break Serbia's economic dependence on Austria by finding new markets in the Balkans, and French capital helped the growth of Serb armaments. As Turner indicates, Serbia became 'potentially the most explosive element in the Balkans' and she regarded covetously Austria–Hungary's Slav provinces—Bosnia, Croatia and Dalmatia. Behind this nationalistic thinking was a strategic motive—the desire to gain an outlet onto the Adriatic.

But if Serb ambitions threatened peace in the Balkans, so did those of Austria–Hungary. With the appointment of Aerenthal as foreign minister and Conrad von Hotzendorff as army chief in 1906, a gambling spirit entered Austrian diplomacy. Austrian policy now aimed at the elimination of Serbia because it was believed to be the nucleus of a South Slav state which would stimulate unrest among the Croats and Serbs within the Empire.

The opportunity for action in the Balkans came with a revolt in Turkey in 1908 by the Young Turk movement which aimed at more liberal efficient government. The arrogant Aerenthal saw in Turkey's discomforture a chance to restore the prestige of the monarchy by annexing Bosnia-Herzegovina, which in any case had been administered by the Austrians since 1878. In September 1908, he secured consent of the Russian foreign minister Izvolsky to the annexation, in return for Austrian support for a revision of the Treaty of Berlin by reopening the Straits to Russian warships. Izvolsky was led to believe that a formal conference of the powers would approve the annexation but instead Aerenthal issued a unilateral declaration on the matter and Izvolsky felt that he had been cheated. Stolypin and Nicholas II, who felt that Izvolsky had in any case exceeded his instructions, were furious and so of course were the Serbian and Turkish governments. Grey expressed the British view that the annexation 'struck at the roots of all good international order'. Even the Germans were annoyed at the Austrian action for they had received little notice of Aerenthal's intentions. However, when the Russians demanded a conference on the question, the Austrians were able to reject it because of a promise of military support from Germany. Moltke, the Chief of the General Staff, with the approval of William and Bulow said that Germany would mobilize as soon as Russia did. Convinced of Russian weakness, the Germans went further and demanded in March 1909 that Russia should recognise the annexation of Bosnia-Herzegovina and make Serbia do the same. The demand contained a scarcely veiled threat of military action and the Russians, who could not be sure of any support from Britain or France, were forced to give way.

Aerenthal's vanity had screwed up tension in the Balkans, which became once more in Anderson's phrase 'the powder-keg of European politics'. The Russians accelerated their military reforms, conscious that if they were forced to surrender in any future confrontation they would lose all credibility as a great power. The German attitude in 1909 boded ill for the future. Convinced that the balance of power in Europe was turning against them, they felt obliged to support Austria–Hungary, their only reliable ally. This clear case of the tail wagging the dog would have disgusted Bismarck. The crisis indicated that the German army would always be on hand to support Austrian adventures and the Austrians knew it. Yet even if Austrian objectives were gained, the only result would be to increase the number of dissident Slavs within the Empire. The crisis foreshadowed that of July 1914 in all its essentials.

Tension in Europe was made even more acute by a second row over Morocco. Franco–German relations over this issue improved after 1905 with agreements in 1908 and 1909. In April 1911, the French were able to extend their control in Morocco by answering the appeal of the sultan for assistance in crushing a revolt in Fez. The Germans would have been well advised to ignore this development but in the propaganda of the Pan-German League Morocco had been built up as a great economic prize. The new German Foreign Secretary, Kiderlen-Wachter, had drafted the aggressive note to Russia in 1909 and believed that similar tactics over Morocco would split the Triple Entente powers. Therefore he persuaded Bethmann-Hollweg and William to declare the French action a violation of the treaty of Algeciras and also to send a warship, the *Panther*, to Agadir, ostensibly to protect German lives and property.

The result of this inept move was only too predictable. In Winston Churchill's words, 'all the alarm bells throughout Europe began to quiver'. The British response was particularly startling for they believed, albeit mistakenly, that the Germans were planning to establish a naval base on the West Atlantic. It was particularly striking that Lloyd George, a pacifist during the Boer War, should refer in a speech at the Mansion House to Britain's resolve 'at all hazards to maintain her place and her prestige'. In the end Kiderlen, who had demanded all the French Congo as compensation for Germany, had to be content with a slice of it in return for recognizing a French protectorate in Morocco.

The Agadir crisis was of profound importance in the events leading up to the war. In France it cemented a previously divided public opinion against Germany, and France's new determination was symbolised by the accession of the hard-liner Poincaré to the premiership in 1912. The Germans, who had wanted to check French control in Morocco, had failed to do so and had received another diplomatic rebuff. Their injured pride rather than World Policy would mean that in future crises they could not back down again. Anglo–German relations dipped sharply and the Conservative leader Heydebrand was cheered when he said in the *Reichstag* that the incident showed who the real enemy was. Tirpitz was able to persuade the German government to plan further increases in the navy and this went ahead despite Haldane's visit to Berlin in 1912 to try to limit the naval race. As a result, the British and French naval staffs held talks and decided that the French fleet would safeguard the Mediterranean while the British fleet would concentrate on the Channel and North Sea. The Anglo–French entente was now virtually a military alliance. All over Europe the feeling was growing that war was just a matter of time.

One of the many unfortunate results of the Agadir crisis was the way in which it incited the Italians to attack Tripoli in 1911 in order to gain compensation for the French acquisition of Morocco. The Italian aggression in turn excited the ambitions of the small Balkan states bordering Turkey. A Balkan League was formed in 1912, consisting of Serbia, Bulgaria, Greece and Montenegro, its objective being to drive Turkey out of Europe. The League had the support of Russia and France because a Slav victory would undermine Austrian security. The risk of the war becoming general was considered worth taking. In October 1912, the League powers attacked Turkey, Adrianople fell, and the Turks were forced to make peace. Germany and Austria–Hungary had stood aside, assuming that Turkey would be victorious, when in fact the victory of Balkan nationalism was a disaster for them. By the Treaty of London of May 1913, Turkey was left with Constantinople and its environs, Albania was reserved for disposal by the great powers and the rest of the mainland was left for the members of the League to distribute among themselves.

But war now broke out among the victors over division of the spoils when Bulgaria, encouraged by the Austrians, attacked Serbia in June. The attack was routed and Bulgarians now found Turkey in the field against them as well as Serbia. Finally, by the Treaty of Bucharest of August 1913, Bulgaria was forced to cede her gains in Macedonia to Serbia and Greece, while eastern Thrace and Adrianople were returned to Turkey. The Serbs also wanted Albania as an outlet to the sea and insisted on keeping troops there despite the disapproval of the great powers. In October they had to yield to an Austrian ultimatum, again backed by Germany, William declaring grandiloquently that he would draw his sword whenever Austria needed help.

Nevertheless, Austria–Hungary's strategic position had declined sharply as a result of the two Balkan Wars, for Serbia was now a formidable Balkan power capable of putting 400,000 troops into the field. Indeed, both the Central Powers were worried at the way in which the military balance of power appeared to be turning against them. Austria's army had a peacetime strength of 475,000 and Germany's 651,000, but this appeared inadequate compared to France's army of 600,000 and Russia's, which numbered 1,200,000 men and was expected to become a force of 2 million men by 1917. The British were expected to join in a general war by the Germans and Moltke admitted that they were opponents 'not to be underestimated'. This situation appears to have created a sense of fatalism in the minds of the German leaders. William, Bethmann and Moltke were pessimistic about Germany's chances in a general war but felt that time would only serve to make the position more hopeless. When war broke out in 1914, the German plan of campaign, as Corelli Barnett demonstrates, was not at all an aggression plotted by a general staff conscious of great power, but a desperate sally by men haunted by numerical weakness.

By 1914 any crisis was likely to precipitate war because of military considerations. The French and the Russians were well aware of the implications of the Schlieffen Plan and their own plans to dislocate it, the French by attacking Lorraine, the Russians by launching a major offensive against East Prussia. All the plans hinged on rapid mobilisation which, once started, would accelerate the whole tempo of any crisis, leaving diplomacy with little hope of solving it.

The July Crisis and the Outbreak of War

On June 28, the Archduke Francis Ferdinand, nephew of Francis Joseph, was murdered by a Bosnian extremist, Princep, while on a visit to Sarajevo. The group to which Princep belonged had been encouraged by Colonel Dimitrievich, onetime Chief of Serbian Intelligence and leader of a Serb Terrorist organisation, the Black Hand. The Serb Prime Minister, Pasich, had known of the plot and had sent a vague warning to the Austrian government which had nevertheless neglected to give the archduke proper protection. Despite the fact that the Serbian government was not guilty of complicity in the plot, most of the Austrian government felt that strong action was needed and indeed on July 5 the Germans urged them to make war on Serbia, though it should be said that the German government hoped that the conflict would be localised.

On July 23, an Austrian ultimatum was sent to Serbia, deliberately framed by the Austrian Foreign Secretary, Berchtold, in terms that no self-respecting state could accept. It demanded the suppression of all anti-Austrian societies in Serbia, the dismissal of all officials to whom Austria objected and the entry of Austrian police and officials into Serbia to ensure that all the demands were being carried out. The Russian government, which had conferred with Poincaré earlier in the month, were now confident of their army's capabilities and of French support; this time they were not going to give way and they initiated military preparations. Serbia, therefore, confident of Russian support, replied in an evasive way to the ultimatum, and Austria declared war on her on July 28. By now the danger of Franco–Russian intervention was clear and Bethmann-Hollweg and others in the German government must be blamed for not restraining the Austrians in a situation where there was little hope of localising the dispute. Bethmann's attempts to warn off the Russians came to nothing for they mobilised on July 30. Only then did Bethmann join Grey in urging restraint on Austria, impressed by Grey's clear warning that Britain would not find it practicable to stand aside in the event of a general war; but while Bethmann urged caution, Moltke urged quite the opposite course on the Austrians.

On July 31, the German government, worried by Russian mobilisation, demanded that Russia should cease her military preparations and in the absence of any reply declared war on August 1. The French were asked for a promise of neutrality in a Russo–German war and as no such French promise was received Germany declared war on France on August 3. On the same day they sent an ultimatum to the Belgian government demanding free passage through Belgium to attack France. The Belgians refused and German troops crossed the Belgian frontier on August 4. It was this moral issue of the violation of Belgian neutrality that united opinion in Britain and led her to declare war on Germany. A general war was under way which was to transform Europe and its place in the world.

Explanations of why war broke out have been many and varied. Underlying its outbreak was a complete lack of comprehension of the implications of total war. On all sides it was assumed that the war would be short and would not destroy the fabric of civilisation. On the contrary, in Russia and Austria it was seen as an escape from domestic difficulties for it was hoped that a successful war would restore the prestige of the monarchy. Lack of any great statesmanship during the July crisis was another factor. 'Again and again in the July crisis,' comments James Joll, 'one is confronted with men who suddenly feel themselves trapped, caught up in a fate they are unable to control.' The disproportion between the talents of the politicians and the gravity of the problems is perhaps symbolised by Bethmann's answer to Bulow soon after the outbreak of war. Bulow asked how the war had come about. 'If only I knew,' was the anguished reply. No one planned a general war in 1914. Therefore the coming of war in 1914 was in one sense a tragedy of miscalculation. Germany's miscalculation lay in the brusqueness and insensitivity of her diplomacy that had created the Triple Entente and it was German support which allowed the Austrians to choose to wage war on Serbia. Yet German hegemony of Europe could have been achieved without war; in fact, it had already been achieved by the early years of the twentieth century through economic advance and the defeat of Russia in the Far East.

But of all the powers it was Austria who did most to provoke war in 1914. She had reopened the difficult Balkan question in 1908 and her ultimatum in July 1914 raised her quarrel with Serbia to the level of a grave international crisis. Finally, it was Austria who, ignoring German calls for caution during that crisis, was the first power to resort to force by attacking Serbia.

The question of responsibility for the war has been an explosive issue since the guilt clause in the Versailles Treaty of 1919 put the whole blame on Germany and her allies. After this, many historians came to agree with Lloyd George that all the nations had 'stumbled into war' and that therefore all nations were in part to blame. In recent years the debate has again aroused strong feelings with the work of Fritz Fischer, who maintained that Germany had specific expansionist aims and that German leaders not only prepared for a major war from 1911 but provoked it in 1914. His views were sharply challenged by other German historians, notably Gerhard Ritter, who stressed that Germany was only partly to blame for the war, the responsibility of the German government lying in its surrender of all political reasoning to military planning.

Further Reading

Anderson, M., *The Eastern Question*, Macmillan, London, 1966

Fieldhouse, D. K., *Economics and Empire 1830–1914*, Weidenfeld and Nicolson, London, 1973.

Koch, H. W. *Origins of the First World War*, Macmillan, London, 1972.

Taylor, A. J. P., *The Struggle for Mastery in Europe 1848–1918*, Clarendon Press, Oxford, 1965.

Turner, L. C. F., *The Origins of the First World War*, Edward Arnold, London, 1970.

Woodward, E. L., *Great Britain and the German Navy*, Frank Cass, London, 1964.

Questions

1. What were the chief aims of Bismark's foreign policy after 1871 and by what means did he pursue them?
2. 'The Treaty of Berlin (1878) left behind it a disastrous heritage of discontent.' Discuss.
3. How important were economic factors in the scramble for colonies after 1880?
4. Assess the effects of colonial rivalries upon the relations of the powers during the period 1890 to 1914?
5. Who was to blame for the outbreak of the First World War?

CHAPTER EIGHT

THE FIRST WORLD WAR 1914–18

The Character of the War

Nothing is more extraordinary to later generations than the rapture with which the onset of war was greeted in major cities all over Europe. Many people no doubt felt that war would bring colour and heroism to their drab humdrum lives and glory and profit to the nation. In the excitement of the hour, old enmities were forgotten in the general patriotic reaction and even the socialists turned from opposition to support. Popular hysteria demonstrated that this was the greatest of all wars of nationality.

The disillusionment was to be swift and terrible. The war was expected, even by the generals, to be short and mobile, and few could have conceived of a conflict lasting four years, bringing with it untold millions of casualties and leaving Europe sadly weakened. It was a war dominated by military technology which made defence stronger than ever before. The new strength of the defence lay in increased fire-power provided by the magazine rifle and the machine-gun. This fire-power, employed by men in trenches behind barbed wire, ended the possibility of the cavalry retaining any military significance and made infantry attacks suicidal. Therefore heavy artillery was required to prepare the attack by pulverising barbed-wire entanglements and well-prepared machine-gun emplacements in an elaborate trench system. Howitzers expended shells at an unprecedented rate and demand soon far outran supply. The shell shortage of the early years of the war was symbolic of the failure to anticipate the nature of modern warfare. There were many other examples; the French army of 1914 went into action in red trousers, which made their wearer an easy target, while on both sides the doctrine of the offensive at all costs still dominated military thinking in a new situation when such offensives would be futile and costly in men's lives.

Once the deadlock of trench warfare was appreciated, ways round the deadlock were sought. In 1915, the German action in using poison gas was soon copied by their enemies and in 1917, partly through Churchill's prompting, the British threw the first tanks into battle at Cambrai. Some old weapons like the mortar and grenade were revived but in the end the deadlock was only broken by the exhaustion of the Central Powers rather than by military innovations.

The misery endured by millions of ordinary men in the trenches of the Western front for nearly four years must be without parallel in recorded history. It demonstrated the truth of Dostoievski's observation, 'Man is an animal that can become accustomed to anything'. Great armies faced each other across a shattered no-man's-land and were smashed by shell-fire, shot, burnt and gassed. Wounded men hung for days on the barbed wire until they died and millions were mown down in the futile offensives.

The Western Front (1914–16)

In 1914 the Germans hoped to win the war in the West by a knockout blow against France launched through Belgium, after which Paris would be surrounded as the German armies crossed the Seine to the north-west of the capital. The French armies attacking Alsace-Lorraine could then be taken in the rear. It was a plan of Napoleonic audacity for it committed nearly seven eighths of the German forces in the west to the pincer movement, while only one eighth would be left in Germany to counter the French offensive. Yet as Ritter and Liddell Hart have shown, the Schlieffen Plan had its weaknesses. It was hardly feasible in 1914 for German soldiers advancing on foot with horse-drawn artillary and rounding the circumference of the circle to move more quickly than the French who were able to switch troops by rail across the chord of the circle. Moreover, the French would have time to destroy bridges and railways in the path of the invasion. Schlieffen's failure to appreciate such factors leads one to conclude that he has enjoyed an exaggerated reputation as a war strategist.

For all that, the Plan came near to success. When the German offensive was launched, the French military under Joffre underestimated the weight of the attack through Belgium and soon the French armies and the British Expeditionary Force under Sir John French were forced to retreat to a more defensible position on the River Marne. Their survival was aided by a number of German errors. Four German divisions in Belgium were sent to East Prussia to help check the Russian offensive so that the right-wing pincer movement was weakened. More seriously, the advance of the Second Army of von Bülow and the First Army under von Kluck had been so rapid that they lost contact and a gap appeared between them. To regain contact, von Kluck veered south-east and exposed his right flank. Joffre seized the opportunity to counter-attack in September and the Germans retreated. In the crisis Joffre had shown admirable coolness and ability to improvise new strategy though his triumph at the Marne was to be his one outstanding victory. The crisis had also demonstrated the quality of the British Expeditionary Force, which by its stubborn resistance at Mons in August had prevented the Germans from outflanking the French left.

Erich von Falkenhayn replaced Moltke as supreme commander of the German army and both sides attempted to outflank each other to the north in a race for the Channel ports. Dogged French and British resistance prevented the Germans breaking through but the losses at the first battle of Ypres in November were enormous. After this, both sides dug in and by the end of the year an elaborate system of trenches ran from the Channel to the Swiss frontier.

In 1915, the Germans were content to remain on the defensive for the most part as Falkenhayn was committed to a major offensive in the east, their attack on the British at the second battle of Ypres being notable for the first use of poison gas. The French and British launched major assaults after this, in Champagne and at Loos respectively, though they did not gain more than three miles at any one point. Yet the war was to take on a more monstrous grimness in 1916 with the most formidable battle of the war, Verdun, which lasted from February to December. Alistair Horne in *The Price of Glory* writes, 'Of all battles of the First World War, Verdun was the one in which most Frenchmen had taken part. Something like seven tenths of the whole French army passed through Verdun. The combined casualties of both sides reached the staggering total of over 700,000. It is probably no exaggeration to call Verdun the "worst battle" in history.'

The French were unprepared for the German onslaught because Joffre failed to discern the German objective in undertaking so titanic an offensive far from Paris. Falkenhayn was not really attempting a breakthrough at Verdun but rather trying to bleed the French army to death through its determination to defend at any cost a city so rich in historical associations. Joffre had not prepared Verdun sufficiently despite the warnings of its commander of its unpreparedness and from military intelligence about German preparations.

When the offensive started, the German artillery wreaked deadly damage, the aim being to create, in Pétain's phrase, 'a zone of death'. Especially lethal were the monstrous 420 mm 'Big Bertha' mortars. Yet the French would not yield Verdun and when the military wished to abandon the Verdun salient, Briand insisted that it be held for otherwise a grave blow would be struck at French morale. The cold, conservative Pétain was brought in to command a new Army of Verdun and he rotated the divisions which had to endure the German shelling. French heroism meant that the Germans did not pass and the battle of Verdun was a heavy strain on both sides.

On the British sector, in an attempt to relieve the French at Verdun, an assault along the line of the Somme by 14 British divisions and five French in July was a disaster. In one day the British lost nearly 60,000 men, including 19,000 dead, and Kitchener's volunteer army was destroyed. The reward for this slaughter was an advance of no more than five miles.

The Eastern Front (1914–16)

In August 1914, the mobilisation of the Russian armies was swifter than expected and by the end of the month there were 2 million Russians under arms. Eight Russian corps were deployed against five German corps in East Prussia, while in Galicia 18 Russian corps faced 12 Austrian corps. The Russians responded bravely to the French plea for an immediate offensive against the Central Powers to relieve the pressure on Russia's allies in the West. The Russian Commander-in-Chief, the Grand Duke Nicholas, ordered the Russian armies into action before they were fully equipped and a second disadvantage was the mutual hostility of the two generals, Rennenkampf and Samsonov, who were to invade East Prussia from the east and the south to effect a juncture.

The Russian advance was an unmitigated disaster. Two German generals, Ludendorff and Hindenburg, were able to exploit the gap between the two Russian armies. Samsonov's army was surrounded at Tannenberg in August and 90,000 prisoners were taken, the commander committing suicide. In September, Hindenburg was able to gain a victory over Rennenkampf's isolated forces at the battle of the Masurian Lakes and East Prussia was cleared of Russian troops.

Better fortunes attended Russian armies in the south. Here the Serbs had parried the Austrian thrust after ferocious battles and had expelled the invaders from Serbia. The Austrian general Hötzendorff could not devote his main strength against the Serbs for he wished to launch an offensive against Russian Poland to divert the Russians while the Schlieffen Plan was put into operation in the west; but the Russians took the offensive first in Galicia and in September took 100,000 prisoners at Lemberg.

This proof of Austrian military incapacity meant that friction between Austria and Germany grew as early as 1914. It also required Falkenhayn in 1915 to help the Austrians by an offensive in the east. In May, Mackensen, on a plan suggested by Hötzendorff, broke through the Russian line at Gorlice in Galicia, taking over 100,000 prisoners and by August Warsaw had fallen. The Russian defeats led to the entry of Bulgaria into the war on the side of the Central Powers and the annihilation of the Serb armies.

In 1916, with the German pressure at Verdun, the Western allies appealed to

Russia for a new offensive. In June came a magnificent Russian response, the great Brusilov offensive which broke the Austrian front and by October had led to the capture of 400,000 prisoners and 500 guns. It was to be the last great feat of arms of the Russian Empire.

War Aims and the Search for Allies

The deadlock after the first battles drove the Powers to consider their war aims. As Taylor has pointed out, 'No power had entered the war with any defined aim except to win. Victory was expected to provide a policy; in fact victory was the policy.' Austria–Hungary was the only power, on the outbreak of war, with a specific objective, the crushing of South Slav nationalism by conquest. The Germans lacked war aims when the war started and sought to work out concrete objectives which once gained would destroy all the forces facing them. In September 1914, Bethmann-Hollwegg's Memorandum showed clearly what this would entail; the loss by France of territory with strategic and economic value, German protectorates over Belgium and Luxemburg, German leadership of a central European customs union and fresh colonial acquisitions for Germany in Central Africa.

As the war continued, German war aims in Eastern Europe became ever more ambitious and resemble Hitler's later demand for 'living-space' in the East. In 1917, at a meeting at Kreuznach attended by Bethmann, William and the Supreme Command, it was decided that Belgium, Poland, Lithuania and Courland should be fully incorporated into Germany. By March and May 1918, when the Central Powers concluded punitive peace treaties with Russia at Brest-Litovsk and with Rumania at Bucharest, it was clear that the Germans wanted complete domination of Eastern Europe.

For the Allies, the general objective sought was the destruction of German militarism and the war was presented as a war for democracy and security. For Britain this meant the destruction of the German fleet and an end to German colonialism; for France it meant the acquisition of Alsace-Lorraine, the Saar and territory on the left bank of the Rhine. The Russians had no specific territorial demands to make of Germany for any territory gained would add to the number of dissident Poles in the Empire; it was the destruction of Austria–Hungary that Russia sought.

Yet the problem of war aims was intimately bound up with the question of alliances, and Allied aims developed markedly once Turkey entered the war on the side of the Central Powers and Italy on the side of the Allies. The Turks entered the war in October 1914 because they feared partition at the hands of Russia if the Allies won the war; in any case they were confident of German victory and German influence in Turkey was strong. Two battle cruisers, the *Goeben* and the *Breslau*, had fled to Constantinople for safety from the Mediterranean in August and in October they entered the Black Sea to attack Russian ports and shipping. At the same time the Turkish action in closing the Dardanelles Straits to commercial traffic led to the Triple Entente declaring war. This was a crucial development and brought nearer the destruction of both the Russian and Turkish Empires. The Turks committed a blunder in joining the war; they could have stayed neutral with complete security for Russia would be fully occupied fighting the Central Powers. The closing of the Straits was a fatal blow to Russia; without the essential supplies from her Western allies her war effort soon came near to collapse and she was to stand on the defensive in 1915.

The Turkish entry into the war soon led to a Russian demand for the Straits and the adjoining territory to be included in the Empire at the end of the war. France and Britain agreed by April 1915 because this was the only way in which they could stimulate the Russian war effort now that direct help was impossible. 'Diplomacy had to make up for the failures of strategy,' says A. J. P. Taylor, 'and a promise for the future was the cheapest coin in which to pay.' By 1916 the Russians were demanding Armenia and Kurdistan, while Britain and France settled their share by the Sykes-Picot agreement of January 1916. France was to have Syria with an extensive hinterland, while Britain would gain Mesopotamia, Transjordan and Southern Palestine.

Meanwhile, the Allies had attempted to entice into the war the most valuable of the uncommitted nations, Italy. It had been no surprise to the other powers when Italy in August 1914 had declared her neutrality in a war which the Italian government regarded as being caused by an Austrian attack on Serbia, for Italy—since an agreement of 1902 with France—had been only a nominal member of the Triple Alliance. Both sides offered inducements, but the Allies could offer more since the main territories which Italy coveted were Austrian. By the secret treaty of London in April 1915 Italy was promised, at Austria's expense, Trentino, the Tyrol up to the Brenner Pass, Trieste, Istria and North Dalmatia and at Turkey's expense Adalia and extensions of territory in Libya.

The Italian intervention in May 1915 gave the war an anti-Habsburg character which otherwise it lacked. Dismemberment of the Austro–Hungarian Empire became an even clearer war aim in 1916 with the promises made to Rumania by the treaty of Bucharest in August which awarded Transylvania, Bukovina and the Banat of Temesvar. It was ironic that a war originally waged by the Allies for the destruction of German militarism had been transmuted by wartime diplomacy into a war waged for the elimination of the Turkish and Austro–Hungarian Empires.

The Balkans and Arabia

The futile bloodshed of the Western front created divisions in the Allied governments on strategy. In Britain several important men in the government became 'Easterners', convinced that the war would be won by opening new fronts in the Balkans where the campaigns would be more mobile and likely to win the support of the neutral Balkan states. Therefore when Grand Duke Nicholas requested relief from the Turkish armies in the Caucasus, Winston Churchill proposed an expedition to force open the Dardanelles Straits so that a lifeline would be opened to munitions-starved Russia.

The Dardanelles campaign was a series of missed opportunities. A partial attack was launched in February 1915 by the Anglo-French fleets but delays meant that the full assault was not attempted until March, by which time the advantage of surprise had been lost and the Turks had stationed four divisions along the waterway. By the time an Allied army arrived in April, Liman von Sanders and Mustafa Kemal had organised the Turkish defences which now numbered six divisions. The Allied forces—British, French, Australians and New Zealanders—performed prodigies of valour but were pinned down on a narrow beachhead at Gallipoli, and in November Kitchener decided to abandon the enterprise. The fiasco caused 214,000 British Commonwealth casualties and had important effects at home, being a factor in the overturning of the Asquith government and the total eclipse of Churchill's career. It led to a suspicion of army 'sideshows' diverting resources from the Western front and it encouraged

Bulgarian intervention in the war in October 1915 on the side of the Central Powers. The sole consolation in the campaign was that it obliged Turkey to divert forces from the Russian front, thus enabling the Russian armies to hold out longer.

The British and the Turks also clashed in Mesopotamia when a British force under Townshend advanced towards Baghdad in 1915 only to be defeated at Kut in April 1916. The British, however, were able to make more capital out of an Arab revolt against the Turks in 1916, seeing in the revolt an opportunity to strike at the Turkish Empire from its vulnerable southern flank. Ronald Storns and Captain T. E. Lawrence were sent on a mission to the Hejaz area of Arabia to help Hussein, the sheriff of Mecca, and his son Feisal, who were leading the revolt. Lawrence already knew the area well and his grasp of strategy, his courage and stamina enabled him to give a great stimulus to the Arab uprising. He persuaded Feisal to attack the Turkish lifeline, the Damascus to Medina railway, by hit-and-run tactics which were admirably suited to the mobile, brave but undisciplined Arabs. While they could be provisioned by the British from the sea, the Turks suffered from malnutrition as they tried to defend the railways. Lawrence's full realisation of this strategy proved his genius and his tactics were later used by, among others, Giap in Vietnam.

In May 1917, Lawrence and Sheik Adudu Abu Taya led the Huwaitat tribesmen across the desert to attack the fort of Aqaba on the eastern coast of the Sinai peninsula. The Turks were taken completely by surprise and with Aqaba as a base, Feisal's army could now function as the east wing of a British advance from Egypt into Palestine. By October 1917, General Sir Edmund Allenby was laying siege to Jerusalem and it was while Lawrence was trying to cut the railway between Jerusalem and Damascus that he was captured, tortured by the Turks and yet was able to effect an escape.

After the capture of Jerusalem in December, Allenby went on to win the battle of Megiddo in North Palestine, which was considered by Liddell Hart to be the 'strategic masterpiece' of the First World War. This victory, won by Australian and Indian cavalry divisions, opened the way to Damascus which was taken in October 1918. At Versailles a system of mandates was created for the Arab Lands. Lawrence was disgusted by the decision and retired into anonymity.

The War at Sea

Technology had transformed naval operations by 1914, with the coming of the torpedo, the mine and the submarine. Guns were bigger, the latest British battleships possessing 15-inch weapons. The latest dreadnoughts, driven by improved turbines and oil-firing, were faster and more armour-plated than their predecessors. On the outbreak of war, Britain possessed the strongest navy the world had even seen with 27 of the new dreadnoughts compared to Germany's 16.

When the war started the British public hoped for a great sea battle with a Nelson-style victory, but as the grand fleet could be lost in one encounter with the enemy or torpedoed by submarines, caution was the watchword. Churchill appreciated this position when he said of the commander of the British Grand Fleet, 'Jellicoe was the only man on either side who could lose the war in an afternoon'. Therefore British naval strategy was more concerned with maintaining the sea lanes than defeating the German fleet. The Germans, conscious of their inferiority in numbers of ships, also wished to avoid battle and aimed at the piecemeal destruction of the British fleet through mines and torpedoes.

The early years of the war then saw no great battles but in 1916 came the collision of the two fleets at Jutland, the only major confrontation of dreadnoughts in the history of sea warfare. Not surprisingly the battle occurred by accident. The German admiral Scheer attempted to lure the British into a trap by sending part of his fleet to sail off the Norwegian coast. This ruse, he hoped, would draw out the southern section of the British Grand Fleet under Beatty, which the bulk of the German fleet would then destroy, but the British intercepted a wireless signal and Jellicoe's force set out from Scapa Flow as well.

The British cruisers, hit repeatedly by the Germans, were shown to be inferior in the accuracy of their fire, the quality of their shells and in the design of their magazines, which were not protected from the danger of cordite-flash. Jellicoe at one point late in the battle had the opportunity to destroy most of the German fleet but refused to take risks with night coming on. The British lost three battle cruisers, three armoured cruisers, eight destroyers and over 6,000 men killed; the Germans lost one battleship, one battle cruiser, four light cruisers and five destroyers and only 2,500 men. Yet though the battle conferred tactical credit on the Germans, the strategic advantage was gained by Britain for the German High Seas Fleet stayed in port for the remainder of the war and its crews mutinied in 1918. Jellicoe was, however, criticised for failing to display the Nelson touch but he wisely maintained an aloof silence on the controversy.

After Jutland, British control of sea communications was challenged only by the submarine. Its menace was seen as early as September 1914, when one submarine sunk three old British cruisers in the space of a few hours. The Germans did not make full use of the new weapon early in the war for fear of offending American opinion. After Jutland they neglected the fleet and concentrated on submarine attacks on shipping, the jugular vein of the British Empire. Supplies of ships and essential imports began to run short in 1916 and when Germany renewed unrestricted submarine warfare in 1917 with more submarines, Britain came near to defeat. In April one out of four ships leaving British ports was sunk; in that month alone one million tons of shipping was lost. The British reserve of wheat dwindled to six weeks' supply, and the supply of pit props from Norway was so interrupted that coal production was threatened.

The Admiralty in this crisis was reluctant to adopt new methods like the convoy system and Lloyd George took over and forced the measure through, retiring Jellicoe when he was slow to implement it. The adoption of the convoy system was Lloyd George's most decisive achievement of the war and enabled Britain to survive. Losses in convoy were under one per cent and by the end of the war British and American yards were building more ships than were being sunk. The German policy of unrestricted submarine warfare boomeranged. It not only failed to bring Britain to her knees but provoked the entry of the United States into the war in April, 1917. Meanwhile, the British navy exercised a fatal silent blockade of Germany which so undermined health and morale there by 1918.

Allied Setbacks (1917–18)

The year 1917 brought the Allies nearer to defeat than at any point since September 1914. At sea losses of merchant ships threatened Britain with starvation while on three major fronts the Allies experienced a series of calamities. Joffre's successor Nivelle was confident that one sharp offensive would break the German lines; as a preliminary to the main area of operations the British attacked at Arras, but with only one success, the taking of Vimy Ridge by the Canadians. The Germans were ready for the French offensives on the Aisne which were repelled with heavy losses. Mutinies now spread among four French armies during May and June, but they were so effectively suppressed by the French command that Ludendorff admitted later hearing little about them at the time. The quelling of the mutinies was the work of Pétain; he called a halt to further offensives, improved conditions generally and meted out ruthless punishment to the mutineers. French official sources stated that only 23 were executed but Haig noted in his diary that there were 30,000 cases to be dealt with.

The failure of Nivelle's offensive left Haig free to determine his own strategy regardless of the French, and he insisted on a great offensive in Flanders. It was launched in July at what was officially called the third battle of Ypres, but popularly known as Passchendaele. The preliminary bombardment churned the Flanders plain into impassable mud, especially as August was the wettest for many years. In this offensive British casualties numbered 324,000 and three British soldiers were killed for every two Germans. The sole gleam of hope was the victory at Cambrai in November, won with the use of tanks.

The Italian task was equally unenviable. Italy went to war on the most difficult front in Europe; it was 400 miles long through precipitous mountains and whenever the Italians attacked, they had to fight uphill and were very vulnerable to counter-attack. Cadorna, the Italian commander, enjoyed a numerical superiority of two to one, but the Austrian defences were formidable. The Italians fought courageously, but lacking training, artillery and machine-guns, lost 66,000 killed and 100,000 wounded in seven months in 1915. In 1916 the Italian offensive also failed and Conrad initiated a counter-attack which destroyed the Italian centre, and seemed likely to envelop the whole Italian army. Cadorna showed his calibre as a commander at this point by stemming the Austrian advance, but the reality of invasion was a grave blow to Italian morale.

Early in 1917 the French and British suggested that they give help to a plan for a knock-out blow on the Italian front. Because the Italians were lukewarm about the plan, it was shelved. 'This,' affirms Christopher Seton-Watson, 'proved the most serious blunder that the Italians committed during the whole war; they threw away the chance of seizing the military initiative and thus forestalling Caporetto.' Their allies went on to plan the offensive under Nivelle on the Western front, leaving the Italians to face a more powerful enemy now that the German troops were available to help the Austrians after the Russian Revolution. Early Italian victories in 1917 persuaded the German High Command to send seven divisions, while the Austrians themselves sent eight, swelling the total number of divisions facing the Italians from 21 to 36. Now the Italians no longer had numerical superiority and in October the German offensive at Caporetto split the Italian armies in two and Cadorna was forced into a 50-mile headlong retreat. He was dismissed as commander-in-chief and 11 British and French divisions were sent to help the Italians, though the front was stabilised by the time they arrived.

On the Eastern front, the Russian war effort lurched to an end in 1917. Russia sustained more casualties than any other belligerent—at least 4 million dead and conceivably twice this figure. The 'human wave' infantry charges, often by troops equipped with bayoneted rifles but no cartridges, had taken a ghastly toll. The Russian shortages of all armaments prevented any successful exploitation of Brusilov's 1916 offensive, which had cost 1 million casualties.

Nicholas II contributed to the military débacle by dismissing Grand Duke Nicholas as commander-in-chief and assuming control himself. At home, his neurotic wife and Rasputin interfered in the running of the war, Rasputin relaying the Russian plans to the Germans. By March 1917 the Russian people had had enough and forced the tzar to abdicate. The March Revolution was received with delight in the West for it was hoped that the new parliamentary régime would prosecute the war with more vigour and encourage American entry into the war. Yet the Provisional Government failed to appreciate the Russian people's yearning for peace and in July 1917, prompted by the Western allies, Brusilov launched another offensive which made some initial headway against the Austrians; but only one soldier in six possessed a rifle and the Austrian and German counter-attack in August drove the Russians out of Galicia and Bukovina.

The army was now demoralised and receptive to Bolshevik propaganda. When the Bolsheviks seized power in November they began immediate negotiations for an armistice with the Central Powers and a truce was concluded in December, followed by the Carthaginian peace treaty of Brest–Litovsk in March 1918. The Russians lost Poland, the three Baltic provinces, Finland and the Ukraine. They were deprived of 40 per cent of their industry, 70 per cent of their coal fields, 25 per cent of their arable land and one third of their railways and population. Perhaps the robber peace indicates the type of peace which the German government, now completely influenced by the military, would have extorted in the West in the event of its victory. Certainly it makes the Versailles Treaty appear moderate in comparison. Only the Allied victory in November 1918 nullified the Brest–Litovsk treaty and justifies the observation of Hugh Seton-Watson that it was Marshal Foch who saved Russia, not Lenin or Trotsky!

The Collapse of the Central Powers

If 1917 was a dark hour for the Allies, it was yet in this year that powerful compensating factors appeared. In France military defeat was compounded by a series of scandals, the most notorious being the activities of Mata Hari who was suspected of seducing prominent personages to extract secrets from them. A mood of defeatism grew and strong leadership was required. The hour brought forth the man. Only Clemenceau could rally the nation and in November 1917 he became prime minister. His motto was 'I wage war' and and he was true to his promise. He visited the front weekly and became a symbolic figure promising victory. He purged the government of defeatists like Caillaux who had been in touch with the enemy, and had spies like Mata Hari executed. In the great German spring offensive of 1918 he showed coolness as the military situation grew critical and backed his Commander-in-Chief Marshal Foch when the cry went up for a scapegoat.

An even more crucial factor was the entry of the United States into the war in April 1917. On the outbreak of war President Wilson had issued a formal declaration of neutrality and his government assumed that owing to the large English, German, Jewish and Irish elements in the population, the nation could never take part on either side without bringing on civil war at home. In any case, it was classical American policy not to become embroiled in European affairs. Events, however, made real neutrality difficult. Though the Americans disliked British seizure of war contraband on neutral ships bound for Germany or Holland, sympathy with the Allied cause grew so that early in the war President Wilson estimated that 90 per cent of American citizens were on the side of the Allies. The German invasion of Belgium meant that from the first Germany forfeited any moral case for her policy, whereas the Allies were given a morally irrefutable case for taking a firm stand against aggression. American indignation grew when the Germans answered the British blockade in 1915 with a counter-blockade using U-boats. 'England wants us to starve,' said Tirpitz. 'We can play the same game.' This policy led to the torpedoing of the *Lusitania* in May 1915, in which 1,198 people died, including 139 Americans, mostly women and children. American determination to stay out of the war at any cost diminished from that day.

For a while Bethmann-Hollwegg managed to restrict U-boat warfare and 1915 and 1916 passed by without German–American relations deteriorating further, but in this period more submarines had been constructed and Hindenburg and Ludendorff were now ascendant in the German government. They shared Tirpitz's belief that full use of the U-boat was Germany's last hope of victory and they believed that it would starve Britain into surrender before any significant American aid could reach Europe. Therefore in February 1917 the German government announced that its submarines would sink without warning all ships, including neutrals, within a broad zone round Britain, France, Italy and the eastern Mediterranean. Wilson now severed diplomatic relations with Germany.

The German Foreign Secretary Zimmermann attempted to pin down the United States by entangling her in a conflict with Mexico. In March, his telegram to the German minister in Mexico City was intercepted by British naval intelligence and divulged to Wilson. In his cable, Zimmermann instructed the minister to propose an alliance to the Mexican government in which Germany would support Mexican reconquest of Texas, New Mexico and Arizona. When Wilson released the note for publication it caused a wave of anti-German sentiment in America. Later in March the Germans sunk three American ships without warning and in April the United States declared war on Germany.

The way for such a declaration had been cleared in March, as the Russian Revolution removed the only obstacle for believing that the European conflict was a struggle between autocracy and freedom. In any case, as F. R. Dulles has shown, 'real neutrality had gone by the board long before Germany adopted unrestricted submarine warfare'. While trade with the Central Powers had dwindled away, the United States had extended vital economic aid to the Allies through the increasing flow of munitions and food. Interruption of this trade would not only have undermined the Allied war effort; it would have had disastrous consequences on many branches of the American economy. By 1917 most Americans feared that a German victory would threaten the United States and they felt that the Allies stood for the things in which they themselves believed.

The American intervention in the war was not a negligible factor as the Germans had fondly imagined. By the end of the war 2 million American troops were in Europe and supplies of essential materials increased. Great psychological encouragement was given to the Allies even when the number of Americans in the fighting was still small in 1917. Wilson's declaration that the war was one fought for democracy seemed to transform it into a crusade which might yet make the tragedies of the previous years worthwhile. For these reasons, and as Ludendorff himself admitted, 'America became the deciding factor in the war'.

The winter of 1917–18 was a long and hard one in Central Europe. By January 1918 the flour ration in Vienna was reduced to 165 grams a day. Left-wing opposition to the war had begun to grow even while German armies were still successful in 1916. In 1918 it combined with the general exhaustion and reached a revolutionary pitch, fostered by three events. The Russian Revolution meant that the war could no longer be represented as a struggle against tzarist barbarism, and it encouraged German workers to hope for similar changes in Germany. The annexationist peace of Brest-Litovsk alienated permanently a large section of the working class and it responded with a wave of strikes in April 1918 which undermined preparations for Ludendorff's spring offensive. The strikers demanded a peace based on 'no annexations', encouraged by President Wilson's enunciation in January of his 14 points which he believed would be the basis of a just peace. His statement had a particularly powerful appeal for the subject races of the Austro–Hungarian Empire, because of its insistence on national self-determination.

With the domestic situation deteriorating so rapidly and with American aid growing inexorably, the German military leadership pinned its last hopes on a great offensive on the Western front in spring 1918. In March, 35 German divisions attacked the British on the Somme, driving them back 40 miles. A second offensive in April in Flanders scored a complete breakthrough and was contained only with great difficulty. In May, a third German offensive broke through the French on the Aisne river and advanced to within 37 miles of Paris. But the German army had now shot its bolt and Allied morale had held. Survival was aided by the belated decision of the Allies to agree to a system of unified command under Marshal Foch. Allied generals had learned the art of elastic defence by holding the front line with a thin screen of troops and conserving their strength for a crushing counter-attack. In July, the French drove the Germans from their salient near Paris and on August 8, the 'black day' of the German army as Ludendorff termed it, the British Fourth Army with large Canadian and Australian contingents, more than 600 tanks and heavy air support, broke the Germans at Amiens. In September, the Americans and Belgians struck at Verdun and Ypres respectively. Foch succeeded in concerting the separate national thrusts into a grand strategy of offense which took full advantage of Germany's lack of reserves as well as her advanced front-line positions.

The final Austrian offensive on the Italian front took place in June but Austrian determination could not offset their lack of reserves. In October, the Italian counter-offensive led to a rout of the Austrian forces at Vittorio Veneto. But now the Habsburg Empire was already in process of disintegration, Czech leaders taking over in Prague, Serb and Croat leaders proclaiming the establishment of a Yugoslav state and Karolyi asserting Hungary's independence.

In Germany, Hindenburg and Ludendorff realised that the war was lost by September 29. They therefore abdicated their power, leaving the *Reichstag* as the responsible body for making the peace. In November, after the Kaiser had abdicated, a new cabinet under Ebert was formed and it negotiated an armistice with the Allies on November 11, it being understood by the Germans that Wilson's 14 points would be the basis of peace terms.

The Results of the War

The First World War had enormous consequences for Europe and the rest of the world. It was, as Lenin said, a mighty accelerator of events and it destroyed the Hohenzollern, Romanov, Habsburg and Ottoman Empires. In the republican régimes that replaced them democracy had only shallow roots and the post-war period was to see a growth of totalitarian government.

Another factor which promoted post-war instability was finance. The war had to be paid for and the device most used was borrowing at home and from abroad. Foreign loans came mostly from allies and were used to pay for imports from one's allies. Therefore, by the end of the war, there was a structure of inter-allied war debts to be paid off with the Western allies deeply indebted to the United

States. This was to vitiate international financial affairs after the war, as governments sought to pay back loans to citizens and other governments. It was a temptation to print more paper money and this hastened the inflation which had already begun during the war. Britain was the only country which sought to finance by increasing direct taxation to any significant degree.

The cost of the war in human and material terms was staggering. Total casualties were 22 million dead and 21 million wounded; thus making the war Europe's cruellest scourge since the Black Death. The casualties were selective since it was the able-bodied, the 'lost generation', who were singled out for combat and death. The optimism of the nineteenth century with its belief in automatic progress could scarcely survive a war which left 10 million widows and orphans.

The war had a levelling effect on customs and manners. A partial compensation for the hardships which women endured was the sudden availability of men's jobs in industry and agriculture. Conscription created labour shortages which had to be filled at once, and women soon dispelled many anti-feminist myths as they proved their capacity to do hard physical jobs in the factories and on the farm. Girls in the munitions industry, subjected to poisonous dust and fumes, found that their skins turned yellow and that in consequence they were ostracised. Yet the world's largest minority group gained a degree of self-reliance which was reflected in their successful demands for the vote in post-war Britain, Germany, Russia and many other countries. If women edged nearer to some kind of equality, the same was even more true of organised labour in nearly all the belligerent countries. For government to mobilise manpower in the war, the cooperation of the trade union movement was essential and by the end of the war unions were in a much stronger position after collaboration with government.

Total war affected the civilian populations, which soon began to suffer food shortages and diseases caused by malnutrition. The inhabitants of Belgium, Germany and Austria suffered most for they were subjected to the slow restriction of the blockade which continued well into 1919. After years of poor diet, influenza killed off thousands of civilians in Central Europe in August 1918, finding easy victims among people worn down by the hardships of war.

It is true that some of the grossest extremes of poverty were eradicated by the growth of planned economies and the inception of the early welfare state. But the power of the state increased vastly during the war and was one factor facilitating the post-war growth of totalitarian governments. In liberal Britain, as in Imperial Germany, the war forced the growth of state intervention into all aspects of life. Walter Rathenau in Germany created a kind of war socialism which directed labour, brought in rationing and allocated resources to the various industries competing for scarce raw materials. Everything was subordinated to the needs of state. Britain more reluctantly gave up its attempt to run the war on 'laissez-faire' principles, but Lloyd George helped to transform the British economy by his work at the Ministry of Munitions. Nothing was sacred; even the opening hours of public houses were restricted and the beer was weakened.

The war weakened the world's centre, Europe, and strengthened the periphery—North America, Russia and Asia. Another war would accentuate this trend by making the United States and Russia emerge as superstates. Europe's primacy was at an end, and its future looked bleak, for the aftermath of war presented huge problems—the finding of employment for demobilised soldiers, the feeding of the populations, the conversion of industry from wartime to peaceful purposes and the danger of incipient revolt. Normal conditions were restored in

Central Europe because the government machinery—the civil service and the police—continued to function. 'One of the most important achievements of the Habsburg and Hohenzollern monarchies,' says F. L. Carsten, 'was the creation of large and well-functioning bureaucracies; they outlived the disappearance of their masters, in complete contrast with Soviet Russia where revolution and civil war destroyed the government machinery totally and irrevocably.' Central Europe avoided the civil war that raged in Russia for years after the revolution; it did not, however, achieve stability. During the war millions of men had become accustomed to systematic violence. Many soldiers found it impossible to return to normal civilian life and when the opportunity occurred they eagerly enlisted in paramilitary organisations like the *Freikorps* or the *Heimwehr.* Violence and insecurity were to be endemic in Central European affairs after 1919.

Finally the European War had developed by 1918 into a World War. In 1917, when the French armies mutinied, large sections of the most important front depended on British contingents, among which were 100,000 Canadians, 150,000 Australians and New Zealanders, as well as Indians and South Africans. By 1918 there were 270,000 Indians in the battleline. Their immense contribution in turn made the war a stage in the decline of colonialism. British rule in India soon faced new demands for independence from the Indian nationalist party. Similar demands for self-determination were to also make the Middle East a storm centre of politics after 1919.

Further Reading

Horne, A., *The Price of Glory*, Macmillan, London, 1962.
Liddell Hart, B. H., *The History of the First World War*, Pan Books, London, 1972.
Marwick, A., *World War I*, Open University Press, Bletchley, Bucks., 1973.
Taylor, A. J. P., *The Struggle for Mastery in Europe 1848–1918*, Clarendon Press, Oxford, 1965.

Questions

1. Account for the deadlock on the Western Front during the First World War.
2. How and why did the war aims of the Allies change during the First World War?
3. In what ways was 1917 a year of crisis for the Allies?
4. What were the chief reasons for Allied victory in 1918?
5. Analyse the most important consequences of the First World War.

CHAPTER NINE

THE POST-WAR SETTLEMENT 1919–25

The Difficulties of Peacemaking

The post-war settlement of Europe provoked furious controversy at the time and has continued to do so ever since. Winston Churchill felt able to claim that Germany got off lightly but in Germany the Versailles Treaty was assailed as a vindictive, dictated peace designed to cripple Germany permanently. Of course, the Allies were bound to demand harsher terms after the German treatment of the Russians at Brest-Litovsk. It was also inevitable after a war of such terrible cost that the victor powers should seek to increase their resources and territories at the expense of the defeated. Only an optimist could have hoped that a benevolent peace would have followed such devastation, especially when it was assumed, as stated in Article 231 of the Versailles Treaty, that German aggression had caused the war. John Maynard Keynes was to write in his book, *The Economic Consequences of the Peace*, that nearly all the major decisions of the treaties were wrong, but he underrated the immense difficulties facing the statesmen of 1919. When these difficulties are borne in mind, the Versailles Settlement appears a more reasonable achievement, despite several serious errors and its failure to establish a permanent order.

One problem that soon emerged was a lack of unity of purpose between the great powers. The self-righteous and idealistic Wilson came to Europe almost in the guise of a prophet and expected his colleagues to make sacrifices in the interests of a just peace. It was easy for him to do this; his country had not been invaded nor had American losses been heavy. The French press turned upon him and subjected him to a bitter ridicule which he found difficult to stomach. Clemenceau was bound to consider only one objective; French security. Twice in just over forty years France had been invaded by the Germans. Germany must be permanently weakened so that never in the future would she be able to mount an invasion of France. Therefore he growled, 'Mr Wilson bores me with his fourteen points. Why, God Almightly only has ten!' Lloyd George, though restricted by unwise election pledges, was able at Paris to display his talents for conciliation; again, it was relatively easy for him to do this. Britain's security problem had already been solved by the surrender of the German fleet and colonies.

Commitments made during the war added to the complexity of the negotiations. Promises made to Italy in 1915 to entice her into the war were clearly at odds with the principles of the 14 points, enunciated by Wilson in January 1918, on which the peace treaties were to be based. The former gave to Italy territory with a large German population, while Wilson had emphasised the principle of national self-determination.

More seriously, the statesmen were under considerable pressure from their respective publics. In the United States, opinion was turning against further involvement in Europe. In Europe, nationalism had become a Frankenstein monster. Popular passions were roused and strident demands were made for a treaty of vengeance on Germany. Lloyd George was no doubt mistaken to promise in the British election of 1918 to 'hang the Kaiser', to 'make Germany pay the whole cost of the war' and to 'squeeze the lemon until the pips squeak'. When he tried to limit reparations during the negotiations of 1919, he received a telegram from 370 M.P.'s holding him to his election promises. In Britain popular feelings were whipped up by the Northcliffe press. In the *Daily Mail* were headlines like 'Hun food snivel', and demands for a harsh dictated peace. Even the narrow patriotism of Clemenceau seemed too moderate for the French. He was later to be refused the Presidency of the Republic partly because of the compromises made during the peace settlement. It was a mistake to choose Paris as the venue for the Conference. Wire netting was required to guard the German delegates from the fury of the mob and when the Allied delegates arrived they had pinned to their coat-tails posters with slogans on them like 'Hang the Kaiser' and 'Make them pay'. This pressure of public opinion must not be discounted. As Harold Nicolson has noted, democratic diplomacy 'possesses one supreme disadvantage; the representatives are obliged to reduce the standards of their own thoughts to the level of other people's feelings'.

In any case, the sheer immensity of the task of reconstructing Europe was appalling. The continent was in chaos and the statesmen faced an impossible task in attempting to appraise a situation which deteriorated daily while the Conference deliberated. By 1918 the Austro–Hungarian Empire had broken up. National committees had been set up in exile during the war by several of its subject nationalities. The Czechs, under Thomas Masaryk and Eduard Beneš, were proclaiming their independence in October 1918. A similar Yugoslav committee under Trumbić represented the Croats and the Slovenes. It agreed in July 1917 with the Serbian government to form a united Yugoslavia under the Serbian monarchy. The statesmen were therefore faced with a 'fait accompli' in a part of Europe where the question of national boundaries was most complex. Wilson was astounded by the deluge of national claims which he received from racial groups of whom he had never even heard. In such a situation errors were inevitable. For example Wilson agreed to the cession of the Tyrol to Italy, not realising at the time that the area in question contained 230,000 Germans.

The fear of Communism did not make for calm deliberation at Paris. By 1919 the red flag waved over the government buildings in Munich and Budapest. It was feared that the menace would spread further—to Berlin or Vienna or even to Italy. In fact, the régimes of Kurt Eisner in Bavaria and Bela Kun in Hungary were short-lived but their existence added to the pressure for a quick peace.

Harold Nicolson, as a member of the British peace delegation, has described the strains of the conference with its 'scurrying cacophony', and 'sense of riot in a parrot house'. Behind all the negotiations was felt 'the ache of exhaustion and despair'. There was, explains Nicolson, a drift away from 'our early peaks of aspiration towards the low countries where figures laboured hurriedly together in a gathering fog'. Nicolson came to believe that the treaties were vindictive but, considering the conditions, the statesmen did well. As Gilbert White, a member of the American delegation put it, 'It is not surprising that they made a bad peace: what is surprising is that they made peace at all.'

Although most attention has been focused on the treaty with Germany, it was only one part of a reconstruction of Europe which took five years. In June 1919, the treaty of Versailles with Germany was worked out. Then came the treaties of St. Germain with Austria and Neuilly with Bulgaria. In 1920, the treaty of Sèvres was signed with Turkey and that of the Trianon with Hungary. In a resettlement with Turkey a new treaty was signed at Lausanne in 1923.

The Treaty of Versailles

The territorial requirements imposed on Germany were moderate and she did not suffer partition as after the Second World War. She lost Alsace-Lorraine to France, West Prussia and Posen to Poland, North Schleswig after a plebiscite to Denmark, and three small areas (Eupen, Moresnet and Malmédy) to Belgium, a move justified on grounds of nationality. All German colonies, which were a liability anyway, were confiscated on the plea that the Germans were unfit to govern backward peoples, and the colonies were turned into mandates for the Allied powers. The separation of East Prussia from the rest of Germany was particularly resented, as was the clause forbidding the union of Germany and Austria unless expressly sanctioned by the powers.

Yet in the main there was respect for the principle of nationality and self-determination. Plebiscites were held in the East Prussian districts of Marienwerder and Allenstein, where the vote went in Germany's favour. The compromise by which Danzig, a German port dominating the commerce of Poland's greatest river, the Vistula, was made into a German municipality with a Polish foreign policy, was a reasonable one. The same solution was found for Memel on the River Niemen. Upper Silesia, a great industrial area, was at first assigned outright to Poland. At Lloyd George's insistence a plebiscite was held there and eventually Poland was given only half the area, though with more of the mineral wealth, while more Poles were left under German rule than Germans under Polish sovereignty. Opportunities in the future were given to Germany in the arrangements over the Saar. It was to be under international control for 15 years with a military force of occupation and French control of the mines. A plebiscite was then to be held. This was duly fulfilled and the Saar was fully restored to Germany in 1935.

The military clauses were more stringent. The army was reduced to 100,000 and volunteers were to enlist for 12 years to prevent the training of reserves by a period of short service. Its armaments were strictly limited. There was to be no military or naval air force and the size of the navy was to be limited to six battleships, six cruisers, 12 destroyers and 12 torpedo boats. The rest of the fleet was to be surrendered to the Allies. In fact, the German crews in a last act of defiance scuttled their ships at Scapa Flow. The French obtained a further guarantee against German aggression. All German territory on the left bank of the Rhine was to be demilitarised. This was seen by the French as a pledge for good behaviour. If a third war broke out between themselves and the Germans, it would be fought on German, not French soil.

Much less wise was Article 231, which raised violent German objections. This was the War Guilt clause which blamed Germany and her allies for planning and provoking the war. It was bitterly resented in Germany because it meant admitting under duress that all Germans who had died in the war had died for an unjust cause. It was also used to justify a demand for compensation for all damage done to the civilian population of the Allies. Lloyd George, supported by Clemenceau, suggested that war pensions should be classed as civilian damages and Wilson gave way on the point. The inclusion of pensions doubled the charge which would be placed on Germany, though to be fair to Wilson he had earlier refused a French and British proposal that Germany should pay the total cost of the war—that is to say, military and civilian damages. No definite figure was fixed at Versailles and a Reparations Commission was established to determine by 1921 the total amount of Germany's obligations. After prolonged haggling, the Commission fixed Germany's liability at £6,600 million with immediate down payments in cash and in kind in the form of coal and shipping. The attempts to extract payment from Germany were to poison the international atmosphere throughout the 1920s.

The Treaty of Versailles was signed in the Hall of Mirrors in June 1919. The German delegates had not been allowed to discuss the Allied proposals, only to submit observations in writing which, apart from the notable exception of the plebiscite question in Upper Silesia, were ignored. Discussion might well have softened some of the harsher aspects of the treaty. The absence of discussion allowed the Germans to claim in the future that as the treaty was a *Diktat* it was not morally binding. Indeed, the treaty could have been improved by a little more consideration for German susceptibilities. The attempt to extradite the Kaiser from Holland and the prosecution of 12 war criminals was bound to keep antagonisms alive. So were the many petty provisions in the treaty which must have galled the Germans, forced to return astronomical instruments taken during the Boxer Rising of 1900, and the skull of an East African Sultan.

But in conclusion the underlying leniency of the terms must again be stressed. The balance of power was not restored, for Germany still dominated Europe. Her steel production by 1925 was twice that of Britain's. Only dismemberment could have destroyed German predominance and this was felt to be impracticable. Machiavelli no doubt would have attributed the failure of the Versailles treaty to the fact that it ignored the rule that an intelligent victor does one of two things to the defeated: he crushes or conciliates. The Versailles treaty did neither. It irritated the Germans but did not deprive them of the means of retaliation. But it would be as fair to say that French policy after 1919, obsessed by the need for security, undermined the Versailles treaty. Versailles failed, says Gerhard Schulz, 'not because the treaties were worthless, not because mistakes were made, but primarily because there was no timely or far-sighted attempt to revise these treaties and to continue the necessarily unfinished work of the Paris Peace Conference.'

The Treaties with Austria, Hungary and Bulgaria

The peace treaties of 1919 and 1920 merely formalised a process that had been generating for a long time, the dissolution of the Austro–Hungarian Empire. For the minorities in central and eastern Europe, the war intensified a desire that had been growing for generations, the desire for national independence. The statesmen of 1919 were determined to respect these feelings but they brushed aside the request of the Austrian delegation, led by Karl Renner, that the new republic of Austria was as new a creation as Czechoslovakia and should not therefore be saddled with responsibility for the war. Both Austria and Hungary, the core of the old empire, were to have treaties imposed on them and were to pay reparations.

At St. Germain, Austria yielded Bohemia and Moravia, with a population of 10 million, to the new Czechoslovakia. Dalmatia and Bosnia-Herzegovina went to Yugoslavia, Bukovina to Rumania and Galicia to Poland. The Trentino, South Tyrol as far as the Brenner Pass, and Istria with Trieste were gained by Italy. The population of Austria was reduced from 22 million to 6½ million, and one third of the German speaking population was assigned to other states. Vienna, with a population of 2 million, was left with an agricultural hinterland which could not easily support it, though the Burgenland, which had been Hungarian, was allotted to Austria as its population was mainly German. No longer was Austria the centre of a free trade area with a population of over 50 million and this caused considerable problems in the future. Yet if Vienna appeared a city that had lost its 'raison d'être', Austria was not regarded with the same hate as Germany and in the 1920s was frequently given economic assistance by the powers and the League of Nations.

Hungary's fate was all too similar to that of Austria's. She lost Croatia and Slovenia to Yugoslavia, and Slovakia and Ruthenia to Czechoslovakia. To Rumania was ceded Transylvania and the Banat of Temesvar. Hungary's population fell from 21 million to 7½ million with a rather greater reduction in territory. Hungary remained an island of feudalism looking out over a sea of peasant states which were not only former Hungarian territory but also states in which were absorbed over 3 million Magyars. The failure to consult all parties on central and east European questions was most unfortunate because the frontier problems were more complicated and the ignorance of the Conference leaders greater. When Lloyd George spoke to the House of Commons on the subject of a territorial dispute between Czechoslovakia and Poland, he was honest enough to admit that he had never heard of the area.

In drawing up the new Bulgarian boundaries in the Treaty of Neuilly, the Allies were influenced primarily by the desire to reduce Bulgaria's capacity to wage another offensive war. Accordingly, she was forced to cede to Yugoslavia four strategic salients in North Macedonia while Western Thrace was given to Greece, which meant the loss of any outlet onto the Aegean Sea. The Dobrudja was returned to Rumania. The Bulgarians complained bitterly that nearly a million of their people were contained in neighbouring states.

The Settlement with Turkey

By the Treaty of Sèvres of August 1920, Turkey was forced to cede Eastern Thrace, her Aegean Islands and Smyrna with its hinterland to the Greeks. Armenia was to become independent and the Straits were to be put under the control of an international commission which would keep the Straits open at all times. Syria was to become a French mandate and Palestine, Transjordan and Iraq British mandates. It was a harsh peace which reflected the Turcophobe opinions of Lloyd George.

Yet the delay in the settlement had crucial consequences because it made possible a remarkable growth of Turkish nationalism from the spring of 1919. The revival was caused by the landing of Greek troops in May 1919 at Smyrna, a move authorised by the Allies to put pressure on the Turks and also to forestall any Italian seizure of Smyrna. The defeat at the hands of the British and French had been seen as a disaster by the Turks but not a dishonourable event, which the Greek invasion certainly was. A national revival took place led by Mustafa Kemal who, though a successful military leader in the war at the Dardanelles and in Syria, had opposed government policy and was therefore free in the public mind of any association with the collapse of 1918. Kemal's nationalist movement, which was to oust the Sultan in 1923 and lay the foundations of a new Turkey, built up its armed strength and demanded the recognition by the Allies of the integrity of Turkish territory, which implied the end of Greek occupation and continued Turkish control of Armenia. None of the Allies had sufficient military presence in the Middle East to crush Kemal and their rivalries in the area prevented any real cooperation over the problem.

In April 1920, the Turks reached an agreement with Soviet Russia for a joint attack on Armenia. By March 1921 a peace treaty was signed between the two countries which settled the Russo–Turkish frontiers in the Caucasus. Turkey returned Batum but retained the adjacent Kars-Ardahan salient. Kemal now turned to his main task, the expulsion of the Greeks from Anatolia. This was achieved by August 1922, for the Greeks were discredited by internal excesses which meant that only Lloyd George among the Allied leaders wished to give aid and he fell from power over the issue.

New peace terms now had to be worked out at Lausanne in 1923. Turkish success at the Conference was due to the stubborn shrewd diplomacy of Ismet. The British representative, Curzon, attempted to use what the American observer Child called Star Chamber tactics to bully Ismet but the Turk stood his ground, using his deafness to ignore proposals which he disliked! He was prepared to make concessions over the Dardanelles Straits because the British still had warships at Istanbul as well as troops in Mosul. The Straits were made free to commercial vessels at all times except when Turkey was at war but there was only limited right of passage for foreign warships. The Turks were to demilitarise zones on both shores of the Dardanelles, and administration of the area was to be under an international commission. The Turks, however, regained East Thrace and the islands of Imbros and Tenedos from Greece. The special legal privileges of foreign governments and individuals in Turkey, known as the capitulations, had been a source of grievance to the Turkish nationalists and were abolished. Turkey was freed from 40 per cent of the public debt of the Ottoman Empire and no longer had to suffer the indignity of foreign supervision of her finances.

The Lausanne settlement faced facts, and its realism enabled it to be a permanent solution of the Turkish problem. Turkey was no longer contracting for she was now an ethnically Turkish unit. Free of pressure from stronger rivals, she was now truly independent, balanced between Russia and the West. The Eastern Question was at an end. For a century or more it had been the most permanent of all sources of international conflict; and yet, as Anderson has stressed, sterility had been its keynote because 'these rivalries were too often fruitless and too often irrelevant to the real interests of the states concerned'.

General Considerations of the Settlement

One of the consequences of the war was to bring democratic ideals and institutions to peoples who had not known them before. But democracy as a rule only works satisfactorily when created by an evolutionary process; the sudden creation of democratic régimes caused by the revolutionary changes in the war and peace settlements was therefore to be yet another factor promoting instability after 1919. Large areas of Europe were committed to a political régime in the working of which they were wholly without experience, and which ran counter to their historical traditions. The liberal assumption that this form of government was in some mystic way appropriate for all Europe was soon proved to be ill-founded and optimistic. Experience was to confirm in Italy, Germany and elsewhere the thesis of Socrates that democracy may all too easily become the parent of tyranny.

The second main strand of the post-war settlements was the vogue for national self-determination. But to apply the principle meant its violation for, in the words of Gathorne-Hardy, 'in the racial and linguistic jig-saw of Eastern Europe there are no clear-cut lines of demarcation'. Wilson's later regret at his pronouncements about self-determination are worth recalling: 'When I gave utterence to these words,' he said, 'I said them without the knowledge that nationalities existed which are coming to us day after day.' Therefore a new patchwork of national minorities replaced the old one. Czechoslovakia, for example, had a total population of 14 million, of whom 4·5 million were Poles, Ruthenes, Magyars and Germans. Poland's population of 32 million incuded nearly ·1 million Germans, 6 million White Russians and 3 million Jews. Rumania now included 1·5 million Magyars. The result was highly unsettling for post-war Europe because it divided the continent into those states which wished to uphold the Versailles Settlement and those which were determined to revise it.

The greatest of the revisionist powers was Germany. Only the continued collaboration of Britain, the United States and France could have guaranteed the settlement against her. The French appeared to have gained an Anglo-American guarantee of military assistance in the event of a German attack but the British–French agreement was contingent on the ratification of the American–French treaty. Unfortunately, the American government failed to secure ratification of the Versailles treaty by Congress and abandoned the guarantee to France. This had grave consequences for the future. The burden of maintaining the Versailles Settlement now lay on the French, who felt that they had been deceived for in return for the Anglo-American guarantee they had given up claims on Germany. The British still attempted to work with the French but they did not ratify the military guarantees which the French so earnestly desired. British interests were still global and Britain sought to avoid entanglements on the continent. Yet the failure to give the military guarantees provoked the French into punitive anti-German policies which undermined the hopes of lasting peace.

The failure of so much of the Settlement has obscured its real virtues. The terms of the Versailles treaty were so moderate as to be a diplomatic defeat for France. Clemenceau had hoped to detach the left bank of the Rhine from Germany but failed to do so. And despite the minorities problem in several of the new states, the treaty marked the triumph of nationalism in the sense that a larger proportion of European people than ever before were ruled by governments to which they would voluntarily pay allegiance and over which they had some direct control. The disaffected minorities probably numbered only three per cent of the population of Europe.

The Germans were wont to claim after the Settlement that it was radically different from the one promised to them as laid down in Wilson's 14 points of January 1918. In fact, only a few of the 14 points actually concerned Germany and these were fulfilled. In Point 5 was stated the intention to adjust colonial claims in the interests of the populations concerned, and this clearly implied the loss by Germany of her colonies. Points 7 and 8 provided for the evacuation of Belgian territory and the return to France of Alsace-Lorraine. Point 13 provided for the creation of an independent Poland with 'free and secure access to the sea', which meant that West Prussia would have to be ceded by Germany. When the armistice was concluded in November 1918, the Germans were informed that they would have to compensate the civilian populations of their enemies for damage done. Many of the remaining clauses in the 14 points were implemented in the Versailles Settlement. Point 10 referred to the right to self-determination of the peoples of Austria–Hungary and the Settlement ratified the creation of Yugoslavia and Czechoslovakia. Point 11 provided for the freedom of Serbia, Montenegro and Rumania, and Point 12 for the independence of the peoples under Turkish rule outside Turkey proper. In Point 14 was expressed the hope that a general association of nations would be formed to guarantee international order. Wilson's persistence here led to the creation of the League of Nations, the necessary machinery for the revision of the treaties. Therefore the 14 points and the Versailles Treaty were not part of a massive Allied confidence trick. On the contrary, they demonstrate the underlying idealism of the settlement.

The French Alliance System

France emerged from the war, suggests Gathorne-Hardy, rather in the situation of a boxer who has laid out the former champion by a well placed blow but who is still too dazed to be certain whether his opponent has been or will be counted out. To a point the metaphor is valid but the French in fact were only too well aware that the opponent had not in fact been counted out and that true security had not yet been attained because Germany might yet struggle off the canvas. Lacking the Anglo-American guarantee or faith in the collective security of the League of Nations, the French attempted to provide their own security.

Three main techniques were used. The French tried to use, or rather abuse, the reparations system so as to strengthen themselves and weaken Germany. Secondly, there was reliance on military methods. The French insisted on keeping the largest military establishment on the continent and were determined to use force if they deemed it necessary, as they did in 1923 when they occupied the Ruhr. They also bolstered their strength through the traditional diplomacy of alliances. A treaty of mutual support was signed with Belgium in 1920, but the area of chief concern was Eastern Europe. A fundamental purpose of the peace settlement of 1919 had been to create a '*cordon sanitaire*' of new states between the two dangerous powers, Germany and Soviet Russia. As Hugh Seton-Watson has shown, 'the permanent nightmare of Western Statesmen during the first decade after the Armistice was an alliance of Germany with Russia'. It was not an unlikely development for the left was strong in Germany and both powers were aggrieved at the Versailles Settlement. The fears of the West were given confirmation by the signing of the Treaty of Rapallo between Germany and Russia in 1922. Provision was made in the treaty for recognition of Russia and the expansion of Russo–German trade.

The Rapallo treaty had two consequences. It hardened the French attitude towards Germany and made Poincaré seize the opportunity to occupy the Ruhr in 1923; it also intensified the French search for new allies in Eastern Europe. An alliance had already been reached with Poland in 1921. Between 1924 and 1927 treaties were signed with the 'Little Entente' powers of Czechoslovakia, Rumania and Yugoslavia. These alliances remained the fundamental features of the East European political situation until the rise of Hitler. France granted her allies financial and military assistance and the French bloc was able to dominate Europe and the League of Nations in the 1920s. Real progress in economic cooperation was made and for a season an illusion of security was created.

But it proved to be a chimera. The alliance of the Little Entente powers had come into existence originally because of a common fear of Hungarian revisionism. When this fear receded, the individual preoccupations of each power became prominent. Yugoslavia looked upon Italy as her chief threat, while Rumania and Czechoslovakia were most apprehensive of Russia and Germany respectively. In any case, no combination of small powers could equal one great state. The strength of the French system, as Cobban has stressed, was the strength of France. It would survive while France had the strength and the will to defend her allies and herself. As German and Soviet strength returned, however, that of France relatively declined and with it the value of the alliances concluded with the East European states. By 1930 the French had again become acutely aware of their weakness and began to construct a chain of fortifications, known as the Maginot Line, along the French–German frontier. But this implied a defensive mentality which was incompatible with the maintenance of France's network of alliances that had formed the cornerstone of her security system since the war.

Locarno

This process of decline in the French alliance system was foreshadowed at the Locarno meeting of 1925, although the meeting appeared to usher in a new era of more cordial relations in Western Europe. After the chaos caused by the invasion of the Ruhr, the more conciliatory Briand replaced Poincaré and worked for a rapprochement with Germany. One rapid result was the Dawes Plan of April 1924, which reduced reparations and made a loan of 800 million gold marks to Germany.

This new French attitude had the approval of the British Foreign Secretary, Austen Chamberlain, and was reciprocated by the German government now that Gustav Stresemann was foreign minister. Stresemann was able and courageous; he came from a nationalistic businessman's world and hated the losses of German territory in Eastern Europe. In February 1925 he made it known that Germany was prepared to conclude a settlement guaranteeing Germany's western boundaries. Stresemann believed that a guarantee of Germany's western frontier was an essential preparation for revision of her eastern frontier.

His initiative led to the signing of the Locarno treaties of October 1925. The frontiers of France and Belgium with Germany were guaranteed not only by all three states but by Italy and Britain. Germany also signed arbitration treaties with France, Belgium, Poland and Czechoslovakia. The agreements induced a mood of euphoria in Europe which was given more substance in the following year when Germany became a member of the League of Nations. Locarno seemed the turning-point between the years of war and the years of peace. The treaties were the result of genuine collaboration between the British, German and French governments during 1924 and 1925 for Stresemann had established a close rapport with Aristide Briand and Chamberlain. The three succeeded in creating an atmosphere in which Germany could again feel an equal partner in the family of European nations. Locarno raised hopes that more revision of the Versailles Settlement could take place so that Germany's aims could be satisfied peacefully, and as Britain was linked to the Locarno agreements, French confidence in Britain's concern for European security was in some measure restored.

But the treaties were criticised at the time and ever since on the grounds that they made one set of European frontiers more inviolable than the others. Britain and Italy were bound to act only if Germany or France tried to change the western boundaries arranged at Versailles. The East was to be the concern only of Germany, France and the Eastern States. The French had of course tried to extract full guarantees of Germany's eastern frontiers but Britain and Italy refused to assume any obligations in that area. Austen Chamberlain defined the British position: 'For the Polish Corridor no British government ever will or ever can risk the bones of a British grenadier.' But the very fact that certain sections of the Versailles settlement were given a privileged position weakened the rest of it. The illusion of security was soon to be shattered. Locarno in a sense reflected the brief period of relative prosperity which Europe enjoyed up to 1929. This prosperity died with the Wall Street Crash and so did the Locarno spirit. Even in 1925 Stresemann had been attacked for his conciliation by the nationalists in Germany.

With the years of depression, extremism was to triumph in Germany and end the prospects of European peace.

Further Reading

Gathorne-Hardy, G. M., *A Short History of International Affairs 1920–1939*, Oxford University Press, London, 1950.
Nicolson, H., *Peacemaking 1919*, Methuen, London, 1964.
Sontag, R. J., *Broken World 1919–1939*, Harper Torchbooks, New York, 1971.
Watt, R. M., *The German Revolution and the Treaty of Versailles*, Penguin, London, 1973.

Questions

1. What were the major difficulties facing the peacemakers in 1919?
2. 'Germany got off lightly'. Do you agree with Churchill's view of the Treaty of Versailles?
3. What were the objectives of French foreign policy after 1919 and how did French governments seek to implement them?
4. Did Locarno make any real contribution to European peace?

CHAPTER TEN

RUSSIA 1914–39

THE REVOLUTION AND THE ESTABLISHMENT OF COMMUNISM

The War and the Fall of Tzarism

The domestic situation in Russia, deprived of Stolypin's strong hand, had been deteriorating before the outbreak of war. Real power was vested in the hands of the court, and ministers were appointed at the whim of Rasputin, who was free to advance incompetent individuals to important posts. Treadgold terms this situation a 'psychopathic tragicomedy' and it lasted until December 1916, when Rasputin was assassinated by a group of courtiers led by Prince Yusupov.

The outbreak of war led to strong demonstrations of loyalty to tzar and country and the Duma voted war credits enthusiastically; but disillusion was swift. Russia was unprepared for war and, unlike Britain and the United States, was incapable of carrying out the necessary planning. The whole economy was strained. The mobilisation of men and the inroads of war in the west diminished the food supply and the railway network, which was not properly maintained, became even more inadequate for wartime emergencies. The lack of comprehension in government circles of the nature of the new crisis is evident in the advice of industry to cut production, as it was believed that demand would decrease.

The Commander-in-Chief of the army was Grand Duke Nicholas, who was popular with the soldiers, but the weaknesses in the army were beyond the wisdom of any one man to repair. Russian troops lacked proper training, equipment and munitions. The problems of supplying them in a theatre of war which was mobile and covered vast distances were never overcome. The offensive of 1914 and 1915 produced staggering casualties, 2 million in 1915 alone. As the army retreated, a refugee problem was created, for 3 million civilians retreated with the soldiers.

The tzar aggravated a deteriorating situation by committing two grave errors. In September 1915 he was goaded by his wife into dissolving the Duma and two days later he assumed command at the front in place of his uncle, leaving the tzarina and Rasputin in complete control of government. In 1916, the Russian offensives cost a million more casualties and the morale of the army began to crumble.

The final crisis therefore began to develop by late 1916. In November, the Duma was reconvened and the Cadet leader Paul Miliukov angrily denounced government failures and asked, 'Is this stupidity or treason?' In December, in a macabre night of horror, Prince Yusupov and other desperate members of the nobility managed with some difficulty to dispose of Rasputin. The monk was poisoned and shot yet was still alive when he was thrown into the River Neva. By 1917 most thoughtful observers foresaw the likelihood of revolution but when it broke out in Petrograd in March its spontaneity took everyone by surprise. Three factors gave the Revolution its first impetus. There were 400,000 workers in Petrograd, and by March they were hungry. Demonstrations on March 8 over bread shortages led to riots which merged with processions celebrating International Women's day and a strike at the Putilov armaments factory. Unlike the

Revolution of 1905, the Cossacks openly sided with the rioters and the situation became serious.

The apathy of the tzar at this point is astounding. He was warned by both the Petrograd garrison commander and the President of the Duma, Rodzianko, that a grave crisis had arisen. He commented, 'This fat Rodzianko has written me some nonsense to which I will not even reply.' He did, however, write to his wife expressing how much he missed his game of patience every evening and stating his intention to take up dominoes again in his spare time! The riots continued and the only move which the tzar made was to dissolve the Duma on March 11. It met in defiance of the order and elected a provisional committee composed of members of the Progressive Bloc with the idea of restoring order, but it was too late. Discipline had broken down and on March 12 the Taurida Palace was invaded by the workers, who set up a Workers' Soviet modelled on the institutions that had proved their worth in 1905. On March 13 most of the ministers were arrested and on March 15 the tzar himself was persuaded to abdicate in favour of his brother, Grand Duke Michael. As Michael refused to take the throne, the Romanov dynasty ended without even a whimper. Nicholas renounced power, calmly enjoying the crisp cold weather and reading the works of Julius Caesar.

The last years of tzarism had seen a number of promising developments in Russian life, particularly in education and industry. It was Russia's tragedy that these developments were soon to be stifled by a new totalitarian régime committed to the monolithic unity of all aspects of life. Tzarist government had stunted political growth but it had left other aspects of life—for example, the arts—to develop freely. Yet with the pressures of twentieth-century warfare, revolution became more and more likely. The Russian economy and bureaucracy could not cope, and by 1916 there were severe food shortages with meat rising in price 149 per cent and vegetables 228 per cent between 1916 and 1917. Russian casualties in the war were enormous and difficult to quantify, but it would be safe to say that 8 million Russians had been killed. The loyalty of the Russian people was at last eroded by such disasters and the régime was seen to have outlived its usefulness. As the poet Mayakovsky expressed it,

'Like the chewed stump of a fag
We spat their dynasty out.'

The Provisional Government and the Bolshevik Seizure of Power

After the abdication of the tzar, real power was divided between the Provisional Committee of the Duma and the Petrograd Soviet of Workers' Deputies. It was a situation that prevented any possibility of effective government and Adam Ulam is right to describe it as 'a perfect prescription for anarchy'. The Provisional Committee was now formed into the Provisional Government, with Prince George Lvov as Prime Minister. He and the Foreign Minister, Paul Miliukov, were Cadets; Alexander Guchkov, the Octobrist, was Services Minister; and Alexander Kerensky, a Social Revolutionary, was Minister of Justice.

Government was difficult for the Taurida Palace was like a madhouse and the Petrograd Soviet, dominated by Mensheviks and Social Revolutionaries, allowed the Provisional Government to exist only on sufferance. The Executive Committee of the Petrograd Soviet soon issued an order providing for the setting up in every army unit of elective committees, and announced that the military orders of the

Provisional Government were only to be obeyed if they did not conflict with Soviet orders. This opened the way for further breakdown of discipline in the army. The relative inertia of the Petrograd Soviet is mainly to be explained by the Menshevik theory of history, according to which the bourgeois liberals should first hold power.

The Provisional Government faced other difficulties. The postponing of a Constituent Assembly caused mounting public impatience and an early dispute about continuing the war led to the resignation of Miliukov and Guchkov in May. Meanwhile exiled revolutionary leaders were returning to Russia—the Social Revolutionary Victor Chernov and Joseph Stalin from Siberia, but most notably Lenin, who arrived at the Finland Station in Petrograd in April after his journey in the famous 'sealed train' which the Germans allowed through in the hope that its cargo would weaken the Russian war effort. He condemned the war as imperialistic and demanded that the Bolsheviks should oppose the Provisional Government and uphold the slogan 'All Power to the Soviets'. This appeared at the time a disinterested action as the Mensheviks and Social Revolutionaries rather than the Bolsheviks dominated the Soviets and the immediate effect was to weaken further the prestige of the Provisional Government.

In May, a new cabinet was formed which included six socialists, including Chernov as Minister of Agriculture. The strong man in this coalition was Kerensky, who believed that a new offensive was necessary so that Russia could demand a victorious peace. He managed to kindle some enthusiasm for the task and even the Petrograd Soviet gave grudging assent. The offensive commenced in July but after initial successes it collapsed and the complete demoralisation of the army resulted. Troops now began to flee home in large numbers and in Petrograd violence erupted spontaneously with the Bolsheviks most prominent. The urban masses were puzzled because the Menshevik and Social Revolutionary leaders had not seized office and one demonstrator shouted at Chernov, 'Take power, you son of a bitch, when they offer it to you.'

Later in the month Lvov resigned and Kerensky became Prime Minister in a cabinet which now contained a majority of socialists. Kerensky was alarmed by the Bolshevik threat, which after the July disorders was seen to be a reality. The government therefore accused Lenin of being a German agent and arrested Trotsky and Kamenev, Lenin being forced to flee to Finland. Kerensky also attempted to gather support by creating his own forum of public opinion. In August he convened a conference composed of Duma deputies, representatives of the Soviets and members of the unions. At the same time he appointed General Lavr Kornilov in place of Brusilov as commander-in-chief of the army and he managed to stabilise the front after the collapse of the offensive.

The latter move, however, led to another fatal fiasco. In September, Kornilov decided that in view of the weakness of the government he would send a force to the capital to effect a governmental reconstruction. Through a mediator it was suggested that he should become prime minister with Kerensky still a member of the cabinet but Kerensky arrested the mediator and tried to dismiss Kornilov who refused to accept the order. By then his troops were already on their way to Petrograd and Kerensky was forced to free Bolshevik captives and use their help in suppressing Kornilov's mutiny, which they did by mobilising their Red Guards and by sending agitators who persuaded Kornilov's troops to abandon him. The general, who was forced to surrender, was probably only trying to strengthen the Provisional Government rather than overthrow it but the whole affair helped the final collapse of discipline in the army and peasants streamed home hoping for land and liberty.

The illegal seizure of land by the peasantry had already started and the legal owners, the gentry, usually left for their own good. Yet the peasant action did not meet the approval of the party which claimed to stand for peasant interest, the Social Revolutionaries, who declared that their programme was not the same as the arbitrary seizure of land for personal advantage. Chernov, their leader and also a member of the government, told a Soviet of Peasant Deputies in May that the solution of the land question must await the decision of the Constituent Assembly and also that the war must go on. The peasants ignored him and continued their illegal division of land.

In the towns bitter rivalry grew up between the factory committees, increasingly under Bolshevik control, and the unions, influenced by the Mensheviks and Social Revolutionaries. The government did little to restrain prices and as the Mensheviks and Social Revolutionaries had participated in the government they received much of the blame. Donald Treadgold puts much of the responsibility for government inaction on Kerensky, whose weakness was that 'oratory became a substitute for action'. Only the Bolsheviks, who had consistently refused to collaborate with the government, seemed to possess a credible set of policies which might solve the crisis.

By the autumn the Bolsheviks had gained in both membership and popular support. The membership now exceeded 200,000 and control of the factory committees had been gained. Bolshevik policies, mainly developed by Lenin, had a realism which the policies of other parties lacked. Bolsheviks urged the immediate seizure of land by the peasants, a rapid conclusion of the war and all power to the soviets. These ideas won them support away from the Social Revolutionaries and Mensheviks, although as E. H. Carr reminds us even in November their 'independent power in the countryside was still negligible'.

The Bolsheviks were more tightly organised than other socialist parties. Kerensky, nominally a Social Revolutionary, demanded loyalty from his party but as he would not follow party decisions himself, that loyalty was not forthcoming. In contrast, Lenin could count on the unswerving support of his party, a vindication of his insistence on a small group of really committed members. By October he was able to declare to the Bolshevik Central Committee that the time was ripe for action. Zinoviev and Kamenev, who opposed such a policy, leaked it to the party press, thereby revealing the plot to the public but the government took no action, harassed as it was by desertions from the army, peasant violence and strikes in the cities.

The man who did the most to plan a Bolshevik takeover was Leon Trotsky, born Bronstein, the son of a wealthy Jewish farmer. He stressed that a rising against the government would have more chance of success if it were made under the auspices of a soviet action against a counter-revolutionary plot than if it were done openly in the name of the Bolshevik party. Working through the Petrograd Soviet, the Bolsheviks challenged Kerensky's right to order troop movements in the capital. This goaded the premier into a denunciation of their tactics and into an attempt to arrest Lenin. Now the Bolsheviks could claim to be resisting counter-revolution and on the night of November 6–7 they seized key points in Petrograd and arrested the ministers of the Provisional Government. Kerensky tried to rally loyal troops outside the capital, failed to do so and fled into exile. Lenin formed a new government with himself as Premier, Trotsky as Commissar for Foreign

Affairs and Stalin as Commissar for Nationalities. Gradually Bolshevik control spread to the other chief urban centres of Russia.

Lenin now attempted to implement Bolshevik policies as well as to ward off attacks by units loyal to the Provisional Government. Private property in land was abolished and all private and church lands were transferred to land committees and soviets of peasant deputies for distribution. In December, after an armistice had been agreed, Trotsky began negotiations with the Germans. As Lenin insisted that they needed a breathing-space the Bolsheviks signed in March the punitive treaty of Brest-Litovsk, by which they ceded Poland, the Baltic States of Estonia, Latvia and Lithuania, the Ukraine, Finland, much of Belorussia and part of Transcaucasia. A total area of 1,300,000 square miles was detached and the loss in population was 62 million, a third of the entire population. One third of the railways and three quarters of coal and iron resources were lost. Three centuries of Russian expansion were undone but Ulam sees the treaty as a blessing in disguise for Lenin's régime. By stripping Russia of its borderlands, these terms made the Bolsheviks concentrate on dealing with opposition in Russia proper without trying to cope with the militant nationalism of the Poles, Finns and Ukrainians. Lenin's wisdom on the matter was in time vindicated and he was now seen as 'the providential leader of the Party and the state, without whom the régime would disintegrate'. There is no doubt that Lenin's concessions to Germany were necessary for any attempt to continue the war would have caused violent opposition in Russia generally. Yet the treaty was denounced even by some Bolsheviks and a Social Revolutionary murdered the German ambassador Count Mirbach in an attempt to provoke a renewal of hostilities. In August Lenin was seriously wounded by Social Revolutionaries who killed two other Communist leaders.

The Bolshevik response was swift and ruthless. A Red Terror was launched through the *Cheka*, the Bolshevik secret police. It was the first of a series of moves to destroy the old state and build a new one. Members of the Provisional Government were deported, and the *zemstvos* and municipal councils in Petrograd and Moscow were dissolved. The Russian Orthodox Church was attacked and the separation of church and state was proclaimed in February 1918. The Constituent Assembly, for which elections were held in November, returned a Social Revolutionary majority, met only once, and then was dispersed by Bolshevik troops.

The task of establishing a new political and social order was immense for the country was in a state of chaos. It was clear that a new army would be necessary to assist the régime and in 1918 Trotsky began to create the Red Army based on conscription, authority and discipline. The death penalty for desertion was restored and the election of officers ceased. Trained officers were required and Trotsky accepted volunteer officers from the old armies and recruited unwilling officers, warning them that desertion would result in harm to their families. About 50,000 officers of the old army were used in the civil war that was about to start. Political commissars were appointed to keep an eye on officers and to carry out propaganda among the recruits. The soldiers fought with devotion for their cause for they were told that death and torture awaited them if they were captured by the Whites (anti-communists), a piece of propaganda which had considerable foundation in truth.

To grapple with the deteriorating economy, the government decided to establish 'Committees of Poor Peasants' all over Russia to requisition grain from the *kulaks* (rich peasants) to feed the cities. In fact, as E. H. Carr suggests, there were far fewer poor peasants than the Bolsheviks had assumed and therefore Bolsheviks from the cities did much of the requisitioning, thus arousing deep anger among the peasantry in general. A number of peasant risings occurred in the summer of 1918 which, with similar events in some cities, contributed to the murder of the tzar and his family at Ekaterinburg by local Bolsheviks in July.

The Civil War

In the early months of Bolshevik rule, there had been little in the way of organised opposition, partly because other parties failed to appreciate what the nature of Bolshevik control would be. After Brest-Litovsk, however, anti-Bolshevik leaders began to resist the new régime more vigorously. They fell into three groups: (1) non-Bolshevik politicians; (2) former officers of the Imperial army; and (3) nationalists seeking independence for their particular minority. As the nationalists were only interested in their own lands and the politicians disliked working with conservative officers, the real core of the opposition were the military commanders.

The Whites (the anti-Bolsheviks) were immensely encourged by the uprising of the Czechoslovak Brigade and its seizure of the area around Omsk in central Siberia in May. The Czechs were troops who had been fighting with the Allies in the European war in the hope of an independent Czechoslovakia after the war. Their action sparked off Allied intervention on a new scale. The Allies had already intervened at Archangel and Vladivostock on the pretext of safeguarding war supplies. Now the scale of intervention was stepped up by British, French, Americans and Japanese in the hope that the Bolsheviks would be overthrown and replaced by a régime willing to continue the war. The Allied intervention gave the Whites opportunities which they were unable to grasp but it was in the main counter-productive as the Bolsheviks, posing as good patriots, were able to undermine White support by using slogans of defence of the homeland against the foreigners. In contrast, the Whites received only half-hearted Allied support, particularly when the November armistice eliminated the need for Russian help against Germany.

The Whites at Omsk were also weakened by internal disunity, for the Social Revolutionaries, Cadets and right-wing elements formed a most uneasy coalition. In November 1918, the conservatives carried out a coup d'état and made Admiral Kolchak, former commander of the Black Sea Fleet, dictator of all forces in Russia. In Estonia General Yudenich organised an army with British help and the stage was set for the decisive battles of the Civil War in 1919 as Denikin and Kolchak attempted to link up their forces.

Denikin struck north from Azov and won major victories as he advanced on Moscow. Kolchak's disadvantages were, however, too much for him. He was not a competent general and had few able men to assist him. Rival generals and Social Revolutionaries refused to obey his orders and swift advance was difficult in the periphery of the country, which lacked industry and communications. After some advances in 1919 his forces were rolled back by a Red offensive in June. Denikin's march on Moscow was halted in October while Yudenich's attempt to take Petrograd also failed. From this point on the Whites collapsed. Decisive factors in their failure were bad relations with the minorities and the brutality used on the peasantry. The American commander in Siberia commented acidly that the Whites killed 100 people in Eastern Siberia to every one killed by the Bolsheviks.

Nevertheless, 1920 was a year of crisis for the Bolsheviks. The new Polish government under Pilsudski was determined to recreate the Poland of 1772 and in April Polish troops swept into Kiev. The Bolsheviks, facing a traditional enemy, were again able to invoke nationalistic slogans and attracted to their side ex-tzarist generals like Brusilov. As a result, they were able to throw back the Poles and advanced towards Warsaw but the Poles initiated a counter-offensive which routed the Red Army. The Bolsheviks were forced to sign the Treaty of Riga in March 1921, which left some of Belorussia and the Ukraine in Polish hands.

Lenin and the New Economic Policy

The miseries of the Russian people were immensely increased by the carnage and destruction of the Civil War, and the terrorism of the Bolshevik dictatorship. In 1920, famine caused the death of about three million people and industrial production was only about one eighth of the 1913 level. As the Red Army was demobilised in 1920, peasant risings erupted in southern and eastern Russia. The climax of the anti-Communist unrest, which involved workers as well as peasantry, came in March 1921 with a revolt at Kronstadt, the naval base, which had been a centre of Bolshevik power in 1917. The revolt was ruthlessly crushed but made a deep impression on Lenin. As always the supreme realist, he realised the need for a Brest-Litovsk, or breathing-space, on the economic front and he adopted the so-called New Economic Policy (N.E.P.).

The essence of this policy was acceptance of a compromise with the peasantry. Peasants were no longer forced into collective farms and the ruthless requisitioning of agricultural produce was abandoned in favour of a tax in kind on a fixed percentage of the production. The peasant was free to sell as much of the remainder as he wished. Lenin's analysis of the peasantry had been incorrect. The poor peasants had not helped the Communists against the rich peasants and, in fact, as E. H. Carr has demonstrated, there had occurred 'a striking equalisation of the size of the unit of production'. As a result, the middle peasants had become the majority of the Russian people and it was they with whom Lenin had to compromise. The compromise was a tactical manoeuvre; the long-term aim of collective farming was not abandoned.

Private enterprise on a small scale was allowed in industry and trade though the state still retained control over the essentials of the economy. These 'commanding heights' were the banks, heavy industry, transport and foreign trade such as it was. Some factories were actually handed back to private owners but state industries employed four fifths of the industrial labour force. What galled doctrinaire Communists was the use in state factories of capitalist devices like piece-work rates, preferential rations and bonuses. Bourgeois experts had to be employed but as Lenin pointed out, 'No price will be too high if we learn intelligently.'

Gradually the Russian economy recovered, helped by the toughness of the Russian people and the enthusiasm of the Communist hierarchy, especially Lenin, who had to goad his followers into implementing the policies. The currency was stabilised and by 1928 the Communists felt able to claim that levels of industrial and agricultural production had overtaken those of 1913.

Meanwhile, groups opposing Lenin's policies in the party were disbanded in 1921 and a nation-wide purge of the party was carried out which resulted in the expulsion of one third of party members. The *Cheka* was abolished and in its place was created the G.P.U., which had the important power, not possessed by the *Cheka*, to arrest party members. These were, however, the last important moves to be initiated by Lenin. In 1921 and 1922 he suffered strokes which forced his virtual retirement and he found it impossible to keep in touch with what was going on in government as his colleagues began to intrigue for power. Lenin died in January 1924, and the deep admiration which ordinary Russians felt for him was demonstrated by the millions who came to pay their respects to his embalmed corpse.

That Lenin was a political genius there can be little doubt. He was close to the average Russian and could influence audiences by the straightforward and clear exposition of his ideas. He was also a humane man who, said Maxim Gorky, declared war on human misery. Two characteristics dominated his career. The first was his complete dedication to revolution and the subordination of his life to that end. This overwhelming sense of service accounted for the modesty of his demeanour, and as E. H. Carr remarks, 'he set an example of austerity and impersonality which long remained a standard of conduct for the party'. Despite his lack of personal vanity or ambition he possessed the unwavering conviction that he alone was capable of leading the party. From this conviction sprang the ability to carry colleagues with him at times of crisis, as in the seizure of power in 1917 or the adoption of the N.E.P. Therefore to Trotsky, Lenin's greatness lay in his capacity for effective action and he was 'the greatest engine-driver of revolution'. The second major characteristic was a unique realism which led Lenin to make correct decisions on a number of vital issues—on the nature of the party, on the question of party policies in 1917 and the tactics by which it was able to take power. These issues reveal Lenin as a great political strategist.

On the other hand, Lenin's lifework boded ill for the future of Russia and indeed the whole world. He had forecast that the state would wither away after revolution, yet the reverse occurred. The élite that had led the revolution added to its power and the result was dictatorship. Lenin may be criticised for his obsessional persecution of opponents after victory had been gained even when they had begun to support his régime for in this way he contributed to making terror a permanent feature of Russian life. 'It must be an indelible stain on Lenin's record', writes Adam Ulam, 'that for all his humane instincts he allowed this cult, a veritable mystique of terror, to develop. While he was quick to intervene when an individual case of injustice was brought to his attention, he allowed mass terror not only to be practised, but to become leritimate and respectable.'

The Emergence of Stalin

Lenin's stroke threw everything into confusion and uncertainty. The governing body had been the *Politburo* (the Political Bureau of the Central Committee) and its members were Lenin, Trotsky, Kamenev, Stalin, Bukharin, Tomsky and Zinoviev. It settled policy and it was then left to the *Orgburo* to implement decisions reached by the *Politburo*. The liaison between the two bureaux had fallen to Stalin, who was now General Secretary of the Central Committee.

Stalin was born Joseph Djugashvili in 1879, the son of Georgian peasants. He was educated in a theological seminary at Tiflis, a period which Isaac Deutscher sees as decisive in his intellectual development, because he reacted against the repressive teaching and absorbed forbidden socialist ideas. Unlike most of the revolutionary leaders, he was not from the middle class and his class hatred was all-consuming. By 1904 he had become a Bolshevik and his gifts as an administrator led to his gradual rise in the party. In 1921 he was Commissar for Nationalities and a member of the *Politburo* as well as General Secretary. This concentration of power worried Lenin, who after his second stroke made a will in which he pointed to the danger of a clash between Trotsky and Stalin. He also mentioned Stalin's rudeness and capacity for stirring up trouble in the party. Lenin was actually preparing an attack on Stalin, with Trotsky's help, when a third stroke immobilised him in March 1923.

'Stalin,' affirms Ulam, 'was a man of uncommonly good sense and unusually vile as well as brooding temper.' He had great gifts as a committee man: brevity and the ability to get to the point. As well as being on the major committees, he was also on most of the important subcommittees like the editorial board of the newspaper *Pravda*, and the committee to deal with the Ukrainian question. It was a strength of Stalin's that he was willing to undertake such tasks which on the face of it were unglamorous and unrewarding. Many Communists liked him because he was not a middle-class intellectual like Lenin or Trotsky but was a coarse peasant like themselves.

His skilful administrative work explains only in part his rise to power. By the mid-1920s he had become a superb politician, possessing an excellent sense of timing, simple but effective oratory and an apparent but misleading joviality. As Commissar for Nationalities, he was able to take most of the credit for the constitutional reform by which, in 1922, a Union of Soviet Socialist Republics was established. He claimed that this achievement was as important as the creation of the Red Army in the Civil War, implying that he was the equal of Trotsky.

With Lenin now incapacitated, a triumvirate of Zinoviev, Kamenev and Stalin began to act together against Trotsky, whose brilliant achievements made him appear a potential Napoleon. His partners underestimated Stalin, as did Trotsky, who on Lenin's death failed to act with any decisiveness as he was ill himself. When Lenin's will was read out in May 1924, Zinoviev said that Lenin's fears about Stalin were groundless, a remark he was soon to regret. This was a decisive moment in Stalin's progress for Trotsky did not seize on the will as a weapon with which to attack him. He was mainly concerned with the hostility of Kamenev and Zinoviev, who clashed with him on major issues like the question of permanent revolution, while Stalin remained in the background. In January 1925, his enemies persuaded the Central Committee to dismiss Trotsky from his post as War Commissar. Trotsky was too loyal to the party to resort to the only expedient left to him—the use of the Red Army. In 1926 he lost his seat on the *Politburo*, in 1927 he was expelled from the party and in 1929 he was expelled from Russia.

Zinoviev and Kamenev soon found that though they had defeated Trotsky they were not in control of the situation. By 1925 Stalin had gained new allies on the *Politburo*—Bukharin, Rykov and Tomsky. The new Commissar of War, Voroshilov, was also his man. Now Stalin was able to move against his partners in the Triumvirate and both Zinoviev and Kamenev were expelled from the party in 1927. Bukharin, Rykov and Tomsky, who had supported Stalin against Zinoviev and Kamenev, were forced out of the *Politburo* by 1930 and Stalin's ascendancy was now complete.

Stalin's Totalitarianism

After 1928 Stalin began to unleash the apparatus of terror against the mass of the population and to carry out a purge of party members in order to revolutionise the economic and social system and to consolidate his own power. By the late 1930s he had built up a totalitarian dictatorship which was more complete and efficient than that in Nazi Germany and which was based on three institutions: the party organisation, the secret police and the army.

In seeking total control of all facets of Russian life, Stalin had to be a working dictator, unlike Hitler who left vast areas of government to others. 'Stalin,' asserts Ulam, 'displayed jealous proprietary feelings for power in all its aspects and details.' As his power grew, the politician in him receded and he became vindictively tyrannical by 1927. This reality was carefully hidden from the Russian people. Stalin was a consummate actor and to the masses he seemed a godlike figure endowed both with iron resolution and genial paternal qualities. He built up this image skilfully and came to represent both the party and the state, thus commanding loyalty almost amounting to worship.

Up to 1927 the Russian people, under the N.E.P., had been for the most part left alone to lead their own lives. The peasantry believed that they had more freedom as they had obtained land; in their eyes the two were synonymous. Some political criticism had been allowed and even those imprisoned for too outspoken anti-Communist views received light sentences. It seemed that the majority of the people preferred what Bukharin called 'the creep at a snail's pace' towards socialism. Stalin's sudden decision to industrialise rapidly both the city and the countryside by converting the peasantry into a landless proletariat shocked the nation. To achieve this state power required strengthening and therefore the first Five-Year Plan inaugurated a new phase in Russian history in which government began to invade every area of life in a manner unparalleled in the history not only of Russia but of any other country up to that time. Thus the first Five-Year Plan marked the real beginning of Soviet totalitarianism.

The secret police, O.G.P.U., an agency increasingly at Stalin's disposal, extended its work. It arrested or bullied independent minds in the party and kept watch on industry and the armed forces. It spied on all foreigners in Russia. It acquired special troops of its own, some of whom ran the concentration camps for political prisoners. From 1928 on, it began to arrest private entrepreneurs, *kulaks* (rich peasants) and members of the intelligentsia, who were often brought before 'show trials'. In July 1934, O.G.P.U. was changed to N.K.V.D., or People's Commissariat for Internal Affairs. In the 1930s it became the biggest employer in the Soviet Union and was entrusted with over one sixth of new construction work by 1941. By then the prison labour force which it controlled numbered about 10 million people.

The Secretariat became a state within a state and its operations extended into every branch of government. It became a web for collecting information, exerting control and cross-spying, and all the threads reposed ultimately in Stalin's hands. A powerful state or party figure could be sure that somewhere in the Secretariat there was a man reporting on his policies and performance. Spying became a way of life. Nor was the moulding of youth neglected. A number of youth organisations were developed: the Little Octobrists for children aged from 8 to 11; the Pioneers for children aged from 10 to 16; and the *Komsomol* (the Communist Union of Youth) for young people over the age of 15. Russian youth was to be conditioned to obey the Communist Party with unquestioning obedience.

The Economic Changes

With the inception of the first Five-Year Plan in 1928, Stalin laid down an extremely ambitious programme. Industrial production, including consumer goods, was to be increased by 250 per cent, agricultural production by 130 per cent and a major start was to be made on the collectivisation of peasant farms. Stalin's motives were not merely economic. The main objective was to convert the entire labour force, rural as well as urban, into employees of state-controlled enterprises as it would then be easier for the government to exert control over the masses. A second objective derived from one of Stalin's obsessions. He felt that the *kulak* was the main enemy of Communism and that the peasantry as a whole was barring Russia's path to industrialisation and socialism. As Ulam puts it, 'a kingdom of darkness must be conquered before the Soviet Union could become the promised land'. A third objective stemmed from Stalin's vision of himself as a modern Ivan the Terrible or Peter the Great. Like them, he wished to modernise Russia for the purposes of great power status and was obsessed with the need for a mighty Russia which would overtake other European states and even the United States. It was a tragedy for Russia that Stalin was profoundly ignorant on economic matters and launched policies which brought economic disaster by the mad speed which characterised them.

By 1928 the peasantry owned 96 per cent of the land and Stalin ordered that the *kulaks* were to be destroyed as a class by collectivisation of agriculture. The government met with the violent opposition of many peasants, especially in the Ukraine and the Caucasus, but opposition was ruthlessly crushed. O.G.P.U. agents and army units would surround villages and machine-gun the inhabitants into surrender, transporting those left alive to concentration camps. Peasants still found ways of retaliation; they ate or sold their livestock rather than put them into a common pool and by 1933 livestock production had fallen to half the 1928 figure. This, combined with the loss of managerial talent, helped to exacerbate the effect of three bad harvests in the years 1931 to 1933, when more than 5 million people died of famine and government action.

Some concessions had to be made to the peasants and they were allowed to keep their own garden plots, but the basic drive for collectivisation continued. By 1940 the 25 million peasant holdings had been replaced by nearly a quarter of a million collective farms on which lived about 75 million people. Individual farms were rare and an immense technical and administrative revolution had been carried out. Russian farming became the most mechanised in Europe, particularly in the use of tractors. Large fields replaced small arable strips and by 1940 the wheat crop was 80 per cent higher than in 1913. The collective farms were to feed the growing population of the towns even during the Second World War, when Russia might not otherwise have withstood the German onslaught. More efficient methods meant that much labour was released for use in industry and it is certainly true that before 1928 the agricultural population was so huge as to encourage wasteful employment, especially as it was a characteristic of the Russian peasant, as Nove has noted, to produce mainly for subsistence. The increased production of grain allowed more to be exported and this furnished extra capital for industrial development.

Against these advantages must be set the human cost, which is self-evident, and certain economic weaknesses. The process of collectivisation caused lasting damage to Russian agriculture; the 1928 level of livestock production was not reached again until 1953. Nor were collective farms always efficient for they were often too large and suffered unduly from the interference of central government. The heavy taxation of the peasant was basic to the system; collectives were left with only about half their produce and this was a serious disincentive to hard work. When Stalin died in 1953, the average income per head of the farm worker was only half that of the industrial worker.

For industry, the first Five-Year Plan envisaged a vast programme of investment, especially in the capital goods industries, to raise production by 20 per cent a year. Targets set for particular industries were unrealistic and that decided for pig-iron was only reached in 1941. Nevertheless, some industries did well, especially machine-making and electrical goods. The standard of living probably declined after 1928 as the state amassed the necessary capital by the intensive exploitation of the Russian people. Nevertheless, it would be fair to pay tribute to the epic nature of the events. Vast projects were begun like Magnitogorsk in the Urals, a great new metallurgical centre created out of a wilderness. Many of the workers and technicians striving in conditions of extreme hardship seemed to have been fired by a real faith in the future.

On the other hand, Stalin's stated aim to make up the difference between Russia and the West in 10 years was optimism run riot. His fear of foreign states is no excuse for attempting the impossible. Targets set were beyond practical possibility and, as Alec Nove has demonstrated, 'the rush, strain, shortages, pressures became intolerable and caused disorganisation'. This made the government tighten its control even more over resource allocation, physical output and credit, but it could not make uneducated peasants into skilled craftsmen overnight.

By the time the second Five-Year Plan was framed, a more realistic attitude had developed in government which now called for overall production increases of 14 per cent instead of 20 per cent. The second plan was carried out more smoothly than the first one, as unskilled labourers hurriedly pulled into the factories were acquiring more competence, and government control of labour intensified. It is difficult to state the degree of success of the plan because of the unreliability of Soviet production figures, which tend to overstate reality. Certainly the plans for consumer goods, housing and real wages were not fulfilled. With Hitler's accession to power in 1933, emphasis was placed on armaments which nearly trebled in the years 1933 to 1938. Excellent growth rates were also achieved in the engineering and metal-working sectors, which diminished Russia's dependence on foreign countries for its capital goods and relieved the strain on the balance of payments. Other industries made considerable gains even if they did not fulfil the forecasts of the planners—for example, coal and electricity. The oil, textile and iron-ore extraction industries were disappointing.

The third Five-Year Plan was overshadowed even more than its predecessor by the growing threat of Germany and the consequent need for more rearmament. The plan called for an annual increase of production of 12 per cent but it ran into difficulties, including labour shortages and the disorganisation created by Stalin's purges. According to Nove, progress was exceedingly uneven with good performances in chemicals, machinery and engineering (including armaments) but with stagnation in oil and steel and an actual decline in sugar output. New plant was located far to the east in the Urals and Siberia. The reasons for this were several; it was a device to cope with the problem of overlarge units and also to reduce the long haul of raw materials from remote areas of Russia. However, the strategic factor was the overriding consideration; the further to the east that Russian industry lay, the more secure it was from German aggression.

Despite all the errors and waste, Russia succeeded in the ten years beginning in 1928 in creating the industrial basis for a powerful arms industry. The production of coal, pig iron and steel was quadrupled in this period, and Russia became a great industrial nation. The base was, however, still too weak to enable civilian investment and consumer programmes to survive the effects of a redoubling of arms spending.

One major problem in the cities was the high labour turnover as the peasant workers, conscripted from the collectives, rootless and bewildered by their new surroundings, wandered around in search of better things. To maintain stable employment, unemployment relief was ended in 1930 and in 1937 workers found guilty of absenteeism were to be dismissed and deprived of their houses, which the régime admitted might mean starvation. In 1930, legislation provided that the worker should go where he was sent by the authorities and the passport system adopted by the tzars to catch runaway serfs was restored. The soviet worker was closely subjected to state control, and collective agreements and strikes were abolished.

Despite this coercion, productivity in the economy rose substantially for three reasons: (1) incentives were made much more effective by the recasting of the wage scales and widening differentials; (2) training schemes at all levels began to transform the quality of the labour force; (3) a new movement developed called the Stakhanovite movement. Stakhanov was a coal miner who by hard work and intelligence achieved an output 14 times the norm. The party took up the example to encourage others to emulate Stakhanov and those who did were rewarded with higher pay and honours. These three factors also tended to help the creation of a new élite, an intelligentsia of about 10 million people who were highly favoured on matters of pay, housing and medical treatment to such an extent that a visiting Spanish Communist, Delgado, wondered at the nerve of the Soviet government in calling Russia a classless society.

Cultural Life (1917–39)

Lenin had stated that the arts should play an important role in the new Russia and that the state would determine developments, but, unlike Stalin later, he did not enforce his conservative preferences. Many writers and artists in the early years were able to make an uneasy peace with the régime and a few, like the Futurist Mayakovsky, were enthusiastic Bolsheviks.

Original creative work was virtually doomed under the Soviet régime once Stalin took control. The arts were to be controlled by the Soviet government as a vehicle for fulfilling its propaganda needs. Writers now had to write novels about the five-year plans or stop writing, so that a growing output of politically motivated trash resulted. In the 1930s, the pressure on artists mounted and some important writers like Isaac Babel disappeared in the purges; others like Mayakovsky committed suicide.

Some creative work of quality somehow survived the onslaught. Michael Sholokhov's *The Quiet Don* was a novel of genuine realism about the Civil War, while Boris Pasternak and Anna Akhmatova did at least survive the Stalinist period, though their work was restricted. In film-making the Soviets could boast a genuine giant, Sergei Eisenstein, whose films *Potemkin* and *Alexander Nevsky* set new standards and won world acclaim. In the field of music both Sergei Prokofiev and Dmitri Shostakovich continued to compose though the latter was roundly condemned in 1936 for the harsh discord in his music.

In some aspects life in Russia improved. Though the consumer was neglected and clothing and other commodities remained drab and expensive, the social services were developed to provide free medical attention and social insurance. Education became compulsory and free with a reduction in illiteracy, though the relatively progressive ideas of the 1920s gave way to a more traditional discipline with an emphasis on ideological goals. Education became indoctrination, intended to produce 'new Soviet man'. Students and teachers were subjected to close scrutiny by the party and the secret police.

The Purges

In 1932 Stalin's second wife, Nadezhda Allilueva, spoke up against the misery that Russia was now suffering. Stalin abused her and that same night she died, apparently by suicide, but she had merely voiced the concern of many leading Communists at the cost of the economic changes. The murder of Sergei Kirov, a member of the *Politburo*, in December 1934 triggered off a wave of purges in the party against any potential opposition. Khruschev stated in 1956 that Stalin had arranged Kirov's murder himself, a view upheld by Robert Conquest in his book *The Great Terror*. Stalin, it is said, was jealous of Kirov's popularity in the party and needed a pretext to liquidate important rivals. The truth of the matter is difficult to establish.

What is certain is that the punishment of Kirov's murderers in 1935 was merely a curtain-raiser for the main drama. In 1936 came the public trial of 16 Old Bolsheviks, including Kamenev and Zinoviev, who were both executed and in 1938, 21 leaders of the Right were brought to trial. Tomsky committed suicide and both Bukharin and Rykov were eliminated. But Stalin had done to death many ordinary people who were utterly loyal and therefore no threat to his power. As Ulam remarks, 'Never since the outbreak of the Black Death in the fourteenth century could so many people have felt so alone and afraid.' Why did Stalin initiate such slaughter?

Perhaps he believed that under a totalitarian régime anyone is potentially disloyal and therefore the régime could only be secure if everyone was so terrorised as to become incapable of independent action. Part of the explanation surely lies in a deterioration in Stalin's character, for by the 1930s the strains of office had made him even more mean and sadistic. The show trials stand as a monument to his vindictiveness. As Ulam points out, 'Many despots of the past killed their victims and desecrated their memories. Stalin in addition killed his victims' self-respect.' This was done by making the prisoner sign a written confession or announce his guilt in public. To extract such confessions, the use of torture was necessary and as failure to obtain such a confession was a black mark against an N.K.V.D. interrogator, he would throw himself into the task with dedication.

Stalin's purge of the army in 1937–8 vividly demonstrates the extent to which he had become omnipotent. Three out of the first five marshals of the Soviet Union, including the Commander-in-Chief Tukhachevsky, three of the four full generals, all the 12 lieutenant-generals, 60 out of 67 corps commanders and 136 of the 199 divisional commanders were shot. The purge was even more extreme in the navy. The liquidations were a hideous insult as the armed forces had always fought loyally for Russia. The architect of the purges carefully disassociated himself from these events by not appearing at the trials. Instead, in 1936 he presented a new Constitution anxious to appear as a philosopher statesman. Probably about 8 million people were arrested during the purges, many of whom were shot or sent to concentration camps, though when in 1938 Beria replaced Yezhov (later shot) as chief of the secret police, the show trials stopped.

Foreign Policy (1917–35)

Hostility towards capitalist states was built into Soviet ideology and western intervention in the civil war merely intensified an existing attitude. The Communists regarded themselves as the agents of a world revolution, which could not be long delayed because of the inherent rottenness of the democracies. Lenin himself believed that the democracies could be brought down by ending imperialism and therefore Russian support was forthcoming for any anti-western nationalist movement like that of Kemal Ataturk in Turkey or Chiang Kai-shek in China. Yet it would be unwise to concentrate on this aspect of Russian foreign policy alone for the Communists inherited an expansionist nationalism from the tzars. In his desire for Russian territorial expansion, Stalin was consciously following in the footsteps of Ivan the Terrible and Peter the Great. By 1945 he had achieved what the tzarist régime had striven for but never achieved—an Eastern Europe under Russian domination. It is therefore clear, as Adam Ulam stresses, that there was 'a strong continuity between the old and the new régime'.

Communist hopes in 1917 that world revolution was imminent were soon shown to be absurd by the course of events. The punitive treaty of Brest-Litovsk, the civil war and the Polish war left Russia in such a state of chaos that the first task was survival. Though the long-term objective of world revolution was never abandoned, tactics had to be flexible and a period of coexistence between Soviet and capitalist states had to be tolerated. Meanwhile, the security of the infant Soviet state could best be protected by exploiting the rivalries between the various capitalist states, especially those between Britain and Germany, and between the United States and Japan. In perceiving the latter area of rivalry, Lenin demonstrated his ability to analyse situations realistically, for in the First World War Japan and the United States had been allies.

The Soviet government refused to give up the revolutionary propaganda which it believed had brought power in Russia. To disseminate the propaganda on a world scale, the Third International, or Comintern, was inaugurated in March 1919. With Zinoviev as its head until 1925, the Comintern was a branch of the Soviet state though its policies were not fully coordinated with Soviet foreign policy for some years. In 1920, Lenin laid down the rules which all foreign Communist parties wishing to join the Comintern would be required to follow. They were to avoid any collaboration with moderate socialists and to support the Soviet republic legally and illegally. They were to exploit parliamentary institutions and unions, and to accept as binding all decisions of the Comintern.

The importance of the Comintern must not be exaggerated. In the 1920s the Soviet government was mainly absorbed in domestic affairs, in the attempt to implement 'socialism in one state'. World revolution was no longer expected in the near future though it continued to be used as a kind of advertising slogan. From 1921 on, a new pattern of Soviet foreign relations evolved, with other countries recognising the Soviet government as uneasy coexistence evolved which caused a great debate in the party. The Communists maintained relations with most European states while at the same time directing within those same countries movements which were designed to overthrow the governments. When accused of such subversion, the Soviet government blandly replied that the Comintern was a private organisation, a fiction which it maintained resolutely. No change, however, occurred in the Soviet hostility towards the League of Nations, which was regarded as a robber league because it was dominated by Britain and France.

When Stalin came to power, the Russian diplomats were more firmly controlled than before through tight organisation and purges. Stalin differed from Lenin, Zinoviev or Trotsky, all of whom had been willing to make sacrifices of Soviet state interest for the sake of revolution abroad. Foreign Communism was now regarded only as an extension of the power of the Soviet Union and eventually as an extension of the power of the dictator. Stalin's cold-blooded realism in foreign affairs was, says Ulam, 'unaccompanied by any lingering ideological compunctions', as his alliance with Hitler was to demonstrate.

The two main areas of concern in Russian foreign policy in the 1920s were Germany and the Far East, for they were regarded as the weak spots in the world order. Initially the Soviet government hoped that a Communist revolution would occur in Germany in 1919, but even when that failed the two countries had much in common. Both were revisionist powers whose common enemy was Poland and whose needs were complementary. Germany was weak militarily as a result of the Versailles stipulations on armaments, while Soviet Russia was weak economically. Both states were diplomatically isolated. In April 1922, the Treaty of Rapallo was signed between Russia and Germany, which restored full diplomatic relations between the two countries and provided for an increase in trade. Both sides emerged from isolation with a diplomatic partner to play off against Britain and France. Later, military contacts were developed. Russia provided bases for German military experiments and in return the Germans erected armaments factories in Russia and shared in their output. The foundations were laid for the rapid recovery of Germany's military predominance in the 1930s which would not have occurred so rapidly without the German army's training on Soviet soil in the previous decade.

The alliance itself was fraught with difficulties. Not unnaturally, the Weimar government resented Soviet encouragement of a Communist coup in 1923, even though the coup itself fizzled out. The Soviet government for its part was disappointed at the German rapprochement with the West at Locarno, which represented a Russian defeat even though the Rapallo agreement was renewed for a further five years in 1926. Russia's diplomatic position worsened in this period, as Communist aid to the General Strike and a raid by police on the Soviet trade mission in London led to a breach of diplomatic relations with Britain. Stalin with his usual skill exploited the situation by a propaganda campaign, explaining to the Russian people that their isolation and suffering were caused by Western saboteurs and spies. Foreign policy, like everything else in Russia, was being integrated into Stalin's totalitarian scheme.

Russian foreign policy in China was many-sided. In one respect it resembled tzarist imperialism as, by a treaty of 1924 with the Chinese Republican government, a virtual protectorate was gained over Outer Mongolia and the Chinese Eastern Railway in Manchuria. The most promising ally was the Kuomintang (Nationalist) party which, the Russians believed, would most weaken Western influence in China. It was assumed that the Chinese Communist party could not at this stage be a mass party, because China was still too rural and a large proletariat had not yet evolved. Therefore the Chinese Communists were told to cooperate with the Kuomintang in 1922 and gain influence in it by stealth. In the next three years, with the help of Michael Borodin, the Soviet's political adviser to the Kuomintang, the Communists did grow more influential in the party and helped to make it more anti-Western in attitude. 'We must squeeze the Kuomintang like a lemon,' said Stalin, 'and then throw it away.'

His policy in China, however, collapsed in 1927. The Kuomintang leader, Chiang Kai-shek, saw the trend of events and, having captured Shanghai with Communist help, he promoted the massacre of large numbers of Communists. The Russians then attempted to mobilise the left-wing of the Kuomintang against

Chiang but the move failed. Ulam's comment that by 1928 'Soviet policy in China was a shambles' is a fair one. Chiang had beaten the Communists at their own game and Stalin's analysis of the whole Chinese situation was faulty. He failed to understand the true potential of Mao Tse-tung's Communist party, which was to be based on peasant support rather than the proletariat.

When Japan invaded Manchuria in 1931, the Russians became even more apprehensive about the security of their Far Eastern possessions. They reacted with a mixture of firmness and conciliation. The Russian army was strengthened in the Far East to show Japan that war with Russia would be costly but, unlike the Western powers, Russia made no criticism of Japanese aggression. The Soviets even offered Japan a non-aggression pact, and sold the Chinese Eastern Railway to Japanese Manchuria (Manchukuo) in 1935. This was appeasement, but appeasement without illusions and from a position of strength. To deflect Japan away from Russia, it was essential that the Japanese armies should be fully involved in China. Therefore Soviet policy again performed some veritable diplomatic acrobatics in 1932 by restoring relations with Chiang Kai-shek, who since 1927 had been the arch-enemy of Communism. For the same reason, the Soviet government urged the Chinese Communists to declare war on Japan, which they did in 1932.

Soviet policy in the Far East was intimately related to developments in Europe. The Soviet government evinced grim satisfaction at the mass unemployment in Germany from 1929 as it appeared to demonstrate that capitalism was bankrupt and only one obstacle stood in the way of Communist power—the Socialist party. Therefore the German Communists were ordered to avoid any collaboration with the Socialists and the net result of their activity between 1930 and 1933 was that they contributed to the failure of the Left and assisted Hitler's coming to power. They regarded the Nazi leader as merely a tool of the Right who would soon lose support to the Communist party. But in 1934, as Hitler's energetic régime tightened its grip in Germany, the Nazi threat to Russia became evident and caused what Ulam has described as an 'agonising reappraisal of Soviet foreign policy'. Faced by the menace of Japan in the Far East and Nazism in Europe, the Soviet government was forced into a radically different attitude towards the democracies and the League of Nations. Russia entered the League in 1934 and had a permanent seat on the League Council. In 1933, formal relations were established with the United States and in 1935 a treaty of mutual assistance was signed with France. Even the Comintern was forced to share in the diplomatic acrobatics. Instead of unrelenting hostility towards socialist parties, communist parties in Europe were now exhorted to support them in a Popular Front against Fascism in 1935.

Further Reading

Carr, E. H., *A History of Soviet Russia 1917–1929,* Penguin, London, 1966.

Hill, C., *Lenin and the Russian Revolution*, English Universities Press, London, 1970.

Treadgold, D., *Twentieth Century Russia*, Rand McNally, Chicago, 1972.

Ulam, A., *Expansion and Co-existence: The History of Soviet Foreign Policy 1917–1967*, Secker and Warburg, London, 1968.

—, *Stalin*, Allen Lane, London, 1973.

Questions

1. Account for the fall of tzarism in 1917.

2. Why were the Bolsheviks successful in seizing power in November, 1917?
3. 'A political genius.' Do you agree with this estimate of Lenin?
4. Explain why Stalin was able to build up a totalitarian dictatorship in Russia by 1939.
5. To what extent was Russia a great industrial power by 1939?

CHAPTER ELEVEN

THE RISE OF FASCISM

Towards a Definition of Fascism

The rise of Fascist movements in many European countries was the great political surprise of the first half of the twentieth century. Fascism remains as one of the most important historical problems of our time and yet its essence is still elusive 30 years after the destruction of Hitler's Germany. Perhaps, as S. B. Woolf suggests, the word 'fascism' should be banned, at least temporarily, from our political vocabulary because its meaning has become so blurred. Communists use 'fascist' as a smear word to discredit any group which appears to be hindering Communist purposes, and the word is too often used as a term of abuse by woolly-minded persons of left-wing views to pillory anyone with views that are remotely right-wing.

Historians find the task of explaining this phenomenon difficult because of the absence of any great philosopher who could expound Fascist ideals as Marx did for Communism. Statements on doctrine by Fascists are usually hopelessly vague. Another problem is that of deciding which countries were fascist. The term is appropriate for Mussolini's Italy but may be considered less so for Nazi Germany. Nazism can certainly be viewed as an aberration from fascist norms, a movement unique unto itself, impelled to nihilistic extremes by the mood of a nation in despair. Without the German experience, fascism would be more acceptable to civilised men. Neither should fascism be considered a singularly German or Italian experience, for several European nations contrived their own expression of the phenomenon, while in others right-wing dictatorships have been mistakenly been called fascist.

Interpretations of fascism have been many and varied and it is only possible in a book of this length to give the gist of a few of them. The Marxists saw fascism as a bourgeois device to prevent the collapse of capitalism and maintain class dictatorship. They fail to explain why, if they were mere agents of the bourgeoisie, the fascists were able to win mass support from peasants and workers. Obviously fascist movements provided emotional satisfaction for the masses to compensate them for the insecurity of the times and therefore an understanding of fascism requires a psychological dimension. Erich Fromm, in *Fear of Freedom*, saw in the lower middle and working classes a desire to give up their freedom which in a period of war and unemployment bred insecurity. They wished to leave decisions to others but at the same time they also craved for power and for domination. They were able to satisfy both desires by joining fascist movements.

Later scholars saw meaningful comparisons between Nazi Germany and Soviet Russia and would define fascism as non-Marxist totalitarianism. The foundations of this new kind of dictatorship lay, they argued, in certain modern developments in technology, ideology and urban growth which enabled total control over men to develop. To Hannah Arendt the essential driving forces of the totalitarian system were ideology and terror, as exemplified in both the Nazi and Soviet régimes. Total terror was the essence of totalitarian government, the means by which the masses could be made to conform. But Arendt's thesis only applies to Nazi Germany and not the other fascist movements which were not totalitarian or guilty of mass murder.

The Arendt thesis appealed to the imagination of the generation of writers working during the worst period of the Cold War as it gave meaning to the great power confrontation between the United States and Russia. In the 1960s, as relations between the two power blocs eased somewhat, a number of writers repudiated the idea that fascism was totalitarian and identified it as a radical form of traditional political protest. Seymour Lipset, in his book *Political Man*, asserted that fascism was a middle-class reaction. Certain groups of white-collar workers like teachers and small traders who normally supported the liberal centre felt trapped between the unions and big business on the one hand, and between the state and their 'social inferiors', the workers, on the other. Therefore they supported fascism which can be defined as an 'extremism of the centre'. Finally, the anti-Marxism of fascism is emphasised by Ernst Nolte who, while pointing to certain similarities between the two ideologies, also stresses the nationalistic elements in fascism.

The author finds aspects which commend themselves in several of the above interpretations and would not restrict himself to any single approach to a complex problem. A clearer understanding may emerge by an analysis of the following characteristics of fascism.

(1) ultra-nationalism and racialism,
(2) mass support,
(3) the leader principle and the élite,
(4) the ambivalent relationship with socialism, and
(5) autarchy and the corporate state.

(1) Nationalism was a springboard for the development of fascism in three ways. A number of countries emerged from the First World War with a profound sense of grievance. In Germany, the peace treaties were stigmatised as a '*diktat*' while in Italy dissatisfaction with Italian gains made nationalists refer to the 'mutilated victory'. This national frustration was a major factor assisting the rise of Hitler and Mussolini because they vigorously condemned the peace settlement. Secondly, in states where there appeared to be a serious threat of communist subversion and violent revolution, nationalists flocked to support fascist parties that promised to keep their countries free from the socialist menace.

One of the worst consequences of the war was the creation of a horde of ex-servicemen who could not settle down to civilian life. Their disappointed patriotism made them natural recruits for the new fascist movements which fully shared their nationalistic aims. A number of para-military organisations supporting fascism grew up, like the S. A. (Brownshirts) in Germany and the Legion of the Archangel Michael in Rumania. In France the Croix de Feu, founded in 1927 under de la Rocque, was an ex-servicemen's organisation. Alan Bullock has demonstrated the importance of Ernst Rohm, the leader of the Brownshirts, in the rise of Hitler. 'Rohm was the indispensable link in securing for Hitler the protection or at least the tolerance of the Army . . . without the Army's patronage, Hitler would have found the greatest difficulty in climbing the first steps of his political career.'

Behind the intense nationalism was the underlying assumption of racial superiority, a constituent part of fascist ideology. The forerunner of Italian fascism, D'Annunzio, wrote in 1895, 'I glory in the fact that I am a Latin; and I recognise a barbarian in every man of non-Latin Blood.' The notion of German racial superiority had its roots deep in the nineteenth century; it was developed in the work of Gobineau and H. S. Chamberlain, who conceived of a hierarchy of races with the Aryan (German) race at the top. By the end of the First World War racial doctrines had become respectable, especially those of Oswald Spengler who, in his book *The Decline of the West*, tried to persuade western civilisation to avoid its fate at the hands of the inferior races.

The most sinister component of the racial myth was anti-Semitism. It was in the late nineteenth century that anti-Jewish feelings, long held in many countries, were erected into a comprehensive doctrine in the work of Chamberlain and Duhring, who stated that Jews corrupted the purity of the German race. Germany replaced Russia as the fatherland of modern anti-Semitism and Hitler's later mass-murder of Jews was foreshadowed. The collapse of Germany in the war gave a new impetus to extreme views like anti-Semitism and it was now that Anton Drexler founded the Nazi Party and adopted a policy of systematic anti-Semitism which attracted important recruits like Ludendorff.

In certain countries—Italy, Belgium, the Netherlands and France—fascist movements paid little attention to anti-Semitism until the eve of the Second World War. It was in central and eastern Europe that anti-Semitism was an integral part of fascist ideology, for there the Jews were more numerous and in Rumania and Hungary a dominant section of the middle class. Hitler has told of his disgust at meeting Jews in Vienna and his reactions may well have been typical. As George Mosse has explained, in the Jews 'fascism had an enemy who could be singled out as symbolising the forces which must be overcome'. The Jews were large enough to be a credible target, but not strong enough to resist.

In a time of insecurity, the middle and lower classes seized on the Jew as the scapegoat for their distress. Four additional factors encouraged this hostility. There existed the old Christian hatred of the Jews as Christ's enemies. The Jews were prominent in international business and finance and could be seen as the national enemy. Social and cultural differences existed which the Jews themselves accentuated by their tight family circles, Saturday Sabbaths and their willingness to help fellow Jews in financial trouble. Finally, by seizing on the fact that many of the avant-garde thinkers in Germany were Jewish, the Nazis were able to exploit the sentiments of the religious and conformist elements in German society.

The assumption of racial superiority boded ill for the hopes of international peace. It was a fundamental supposition of most fascists that their state could do no wrong and that might was right. Fascist foreign policy was therefore to be aggressive and expansionist.

(2) Fascism has often been identified as merely a reactionary movement but this definition is unsatisfactory because the fascist movements won support from all classes. Fascist leaders themselves came from every class. Quisling, the Norwegian fascist, was an army officer while Mussolini was the son of a blacksmith. As we have seen, fascism had a strong nationalistic appeal which, with its uniforms, flags and historic symbols like the fasces and the swastika, won the support of ex-servicemen. But the war had undermined the economic stability of Europe and brought about social mobility which induced a sense of insecurity in many classes. 'Fascism,' says Trevor-Roper, 'was born of fear, the fear of a proletarian revolution', and the normally moderate middle class supported fascism.

Fascism had a special appeal for youth, which welcomed the opportunity for action and rebellion. Fascist ideas seemed new, vital and patriotic and no other party had such an attraction for young people who formed an important element in a number of fascist movements—Antonio's Falange in Spain, Degrelle's Rexists in Belgium and Jeunesses Patriotes in France. In both Italy and Germany the fascists had their youthful martyrs. The Nazis made a hero out of Horst Wessel, killed in 1930 in a brawl with the Communists over a prostitute, and the Horst Wessel song became the anthem of the Nazi Party. In Italy the fascist youth organisation was called after the boy hero Balilla, who had thrown a rock at the Austrian police in the eighteenth century.

The fundamental violence of fascism appealed to the socially uprooted and maladjusted. By joining fascist movements, they could vent their frustration by causing trouble and beating up opponents. A. J P. Taylor, in reviewing Kirkpatrick's study of Mussolini, called Mussolini the first of the Rockers. 'Mussolini and the Rockers had much in common: blackshirts, a love of speed and violent gesture, a persistent craze to race after nothing in particular.'

(3) In the nineteenth century, Hegel had affirmed the need for leaders to stand out from the multitude and the ideas of Gobineau and Pareto supported and triggered off interest in élites. The leading figure in the establishment of the theory of the élite and the leader was, however, Nietsche. 'God is dead', he wrote, and proclaimed the need for man to fuse his passion and self-discipline. Then a new race of supermen would be created and redemption would only come through them. In also expressing the need for new breeding methods and violence, Nietsche anticipated two other parts of the Nazi doctrine. In France, élitist ideas were subscribed to by Sorel and Déroulède although Sorel looked to the proletariat for his élite. The fascists seized on the concept of the élite and proclaimed their desire to establish a new hierarchy. This policy proved to be a significant asset, for potential recruits could be convinced that they would become important cogs in the new order.

Soon after the war charismatic leaders began to emerge. In a period of insecurity they were a focus of loyalty, especially in Germany, where the expulsion of the Imperial family had left a vacuum in national life. At a time when liberal government had patently failed, many Germans and Italians wanted to feel that there was a strong hand at the helm. But the real genius of these leaders lay primarily in their ability to play on the emotions of their followers. Mack Smith calls Mussolini 'an artist in propaganda', able to create, for some years at least, an image of himself as the strong, efficient but cultivated leader. Albert Speer has recalled how at party gatherings Goebbels and Hitler were able to rouse the workers, bourgeoisie and students, and mould them into a new unity. In its frenzy, the mob demanded victims and Hitler provided them in the form of Jews or socialists.

(4) Most of the fascist leaders had been socialist earlier in their career, including Mussolini, Mosley, Déat, Doriot and Quisling. Fascist programmes had a considerable socialist content, particularly in Germany through the influence of Hitler's rivals in the Nazi Party, the Strasser brothers. Fascism was therefore able to offer nationalism and socialism together, a combination which produced a tremendous appeal.

But at the same time fascism was born out of fear of socialism. The threat of Bolshevik revolution frightened the European middle and upper classes and swung them over to support fascist parties which promised to contain the socialist threat.

In several countries valuable financial aid was donated to the fascists by leading industrialists. It was after the success of the socialists in the elections of 1919 in Italy that fascism became a political force. Hitler's rise to power followed the world depression of 1929–32, when revolution again appeared to be dangerously close. Therefore before all else fascism was anti-communist and it was anti-communism that was the true uniting factor in a heterogeneous movement.

(5) The central principle in fascist economics was autarchy (economic self-sufficiency). In the nineteenth century the concept had been developed by St. Simon and List, and during the First World War by Naumann, who supported the idea of a *Mitteleuropa* which would allow Germany to be self-reliant and dominate Europe. To pursue autarchy implied the need for state direction and extra living space. From this need was derived the concept of the corporate state, i.e. a system of government in which all national life would be concentrated in the hands of the state. In practice, fascist economic policy became a series of improvisations rather than a system, though fascism did seem to provide an answer to some of the contemporary economic problems like unemployment. However, to rule effectively and dynamically and actually to implement the promised improvements involved internal and foreign aggression—the spoliation of the Jews at home and foreign conquest abroad.

Before surveying the rise of Fascism in Italy, it is necessary to analyse briefly the many difficulties facing Liberalism in Italy after 1871, because they to some extent explain why the fascists were able to gain power.

The Problems of Liberalism in Italy (1871–1919)

The history of Italy in this period presents in general a most melancholy spectacle. The high hopes of the Risorgimento were confounded and unity seemed to bring few real benefits to the Italian people.

One factor causing disillusionment was the failure to develop effective parliamentary institutions. Power remained in the hands of two coalitions of parties, the Left and the Right, but there was no essential difference between these groupings and therefore no possibility of constructive debate or alternation of power. In practice, a few politicians avid for office kept themselves in power by the technique of '*transformismo*'. They disregarded party labels and made bargains with deputies from both the Left and the Right to create a parliamentary majority. The chief practitioners of this method were Depretis, Crispi, and Giolitti, who was perhaps the most skilful of the three.

Parliament became an amorphous mass of deputies led by ministries whose members changed constantly. Between 1871 and 1914 there were 31 different ministers of finance alone. As parliamentary government seemed to have little relevance to Italy's real problems, public apathy towards parliament resulted, and one third of the electorate habitually abstained from voting.

Under this system the problem of the South was not really tackled. Southerners resented the centralised government of the new Italy and brigandage on a large scale led to the loss of more lives than in all the wars of the Risorgimento put together. Northern Italians did not understand the problems of the backward South yet its poverty was only too real. Most of the huge emigration from Italy in this period was from the South and in the peak year of 1913, 873,000 people left Italy.

The hostility of the Church continued to embarrass Italian governments. Not until 1904 did the Pope officially allow Catholics to vote, and even then only in areas where otherwise there might be a socialist victory. No Catholic party was founded until 1919.

From the late 1880s national discontent showed itself in the growth of an extreme socialist movement. The resort to violence in national life was distressing. In 1898, riots in Milan led to the death of 80 people, and in 1900 King Humbert was murdered.

There was no relief from such tragedies in the field of foreign and Imperial affairs. Though she joined the Triple Alliance in 1882, Italy was still regarded as a second-class power, while her colonial ambitions led to the annihilation of an Italian army at Adowa by the Abyssinians in 1896. Such humiliations helped the rise to prominence of a group of nationalist writers who saw Italy's future as one of expansion in Africa and the Balkans. The chief figures of this movement were Corradini, Marinetti and Gabrielle D'Annunzio.

It would be wrong to view the period in question as one of complete failure. Depretis and Crispi both initiated reform of the franchise and transport, while Giolitti laid the foundations of a Welfare State and made genuine attempts to help the South. The improvement in the quality of life was matched by the radical progress of the Italian economy, industrial production increasing by 87 per cent between 1901 and 1913.

The Impact of War

On the outbreak of the First World War, Italy's initial attitude was careful neutrality. The government feared Germany's power and did not wish to antagonise Austria-Hungary for fear of prejudicing its chances of compensation in the Trentino or Albania. Its decision pleased the majority of the Italian public but neutrality had its dangers. Whichever side won the war would have scant regard for Italian ambitions, especially the Central Powers, who felt that the Allied victory at the Marne was due to the removal by the French of 10 of their divisions from the Italian frontier. Therefore Salandra's government bargained with both sides to extract generous terms by which Italy might enter the war. The Allies were able to offer more and in April 1915 the Treaty of London was signed, committing Italy to enter the war on the side of the Entente. Italy was promised South Tyrol, Trentino, Trieste, Istria, Dalmatia, Valona and the Dodecanese.

The high hopes with which Italy went to war in 1915 were soon destroyed. Her armies had to fight on Europe's most difficult front, which was 400 miles long and so mountainous that wherever the Italians attacked they had to fight uphill. Therefore the brave efforts of 1915 and 1916 were futile and in October 1917 an Austro-German offensive routed the Italians at Caporetto.

A belated victory at Vittorio Veneto in October 1918 could not make up for the years of defeat or for the cost of the war. More than 5 million men had been mobilised and 680,000 had been killed. Italy found at the peace conference that her defeats had depreciated her stock in the eyes of her Allies. In any case, the United States refused to be bound by the Treaty of London and therefore Italy was disappointed over her claims to Fiume, Dalmatia, and African territory. This was galling when Italian gains were set beside those of Britain and France and seemed puny in comparison. The considerable gains which were made, including the disappearance of Austria-Hungary, were overlooked. As Seton-Watson points out, 'What was not achieved loomed larger than what was, and more and more Italians came to believe that victory had been mutilated and the war fought in vain.'

A second factor undermined national life—the impact of the war on the standard of living and social stability. The war had strained government finances and the public debt had risen nearly sevenfold. The war hit the middle classes—small landowners, tradesmen and members of the professions—whom Chabod describes as 'the real backbone, in the political sense, of the Italian State'. They suffered from higher taxation and the decline through inflation of the real value of their incomes and pensions. The cost of living rose sharply because of the decline in the value of the lira. In 1914 the dollar was worth 5 lire but by 1920 it was worth 28 lire, a serious factor since Italy had to import huge quantities of coal, wheat and oil. Between 1914 and 1921 the cost of living rose 560 per cent. The $2\frac{1}{2}$ million demobilised soldiers added to the ranks of the discontented.

The immediate post-war years were therefore characterised by social unrest. In 1919, 18·8 million workdays were lost by strikes and the figure was almost as high in 1920. The Italian trade unions called for workers' control of factories and when Alfa Romeo implemented a lock-out in August, 280 factories were taken over by workers of Milan. The Prime Minister, Giolitti, followed a deliberate policy of allowing the workers their head to discover for themselves the difficulty of running factories. The policy had begun to work in 1921 for the number of days lost by strike had been halved. Nevertheless, the fear of a Bolshevik revolution remained strong in the minds of the middle and upper classes and was a factor which an able leader might exploit.

A third factor undermined the hopes of effective liberal government. In 1919 proportional representation had been introduced and it helped the creation of two mass parties, the Socialist party and the Catholic Popular party. Neither could on their own provide the nucleus of a stable coalition. The socialists were averse to parliamentary procedures anyway and were fragmented by disputes over whether to work within the system or not. In 1921 the extremists broke away to form a Communist party. The Popular party also lacked unity for its members ranged from clerical reactionaries to Christian Democrat radicals. The two parties were too far apart ideologically to allow the moderates of each to create a coalition. Between 1918 and 1922 there were five governments with constant cabinet reshuffles between the major changes. Therefore by 1922 there was a power vacuum at the heart of Italian politics and a demagogue arose to exploit it.

Mussolini and the Fascist Seizure of Power

Mussolini was born in 1883 at Dovia, son of a socialist blacksmith and a schoolmistress. In 1912 he became chief editor of the socialist party newspaper *Avanti*, having developed a violent style of socialism which bordered on anarchism. When the First World War began, Mussolini broke with the official socialist line of opposition to intervention in the war, a move which he justified on the grounds that the Allies represented the Left. The socialists expelled him from the party and from his job as editor of *Avanti* so he started a new paper *Il Popolo d'Italia*.

At the end of the war, Mussolini searched for new means of self-aggrandisement. Influenced by Sorel, Corradini and D'Annunzio, he felt a need for constant action. Mussolini was not, however, merely a thug; he had some genuine political talent. As Chabod has pointed out, 'his strength lay in large part in his undeniable ability to rouse the masses by means of an oratory which was always polemical and violent, often vulgar, but never obscure or colourless'.

After the armistice, with the encouragement of the syndicalist Michele Bianchi and a few *Arditi* (daredevil military corps), Mussolini summoned a meeting in Milan and with Marinetti proclaimed the birth of the *Fascio di Combattimento*. The term *fascio* derived from the insignia that the lictors of ancient Rome carried (a bundle of rods with a protruding axe blade, symbolising authority and discipline). In the elections of 1919, not one Fascist was elected despite the movement boasting the names of Marinetti and Toscanini. Mussolini was still hoping to be the Lenin of Italy and the extremism of his policies alienated respectable people, while the workers regarded Mussolini as a renegade.

In 1920, Mussolini therefore moderated his policies, cutting down his tirades against the Church, the monarchy and capitalism. But it was the scare brought about by the occupation of the factories by the workers that brought widespread support for the Fascists, who claimed to be the saviours of the nation in the face of the socialist menace. The industrialists began to give financial support, which formed about three quarters of Fascist revenue. Important contributors included Giovanni Agnelli of Fiat, Alberto Pirelli, the tyre magnate, and the Perrone brothers of the armaments firm Ansaldo. The largest sum, the equivalent of £1½ million, came from the Banking Association. These contributors were not fascist by conviction; they were simply anxious to protect their interests by any means possible. As Denis Mack Smith put it, they 'evidently put riches and comfort before liberty'. Mussolini meanwhile tailored his programme to please his industrial backers, and by January 1921 was advocating a return to private enterprise with a minimum of state interference. By this stage Fascism was also bidding for the support of the landowners for fascist action squads were moving into the countryside and attacking socialists with liberal doses of castor oil and muggings. Mussolini clearly rejected the policy of land for the peasants and stated that the land rightly belonged to the person investing in it, not the person working on it.

Events began to play into Mussolini's hands for in January 1921 the Socialist party split. The Communists formed their own separate party and the consequence of the breach was that membership of both parties was halved in 1921. In May Giolitti, the Prime Minister, sprang elections on the country in the hope of breaking the Socialist and Popular parties and he included the Fascists in a new coalition 'National Bloc'. This gave the stamp of respectability to the Fascists, and Mussolini with 34 of his colleagues was elected after an election campaign characterised by the violence of the fascist squads.

Despite a peace pact with the Socialists in August 1921, violence continued and opposition from his own ranks forced Mussolini to denounce the pact in November, and a new campaign was launched against the Socialists. The violence used was connived at by many sectors of public opinion and by late 1921 the Fascists had a considerable measure of mass support. An analysis of about half its membership of 320,000 shows that 18,000 landowners, 14,000 tradesmen, 4,000 manufacturers, 10,000 from the professions, 7,000 state employees, 15,000 private employees, 36,000 agricultural labourers and 23,000 industrial workers supported the party. There were therefore in the Fascist ranks many of the lower middle class who felt caught between capital and labour. They were, says Seymour Lipset, 'the displaced masses of the newly industrialising countries', who in their insecurity turned for protection to the radical forces outside the traditional Left or Right. Thus the popular support that Fascism gained was 'an extremism of the centre' and, able demagogue that he was, Mussolini was able to exploit the lower middle-class neurosis.

With large sections of the army and police also approving his 'stand' against socialism, Mussolini now required the benevolent neutrality of the Church and monarchy. In 1922 direct approaches were made to the Vatican and in September Mussolini made a speech in which he indicated that he was now ready to renounce his republican ideas and support the House of Savoy. By October the Fascists had the scent of real power in their nostrils. In August, a general strike had been called for by the socialists as part of a counter-attack but it was such a failure that it became known as 'the Caporetto of Italian socialism'. It gave Mussolini an even better claim for standing as the bulwark against the Red menace and the Fascists took control in Milan. As Giolitti had retired in June 1921, the government under Facta lacked both firmness and wisdom.

In October, Mussolini at last nerved himself to implement what extremists like Farinacci had long desired, a move towards power. When 50,000 Blackshirts began to converge on Rome, many of the political leaders still failed to realise the danger. When Facta asked the king to sign a proclamation of martial law in the emergency, Victor Emmanuel refused. Instead the king sought to entrust the task of forming a new government to Salandra and Mussolini. When Mussolini refused, the king invited him to come from Milan on October 29 to form a new government.

What is striking about these developments is the way in which the various authorities stood aside and connived at the Fascist victory. The police and the army made no move to stop the Blackshirts and when they entered Rome it was not a battle, merely a parade. Victor Emmanuel III's motives for not giving a lead require explanation. He appears to have doubted Facta's determination or ability to resist Mussolini. Moreover, he was uncertain whether the army would support the government in proclaiming martial law. But he was already half disposed to accept the Fascists anyway, for he feared the possibility of losing his throne to his ambitious cousin, the Duke of Aosta, who enjoyed great popularity because of his war record and could be sure of Fascist backing if the king were difficult. Finally, the Queen Mother Margherita, an iron reactionary, was by 1922 a fervent Fascist supporter.

The influence of the Roman Catholic Church too was being used on behalf of the Fascists. Pius XI saw the Fascists as a lesser evil than the Socialists and assumed that in power they would grow more responsible. Accordingly, the Pope ordered all priests to withdraw from politics on the eve of the March on Rome and gave no support to the Popular Party. It is clear that, as Alan Cassels demonstrates, 'by 1922 there was hardly any section of the Italian establishment not ready to collaborate with Fascism either for nationalistic or anti-bolshevik reasons or both'.

The Implementing of Dictatorship

Mussolini now announced the formation of a coalition cabinet, including members from the Liberals, Nationalists, Popular and Socialist parties. Technically he had come to power legally and his government was a compromise arrangement. True revolution was only to come in January 1925. Meanwhile Mussolini moved carefully in the direction of more totalitarian power, lulling the opposition into believing that he was not really different from past premiers. More rigid control of the press was brought in and local Fascist party bosses, the '*ras*', acquired more control in many areas than the government-appointed prefects. In 1923, Acerbo drafted a new electoral law enacted in November. It provided that whichever party received the largest number of votes would obtain two thirds of the seats in the Chamber. Fascist violence in the election campaign of April 1924 ensured that the party obtained 64 per cent of the votes. An important development was the formation of the Blackshirts into a permanent Fascist militia, the Volunteer Militia for National Security (M.V.S.N.), which swore allegiance to Mussolini—not to the king—and whose support was to help Mussolini stay in power during the great crisis of 1924.

In May of that year a young socialist Giacomo Matteotti denounced Fascist abuses during the election and challenged the validity of the results. In June, he was kidnapped by Fascists in Rome and stabbed to death. When his body was found later, a great storm of indignation arose and for the next six months Mussolini faced a political crisis with which he could not cope. He had not in fact ordered the murder but the gang responsible had worked for Rossi, head of Mussolini's press bureau, and as Mussolini had given instructions that life should be made difficult for socialists, he was morally guilty.

With public revulsion against Fascism now so great, there was a supreme opportunity for the opposition to unseat Mussolini. They failed to grasp it. A substantial minority of Socialists and Popularists withdrew from Parliament, an action dubbed the 'Aventine secession' as it recalled the last stand of Caius Gracchus and his followers on the Aventine Hill. Amendola, the head of this movement, hoped to topple Mussolini's regime by making it completely isolated. It was hoped that Victor Emmanuel would dismiss Mussolini but the king refused to act. As the Aventine lacked key figures like Salandra and Giolitti, its action merely weakened Parliament and helped Mussolini's political survival. Finally, the attitude of the Church was again of assistance. In 1923, the Pope had forced the resignation of the Popular Party's most determined figure, Sturzo, and in 1924, after Matteotti's murder, he condemned the Popular Party itself and ordered all priests to resign from it. Pius XI saw the Fascists as the only force capable of resisting socialism, but as S. B. Woolf notes 'by these successive acts the Papacy destroyed the only popular movement which might have outbidden Mussolini'.

Mussolini gradually regained his composure and in January 1925 was able to launch his régime on a truly dictatorial path. All pretence at collaboration was now ended. Amendola was beaten up and died soon after. The political parties, Masonic Lodges and opposition newspapers were all suppressed. In December, a degree made Mussolini head of the Fascist Grand Council and he was no longer accountable to parliament. Only the king had the power to dismiss him. Mussolini decided what questions might be debated in parliament which was now a cypher. The bureaucracy was filled only with his appointees and a secret police (O.V.R.A.) was established.

Individual liberty was now circumscribed and Italians were deprived of their citizenship if the government wished. One of the first victims was Professor Salvemini of the University of Florence. A special tribunal was set up to judge political crimes in 1927. Between then and 1943 some 5,000 people were sentenced by this court but its severity is put into perspective when one considers that only 29 death sentences were passed. Many political cases were still heard in the regular courts, where the accused could often obtain a fair hearing.

The Acerbo Law of 1923 was replaced by a new law in 1928. There was one list for which candidates were to be nominated by the labour syndicates and other organisations. From the list the Fascist Grand Council would choose 400 and present them to the electorate for approval. In effect, this law ended the liberal system and replaced it with a rubber-stamp plebiscite. The right to vote depended on membership of a fascist syndicate, a rule which disqualified 3 million people. Italy was now a one-party state under the dictatorship of Mussolini and in practice the Grand Council merely approved what he had already decided.

The Corporate State

Since the First World War Mussolini had been intrigued by the possibility of instituting a system of representation that would rest on the national syndicates instead of the old parliamentary system. This was not a new idea for it was derived from two currents of thought. Catholic supporters of corporativism looked back with nostalgia to a revival of the medieval guilds or corporations, in which there would be cooperation between employer and workers, even profit sharing and part ownership. The second current was Syndicalism, which had been most cogently argued by Georges Sorel.

Originally syndicalists had supported the idea of class warfare and government based on labour syndicates alone, but some moderation of this view had taken place. Some syndicalists had become friendly with Mussolini during the war and one of them, Edmondo Rossoni, conceived of a syndicalist organisation which would include producer syndicates as well as the labour unions. It was argued that if the government coordinated the work of the syndicates, it would end class warfare at a stroke while at the same time preserving capitalism. In practice, in Italy capital was to be treated more leniently than labour and therefore the corporative system can be seen as designed to win the support of employers. In this sense, Woolf is right to call Italian fascism 'a mass party of reaction' because it employed its power in the interests of capitalism.

Mussolini had established a committee made up of members of the employers' federation and the Fascist labour syndicates in 1923 to study the issue, and in 1925 the employers' federation agreed to deal only with Rossoni's Fascist labour syndicates. The rival socialist and Catholic labour unions were to be outlawed. The government would choose the officials of the labour syndicates rather than allow workers to do so, whereas the employers' federation was free to choose its own representatives. In 1926 the Minister of Justice, Alfredo Rocco, who was perhaps the most coherent thinker in the government, began his attempt to subordinate all elements in the country to the state. Strikes and lock-outs were prohibited and the syndicalist state came into existence, for the state, acting as umpire, recognised producers' and workers' syndicates in six fields of the economy (industry, agriculture, commerce, maritime and air transport, land and inland-waterway transport, and banking). In 1934, the system underwent further change when 22 corporations were set up for particular fields of economic activity—for example, wine and textiles. In each corporation, the P.N.F. (National Fascist Party), employers and employees were represented, and in 1939 a Central Committee of Corporations replaced the Chamber of Deputies.

The theory behind the Corporate State was very fine; it would bring social justice and real planning of the economy. In practice it had two essential features. It was a device through which the political dictatorship of the P.N.F. could be exercised and it ensured the pre-eminent position of employer over employees. Ironically, even the industrialists began to lose faith in Mussolini in the years when the system was created. There was too much bureaucratic bungling and perhaps even more graft, and the system was no answer to Italy's economic problems.

The Economy

As with many parts of their programme, the Fascists had kept their ideas on the economy rather vague prior to office. Their period of power was to see an initial liberal phase in economic policy which was followed by a growth in state intervention and a programme of autarchy.

Under the liberal economist De Stefani, who was Minister of Finance from 1922 to 1925, Italy's finances recovered from the strain of the previous years. De Stefani brought in a simpler tax system and attracted foreign capital by exemptions from taxation. He also sought to withdraw government from business wherever possible and abolished price-fixing, rent controls and subsidies. By his reduction in government expenditure he achieved a budget surplus for the first time since the war. With a revival in trade there was a fall in unemployment from over 500,000 to 122,000. 'This recovery from the deep depression of the postwar years,' says Clough, 'was remarkable and greatly aided the Fascists in winning favour and in establishing themselves in power.'

Mussolini could not leave well alone and at the behest of some industrialists dismissed his minister in 1925. His policy in the next few years was based on considerations of prestige rather than the economic welfare of Italy. In August 1926, he made a speech in which he declared, 'I shall defend the Italian lira to my last breath—to my last drop of blood'. The lira was revalued at ninety to the pound sterling instead of one hundred but this made it more difficult for Italy to export and pushed the country towards depression, two years before the Wall Street Crash. Not until 1936 did Mussolini devalue the lira and meanwhile unemployment rose to 1·1 million by 1932, with perhaps half the total labour force underemployed. The government added to the deflationary spiral by cutting the wages of public employees by 12 per cent and raising tariffs, which led to foreign retaliation. A reduction in the number of foreign tourists owing to the world depression aggravated the balance of payments problem.

Another government response was to attempt a policy of national self-sufficiency, especially in food production. Mussolini called for a victory in the 'battle for grain', an attempt to reduce Italian wheat imports by the bringing into cultivation of marginal land and better methods. Wheat imports were cut by 75 per cent between 1925 and 1935 but the resources deployed in this effort would have been more productive in the cultivation of other crops. The serious problems of agriculture were not tackled and the real wages of agricultural labourers fell by about 50 per cent.

In industry the worst phase of the Depression was reached in 1932. The depression years saw an increasing tendency towards monopoly in industry with small firms swallowed by large concerns with government blessing. The large firms were able to act like cartels in matters of price-fixing and production quotas. In 1933 the government organised the Institute for Industrial Reconstruction to provide subsidies for firms in difficulty, with the result that by 1940 the government held a 20 per cent interest in Italian industry. Thus state capitalism was encouraged by Fascism and was conspicuous in shipbuilding, aviation and petroleum production.

In 1934, the government reduced the working week to 40 hours to spread out employment but, as hourly pay was not increased, workers took a cut in their real income. No real attempt was made to raise purchasing power as a means of combating depression, though the government did spend considerable sums on public works. Land reclamation to increase arable land and reduce malaria had some success, notably the draining of the Pontine Marshes. The electrification of the railways was begun and a new development in road building, the *autostrada*, was pioneered. In Rome itself new archaeological projects opened up the area around the Coliseum, and many new government buildings were constructed, usually on the principle that what was massive was beautiful. An attempt was made to provide help for the South and 57 per cent of revenue was spent in that area.

The advent of the Ethiopian war cut unemployment and stimulated the economy in the short run but intervention in the Spanish Civil War and Albania strained Italy. By 1936 the budget was badly in deficit and the government was forced to devalue the lira and increase taxes. An inflation rate of 20 per cent was reached in 1937 and the programme of autarchy was proved to be an absurd one, given Italy's limited resources. Genuine economic growth in the Fascist years was small and real incomes fell generally between 1925 and 1938.

The Church and the Jews

In his youth Mussolini had been violently anti-clerical but even before the March on Rome he had moved towards friendlier relations with the Church which, as we have seen, materially helped him to establish his power. The Duce fastened on the deeply rooted sentiments of many Italians who were disturbed that the Church was not yet formally reconciled with the government and he tried for even closer relations with the Vatican. The crucifix was restored to schools and courtrooms, and masses were scheduled for public functions. Negotiations went ahead for a full solution to the problem of relations between Church and State despite dispute over youth organisations which led to the virtual disbanding of the Catholic Boy Scouts in 1928.

In 1929 a concordat was at last signed. The Pope's temporal power over the Vatican City and St. Peter's was restored in return for papal recognition of the Kingdom of Italy and a renunciation of papal claims to former papal estates. The government agreed to compensate the Church for ecclesiastical property which had been confiscated during the Unification of Italy and the Pope was given the right to appoint all bishops in Italy after consulting the Italian government. The State was to continue to pay the salaries of churchmen and was not to molest Catholic societies. The agreement was Fascism's most enduring legacy and devout Italians were overjoyed that after half a century of hostility between Church and State peace was now achieved. Mussolini reached a new peak of popularity in Italy and his reputation soared throughout the Catholic world.

The peace was, however, an uneasy one. Indeed, as Daniel Binchy has pointed out, the experience with Fascist Italy and Nazi Germany in the 1930s eventually 'led Pius XI, although by temperament inclined to sympathise with authoritarian government, to recognise in modern dictatorships the most formidable danger to Christianity in our time'. The issue which most divided the Fascists and the Church in the early 1930s was the status of the Catholic lay organisation, Catholic Action. It had grown when the Popular Party disintegrated and by 1929 possessed 4,000 adult centres and 5,000 youth clubs. Mussolini was jealous of its influence for in many rural areas it was stronger than the P.N.F. Therefore, despite recognition of its independence in the Concordat, Mussolini sought to destroy it and began by accusing it in 1931 of harbouring leaders of the outlawed Popular Party. He then closed down the university branch of Catholic Action, a move for which he was vigorously denounced by the Pope. The Fascists then declared that participation in Catholic Action was incompatible with party membership but this merely led to mass resignation from both the party and Catholic Action. To the relief of both sides a shaky compromise was reached whereby Catholic Action fell more under the control of the bishops, who were not to select lay officers in any way hostile to the régime.

Up to 1938, despite such difficulties, the Church had not been opposed to Fascism and in 1929 Pius had even referred to Mussolini as the 'Man of Destiny'. Unfortunately Mussolini, who had in earlier years expressed disgust at Hitler's racial ideas, proclaimed a racialist manifesto in 1938 setting out reasons for an Aryan racial policy in Italy. It was this new racialism that provoked the great breach between Church and State. The Pope had already expressed sorrow in 1937 over Hitler's racial programme and now he condemned anti-Semitism as a denial of the brotherhood of man. He infuriated Mussolini by taunting him for imitating the Nazis and in September he remarked to some Belgian pilgrims, 'Spiritually we are Jews.' Unwisely, Mussolini brought in a law for the 'Defence of the Italian race' which prohibited marriage between 'Aryan' Italians and 'Jewish' Italians and insisted on public registration of Jews. Jews were forbidden to own important industry and were banned from a number of occupations including education and the armed forces. But in comparison to their brothers in Germany, Jews in Italy were not greatly affected until 1943, thanks to the attitude of most Italians and discreet help from the Church. When the Nazis seized Northern Italy in 1943, about 9,000 Jews were murdered.

In 1939, Pius XI died and Cardinal Pacelli, an aristocrat who had seen service in Germany, was elected Pius XII. He was more suave and cautious than Pius XI or his successor John XXIII and he made it clear that he intended to follow a more conciliatory policy towards Germany and Italy than had Pius XI. When the Pope quickly ended lay direction of Catholic Action, Ciano wrote in his diary, 'I believe that we can get along with this Pope'. As C. F. Delzell explains, 'Pacelli's cautious diplomatic behaviour and training were to prevent him from being a first-rate moral leader of the Church during a time of unprecedented violence and destruction'. The Pope, it is true, did try to prevent war breaking out in 1939 and then threw his influence on the side of Italian neutrality. It is his silence over Nazi atrocities which has been criticised. In a recent book *Into That Darkness*, Gitta Sereny has claimed that the Vatican knew of Nazi genocide programmes from an early point in the war and only in 1943 made any clear protest about them. Sereny gives four possible reasons for the papal attitude. The Pope feared Bolshevism above all else as the arch-enemy of the Church and for this reason did not condemn the murder of Russian civilians. He also feared that if he did attack the Nazis, they might wipe out Catholicism in Europe. Perhaps he did not believe the stories of German atrocities despite their thorough documentation, because he had spent his happiest years in Germany. Finally, claims Sereny, the Pope was instinctively anti-Semitic himself and kept silent when a firm stand from the beginning might have rallied European Catholic opinion sufficiently to force the Nazis to change their policies.

Sereny's views are conjectural and one-sided. It is natural that the Pope should feel concerned to act in a way that did not increase the risk of more Nazi mass murder of Catholics. By following a cautious policy he would retain some chance of mediating in the war whereas had a clear denunciation of the Axis powers been made, Mussolini could have cut him off completely from the outside world. Furthermore, the Pope did at times act courageously. The German invasion of Scandinavia in 1940 was condemned and when Pius learned of the impending German attack on the Low Countries he informed representatives of the states concerned. Pius also saved the lives of some thousands of Jews in Italy by hiding

some in the Ardeatine Caves in 1944 and by instructing monasteries
to Jews in flight.

Only scrutiny of the Papal archives can reveal the full truth on this v
tion but it may well be that the Church has been particularly criticised on
because of its pretensions. If over the centuries it had claimed less for its w dom, less might have been expected of it in a difficult position. The Roman Catholic Church claimed the highest standards and was therefore judged by them. It was, in fact, no worse and no better than the other appeasers of Fascism. As Kedward has remarked, 'Fascism revealed the insecurity and fallibility of many well-established historic institutions.'

The Nature of the Fascist Régime

Fascists claimed to have created a totalitarian one-party state in Italy but it is clear that in comparison with Nazi Germany or Soviet Russia the power of the régime was very limited. Gentile, in an article in the *Italian Encyclopaedia*, gave the chief criterion of totalitarianism: 'No individuals or groups outside the State'. But in Italy the Church and the monarchy retained a large measure of real independence and Italy was as much dynastic and Catholic as totalitarian. Other important groups like the industrialists and the armed forces kept much of their autonomy.

Nor did the Fascists convert the masses so as to win their allegiance. Italians viewed Fascism with the same scepticism as they had viewed earlier régimes. One reason for this was the lack of a clear-cut Fascist ideology. The Fascists claimed to worship action and Ernst Nolte emphasises 'the priority of action over doctrine' in Fascist Italy, but in practice this merely meant opportunistic and inefficient government. We must agree with Hannah Arendt's verdict on Mussolini's régime as 'not totalitarian, but just an ordinary nationalist dictatorship'.

The limits of the Fascist dictatorship can be seen in the relative freedom which was allowed the liberal philosopher Benedetto Croce. When his former friend Gentile proclaimed the 'Manifesto of the Fascist intellectuals' in 1925, Croce made a scathing attack on Fascist ideas as 'an incoherent and bizarre ragbag', and he was backed by many of Italy's leading intellectuals. Though irritated, Mussolini did not dare to arrest Croce partly out of fear of foreign criticism, and the philosopher continued to publish freely in his review *La Critica*.

When Italy entered the Second World War in 1940, the pretensions of the régime were brutally exposed. Fascism had been very much the creation of one man whom Denis Mack Smith describes as a 'stupendous poseur'. Mussolini lacked real administrative ability and was too concerned in womanising or in projecting an image of himself as a superman. He held nine ministries and claimed to work a 14-hour day, though his personal secretary has revealed that he slept at his desk during office hours and was in bed by 10 p.m. Mussolini's one talent lay in propaganda which prevented the sheer inefficiency of Fascism from being appreciated and remedied. His warlike pretences deceived foreign statesmen into an exaggerated view of Italian power because Mussolini spoke of his capacity to mobilise 8 million bayonets in a few hours and how his aircraft would blot out the sun. The press was used to showing Mussolini's prowess at fencing, riding, driving and playing the violin, but he was far from being a dynamic man of action in 1940. By then he was myopic and his ulcer necessitated a milk diet. Unfortunately, he had begun to believe his own propaganda and his one genuine skill contributed to his ruin.

Fascist Foreign Policy and the Road to Disaster

'Better to live one day as a lion than a thousand years as a lamb,' Mussolini told his Blackshirts in 1935. By then an aggressive militarism and active foreign policy had become the most obvious features of Fascism. In contrast, one might view the first decade of Fascism as one of good behaviour, but this would be a half-truth. In the early years Mussolini was still feeling his way and did not have a coherent foreign policy. He had a mania for signing pacts with foreign countries and eight such pacts were signed between 1926 and 1930. This supports the contention of Stuart Hughes that Mussolini was striking out in all directions in the hope of scoring points on the cheap; it was a policy of improvisations without a definite aim.

Mussolini knew that he had to improve Italy's international status for in the last resort this was the criterion by which his régime would stand or fall. Therefore despite his domestic concerns, he did indulge in a number of diplomatic adventures in the early years. In August 1923, at a conference delimiting the frontier between Albania and Greece, the Italian representatives were murdered by a terrorist. This atrocity gave Mussolini the opportunity to display the Fascist spirit. He dispatched an ultimatum to the Greek government and despite a conciliatory reply occupied Corfu. A conference of ambassadors arranged compensation for Italy which Mussolini was forced to accept. He had wished to annex Corfu but a veiled British threat to use the Mediterranean fleet made him withdraw from the island.

Italy was more successful in a second escapade. Two weeks after the Corfu incident Mussolini sent a military commandant to govern Fiume on the pretext that negotiations between Italy and Yugoslavia to found an independent Fiume had reached deadlock and that the town was falling into anarchy. The Yugoslav government accepted this high-handed action as France, Yugoslavia's protector, was engaged in the Ruhr and also because King Alexander of Yugoslavia admired Mussolini. Italy therefore won a certain prestige but it was a Pyrrhic victory as it aggravated the rivalry of the two countries in the Balkans.

Mussolini worked with some success to win the approval of British statesmen. He assisted the British in putting pressure on Turkey to cede the Mosul area to Iraq and in return Britain gave Jubaland to Italy in 1924. But Mussolini's patience declined as the 1920s went by without any major Italian successes. He was irritated by the failure to gain a guarantee of the Brenner frontier at Locarno in 1925 and became, as Elizabeth Wiskemann terms it, 'the chief anti-democratic conspirator of Europe' by 1927. He quarrelled with France and Yugoslavia and gave military assistance to revisionist powers like Hungary and Austria.

A new phase of Italian foreign policy began in 1930, when Mussolini declared that the struggle had moved beyond Italy to a world arena and he called for rearmament, revision of treaties and expansion towards the Danubian basin. Soon he was talking about 'Fascism for export', declaring that in another decade all Europe would be Fascist. In 1932 he took over the foreign ministry himself and moderates like Grandi were sacked. By 1936 he had taken command of all the service ministries and therefore he allowed his son-in-law Count Ciano to become Foreign Minister.

For a brief period Mussolini acted as the principal champion of Austrian independence in the face of the threat from Nazi Germany. Since 1928 he had tried to make Austria an Italian satellite, first backing Prince Stahrenberg's Heimwehr movement and later the dictatorship of Dollfuss. In March 1934, the Rome

Protocols to promote trade were agreed between Austria, Hungary and Italy, but this was more than offset by Mussolini's fatal error of encouraging Dollfuss to crush the Austrian Socialists. A four-day civil war occurred in February in Austria which resulted in the destruction of the socialist movement. Many Austrian workers joined the Nazis in desperation against the Dollfuss government. In July, the Nazis murdered Dollfuss and tried to take over Austria, but they called off their '*putsch*' when Mussolini ordered Italian troops to the Brenner Pass.

With such an obvious threat to Austrian independence, Mussolini should have avoided any wild Imperial adventures, yet it was at this precise juncture that he chose to involve himself in Abyssinia. His motives are not hard to fathom. The years of depression and the failure of the corporate state had sapped his popularity in Italy. He now wished to employ the classical device of dictators to draw public attention away from domestic troubles, a successful war abroad. Italian nationalists still nurtured a desire to revenge the Italian humiliation at Adowa in 1896 and the war could be justified with arguments that Abyssinia would provide Italy with raw materials and markets and furnish the base for a new Roman Empire.

To initiate the war, Mussolini required both a pretext and an assurance of French neutrality. A clash at the oasis of Walwal near the border of Italian Somaliland gave him the first requirement. In January 1935, Pierre Laval came to Italy and in return for Italian renunciation of privileges in Tunisia, he gave tacit French approval of undefined Italian action in Abyssinia. The stage was now set and in October 1935 war was declared.

It can truly be seen as a turning-point in the inter-war years. At the League of Nations a sanctions policy was adopted, mainly at Britain's prompting, and the long friendship between Italy and Britain was ended. In December, Hoare, the British Foreign Secretary, and Laval concluded a deal which would have given Mussolini two thirds of Abyssinia. When news of the deal leaked out it inflicted a lethal blow at the League and caused the fall of Laval's government. The war had for once diverted attention away from Europe and encouraged Hitler to occupy the Rhineland in March 1936. Meanwhile, Emperor Haile Selassie had been driven out of his country and in May Mussolini was able to proclaim victory and grant his king a new title, Emperor of Ethiopia. For a short period the Duce was again popular in Italy.

Mussolini's victory went to his head and he became overconfident, but perhaps the most fatal consequence of the war was its effect on German-Italian relations. Hitler was the only major leader not to have criticised Italian aggression and the two countries drew closer together through joint aid to General Franco during the Spanish Civil War. Mussolini supported Franco in order to spread Fascism, to encircle France and increase Italian influence in the western Mediterranean.

In November 1937, Mussolini made his first visit to Nazi Germany, and it was a great success despite a torrential rainstorm reducing his text to a sodden rag as he tried to read it faster and faster to the great confusion of the crowd! He was most impressed at the spectacle of German efficiency and from this point fell more and more under Hitler's influence. Italy joined Germany and Japan in the Anti-Comintern Pact and in March 1938 made no move to prevent Hitler's annexation of Austria. This passivity, combined with the rapprochement with Germany, ruined Mussolini's prestige at home and abroad, yet he remained blind to his real interests. His last triumph, his part in the Munich settlement, should have demonstrated to him the means by which he would win and retain public support in Italy. There was great relief in Italy that Mussolini had helped to save the world from war but he failed to learn the right lesson. After Hitler had absorbed the rest of Czechoslovakia in March 1939 without informing Italy, Mussolini responded by invading Albania in April. The war was quite unnecessary for Albania was already an Italian vassal and the war, though successful, further dissipated Italy's resources. In May, Ribbentrop came to Italy to conclude a full alliance. By the terms of the 'Pact of Steel' Italy found herself pledged to support Germany even in a war of aggression. Ribbentrop promised that Hitler would not go to war for at least three years but when the Germans signed a non-aggression pact with Stalin in August, both Ciano and Mussolini realised the imminence of war. They sent to Berlin a long list of reasons why Italy could not go to war at this juncture and requested huge amounts of aid. 'It's enough to kill a bull, if a bull could read,' Ciano wrote in his diary.

When the Second World War broke out Mussolini announced that Italy would be a non-belligerent but when Hitler's armies began to overrun France Mussolini was desperately afraid that he would lose his share of the booty and declared war. It was his most fatal error and led to the fall of his régime. The war was most unpopular in Italy and, in Chabod's words, enlarged 'the profound abyss that had opened up between the country and Mussolini'. In any case, Italy was patently unprepared for a major war. The army, nearly one third of which was serving overseas, was still equipped with rifles of 1891 vintage and First World War artillery. The air force had more than 3,000 planes on paper, but only 980 of them were ready for service. The best prepared of the services was the navy, but it did not possess any aircraft carriers, so vital in modern warfare at sea. In 1943, Mussolini belatedly confessed that Italy had been better equipped for war in 1915 than in 1939.

The sham of Fascism was now cruelly exposed. Mussolini's hopes of obtaining territory from a defeated France were treated with contempt by Hitler. By 1942 Mussolini was physically spent and his authority shattered. Most Italians had come to hate what F. W. Deakin has called the 'brutal friendship'; the German alliance had reduced Italy to the status of a vassal. By early 1943, three interlocking conspiracies were developing against Mussolini. Army leaders plotted to replace him with Marshal Badoglio, while certain Fascists wished to put government in the hands of Ciano and Bottai. Anti-Fascists were still hoping that the king would act to end Mussolini's rule and restore liberal government, but as ever he was indecisive. In July, at a meeting of the Fascist Grand Council, Mussolini faced a determined party revolt led by Ciano and Grandi which give the king the opportunity to arrest him and replace him with Badoglio.

The German response was an invasion of Italy which forced the government to flee from Rome and conclude an armistice with the Allies. In October, Italy re-entered the war on the side of the Allies. Meanwhile Mussolini had been liberated in July by German paratroopers and flown to Germany, where in humiliation he confronted Hitler. In September he was sent back to Northern Italy to organise the 'Italian Social Republic' with its capital at Salo. Supported by the most fanatical Fascists, he tried to win support by new socialist measures but both the workers and middle class were rightly sceptical of this transformation. The neo-Fascist régime had a new brutality which was made evident in January 1944, when several of the rebel Fascists, including Ciano, were shot. A genuine resistance movement now grew up and in April it was able to launch an insurrection in Milan as the Allies moved north from Bologna. Mussolini, with his faithful mistress Clara

Petacci, headed for Switzerland but they were stopped by partisans and shot. Their bodies were hung upside down in Milan for the infuriated mob to kick and spit upon.

Italian Fascism was now formally defunct but in truth it had been moribund since 1941. Little of the régime's works remained by the end of the war—the agreement with the Church, a few public works and some social welfare. The only remnants of the vaunted corporate state in modern Italy are a few practices like state intervention in labour disputes and industry. But though to later observers Mussolini may appear a mere windbag he was founder of a formidable political movement which was imitated in other countries, and but for him history would have been very different. Hitler always admired Mussolini and said that but for his example he would not have had the courage to seek power himself.

Further Reading

Binchy, D. A., *Church and State in Fascist Italy*, Oxford University Press, London, 1970.
Cassels, A., *Fascist Italy*, Routledge, London, 1969.
Chabod, F., *A History of Italian Fascism*, Cedric Chivers, Bath, 1974.
Clough, S. B., *An Economic History of Modern Italy*, Columbia University Press, London, 1964.
Seton-Watson, C., *Italy from Liberalism to Fascism*, Methuen, London, 1967.
Woolf, S. J., *European Fascism*, Weidenfeld and Nicolson, London, 1970.

Questions

1. What did the various fascist movements have in common?
2. Account for the relative failure of parliamentary democracy in Italy between 1871 and 1914.
3. Why was Mussolini able to seize power in Italy in 1922?
4. Did Italian Fascism confer any real benefits on Italy?
5. To what extent was the Fascist régime in Italy totalitarian?

CHAPTER TWELVE

THE GERMAN TRAGEDY 1918–39

The Revolution of 1918 and the Founding of the Weimar Republic

With the failure of Ludendorff's spring offensive in 1918 Germany began to crack under the strain of war and blockade. The public wanted more say in the affairs of a nation run more and more by a military clique, and opinion turned against the Kaiser, who was regarded as an obstacle to peace. Discipline began to break down, a phenomenon which for Germany was novel and horrifying. In October, mutiny broke out at the Kiel naval base when it was rumoured that the German High Seas Fleet was to be ordered to sea to make a last stand against the British. A. J. Ryder notes the special irony that the revolt began in the navy, 'which more than anything else had symbolised the pride and ambition of the Hohenzollern régime'. A workers' council on the Russian model was founded in Kiel and the example was imitated in other German towns. In Bavaria, Kurt Eisner's action in proclaiming an independent communist republic in November seemed to foreshadow the dissolution of Germany itself.

With Germany's allies in even worse straits, it had become clear to Hindenburg and Ludendorff in late September that the war must be ended. They suggested that a new parliamentary régime should be set up which would bear the responsibility for a peace settlement. The German parliament and public had been kept in the dark about the true seriousness of Germany's position and, when the *Reichstag* was so informed, the Conservative leader Heydebrand expressed the general bitterness: 'We have been lied to and cheated.'

Germany's first full parliamentary government was a compromise. It was headed by Prince Max of Baden but most of his colleagues were from the Centre, Progressive and Social Democratic Parties. It began negotiations for an armistice in October and when Ludendorff opposed the armistice terms, Prince Max obtained his dismissal. Later in the month, William himself had to abdicate and go into exile, as did the other crowned heads of Germany. There was really no alternative; the Allies were insisting on this course of action and in any case many Germans hoped for a more lenient peace if a republic were set up. At first William refused to go and the socialists in Prince Max's cabinet resigned in protest. This in turn forced the prince to hand in his resignation and the socialist leader Ebert became chancellor.

Unfortunately, the parties of the Left contained divisions which were to prevent the consolidation of a really sound democracy in Germany. The revisionist socialists under Ebert wanted a moderate parliamentary régime while the Independent Socialists sought the immediate socialisation of the economy and radical changes in the army and civil service. The most extreme group, led by Karl Liebknecht, were the Spartacists, who wanted a soviet régime on the Russian model and they rejected Ebert's offer to join his government hoping that he would fall as Kerensky had in Russia. The new government therefore needed the support of the army and it was forthcoming. On November 10, General Groener, in a historic telephone call, offered the army's help in maintaining Ebert in office in return for the preservation of the officer's authority in the army. Ebert accepted and also authorised his colleague Gustav Noske to recruit volunteer forces to keep order should an emergency arise. These volunteer bands came to be known as Free Corps and were made up of ex-soldiers whose political convictions were anti-Bolshevik and anti-democratic. Ebert's reliance on the army and the Free Corps was to be a serious handicap for the new democracy.

Ebert's fear of the Spartacists was well-founded. They had now constituted themselves as the German Communist party (K.P.D.) and in January 1919 they attempted an armed revolution in Berlin. Ebert's government was saved only by the aid of the Free Corps, who brutally murdered the Spartacist leaders Liebknecht and Rosa Luxemburg. Other cities where communist resistance had broken out were purged and in June Eisner's régime in Bavaria was ended and the leader himself murdered. Though now supported by the Independent Socialists the K.P.D. lacked mass support and in the white terror that followed their defeat the Communists lost most of their leaders.

The Problems of the New Republic

Order was now restored, but as Hannah Vogt has stressed, 'the men who were to pick up the reins of government faced a tremendous, thankless task'. The consequences of the war were grim. Germany had lost 2 million dead, the people were half-starved, and with the demobilisation of the army fears of unemployment and inflation grew. A legend was already growing that the army had been defeated not by the Allies but by the treachery of the government at home. This was the 'stab in the back' or '*dolchstoss*' myth. When the same government signed the Versailles treaty, the German people who had been led to expect a lenient treaty condemned it as a robber peace.

From the beginning the Weimar Republic was attacked by inveterate enemies at both ends of the political spectrum. The Communists never forgave the moderate socialists for the thorough repression of the Spartacist revolt and the gulf between the two parties widened.

On the radical right, the German National People's Party (D.N.V.P.) and the National Socialist German Workers Party (N.S.D.A.P.), led by Adolf Hitler, depicted Weimar politicians as betrayers of their country. It was vital therefore that the republic be able to rely upon the fundamental institutions like the judiciary, the civil service and the army, but such was not the case. The revolution of 1918 had left intact the pillars of the former régime—the junkers, the army, the bureaucracy, the great industrialists and the judges. These were more often in opposition to than behind the infant republic.

Few changes had been made in the judiciary and the judges were anti-democratic in spirit. They abused their discretionary powers, condoning crimes committed by the Right while dealing severely with the excesses of the Left. Of 354 political assassinations by the Right between 1918 and 1922, 326 went unpunished whereas only four of 22 assassins of the Left went unpunished. This degree of bias was an incitement to the radical Right to indulge in further acts of violence. The Weimar system of justice prepared the way for the total breakdown of legal standards which was to follow Hitler's accession to power, and Franz Neumann is right to describe political justice as 'the blackest page in the life of the German republic'.

The most crucial institution was the army. In view of the nation's experience with generals like Ludendorff during the war, it was essential that the army should be firmly under political control. With a reduced army, a corps of officers upon whom the republic could rely might have been selected. The opportunity was missed because, as we have seen, the new government relied on the army to suppress the menace from the Left. Thus the army remained a state within a state and, though it could be relied upon to crush Communist subversion with alacrity, it was most reluctant to act against right-wing movements. The intrigues of army leaders were to become a major factor in the paralysis of the Weimar democracy in the 1930s when, as F. L. Carsten has shown, loyal support by the army might have enabled democracy to survive. 'If the republic after 1930 had possessed an army entirely loyal to it, the great crisis would have taken a different course. A Reichswehr which in the hour of peril would have cooperated with the Prussian police and the republican organisations instead of intriguing against them, could have been the rock on which the waves broke.'

The attitude of the army towards the republic was soon demonstrated in the affair known as the Kapp Putsch. Passions had been revived in the army and the Free Corps by the military clauses of the Versailles Treaty. In March 1920, a plot was hatched by a rabid nationalist, Dr Kapp, and certain army officers who wished to set up a military dictatorship. When the government requested help in crushing the rebellion, the army leaders refused. General von Seeckt, shortly to be Commander-in-Chief exclaimed tersely, 'Reichswehr does not fire on Reichswehr.' The government was forced to abandon Berlin and only a general strike by the unions paralysed the putsch and saved the republic. Little was done to punish the Kapp rebels or those in the army like von Seeckt, who had been less than loyal to the republic. Of 775 officers implicated in the affair, a mere 48 were relieved of their duties. The army continued to operate as a state within a state and under von Seeckt's intelligent direction a nucleus of the future German army was created in the 1920s which stressed the need for mobility and evaded the restrictions of the Versailles Treaty where possible.

Another unfortunate feature of the Weimar years was the introduction of a totally new level of violence in national life. Political murder had been rare in Germany before the war, but 376 political murders were committed between 1918 and 1922. Free Corps officers murdered the Communist leaders and Matthias Erzberger, the Centre party leader, and Walther Rathenau, the industrialist, were both assassinated. The larger parties had their private armies, formed initially to recruit members and guard party meetings. The largest was the *Stahlhelm* (Steel helmet), founded as an army veterans' organisation and very right-wing. The parties with republican sympathies countered with the *Reichsbanner*, the Communists formed a Red Veterans League, and the Nazis formed the *Sturm Abteilung* (S.A.) or Storm Troops. In the last years of the republic election campaigns became veritable battles in the halls and streets as verbal battles gave way to brutal terrorism.

The New Constitution and the Parties

In 1919, the National Assembly approved a new constitution which its author Hugo Preuss, a professor of constitutional law, hoped would embody liberal ideals. Germany remained a federal state but central government was given more power than before in its control of foreign affairs and finance. Prussia lost its old predominance as the upper house was subordinate to the *Reichstag*, and inside Prussia the junkers lost their monopoly of power with the abolition of the three class franchise. Power rested with the *Reichstag*, elected by citizens of both sexes over the age of 20. The president was to be elected by the nation, not the parliament. He did not head the executive but was to command the armed forces and had the power to dissolve the *Reichstag*. In a state of emergency he possessed the authority under Article 48 of the constitution to suspend civil rights and use the armed forces.

It seemed a genuinely democratic system, but certain weaknesses were revealed in its working. Candidates for the *Reichstag* were elected by proportional representation, a method which encouraged the growth of small parties. In 1932, 27 parties contested the election, and 15 gained seats in the *Reichstag*. It was therefore necessary to form coalition governments which were often weak and short-lived, and between 1919 and 1933 there were 21 different cabinets. Even more serious were the special powers given to the president under Article 48. The first president, Ebert, acted constitutionally but when Hindenburg became president in 1925 he began to exploit these powers in an undemocratic way. Whether any constitution could have worked effectively in the dark period after 1930 is, however, questionable.

The four chief democratic parties were the Social Democratic party, the Catholic Centre, the German Democratic party and the German People's party. The socialists, as we have seen, were weakened by divisions and the most stable party was the Catholic Centre; it drew votes from all strata of society and, therefore, having to compromise between the various interests within the party, was moderate. It played an important part in Weimar politics since its position in the middle of the political spectrum meant that no government could be formed without its participation. The German Democratic party was liberal and boasted outstanding individuals like Rathenau and Max Weber. The German People's party, with Stresemann as its outstanding personality, was more moderately liberal. These four parties entered into various coalitions with each other and formed 17 governments, but from 1930 they all lost seats to the more extremist parties on the left and the right. In 1920, the democratic parties had gained 82 per cent of the votes cast but by 1932 the figure had fallen to only 39 per cent.

The Inflation of 1923

Germany's recovery from the war was a slow process made more difficult by Allied efforts to extract reparations from her. Living standards remained low and inflation was rampant. By July 1922 the mark was worth less than one hundredth of its 1914 value. The Allied attitude to Germany stiffened after Germany signed the Treaty of Rapallo with Russia in 1922. The French obsession for security was revived and in January 1923, Poincaré, convinced that Germany could pay reparations if she wanted to, seized the opportunity to send troops into the Ruhr when Germany defaulted on her payments of timber. The ostensible reason for this action was the extraction of reparations but the French also hoped to weaken the German economy and detach the Rhineland from Germany by supporting a separatist movement there. The German government replied with passive resistance and clashes between French soldiers and German civilians resulted in the death of 132 people.

The affair paralysed the German economy, causing more shortages and runaway inflation. The inflation was fuelled by the German government which, in trying to balance its budget, printed vast quantities of notes and allowed easy credit. A crazy world was now created in which the value of money fell by the hour. The dollar had been worth 14 marks in July 1918; by November 1923 it was worth 4,200,000,000 marks. A typical story of the period is of a woman who left a basket full of notes outside a shop; when she returned the notes were still there but the basket had been stolen! William Guttman recalls how at this time he went into a café for a cup of coffee which cost 5,000 marks. By the time that he had finished his coffee, the price had risen to 8,000 marks. In a period of collective insanity people insisted on being paid by the day and then rushed off to convert their paper money into goods. As no one wanted to accept the worthless paper, a barter economy developed. The fabric of German life appeared to be crumbling away.

It was at this point that Gustav Stresemann, leader of the German People's Party, became chancellor, the first genuine liberal to do so. This courageous realist took a number of steps to end the crisis. The policy of passive resistance was ended and a new bank was set up to issue controlled amounts of a new currency, the Rentenmark, said to have the backing of farmland. The 'miracle of the Rentenmark' now occurred; the German people believed in its stability and it gradually replaced the old mark. It was, in the words of Stolper, 'a psychological device' as there was no way in which the land backing the new currency could be converted into cash. Anyway, confidence was restored, especially as government expenditure was drastically cut and the budget balanced.

The consequences of 'the death of money' in 1923 were, however, grave for the régime which faced a fresh wave of disorders. In November, the Nazis under Hitler staged their Beerhall Putsch in Munich, a move checked by the loyalty of the Bavarian police. The inflation was a traumatic experience for the German people, already demoralised by war and disunion. The poverty caused by the inflation was extreme and those on fixed incomes were hit incredibly harshly. Unlike wages, salaries were not revised upwards twice a week, and pensions and insurances became worthless. It was therefore the middle classes who were dealt the hardest blow and their confidence in the republic was shattered. They had become proletarianised and therefore 1923 was a more genuine revolution than the political collapse of 1918. 'From the ranks of the disinherited bourgeoisie,' affirms Ryder, 'much future support for Hitler was to come.'

Some groups, of course, gained from the tragedy. It was galling for Germans who were forced to beg and were suffering poor health that foreigners could live in the best hotels for next to nothing. Speculators and businessmen took advantage of cheap credit to invest in industry and amass gigantic fortunes rapidly. Hugo Stinnes, the iron and coal magnate, was the chief example of this phenomenon. Finally, government circles could not easily forget the events of 1923 and their fear of inflation explains the timid reaction to the problems of mass unemployment after 1929.

Recovery and Collapse

With the conclusion of the Dawes Agreement in 1924 came a loan of 800 million dollars, mostly from America, which enabled Germany to re-equip her industries and initiate a general economic recovery helped by the introduction of scientific management and mass production methods. 'It is not merely a figure of speech,' asserts Stolper, 'to say that in these fat years a new Germany was building up.' Real wages rose above pre-war levels, hours were shortened and social insurance was improved. The inflow of foreign capital enabled local authorities to build new schools and hospitals, while the extension of public ownership to gas and electricity reflected the socialist influences in the republic. The concentration in big business continued. In 1925, the giant chemical combine I. G. Farben came into existence, followed in 1926 by a similar combine of steel firms, Vereinigte Stahlwerke.

The extent of the economic recovery should not be exaggerated; even in the peak year of 1928 unemployment stood at 1·8 million and Germany was dangerously reliant on short-term foreign loans. Stresemann uttered a prophetic warning in 1928. 'Germany is dancing on a volcano. If the short-term credits are called in a large section of our economy would collapse.' His advice was ignored and easy borrowing from abroad ended with the Wall Street Crash of October 1929. Stresemann's worst fears were now justified as an appalling depression gripped the German economy. At the trough of the depression in 1932, when over 6 million people were out of work, the unemployment rate was almost one in three of the male working population. The depression discredited parliamentary government, which seemed unable to take any effective action against the problem. Businessmen came to believe that only an authoritarian régime could help them while hunger and despair drove millions of voters to support the Nazis and the Communists.

Meanwhile, the republic had suffered irreparable losses with the deaths of Ebert in 1925 and Stresemann in 1929. The German liberal historian Erich Eyck has asserted that Germany should be proud of Ebert because 'a man who excelled in political common-sense, mature judgement and moral integrity had risen from the lower ranks'. He was succeeded as president by Hindenburg, now 78, a man who had fought in the campaigns of 1866 and 1870, more a myth than a man, with an undeserved reputation for patriotism that the next few years were to belie. At the time it appeared that he was providing a focus of loyalty which the German people had lacked since 1918. As Stresemann had commented, 'The truth is that the German people want no President in a top hat. He must wear a military uniform and plenty of decorations.' But Hindenburg was a monarchist who disliked the republic and he was to depend totally on his military clique for advice, with disastrous results in Germany.

The death of Stresemann in October 1929 from a heart attack brought on by years of overwork and abuse was truly tragic. His death, affirms Ryder, was a turning-point in the life of the republic because he had no successor. No later foreign minister 'combined his unflagging pursuit of national aims with the diplomatic skill that won foreign confidence'. His realism had contributed to the one period of real peace in the inter-war years and if he had lived to guide Germany through the approaching world depression, Hitler might never have become chancellor.

The last truly democratic cabinet in the Weimar Republic was that of the Social Democrat Hermann Müller. It was formed in 1928 with Stresemann as Foreign Minister until his death and General Groener as Defence Minister, as he had the confidence of Hindenburg. The government was bitterly attacked by the Left and the Right for accepting the Young Plan on reparations in June 1929 despite the fact that it reduced Germany's payments. Unemployment was, however, a much more acute problem as the winter of 1928–29 saw unemployment rise to 2·6 million and in the following winter the 3 million mark was passed. Unemployment insurance was hopelessly inadequate as it was designed only to build up a fund sufficient to sustain 600,000 unemployed for only three months. The unemployed had to rely more on the hand-outs provided by municipal welfare agencies, though there was another choice: membership in the private army of one of the extremist parties.

The unemployment question finally cracked the Müller cabinet. It was composed mainly of Social Democrats and members of the German People's Party and had therefore always been an uneasy coalition because the latter group represented the interests of the propertied classes. In March 1930, the government parties spilt over a proposal to cover the budget deficit by increasing unemployment insurance contributions, a move which the German People's party opposed. When the socialists refused to consider a compromise suggested by the Centre Party leader Brüning, the Müller cabinet resigned. It was a grave moment in the history of the republic for after this no party combination existed that commanded a majority in the *Reichstag*. The way now lay open for Hindenburg to use, or rather abuse, his emergency powers.

Hindenburg, who liked the Centre Party leader Brüning as he had a good war record and was an austere Catholic, nominated him as the next chancellor. Brüning formed a government made up of members from the Centre and Conservative parties but it relied on the confidence of the president who listened increasingly to the advice of Generals Groener and von Schleicher. Kurt von Schleicher was a shrewd manipulator and urged Hindenburg to make use of his presidential powers under Article 48 from this point with Brüning as merely a front man. Thus in a very real sense parliamentary government ended in March 1930. Brüning's reliance on Hindenburg increased after the general election in September, which increased greatly the strength of the extremist parties. The Communists added 23 to their existing 54 deputies but the most astonishing phenomenon in the elections was the rise of the National Socialists. They increased their seats from 12 to 107 and were now the largest party after the Social Democrats. Hitler at this point demanded a place in the cabinet but Hindenburg refused, declaring that the best position that he would give Hitler was postmaster-general so that he could lick stamps!

Brüning's position as chancellor was now even more hopeless. The economic situation grew worse as both unemployment and the balance of payments deficit grew. The chancellor was not helped by issues in foreign affairs. When he suggested an Austro–German Customs Union in 1931, the French forced the scheme to be dropped on the grounds that the customs union might foreshadow closer political ties. This latest revelation that Germany was still under the tutelage of the Allies further inflamed national passions. Brüning also tried to persuade the powers to put an end to reparations. All he gained while in office was President Hoover's declaration in June 1931 of a year's moratorium on all international debts. He did in fact negotiate an end to reparations but by the time this was ratified at the Lausanne Conference of July 1932 he had already fallen from office. At home, Brüning was forced to use deflationary policies which Stolper condemns as 'one of the strongest contributing factors in the downfall of the Republic'. Yet if Brüning had used reflationary policies, the balance of payments deficit would have worsened and caused a loss of confidence in the mark. The fear of a repetition of 1923 cast a long shadow over the government's fiscal attitudes. His policies made the majority of the *Reichstag* more hostile and the chancellor ever more dependent on Hindenburg, who was re-elected president in 1932 in preference to Hitler who nevertheless won nearly 37 per cent of the votes cast.

In the state elections of April 1932, the Nazis became the leading party in the Prussian state parliament and this success convinced the military clique behind Hindenburg that it would be advisable to do a deal with Hitler. In May, Schleicher persuaded Hindenburg to dismiss Brüning, a move that the President was only too willing to make as Brüning had recently suggested settling the unemployed on estates in East Prussia, a plan which smacked too much of Bolshevism for the old man. Hindenburg's brutal dismissal of Brüning demonstrated his own ingratitude and his toleration of Schleicher's intrigues. German liberal historians condemn Hindenburg's 'stab in the back' of the man who had served him well. With this act, says Erick Eyck, Hindenburg 'killed not only the German Republic but the peace of Europe'.

Schleicher now suggested as the next chancellor Franz von Papen, an aristocratic member of the Centre party and a political lightweight. Schleicher himself was defence minister in a new government dubbed 'the cabinet of barons', which had even less support in the *Reichstag* as the Centre party was furious at the way Brüning had been dismissed. The choice of such a government at a time when the unemployed numbered over 6 million was utterly irresponsible. Schleicher had nominated von Papen as he seemed the right man to do a deal with the Nazis and one of the chancellor's first measures was to lift the ban imposed by Groener during the life of the previous government on Hitler's private armies, the S.A. and the S.S.

The consequences were only too predictable. The Nazis increased their violence and in July they clashed with the Communists at Altona in Prussia. Von Papen seized on the incident as a pretext for dismissing the Prussian socialist government under Otto Braun on the grounds that it was incapable of keeping order. When the socialists indicated their determination to resist what was after all an illegal move by von Papen, the army was brought in to settle the question and the socialists had no other course but resignation. Prussia had been a stronghold of republicanism and socialism since 1919 and von Papen's action dealt a heavy blow at what remained af the Weimar régime.

Despite his attempt to pose as the champion of order, von Papen still could not handle the *Reichstag* and had to ask Hindenburg to dissolve it. The elections in July merely made his position worse as the Nazis, who became the largest party, won 220 seats and the Communists 89 seats. Hitler's bargaining position was now great; he demanded that he be appointed chancellor but Hindenburg was not yet willing to accept a Bohemian corporal as premier and Hitler would accept no other position. At the first meeting of the new parliament, a vote of no confidence was passed by 512 votes to 42, and the humiliated von Papen was forced to request another dissolution. In the next elections, held in November, the Nazis lost ground quite significantly, the number of their seats falling from 220 to 196. Nevertheless, Hitler remained as stubborn as before on the issue of the chancellorship.

The atmosphere of rumour and intrigue now thickened. As von Papen had failed to gain Hitler's support and faced the opposition of nine tenths of the *Reichstag*, Schleicher now engineered his dismissal and became chancellor himself in December. He hoped to split the Nazis by winning over the support of the genuine socialists in the party like the Strasser brothers, as well as the trade unions. These rather amateurish moves merely aroused the suspicion of the Left. Meanwhile, in early January, Hitler and von Papen, eager for revenge on Schleicher, had begun to negotiate for a joint government. Schleicher, unable to gain the cooperation of the *Reichstag*, asked Hindenburg to dissolve it and give him special powers to govern without it. This Hindenburg refused as he feared that civil war might result, and Schleicher, having lost the president's confidence, resigned on January 28. Von Papen and other advisers at last persuaded the president that the next government would have to include Hitler and on Hitler's terms.

On January 30 a new government was formed, with Hitler as chancellor, in a cabinet comprising three Nazis and 10 conservatives. Hugenberg was minister of economics, General von Blomberg war minister and von Papen vice-chancellor. The army clique was convinced that only a régime founded on mass support could govern Germany and only the Nazis possessed such support. At the time there seemed no alternative to admitting the Nazis into power. In the evening of January 30 the Nazi storm troopers held a seven-hour torch parade in Berlin in celebration of Hitler's triumph. The hour of National Socialism had arrived.

Why did Hitler gain Power?

Many reasons have been put forward for a development which was to have such disastrous consequences. The Versailles Treaty, the weakness of the party system and the economic catastrophes of the period all gave Hitler opportunities which he readily accepted. His success marked the failure of the Left, on whom considerable blame can be placed. The Soviet government forbade German Communists to cooperate with the Social Democrats, underrating the danger which Hitler presented. The result was a failure of the Left to combine against him. The Social Democrats themselves are far from blameless. Their policies were, in fact, moderate but they still shouted revolution and Hitler was able to pose as the saviour of Germany against Communist subversion. Socialists never mustered the courage to drop either their Marxism or their gradualism. To have dropped Marxism would have meant losing votes to the Communists while the abandonment of gradualism would have meant cutting the party's links with the existing state. By 1933 the S.P.D. was dispirited by recent election failures.

But if the Left was guilty of a sin of omission—the failure to unite against Hitler—the Right, by actively inviting Hitler into high office, was guilty of a far greater sin of commission. Hitler in fact never won a majority at the polls. 'Despite the mass support he had won,' writes Alan Bullock, 'Hitler came to office in 1933 as the result, not of any irresistible revolutionary or national movement sweeping him into power, nor even of a popular victory at the polls, but as part of a shoddy political deal with the "Old Gang" whom he had been attacking for months past. Hitler did not seize power; he was jobbed into office by a backstairs intrigue . . . the heaviest responsibility of all rests on the German Right who not only failed to combine with the other parties in defence of the Republic but made Hitler their partner in a coalition government.' For Hitler, this success came in the nick of time for in the previous November his party had lost 2 million votes, was short of funds, and was exhausted.

Perhaps the conservative politicians like von Papen assumed that Hitler in power could be tamed. Hitler would be the front man; real power would be exercised by von Papen and Hindenburg. 'In two months we'll have pushed Hitler so far into the corner that he'll be squeaking,' von Papen told a friend. Yet Hitler had proclaimed often enough his determination to destroy the constitution once in power, and his followers had demonstrated by their brutal murders what the nature of a Nazi régime would be. Bearing this in mind, one can only say that the 'Old Gang' was guilty not only of gross dereliction of duty but of gross political blindness as well in underestimating Hitler's talents.

In six months Hitler had set up a dictatorship which was a total denial of all the traditional values of European civilisation. It was to transform Germany and its destructive urge to wage war ended most of Europe's remaining power in the outside world.

Hitler's Rise to Power

Hitler was born the son of a civil servant at Braunau in Austria in 1889. Though he later claimed that he lived in poverty and was beaten by his drunkard father, it would appear that the family was comfortably placed and his father quite progressive. Hitler was lazy, and went to the *Realschule* (Secondary Modern School) rather than to the *Gymnasium* (Grammar School). His record was poor and he failed to learn Latin or gain the customary school-leaving certificate which for most Austrian boys was the passport for a career. By the time he had reached the age of 18 both his parents were dead and his attempts to become an architect in Vienna had failed.

Hitler lived in Vienna in obscurity for four years from 1909 to 1913. They were the formative years, believes Alan Bullock, in which his character and opinions were given definite shape. He soon ran through his inheritance and mixed with the flotsam and jetsam of Vienna. Here he learned the need to be brutal and unscrupulous, to feel contempt for the masses, and to hate the Jewish race and Socialism. By the time he left Vienna he was a convinced Pan-German, living in a fantasy world all of his own.

It was the outbreak of war in 1914 that rescued Hitler from a life of frustration. He joined the Bavarian army and spent four years on the western front, winning the Iron Cross, First Class, a distinction rare for a corporal. Like many other servicemen he was profoundly shaken by Germany's surrender and returned to Munich where he had lived just before the war. He was now interested in politics and in 1919 he joined the German Workers' Party which soon adopted a new name, the National Socialist German Workers' party. Hitler's personality made him its leader, despite the socialism of much of its programme which appealed to many of the early Nazis like Gregor Strasser. As far as Hitler was concerned, he was the Nazi programme and his aims were the overthrow of the Republic, an end to the Versailles Treaty, the union of all Germans, living-space for Germany's surplus population and the elimination of the Jews. The times favoured such extremism and Hitler's audiences grew in size. As Alan Bullock has shown, 'Nazism was a phenomenon which throve only in conditions of disorder and insecurity.' Many ex-soldiers who could not adjust to civilian life joined the military wing of the party, the S.A., led by Ernst Röhm.

The catastrophic events of 1923 highlighted the fragility of the Republic and in November Hitler attempted to overthrow the Bavarian government with the help of Ludendorff. The abortive 'putsch' was a fiasco but so unfortunately was Hitler's trial where his eloquence won him a light five-year sentence of which he only served nine months. During his term in prison he wrote *Mein Kampf*, in which he expressed his most deeply felt convictions.

Hitler now perceived the need to adopt parliamentary tactics and between 1925 and 1929 the party grew slowly, despite these being the 'fat' years of the Republic. The socialist element in the party lost influence as new men came to the fore. Three men may be singled out here as they each represented one of the chief Nazi 'types'. The able but malevolent Goebbels, a dwarfish individual with a club foot, found his métier in propaganda, persuading Hitler to use the new techniques available in the mass media. The unscrupulous Göring was a manipulator of power and led the Nazis in the *Reichstag* from 1928, as Hitler, still an Austrian citizen, was debarred. Unlike the first two, Himmler had a doctrinaire belief in Nazi racial theories and organised the S.S. as a military élite.

In 1929, the Nazis gained considerably from a tactical alliance with the conservative and respectable German Nationalist party led by Hugenberg. W. S. Allen, in his book *The Nazi Seizure of Power*, looks at Thalburg, a fictitious name for a real German town, and points out that the alliance with the Nationalists helped the Nazis in two ways: (1) as all the 'best' people belonged to the Nationalist party, the Nazis gained in respectability while still appearing revolutionary; (2) the Nationalists provided much needed cash for the Nazi propaganda machine.

Hugenberg, like many others, believed that he could exploit the Nazis but he was sadly disappointed in the elections of September 1930, when the Nazi seats leapt from 12 to 107. The chief reason for this success has been well emphasised by Alan Bullock. Hitler's speeches in 1930 had 'a psychological perception of the mood of a large section of the German people which was wholly lacking from the campaigns of the other parties'. He believed that a political leader needed to be able to move the masses and Hitler knew how to move them. In *Mein Kampf* he had outlined the method. Effective propaganda must be confined to a few bare necessities, lies should be big lies, all points should be painted in black and white, and hammered home with passionate and violent rhetoric. Hitler followed this method only too well and he was unsurpassed in modern times in his ability to win over mass audiences. He played on their fears and told them what they wanted to hear. Rarely has a political leader promised so much to so many. To the unemployed among the embittered middle and working classes he offered jobs, to the peasantry he offered more land, to big business he offered government contracts and a free hand for private enterprise, to the army he offered rearmament, to the nationalists he offered the recovery of German greatness, to youth he offered action and commitment, and to all he offered strong leadership, economic recovery and the re-establishment of law and order.

The verbal impact was buttressed by the visual. At Nazi meetings the posters, the swastika emblem, the flags, the salutes, the uniforms all combined to create a sense of power, a sense of belonging to a movement whose success was irresistible. Hitler, affirms Bullock, hit on a psychological fact of the greatest importance; 'that violence and terror have their own propaganda value and that the display of physical force attracts as many as it repels.'

Hitler of course craved for power but this craving was allied to a sense of mission which was perhaps the greatest source of his strength. He had a fanatical belief that he had been selected by destiny to lead Germany to a new and secure greatness. Such faith in himself gave him a hold over his followers and the confidence to take risks.

Revolution After Power

Hitler had come to high office in January 1933 with a veneer of legality and the odds on his acquisition of dictatorial power seemed unfavourable as only three of the 11-man cabinet were Nazis—Hitler himself, Frick as Minister of the Interior and Göring as minister without portfolio. Also ranged against Hitler were the powers of the president and the majority of the *Reichstag*.

Despite this situation, Hitler was to concentrate dictatorial power in his own hands in six months, continually taking his opponents by surprise in his use of force as the first, not the last, resort. He persuaded Hindenburg that new elections were necessary and during the campaign the Nazis besieged the electorate through their control of the police, press and radio. Opposition party meetings were banned and 400,000 S.A. and S.S. men were drafted into the Prussian police so that Nazi terror could be used legally.

Hitler claimed that such terror was necessary if he were to fulfil his task of saving Germany from Communism. His lie was made to appear truth when in February a young Dutchman, van der Lubbe, was accused of setting fire to the *Reichstag*. Whether he was the guilty party is a question that still intrigues historians. Recent research by German historians like Bracher and Hofer indicates that it was impossible for Lubbe, who was half-witted and almost totally blind, to have started a fire of such magnitude in so short a space of time. As he was known to associate with S.A. men, it seems likely that the Nazis started the fire. They of course claimed that Lubbe was a Communist and used the incident as a pretext to outlaw the Communist party and arrest 4,000 of its leaders.

Despite their frenzied propaganda the Nazis polled only 43·9 per cent of the votes which, with the Nationalist party vote, gave them a bare majority. In practice, this turned out to be a good working majority as the 81 Communist deputies were debarred from sitting. At the opening of the new *Reichstag* in March, the Third Reich replaced the unlamented Weimar Republic in a ceremony brilliantly stage-managed by Goebbels.

Wishing to be free of the president's emergency powers, Hitler now presented the *Reichstag* with an Enabling Bill which would authorise the government to pass laws without consulting the *Reichstag*. To their eternal credit, the Social Democrats, led by Otto Wels, voted against the bill despite the fact that the *Reichstag* was surrounded by baying S.A. and S.S. men. No other party displayed similar courage, the Centre party approving the bill after it had received vague promises from Hitler about the rights of the Roman Catholic Church. Had the Centre opposed the bill, Hitler would have lacked the two-thirds majority required for constitutional changes, though it seems almost inevitable that he would have forced the bill through by one means or another.

The *Reichstag* was now a rubber-stamp and the parties who had approved the Enabling Law had signed their own death-warrant. Hitler was now president and independent of the *Reichstag*. As Bullock remarks, the gutter had come to power. Nazi governments were appointed in all the states, and opposition parties were liquidated. Socialist leaders were arrested, the party's funds seized and its press banned. The Centre and Nationalist parties were not spared either, in spite of their cooperation with the Nazis. By the end of 1933 Germany was a one-party state. The unions too were simply dissolved and in May in their place was set up the Labour Front to which all people engaged in industry or trade, including employers, would belong.

There was little opposition to these developments. Hindenburg was so old and lethargic that he did not appreciate the trend of events, nor was there any public reaction to the Nazi brutality. This was no doubt due partly to self-deception or fear but an important factor must have been a willingness to respond to the appeal of a magnetic leader. By identifying National Socialism with Germany and in calling for a national revival, Hitler touched on people's deepest loyalties at a time of national crisis.

Hitler's chief worry by 1934 was growing unrest in his own party. Some members were disappointed at their failure to gain the rewards of office and many storm troopers who took the socialist ideas of the movement seriously were chagrined at how little of the socialist programme had been implemented. Hitler clashed with the S.A. leader Ernst Röhm on this question and also on Röhm's proposal that the S.A. and the army should be united, presumably under his leadership. This also alarmed the army, on whose benevolent neutrality Hitler still relied. When he heard from Himmler and Göring that Röhm was planning a coup d'état, Hitler acted swiftly. On June 30 the Nazis murdered about 400 people, including members of the S.A. like Röhm, socialists in the party like Gregor Strasser, several leaders of the Centre party and Generals von Schleicher and von Kahr.

The 'Night of the Long Knives' revealed the true nature of the Nazi régime but Hitler's power was consolidated when Hindenburg died in August 1934. Hitler simply merged the office of president and chancellor, and made civil servants and army personnel swear an oath of allegiance to him personally.

The Nature of Hitler's Rule

Hannah Vogt has remarked on the contrast between the present image of life in the Third Reich and what many people who lived through it report about the good features of the period. Even discounting the claims of Nazi propaganda, the régime became popular. The skill of the propaganda itself was one reason for this. Goebbels controlled the mass media and was able to kill most criticism in Germany stone dead in two years. Of more importance was the capacity of the régime to live up to its promises. Germany was given strong leadership, unemployment vanished, big business received contracts, Germany rearmed and moved from triumph to triumph in foreign affairs. Hitler seemed indeed the national saviour that he claimed to be.

The outstanding feature of Nazi rule was Hitler's own unquestioned authority. Other Nazis fought each other for influence but there was never any question of challenging Hitler and indeed conflicts were taken to him for arbitration. Not that the power he wielded was used efficiently. Delow describes Hitler as the 'antithesis of an effective bureaucrat' because he disliked administration and shirked difficult decisions. He preferred public speaking or leisure in company with friends from his Munich days and his mistress Eva Braun.

The administrative confusion already existing in Germany due to the overlapping institutions of the central and state governments was made worse by the Nazis when they created a third competing authority, their own party machine. Nor did Hitler's practice of deliberately causing quarrels among subordinates help efficiency. Those who came to the top built up their own administrative empires so that Germany became a veritable administrative maze. It would be fair to say that German government in the period was less efficient than before 1933, was less totalitarian than Soviet Russia, and is best described as 'authoritarian anarchy'.

Hitler's supreme authority was exercised through the Nazi Party Central Office while in the regions Germany was divided into *Gaus* headed by a *Gauleiter* responsible for ensuring the authority of the party in his district. In addition to this territorial organisation, the party maintained many functional organisations like the Hitler Youth and the party militia through which most aspects of the German life could be controlled. It was the task of Central Office to supervise these organisations. In the early years, the Central Office was under Hitler's deputy, Rudolf Hess, who had the right to initiate legislation, select personnel and settle differences between party members. When Hess flew to Scotland in 1941 in a vain attempt to persuade Britain to make peace with Germany, he was replaced by Martin Bormann, an efficient fanatic who served Hitler with devotion and whose easy access to Hitler gave him an immense amount of power.

The most important of the functional organisations in the early years were the *Sturm Abteilung* (S.A.) or storm troopers, and the *Schutz Staffel* (S.S.) or Elite Guard. After the Night of the Long Knives, the S.S. under Himmler was the more influential and it now kept watch on all political life. Himmler built it up as an élite force within the party and the state. Members were selected with great care for their physical fitness and racial pedigree but above all for their fanatical devotion to the person of Hitler. The S.S. motto was 'My honour is true', which meant absolute loyalty to Hitler and Himmler. At the beginning of the war, entire units of the S.S. were introduced into the army and were called the *Waffen S.S.*

The Prussian Minister of the Interior, Göring rapidly purged the Prussian police and established reliable Nazis in key positions. It was this control of the police that enabled the Nazi revolution to retain its sham appearance of legality. Göring also reorganised the political police, better known as the Gestapo. Himmler was soon its commander and he appointed S.S. men to the key positions in all the police organisations. In this seizure of this power, Himmler was helped by the head of S.S. intelligence, Reinhard Heydrich. A gifted and handsome individual of perhaps some Jewish ancestry, Heydrich was one of the few Nazi leaders who matched up to the Nazi ideal of German youth! He saw the advantage of compiling files on all the prominent figures in government. When the Nazis moved into other countries after 1938, Himmler and Heydrich organised special task forces to accompany the army into occupied areas to round up Jews and potential opponents.

A number of agencies were set up for racial questions, including the Ancestral Heritage Office to investigate the racial credentials of Germans, and the Well of Life (*Lebensborn*), which were orphanages for racially valuable children. In 1939, Himmler set up a supreme supervisory office for all racial questions—the Reich Commission for the Consolidation of the German People. It was designed to carry out the Nazis' racial programme, which meant the provision of land for Germans in newly acquired areas, the seizure of Polish and Jewish property, and the mass execution of the Jews. The implementing of this programme did much to disrupt the economy as it used vast resources, but Himmler was moved by ideological considerations only.

The judicial system was twisted so as to serve the régime's perverted ends. Sentences became more severe and 43 offences carried the death penalty by 1945. Special courts were established and staffed only by judges of proven loyalty to Nazism. The onus was now on the accused to prove his innocence, a difficult task against a bullying judge. At their worst, trials were conducted in the spirit of the trial of the generals who attempted to murder Hitler in July 1944, at which Roland Freisler, the President of the People's Court, screamed violent abuse at the defendants.

The régime increasingly used torture, execution without trial and the concentration camp. The full extent of the horror was hidden from most people but the existence of such camps was common knowledge. As Hitler himself said, 'Terrorism is an effective political tool . . . people will think twice before opposing us, if they know what awaits them in the camps.' In the camps, the power of the guards was limitless and brutal torture common. A number of methods were used for killing the inmates including injections, drowning and electrocution, and it is small wonder that prisoners on average only survived for nine months in the camps. It was a system that attracted sadists, who were positively encouraged by the chief authorities like Freisler to indulge in more cruelty. The horrors of Belsen and Auschwitz were a natural result.

The Economy

Hitler's most urgent task was a reduction in the number of unemployed with rearmament as a second, more long-term, aim. He expanded the work of previous governments in the provision of public works programmes and financial incentives to businessmen to invest and therefore employ more labour. Motorways, airfields and frontier defences were built by cheap labour provided by the National Labour Service, which was compulsory for all men between 18 and 25 after 1935. Rearmament added to the demand for labour, as did conscription which came in in 1935. Hitler was also supremely fortunate that by the time he came to power the trade cycle had reached the trough of the depression and recovery had already started. Unemployment fell in the first year from more than 6 million to less than 4 million, and by 1938 only 400,000 people were unemployed. By this time industrial output had nearly doubled and national income had risen by 87 per cent. Ironically, there was now a labour shortage, which caused an influx of foreign workers and renewed fears of inflation. The Minister of Economics, Schacht, quarrelled with Hitler over the inflation question and resigned in 1937 when he found that his authority was being diminished by Göring, who was controller of a four-year plan launched in 1936.

With unemployment solved, Hitler, remembering the effects of the Allied blockade in the First World War, made German self-sufficiency in food and essential raw materials his next objective. Autarchy was to some extent achieved as Germany's dependence on agricultural imports fell from 35 to 25 per cent, and German scientists struggled with varying success to produce synthetic rubber, wool and oil. Steel output rose impressively from 7 million to 19 million tons between 1932 and 1937.

The German economy was helped by a number of windfalls. World trade revived in 1937, and when Austria and Czechoslovakia were absorbed into the Third Reich, their assets were seized. The plunder of the Jews, which increased dramatically from 1938, also swelled the coffers of the *Reichsbank*. Yet when war broke out in 1939, German reserves of essential oil, copper and rubber were still inadequate. Autarchy demonstrates the reason for Hitler's ultimate failure, his refusal to face realities.

The main feature of Nazi policy towards the economy was *Gleichschaltung* (regimentation). Trade unions were dissolved and workers now joined the German Labour Front, led by Robert Ley. Factory owners were given complete authority over their workers though party officials were also appointed to keep a watch on economic enterprises. From 1935 all workers were to possess a labour book with their job record and racial background.

One of the most important activities of the Labour Front was the organisation for welfare and leisure known as 'Strength through Joy', a name that gave rise to not a little mockery. The organisation enabled more Germans than ever before to enjoy subsidised foreign holidays, sport and concerts.

In the drive for autarchy the consumer came off second best. The diet of the German people deteriorated though the housing and consumer durables sectors improved. Taxation remained high as only 63 per cent of Germany's net national product was spent on personal consumption compared with 79 per cent in Britain. Real incomes still rose before the war for Hitler was aware of the need for popularity. Thus expenditure on armaments, though it was considerable and reached 27 per cent of the gross national product in 1938, was not as thorough as Germany's enemies feared. The real difference lay in the quality and modernity of her weapons. Only late in the war was consumption really held down as Germany began to rearm in depth.

The unity imposed on the economy was more apparent than real. The different agencies competed for influence and scarce resources, and issued such a flood of orders that by 1939 confusion reigned supreme. Hitler shut his eyes to the need for long-term planning and even in 1945 Germany was still not making maximum use of her resources.

Cultural Straitjackets

The Nazis aimed at full control of all aspects of cultural life and a Reich Chamber of Culture was created with authority over all the arts, the press and the radio. Goebbels presided over this organisation and tried to crush the artistic developments that had been Weimar's chief achievement. Those intellectuals of independent mind rapidly found that they faced two choices—emigration or the concentration camp, especially if they were Jewish. The few like the poet Stefan George who attempted to cooperate with the régime were rapidly disillusioned. That thinkers of the quality of the novelist Thomas Mann and the scientist Einstein had to emigrate was Germany's loss and the gain of the outside world. An inevitable decline of intellectual standards occurred.

In the view of the Nazis, the task of the intellectual was service to the state. Scientific objectivity or art for art's sake were regarded as hangovers from discredited liberalism. German art was to be functional and should highlight Nazi ideals. Artists like Adolf Ziegler and Johannes Beutner contributed work on the Aryan figure and typical paintings featured chaste nudes and peasant girls stripped to the waist working in the fields. Hitler's particular interest was architecture and he employed Albert Speer to design plans for the rebuilding of Berlin and other cities on a monumental and classical scale. The culture was reflected in the gigantic columns of the Nuremberg stadium and the Chancellory.

The new art of film-making was also twisted to serve the régime. Leni Riefenstahl produced a memorable film, *Triumph of the Will*, a study of the Nazi rally at Nuremberg in 1934. Goebbels appreciated the importance of the cinema as a means of indoctrination and many films were produced glorifying the German race and heaping scorn on Jews and Slavs.

The attitude of the Third Reich to creative thought was made evident in May 1933, when students took part in a ceremonial burning of 'un-German' books in Berlin. Jewish or left-wing lecturers were dismissed from the universities and the number of students fell from 116,000 in 1933 to 67,000 in 1937, mainly as a result of Nazi pressure. A grotesque perversion of the curriculum resulted as each subject was used merely as a tool for propagating Nazi ideals. The academic world failed to protest at this development.

A similar concern for indoctrination was demonstrated in the schools. Teachers had to belong to the Nazi Teachers' Association and many Jewish teachers were arrested, often as a result of being exposed by their pupils. The new emphasis in the curriculum was on physical training. New schools were built for children chosen for their leadership potential and racial purity. For older pupils destined for high position in the party were set up residential schools called *Ordensburg*, a name which recalled the castles built by the Teutonic Knights in the Middle Ages.

For the indoctrination of the mass of German youth the main instrument was the Hitler Youth to which boys were admitted at the age of 10. The movement was led by Baldur von Schirach and reached a membership of 6 million by 1936. Military training was a cardinal feature of its activity and by 1938 more than 300,000 young Germans were organised in units serving the needs of the armed forces.

The Nazis and the Churches

National Socialism was a substitute religion. Hitler's genius lay in his ability to strike responsive chords among the German people, appealing to their idealism as well as their greed and hatred. In Nazi ceremonies, 'Heil Hitler', and 'Sieg Heil' gave staccato fury to the rituals of obedience, while the use of the swastika emblem and special uniforms gave the Nazis the appearance of a special order set apart. Given this factor and also Hitler's contempt for Christianity with its 'effeminate pity-ethics', relations between the Nazis and the Churches were inevitably uneasy.

Both Protestants and Catholics were slow to grasp the full threat posed by the Nazis and indeed there was much initial goodwill towards Hitler, who was regarded as a bulwark against Communism. Not until the war was the full horror of the régime revealed and by then the Churches had made fatal compromises. Hitler acted shrewdly in not provoking them; indeed, in his original programme 'Positive Christianity' was proclaimed as a Nazi aim and as a result the two Churches failed to unite against him.

In 1933, Hitler won some acceptance from German Catholics by promising a Concordat with the Pope and he managed to persuade the Centre Catholic party to vote for the vital Enabling Bill. When the Concordat was signed in July, the Roman Catholic Church was promised freedom of activity in Germany. The Catholic hierarchy now intended cooperation with the régime despite its violence and its dissolution of the Centre party. It is clear that many German Catholic leaders had disliked the Weimar democracy and were more concerned about the rights of the Roman Catholic Church than civil liberties.

The Protestant or Evangelical Churches were already weakened by 300 years of cooperation with government. Neither was there organisational unity; there were 28 Protestant Churches, some Lutheran, a few Calvinist, and the largest, the Old Prussian Union, was a combination of the two. The Protestant Churches were nationalistic in outlook, believed in obeying the secular power and were taken in by Hitler's promises. Inside the Lutheran Church a group grew up called the German Christians who proclaimed that Jesus Christ was not Jewish but Aryan. Hitler, in his desire for control and uniformity, appointed a German Christian, Müller, as Reichsbishop for all the Protestant Churches.

This move did arouse opposition from some Protestants, led by Martin Niemöller, who formed a new body, the Confessional Church. It resisted successfully a proposal to exclude Christians of Jewish origin from the Church and in 1935 issued a clear warning of the dangers that the Nazi régime posed for the Church. Hitler retaliated by arresting 800 leading churchmen, including Niemöller, who was eventually sent to Dachau concentration camp. The Protestant youth movement was merged with the Hitler Youth, church property was taken over and clergy dismissed. Most of the clergy tried to take up a middle position, rejecting the German Christian but unwilling to join the Niemöller group.

In one year alone more than 100,000 people left the Roman Catholic Church as the Nazis mounted an attack on Catholic charities, schools, monasteries and press. In 1937, Pius XI gave voice to Catholic disillusionment when he denounced the evils of the Nazi state in an encyclical *With Burning Anxiety*. Nevertheless, there existed a fatal ambivalence in Catholic attitudes despite the arrest of several hundred priests. Both Churches failed to react vigorously to the agonising moral problems facing them. With a few exceptions like Niemöller, Bonhoeffer and von Galen, the Catholic Bishop of Münster, the Church leaders allowed Nazi atrocities to go unchallenged. In the greatest crisis which they had ever faced, the German Churches had been tested and found wanting.

The Army

The greatest single obstacle to full Nazi dictatorship within the German state was the army but it failed to move against Hitler in the early years when it had both the opportunity and good reason to do so. In the 'Night of the Long Knives' two generals were killed but despite their anger, the army leaders failed to act. General Beck typified their attitude when he said, 'Mutiny and Revolution are words that do not occur in the vocabulary of a German soldier.' In any case these gentlemen of the old school shared many of Hitler's aims, even if they despised the man himself as proletarian and crude.

As time went on the chances of an effective army revolt receded rapidly. In March 1935, universal military service was reintroduced. Now Nazified youth filled the army, thus making any moves by the army leaders against Hitler's régime extremely risky as they could not trust their soldiers to carry out orders.

Hitler for his part did not trust the generals, who challenged his plans for war at an important conference in November 1937. Therefore he contrived to remove both von Blomberg, the War Minister, and von Fritsch, the Commander-in-Chief of the army, within a few months. Blomberg was disgraced following allegations that his wife had in the past been a prostitute. Fritsch was accused of being a homosexual and was forced to retire into private life, despite the chief witness against him confessing in court that the Gestapo had made him incriminate Fritsch. Hitler became his own War Minister, appointing to his own military staff obsequious officers like Wilhelm Keitel. In all, 16 generals were dismissed and Göring became head of the *Luftwaffe*. The army's indignation at these moves might have crystallised into actual revolt had Hitler suffered a setback in his foreign policy but in 1938 he was able to absorb both Austria and the Sudetenland. With the army subservient to his wishes there was now no effective check to Hitler's dictatorship.

Further Reading

Bullock, A., *Hitler: A Study in Tyranny*, Penguin, Harmondsworth, 1969.
Carsten, F. L., *The Reichswehr and Politics 1918–33*, Oxford University Press, London, 1966.
Ryder, A. J., *Twentieth Century Germany from Bismark to Brandt*, Macmillan, London, 1973.
Stolper, G., *The German Economy 1870–1940*, Allen and Unwin, London, 1940.
Vogt, H., *The Burden of Guilt. A Short History of Germany 1914–1945*, Oxford University Press, New York, 1965.

Questions

1. What were the fundamental weaknesses of the Weimar Republic?
2. How far did economic developments prepare the way for Hitler's accession to power?
3. To what extent was Hitler's success a result of his own talents as a political leader?
4. How truly totalitarian was the Nazi régime by 1939?

CHAPTER THIRTEEN

INCIPIENT CIVIL WAR IN FRANCE 1918–39

France in 1919

'If Spain became the classical case of open civil war, it was France which offered the most striking example of the wider tendency to incipient civil war,' writes David Thomson. The inter-war period was one in which parliamentary institutions were discredited in France as short-lived governments failed to stem the rising tide of violence, especially in 1934 and 1936. National unity was destroyed by class warfare and France entered the Second World War psychologically and materially unprepared for another major struggle with the Germans.

It is tempting to ascribe the root cause of France's malaise to the terrible cost of the First World War. As Clemenceau himself lamented, 'the élite of her youth was at rest in a shroud of glory'. A total of 1,390,000 men (10 per cent of the active male population) were dead or missing; 740,000 were maimed. These losses hit France particularly severely for she was already a country suffering, in Kemp's phrase, 'demographic anaemia'. Her population was increasing very slowly before 1914; as a result of the war her total population in 1921, excluding the lost provinces of Alsace-Lorraine, was lower than in 1891 and contained the lowest proportion of young and the highest proportion of the elderly of all European countries. Germany still retained her demographic superiority with a population of more than 60 million compared to France's 39 million. With the collapse of Russia and the French failure to obtain the Anglo-American guarantee, Germany's potential international strength was greater than in 1914. It is small wonder that security obsessed the French. 'This is not peace,' Marshal Foch said of the Versailles Settlement. 'It is an armistice for 20 years.' In a similar vein, Clemenceau remarked that France was condemned to eternal vigilance. The determination with which French governments pursued reparations is explained by the underlying feeling of weakness. France was to receive 52 per cent of any sum extracted from Germany and it was hoped that this would finance the costs of repairing the devastated provinces; time was to show that such hope was vain.

The war had been a traumatic experience for Frenchmen in other ways. It had led to the loss of investments in Russia, necessitated huge government loans and put the nation in debt to the United States. It ended currency stability, which had lasted for over a century, and by accelerating the increase in the proletariat raised the spectre of socialist revolution. Even the peasantry was now an embittered and discontented force.

The Elections of 1919 and the *Bloc National*

Rather like Lloyd George's 'Coupon' election in England in 1918, the French elections of 1919 smacked of declining national standards. The right-wing parties formed a '*Bloc National*' supported by the cartels of big business, the most famous of which was the steel cartel, the *Comité des Forges*. The menace of Communism was denounced and a brilliant election poster depicted a savage Bolshevik with a bloody knife between his teeth. This, combined with a strange version of proportional representation, gave the Right a specious election victory. According to this system, each department returned a group of deputies in proportion to the votes cast but if any list of candidates gained a majority of votes, it gained all the seats in that department. As the *Bloc National* was more united than the Left, it won a landslide victory.

The results were most disappointing to the French labour movement, which during the war had seen the membership of the C.G.T. rise to over two millions. The Left were as usual divided between the revolutionary and gradualist elements; the revolutionaries aimed at close links with the Soviet government and the overthrow of the Republic, policies which were anathema to the moderates led by Léon Blum. After a conference at Tours in December 1920, the two wings went their separate ways. The extremists set up a Communist party with its own trade union organisation, the *Confédération Générale du Travail Unitaire* (C.G.T.U.). 'The significance of the schism,' remarks Cobban, 'was that it created two left-wing parties in bitter rivalry with one another. Henceforth the presence of the Communists on their left prevented the Socialists from cooperating whole-heartedly with the Radicals for fear of losing their own clientèle to the former.'

Yet the *Bloc National* was also doomed to weakness through division. Its cohesion was weak because it was made up of men of all parties including moderate Socialists and Radicals. Many were Catholic and political amateurs who made a number of serious errors in financial and foreign affairs.

Relations with Britain deteriorated over the Middle East and also as a result of the Washington Conference of 1922, which gave Britain the right to a battleship tonnage twice that of the next two greatest European naval powers, France and Italy, combined. This acquisition of British security only served to throw light on the relative flimsiness of French security and relations between the two countries became acrimonious over the German reparations question. The British protest at the French invasion of the Ruhr in January 1923 seemed hypocritical to the French; it appeared that the British were only interested in a revival of business with Germany at the expense of justice for France. The invasion of the Ruhr was, however, an error. The French troops resented having to serve in peacetime and the public resented the higher taxation that resulted from Poincaré's move. In the future, French governments were to be reluctant to use the military supremacy gained at Versailles. As Denis Brogan says, 'Germany was still open to French invasion but the will to invade was dead'.

The *Cartel des Gauches*

Even before the invasion of the Ruhr, the *Bloc National* had become unpopular because of its moves to prevent civil service employees having the right to strike and its attempts to extend the Church's influence in education. Therefore the elections of 1924 saw a decided swing to the Radical-Socialist coalition, the '*Cartel des Gauches*', which won 270 seats against 210 to the *Bloc National*. The results demonstrated the desire of the French public to return to the easier days before the war. Irritation with rising taxes made inevitable by the Ruhr invasion combined with a genuine horror of war. The inflexible Poincaré was now unpopular and Herriot became premier; in sharp contrast to his predecessor he was a warm friendly individual with a genuine desire for the well-being of the ordinary Frenchman. Unfortunately, the Cartel's troubles only began with victory as it faced several difficult problems.

The alliance between the Socialists and the Radicals, though a natural combination at election times, did not operate easily in office. The two elements clashed over the question of the economic role of the State. To the Radicals the State was a dangerous machine whose use was to be kept to a minimum, a view that won Socialist contempt. Matters came to a head over finance, which Herriot had assumed France could 'muddle through'.

The French had steeled themselves during the ordeal of war by the thought that when victory was won, Germany would pay the cost of the war. By 1924 it was clear that she could not do this. With inflation rampant, something urgent was required to restore solvency to French finance. The Herriot government attempted to impose a capital levy, a tax on property-holders which appealed to the Socialists but not to the Radicals. The government fell on the issue and was succeeded by another short-lived ministry in 1925 at a time when the franc was falling rapidly in value and the cost of living rising rapidly. Only in 1926 was confidence restored when Poincaré became premier again. His firmness rather than any actual measure impressed the French public and helped stabilise the franc. As the extra taxes he imposed fell on the poor, the Socialists were displeased and the unity of the *Cartel des Gauches* undermined.

The Cartel also had to contend with the delicate question of Alsace, which Dennis Brogan describes as 'in some ways the greatest cause of French disillusionment with victory'. Under German rule the province had become accustomed to far more local freedom than the French system permitted. The Radicals disliked the continuation of the Concordat in Alsace and the existence there of clerical education. In 1924, Herriot denounced the Concordat and prepared to laicise education in Alsace. These moves antagonised not only Catholics but the Alsatian public in general and the proposals were dropped.

A linguistic division still existed to prevent good relations between the central government and the people of Alsace. The government wanted all instruction to be in French while the Alsatians, including the clergy, wanted at least part of the instruction in German. As German was the mother-tongue of the population, the French should have perceived the deep emotional attachment to it in Alsace instead of enforcing linguistic uniformity. This lack of tact by the French government caused the growth of an Autonomist movement in the province which was to some extent stimulated by the recovery of Germany after 1924. In 1928 came the unedifying spectacle of the trial and pardon of several Autonomist leaders.

The problem of Empire also taxed French government in this period. Interest in the Empire had been increased by the war, which had illustrated dramatically the numerical inferiority of the French population to the German. The Empire had provided men and supplies on a considerable scale but promises of political change had been made to the colonies and in the post-war years the growth of colonial nationalism became a serious issue. Therefore in Indo-China, North Africa and Syria the French faced the necessity of suppressing armed uprisings.

Reconstruction

A more pleasing feature of the 1920s was the rapid recovery of the French economy. The zones of France over which the war had pursued its course had been terribly devastated and in the ten Northern departments the population had been nearly halved. But 80,000 million francs were spent on reconstructing the devastated areas by 1925, a feat which Brogan calls 'the greatest economic achievement of post-war Europe'. The recovered areas again became the richest producers of crops in Europe, particularly in wheat and beetroot. Against this, the drift to the towns continued and some land went out of cultivation because

673,000 peasants had been killed in the war. The shortage of labour did, however, begin to encourage improved farming methods and France, despite a falling rural population, was more nearly self-sufficient than other West European nations.

The damage caused by the war had a more lasting effect on French industry as the areas destroyed by the war contained France's chief industrial zones, but by 1925 much rebuilding had been completed. Starting from scratch, French industry was able to benefit from new capital equipment. The war had encouraged the expansion of industry elsewhere in France and the recovery of Alsace-Lorraine gave her new sources of iron ore and potash. The French motor industry expanded rapidly with new names like Renault, Citroën and Peugeot coming to the fore. An annual production of 200,000 cars was attained and France for a time was a leader in the cheap car as well as the luxury car market.

France's role as the playground of Europe was of considerable benefit to the balance of payments though it led to a growth of American influence on French culture. Unemployment was low in the 1920s and wages by French standards were good, with the worker now receiving a larger share of the national income than ever before. Increasingly, France imported labour from North Africa and other parts of Europe, including 800,000 workers from Italy alone in 1931.

Thus the 1920s were a comparatively brilliant period for the French economy. Government help had accelerated modernisation in the metallurgical, engineering and chemicals industries though backward areas remained. A shift had taken place towards heavy industry but as much of the new growth depended on export markets the French economy became more sensitive to changes in the level of world trade.

The Depression

By 1926 serious divisions had opened up in the *Cartel des Gauches*, while at the same time its achievements in foreign affairs—the Locarno and Kellogg Pacts—were neglected. Therefore in the elections of 1928 the parties of the Right won 330 out of 610 seats. Another feature was the steady growth in the strength of the Communists, who won significant support from many of the 3 million immigrants in France. The Right was fortunate in that for a time France seemed immune from the world slump. The Left, however, was singularly unfortunate in this respect. By the 1932 elections, the Socialists and Radicals had reunited and won 334 seats against 257 for the Right and only 12 for the Communists. Once again, as in 1924, the Left inherited difficult economic problems from the Right which it could not tackle.

Though France suffered a less profound shock than the United States after the Wall Street Crash of 1929, the depression was causing serious distress by 1932 and the stagnation of the economy provided a grim contrast with the brilliant performance of the previous decade. French exports, which were largely luxuries, could not be afforded by foreign customers, especially after the sterling crisis of 1931 resulted in the overvaluation of the franc and the pricing of French goods out of world markets. Cheap imports from other countries desperate to sell at any price hit the home market. With the decline in tourism, the balance of payments grew more unfavourable and unemployment figures rose. By 1932 the number of registered unemployed was 433,000 but to this figure should be added the 600,000 foreign workers who left France.

Attempts to combat the depression were hampered by the economic sacred cow—sound money. The franc should have been devalued but opposition to this course was general in government and the capitalist classes, an opposition which Kemp condemns as exceeding all rational limits. Sound money was considered one of the foundations of the social order; to lose it would result in social revolution. Therefore to save the franc the governments of the early 1930s added to the deflationary spiral by cutting government expenditure at a time when they should have increased it.

Such policies were fatal to the unity of the Left coalition. When Daladier's government in 1932 cut the salaries of civil servants, the Socialists were furious and were not appeased by Daladier's promise of socialist measures in the future—for example, the nationalisation of the armaments industry and insurance companies. The depression, which had been the major reason for the Left's electoral victory, was now proving a liability. Its disunity resulted in rapid changes of government, six different cabinets taking office between May 1932 and February 1934. This game of musical chairs, as Brogan calls it, was highly discrediting to parliamentary institutions and gave the opportunity to several right-wing leagues to mount a vicious campaign against democracy.

The Leagues, the Stavisky Affair and the Riots of February 1934

We have already seen in Chapter Three how the *Action Française* aimed at the restoration of royalist authority and national greatness. Though its policies did contain elements of socialism, *Action Française*, as Eugen Weber has stressed, remained a group rather than a political party seeking power and with its traditionalism it came to seem rather old-fashioned. In the 1920s many monarchists and Catholics rejected its violence and in the 1930s it was outdistanced by new authoritarian groups.

Georges Valois, who had been a member of *Action Française*, left the movement in 1925 to found *Le Faisceau*, a French copy of Mussolini's Fascist party. Into his organisation flocked war veterans disillusioned by a world unfit for heroes to live in. After Poincaré restored confidence in 1926, the movement lapsed into insignificance and other groups moved into the limelight. Marcel Bucard's *Francistes* claimed to be fascist but had only a very small membership. Larger leagues were the *Jeunesses Patriotes*, the *Solidarité Française* and the *Croix de Feu*. *Jeunesses Patriotes* was founded by a Paris deputy Pierre Taittinger in 1924; it was anti-communist and tried to copy the Italian fascists. By the early 1930s it claimed to have a membership of 90,000 including 6,000 in Paris. *Solidarité Française*, which was founded in 1933 by talcum powder tycoon Francois Coty, was violently anti-Semitic.

The most important of the leagues was the *Croix de Feu*, an organisation for ex-servicemen who had been cited for gallantry in battle. It was founded in 1927 and was led by Colonel de la Rocque. Its success was due to three causes: its discipline, the vague nature of its programme, which gave it a wider appeal than other right-wing groups, and its position as a number one target for the Left. Though its rallies and use of cars and planes were impressive, the *Croix de Feu* was not truly fascist. It lacked mass support and Weber is right to call its members 'patriotic conservatives'. After 1936, the movement was to go into a decline and Jacques Doriot's genuinely fascist *Parti Populaire Français* became prominent.

Membership in one of the Leagues offered to the man of the Right what Communism offered to those of the Left—an opportunity for action, entry into the élite and the charismatic attraction of the leader. The appeal to youth was particularly strong in a country where the political leaders like Herriot and Blum were in their 60s while fascist leaders like Doriot were in their 30s.

Anti-democratic as these movements were, their threat to the Republic should not be overestimated. They never gained a mass following as in Italy or Germany because the different groups failed to unite and also because France escaped the worst consequences of the depression. What they did have in common was a righteous indignation at national decadence which they believed was caused by democracy. Right-wing papers like *Le Matin, Candide* and *Je suis partout* whipped up public opinion with indecent invective against republican government. Their campaign might have fizzled out but for the Stavisky Affair, which seemed to prove, in their eyes anyway, that their diagnosis of French democracy was only too correct.

Serge Alexandre Stavisky was a professional swindler whose activities had come to the notice of the police as early as 1927, when he had been arrested and released pending trial. In 1933, he was still at liberty having been granted 19 'provisional' releases, probably through the aid of influential friends. Now, however, he overreached himself by floating a loan of 200 million francs worth of bonds, allegedly to finance a small municipal pawnshop at Bayonne. In December, the scheme collapsed and after a warrant had been issued for his arrest Stavisky disappeared. In January 1934, he was found dead, apparently having committed suicide. The parties of the Right now claimed that Stavisky had been murdered to prevent him disclosing the names of his influential protectors. The prime minister at the time, Chautemps, tried to hush the matter up, an unwise policy as his brother-in-law was head of the judicial department responsible for Stavisky's provisional releases. When the premier refused a committee of enquiry into the affair, the leagues organised large demonstrations as a protest against Republican corruption.

On January 27, Chautemps was forced to resign and Daladier became prime minister. To please the Socialists, he dismissed the rabidly right-wing Prefect of the Paris Police, Chiappe, who had persistently made life difficult for the Left. It was the dismissal of Chiappe that sparked off serious trouble on February 6. When the new government made its first parliamentary appearance, there was utter disorder in the Chamber caused by the Right and the Communists. Across the river from the Chamber great riots organised by the Leagues broke out which the police contained only with difficulty. As a result of the riots 15 people were killed and 328 seriously injured. Daladier was forced to resign and further demonstrations took place in the next few days.

The riots intensified the bitter struggle between the Left and the Right in France. The Left believed that the Leagues had organised the trouble to overthrow the Republic, but the riots were so uncoordinated that this explanation is unlikely. The events of February 6 were merely an explosion of latent anti-parliamentary feeling in Paris, sparked off by a succession of weak governments and the revelations of the Stavisky Affair. Probably the only real political objective was the overthrow of Daladier's cabinet.

The affair was slow to peter out. Doumergue's government initiated enquiries into Stavisky's activities and put much of the blame on the real sinners, the detective police and judiciary. Stavisky had worked as a spy for the Sûreté, which had given him some immunity, while his links with the Radical deputy and lawyer Bonnaure had made the judiciary reluctant to move against him. Public interest in the affair was kept at fever pitch by the death of Albert Prince on February 21. This important legal official was found fastened to a railway line and horribly mutilated. Again there was speculation about criminal activities in high places but though the mystery was never solved it may well be that Prince committed suicide.

The Popular Front

'The most important consequence of the 6th of February,' asserts Cobban, 'was the traumatic effect it had on the French Left.' The threat which the Right seemed to pose to the parliamentary system angered the Radicals and Socialists and sobered the Communists, who had begun to appreciate the lesson to be learned from the triumph of the Nazis in Germany. In any case, they were now under instruction from Moscow to collaborate with socialist and liberal groups against fascism. The Communists now became belligerently nationalistic, a pose that did not entirely convince the Socialists, who for so long had been the target of Communist slander. Nevertheless, the *Croix de Feu* did appear such a threat to parliamentary government that an alliance on the Left seemed essential.

In July 1934 Socialists and the Communists therefore agreed on common political action and in July 1935 a common front was formed between the Radicals, Socialists and Communists, with Daladier and Blum addressing a great combined meeting of the three parties on July 14. By January 1936, a Popular Front programme had been constructed. It called for a return to a system of collective security, the consolidation of the Franco-Soviet pact, for the dissolution of the Fascist leagues, and extensive measures of economic and social reform. The slogan of the Popular Front was 'bread, peace, and liberty' and it particularly attacked the 'two hundred families'—the Regents of the Bank of France who embodied the power of organised wealth.

The programme was ideally suited for a country which after years of depression was prepared to consider real political change. By 1935 the slump had bitten hard in the agricultural as well as the industrial sector and a catastrophic fall had taken place in farm prices. Another factor was swinging opinion towards the Left. Ordinary people were becoming increasingly alarmed by the appeal of the Right to violence. Shortly before the elections in 1936, Léon Blum, happening by chance to meet the funeral procession of the *Action Française* historian Jacques Bainville, was beaten up and nearly lynched by the mourners. He became a martyr figure and the Right was discredited by such an ignoble attack on an elderly and defenceless victim. A third factor made victory for the Left certain: while its parties had gained some cohesion, the Right had not, for the *Croix de Feu* refused to run candidates. Thus the elections resulted in a shift of seats to the Left which gave the Popular Front about 380 deputies against their opponents' 237. The Communists gained 62 seats, the Socialists 39 but the Radicals lost 43 seats and their loyalty to the Popular Front became a matter of some doubt.

The new government was headed by Léon Blum. With a shrill voice, he was not a great orator but he deserved his position by virtue of his integrity and considerable intellect. His period in office was to see important measures passed but the early optimism aroused by the sweeping electoral victory was soon to cool. The Communists refused to take office despite playing a large part in the election victory and were therefore in a position to profit from the errors made by the government.

The government was immediately embarrassed by a rash of strikes in May and June at a time when it wished to reassure the employers that they would not be expropriated. The victory of the Popular Front had aroused hopes of better conditions among the workers, the more militant of whom believed that the factories were to be handed over to them to run. Starting in the aircraft factories, sit-down strikes spread from industry to industry, paralysing the economic life of the country. It was therefore Blum's first task to restore industrial peace.

A conference of employers and union leaders was held at the Hotel Matignon in June, at which Blum won a great personal success by persuading the employers to make far-reaching concessions. He saw that the economic stagnation might be solved by increasing the purchasing power of the masses. Accordingly, the Matignon agreements awarded an average pay rise of 12 per cent in wages and civil service salaries, and brought in compulsory collective bargaining (a development which encouraged a rise in the membership of the C.G.T.), holidays with pay and a 40-hour week. To help the peasantry, a Wheat Board was to be set up to fix a fair price for the producer. The government also stated its intention to nationalise the armaments industry and implement closer control over the Bank of France. These policies were to leave a permanent mark on France and as Tom Kemp says, 'they broke with the deflationary policies of the previous five years and established the foundations of a welfare state'.

Blum's government also brought in some rationalisation of the executive machinery and in October devalued the franc by 25 per cent. This necessary step brought in a more realistic exchange rate and increased the possibilities of economic recovery by cheapening French exports and encouraging tourism. But there were unfortunate results as well. Devaluation, allied with a high level of government expenditure, was inflationary. Retail prices in December were 17 per cent higher than in May. Nor did devaluation stimulate French industry as much as had been hoped. Blum was still distrusted by the employers, who remained reluctant to carry out new investment. The level of unemployment remained high and in 1939, even with an armaments drive, industrial production was only 86 per cent of what it had been before the slump and at the same time capital equipment was becoming increasingly obsolescent. France's economic decline relative to other countries was even greater.

The Right, baulked at the polls, was still a threat to stability because it turned to more ruthless measures. Soon after the 1936 elections members of *Action Française* and the *Croix de Feu* set up the C.S.A.R. (*Comité Secret d'Action Révolutionnaire*). They became known as the *Cagoulards*, or Hoods, from their cult of secrecy and were led by an ex-member of *Action Française*, Eugène Deloncle. The *Cagoule* was a secret military society whose objective was the establishment of a dictatorship in France to forestall the imminent threat of a Communist revolution. It received large sums of money from big businesses like Michelin and committed a number of acts of terrorism but at the end of 1937, after an abortive 'coup', 71 *Cagoulards* were arrested, though they were still awaiting trial when war broke out.

The activities of the Right were only of nuisance value; the worst problems facing the Popular Front lay in foreign affairs. The outbreak of the Spanish Civil War in 1936 posed a thorny question of whether the French should actively support the Republicans. The French government, though sympathetic to the Republican cause, decided against intervention because such a policy would alienate Britain. Blum was able to gain some measure of public support for the government line by playing on the general horror felt in France at the prospect of war; but the Spanish Civil War continued and made deeper the divisions in French society. While the Left sympathised with the Spanish Republicans, the Right, which approved of Franco, condemned their attitude and tried to depict them as the dupes of the Russians. The course of the Spanish war also made French Radicals ponder over the advisability of any association with the Communists.

By February 1937 the Popular Front government was suffering increasing pressure from its enemies on the extreme Left and Right. Despite the Matignon agreements, industrial peace was not maintained, while the Right was antagonised by the government's nationalisation policy and by its decision to dissolve the leagues. Blum came to feel that the only way to restore confidence was to call a temporary halt to reform with a cut in government expenditure. This merely encouraged the government's enemies to fresh acts of violence. When a Leftist mob attacked a *Croix de Feu* meeting at Clichy, the police were forced to open fire on the mob and six people were killed. The C.G.T. response to this 'massacre' was to call a General Strike. In June, Blum was forced to resign when his proposals for foreign exchange control to protect the franc were defeated in the Senate.

The optimism of 1935 and 1936 was now dead and France experienced more rapid changes of government; the instability of French politics was dramatically demonstrated by the absence of any French government at all when Hitler marched into Austria in March 1938. Only in April, when Daladier became Prime Minister in a Government of National Defence, was some semblance of stability restored. By this point, foreign affairs were absorbing most of the government's attention. Daladier and his Foreign Minister Bonnet were content to follow Britain's lead in the attempt to win back Italian support and appease Hitler. Only the Communists attacked appeasement with any vigour; the French public sincerely feared another holocaust and doubts about the effectiveness of the armed forces grew each year.

When the Second World War broke out in September 1939, France was unprepared for a fresh struggle. The downfall of the Third Republic in the summer of 1940 startled the world but it cannot be explained solely by reference to military factors. Rather the French collapse represented the culmination of a long process of inner decline which was partly economic, partly political, partly psychological. 'It can hardly be contested that the economic decline of the interwar period prepared the way for, if it did not make inevitable, the military defeat which ended the life of the Third Republic,' asserts Tom Kemp. But to this factor must be added the acute divisions in French society between the Left and the Right. Afraid of socialist measures, the Right for years before 1939 had been spreading the slogan 'better Hitler than Blum', while the workers were in no mood to support a government which had allowed the gains of the Matignon agreements to be eroded by inflation. Finally, a psychological dimension is required to explain the paralysis of will which seized France on the outbreak of war. A universal pessimism at the prospects of success gripped both the political and military leaders. The real test of any régime is how well it can face up to crisis; in 1939–40 the Third Republic was tested and found wanting.

Further Reading

Brogan, D. W., *The Development of Modern France 1870–1939*, Hamish Hamilton, London, 1967.

Cobban, A., *A History of Modern France* (Volume 3), Penguin, Harmondsworth, 1970.

Kemp, T., *The French Economy*, Longmans, London, 1972.

Questions

1. Account for the feeling of insecurity in France after 1919.
2. Why did France experience disorder in 1934?
3. What were the chief successes of the Popular Front government?
4. Why was France so unprepared for war in 1939?

CHAPTER FOURTEEN

THE REPUBLIC AND THE CIVIL WAR IN SPAIN

The Fundamental Problems of Spanish History

Spain was the first European power in modern history to acquire an empire and the first to lose it. This factor meant a loss of national purpose and self-absorption in parochial issues which caused many of the fierce ideological conflicts of the modern era. Spain also faced an acute lack of natural resources with many areas being arid and barren like Andalusia. Such mineral wealth as Spain possessed was hardly exploited in the nineteenth century because she lacked good communications or a large middle class. Foreign investors were chary of using their capital in a country continually racked by disorder.

Another source of national weakness was the strength of municipal and provincial feeling, which led to a man's allegiance being first of all to his native place and only secondly to his country and government. Spain has always been at heart a collection of small republics held together in a loose federation. It has always been a difficult country to govern because of the need, in the words of Brenan, 'to strike a balance between an effective central government and the needs of local autonomy'. If too much central control is exerted, the provinces revolt and proclaim their independence; if too little control is exerted, the provinces withdraw into themselves and practise passive resistance. In the case of Catalonia, there was an extra difficulty in that the province was culturally and linguistically an extension of France rather than a part of Spain.

Spain has rarely achieved political stability owing to the unending struggle between the forces of reform and reaction. In the late nineteenth century, the country experienced a rather corrupt form of parliamentary government but in 1898 there occurred an event which brought the smouldering resentment with the system to a head. Spain lost the last of her colonies outside Africa—the Philippines and Cuba—in the war with the United States. It was a traumatic experience and brought to the surface forces which had been growing for some time—regionalism, anti-clericalism, frustration in the army, militant anarchism and a general contempt for parliament. Bakunin's anarchism had established itself among the industrial workers of Barcelona and the agricultural labourers of Andalusia. The anarchists were imbued with a moral fervour and hated the Church which, they felt, had deceived them. They rejected compromise and used the strike as a political weapon. Their leaders, Durruti and Ascaso, were such specialists in political assassination that anarchism came to seem mere gangsterism. In 1911, a nationwide anarchist organisation was founded—the C.N.T. (*Confederación Nacional de Trabajo*). By 1930 the C.N.T. was extremely strong, despite the deaths of both Ascaso and Durruti, and it prepared for the social revolution.

Socialism took longer to establish itself. In 1888, the U.G.T. (*Unión General de Trabajadores*) was formed, slowly expanding its membership to a quarter of a million by 1918. It was strong in Madrid, Bilbao and the Asturias but like most socialist movements was weakened by inner divisions.

The most explosive issue was the growth of regional feeling which resented the attempts of the government to centralise administration. In the Basque provinces and Catalonia claims were put forward for more autonomy. Regionalism was one of the factors which led to the 'Tragic Week' of 1909, the first of the crises in Barcelona which rocked Spanish politics in the next 15 years. Between 1919 and 1923 there were 700 political assassinations in Catalonia, most of them committed in Barcelona.

Primo de Rivera and the Fall of the Monarchy

In 1921, a Spanish army of 7,000 was massacred by the Moors in Morocco. King Alfonso XIII must bear much of the blame for this tragedy as he had ordered a reckless advance and told the generals to ignore the cautious advice of the war minister on the grounds that he was an imbecile! To protect the king from the damaging revelations of an enquiry into the disaster, the Captain-General of Catalonia, Primo de Rivera, staged a 'coup' in 1923. It was a bloodless affair as the parliamentary régime had already ground to a halt. For the next seven years. Primo ruled as a genial dictator, his vices endearing him to a large part of the population. 'He would be observed almost alone in Madrid,' writes Hugh Thomas, 'swathed in an opera cloak making his way from one café to another and on returning home would issue a garrulous and sometimes intoxicated communiqué which he might have to cancel in the morning.' Favoured by a period of boom, Primo cooperated with the Socialists and initiated many public works, the result being a period of unparalleled industrial peace. It was of great benefit to Spain that he ended the Moroccan War with the help of the French, the Moorish leader Abd-el-Krim being imprisoned.

But Primo's régime was institutionally weak. He failed to win the support of the old politicians so he tried to create a new party, the *Unión Patriótica*, and set up a corporate assembly (copying Mussolini's Italy) in 1927. Neither device had time to develop for with the advent of the slump, the middle class and the army grew increasingly restive and it was their demands that led to the dismissal of Primo in 1930. Tired and disillusioned, he went into exile and died a few months later.

Primo's historical function had been to protect the king against his opponents and after his removal Alfonso faced bitter republican criticism. In April 1931, municipal elections were held which resulted in an overwhelming republican vote in the towns. When it was clear that the army and the Civil Guard would not support him, Alfonso abdicated without waiting for the final results to come in from the rural areas, although they would have shown an overall monarchical majority. In this decision, Alfonso was probably correct; no government in Spain could survive without support from the large towns. The abdication demonstrated the degree to which monarchical sentiment had been eroded in Spain. Even the aristocrats observed the fall of the monarchy, as one of them remarked, as they might have watched a bad film. It was a highly significant moment in Spanish history for a new régime had been ushered in without the active support of the army. In June, elections were held for a Constituent Cortes.

The Republic (1931–36)

Until the outbreak of the Civil War five years later, Spanish politics were divided into three main periods: (1) until mid-1933 a period of progressive republicanism prevailed; (2) from November 1933 to February 1936, Spain was dominated by right-wing republican government; (3) from February to July 1936 politics continued to polarise, a descent into violence occurred and civil war resulted.

After the 1931 elections, the strongest groups in the Constituent Cortes were republican and included the socialists. The most important republican politician was Azana, leader of the Left Republicans. A politician with a shady past, Lerroux, led the Radicals, who were, despite their name, right-wing. More than half the deputies came from the professional classes, who were idealistic and politically immature. Azana, first Minister of War and then Prime Minister, typified this group in his combination of verbosity and integrity. This lack of experience, combined with a lack of consensus for a moderate republic, soon led to disillusionment with the new régime. Zamora, a conservative Catholic, initially Prime Minister, became President and might have been a guarantee of moderate government but his powers were very limited through fear of the executive abusing the right of dissolution as Alfonso had done. The absence of an Upper Chamber removed another check on the legislature, which on a number of issues alienated support by its radical policies.

Four major problems had to be tackled by the new republican government: the land; the Church; regionalism; and the army. Unfortunately, its efforts on these questions alarmed the capitalist classes without weakening their power. In the words of Raymond Carr, 'the weakness of republican legislation, both in the spheres of finance and labour, was that it threatened fundamental change which the government lacked the will or the desire to implement'.

The new régime suffered by coming to power in a period of depression when agricultural prices fell and unemployment rose as land went out of cultivation. A quick solution to the land question was therefore required but this proved difficult because of regional variations and a lack of skilled technicians. As a result, the Agrarian Law of 1932 only applied to the central and southern provinces. It laid down that unworked estates of over 56 acres were to be expropriated by the Institute of Agrarian Reform which would distribute the land to individuals or cooperatives. But by 1934 only 12,500 people had been settled on such estates and Caballero, the Socialist leader, dubbed the law as an aspirin to cure appendicitis because it gave no real help with credit or irrigation. Then the Lerroux administration withdrew funds from the Institute so that agrarian reform in Carr's phrase turned out to be 'a disappointing muddle'.

The republicans were urban in attitude and did not understand rural problems. Many were more interested in other areas of government such as anti-clerical legislation. Division hampered the formulation of an effective policy; the republicans wished to create an independent peasantry as in the Third Republic, whereas socialists argued in favour of collective agriculture. The problem of Spanish agriculture remained as a major cause of discontent. It was a source of Anarchist strength as the C.N.T. gained many supporters from the landless labourers of Andalusia.

That the influence of the Church had grown in the late nineteenth century was chiefly due to the Jesuits, who owned railways, banks and shipping companies. Their quarrel with the Liberals was bitter, particularly over education. In the complete Church catechism published in 1927, Liberalism was defined as 'a most grievous sin against faith'. Combined with this intransigence was a great laxity of conduct which led many Spaniards to see in the Church everything that was vile and hypocritical. In the Civil War this hatred of the Church was to have tragic consequences.

The republicans also disliked the Church because it had openly preferred the monarchy to the new régime. All the cabinet were anti-clerical if not atheist, with the exception of Zamora and Maura (Minister of the Interior). In the past, Lerroux, as a demagogue in Barcelona had called on his followers to destroy churches. Typical of the republican lack of tact was Azana's unwise remark that 'Spain had ceased to be Catholic' when he meant that Spain was not totally Catholic as in the sixteenth century. The Church leaders reacted strongly. Cardinal Segura, Archbishop of Toledo and Primate of the Spanish Church, in a violent pastoral letter warned the faithful of the need to fight the Church's enemies. As a result he was asked to leave Spain.

The republican government made a grave error in creating a Constitution that was highly controversial, full of emotional phraseology and containing many articles that offended the Church. Article 26 separated Church and State, payment of priests was to end in two years and religious orders could be dissolved if the Minister of Justice judged them to be a danger to the State. Jesuits were to be banished and their property confiscated. Religious education was to end and divorce was to be made easier. Such terms were a clear challenge to the Church. Potential supporters among the clergy were alienated and the government itself split on the issue. Zamora resigned as Prime Minister and the Basque deputies left the Cortes. The forces of reaction were provided with a rallying cry which they badly needed and their anger was increased by an outbreak of church burning in May 1931 which spread from Madrid to Andalusia.

The problem of regionalism became serious in 1931 when the Catalan party declared for independence. The government forced the Catalans to back down on the matter but as it had promised more autonomy for Catalonia it did draw up a Catalan Statute, which was endorsed by a referendum in Catalonia in August. This was a solution to a difficult question but it alienated the Right, especially the army, which felt that its achievement in crushing Catalan opposition between 1917 and 1923 had been undone.

The government was determined in fact to reduce the power of the army and offended it in other ways. Press criticism of the army was now permitted and breaches of the civil code by soldiers now came under the jurisdiction of the ordinary courts. As there was a ridiculous proportion of officers to men of one to ten, a number of officers were compulsorily retired. Unfortunately these officers, with time on their hands, were tempted to plot against the government. Cabals of right-wing officers were formed and in 1932 General Sanjurjo, the hero of the Moroccan Wars, outraged at the Catalan Statute, staged the first revolt against the republic at Seville, which ended in abject failure.

The government was strengthened by the army revolt but its unity was badly shaken by the Casas Viejas affair in January 1933. An anarchist group in the village of Casas Viejas in Andalusia was murdered by the Civil Guard, 25 villagers being killed. 'It was the long-term effects of Casas Viejas which destroyed Azana's government in September 1933,' asserts Carr. The repression alienated the working class and gave the Right an opportunity to attack the Republic as violent and disorderly. Scurrilous attacks in the press helped to sway opinion to the right. The affair split the coalition itself; Lerroux's Radicals attacked the government over the massacre but more serious was the desertion of the Socialists, who were to fight the next election as a separate party. To complete the disarray of the Left, the C.N.T. carried on a campaign of non-cooperation with other parties. With the republican unity so shattered, the Cortes was dissolved in September and elections held in November.

With the government so unpopular it was only too predictable that the elections resulted in heavy republican losses as the political initiative passed to a new party, the C.E.D.A. (*Confederación Española de Derechos Autónomas*). The brain child of the Jesuits, the party was an alliance of right-wing groups and its main objective was to resist the anti-clerical legislation of the Constituent Cortes. It was led by Gil Robles and tried to copy the German Centre Catholic party. Reactionary elements were, however, influential in the C.E.D.A. so that its devotion to republican ideals was debatable. It depended on the funds of landowners and therefore, though it claimed to be a mass Catholic party, it was really a front for the extreme Right.

As the C.E.D.A. did not have an overall majority, the Radical Lerroux formed a centre government which seemed to truckle to the Right in the way it slowed down educational and agrarian reform and in its amnesty for rebel officers. In return, the C.E.D.A. supported Lerroux, though C.E.D.A. members were not in the government. The Anarchists found this situation intolerable; in December 1933 they instigated a rising at Saragossa and led a great strike in March 1934. The Anarchist revival worried the Socialists, who were afraid of losing influence, and after 50 years of relatively moderate policies the Socialist party became revolutionary.

The pretext for more revolutionary action on the Left came in October 1934 when three C.E.D.A. members were allowed into the government. Caballero, afraid of Spain going 'fascist', joined with the Anarchists in an armed revolt. The rising was easily crushed except in the Asturias, where harsh repression resulted in the deaths of 3,000 people. The October Revolution was a turning-point in the history of the Republic and can be seen as the prelude to the Civil War in the way that it sharply polarised political opinion. Many middle-class moderates moved to the Right to conserve their lives and property, terrified by stories in the press of atrocities committed by the workers. The Left were alienated by the repression, especially as the Foreign Legion and the Moors, Spain's hereditary enemies, were used to put down the revolt. Many workers were tortured and shot without trial.

Lerroux's government tried to steer a middle course in the crisis and did stop the political executions in 1935, though forced to admit five C.E.D.A. members into government when a new cabinet was formed. The reputation of the Radicals was, however, ruined by a financial scandal over a new roulette wheel—the *straperlo*—which would have made money for government members. Lerroux's government was forced to resign and new elections were held in February 1936. The Left had learned from its disunity in 1933 and formed the Popular Front—an electoral coalition of Republicans and Socialists which won a majority of votes. The further polarisation of political forces was reflected in the virtual annihilation of the Centre parties like Lerroux's Radicals.

This polarisation was also reflected in the growing importance of two extremist parties—the Falange and the Communists. Up to the February elections, the Spanish Fascist party, the Falange, had not been a serious political force. Its creator, José Antonio de Rivera, the son of the former dictator, had entered politics to defend his father's memory from republican attacks. A man of charm and authority, he founded the *Falange Española* (Spanish Phalanx) in 1932 and two years later it merged with another group, the Nazi-influenced J.O.N.S. (*Juntas de Ofensiva Nacional Sindicalista*). José Antonio believed that an élite should pave the way for the restoration of Spanish greatness and hoped to attract the workers by setting up a corporate state. Financed by Bilbao industrialists, the movement initially attracted only university students in Madrid and Seville. They indulged in street violence against the Left, tactics which José Antonio himself disliked. Gradually the Falange gained support at the expense of C.E.D.A. and forces on the Right, like the army, began to take it seriously. The Falange contributed to the outbreak of the Civil War by its gang warfare which seemed to prove to the Right that orderly government was impossible under the Republic.

The Communists had been insignificant in the 1920s but with the change of Comintern policy in 1934 they began to cooperate with other parties on the left. Their participation in the Asturian rising increased their prestige, especially as one of the heroines, Dolores Ibarruri, nicknamed 'La Passionaria', was a Communist. By the time the Popular Front was formed they had gained influence out of all proportion to their numbers. They could claim to be more modern, European and dynamic than the old Spanish parties and behind them stood Russia to provide material assistance.

From the February elections to the revolt of the generals in July, Spain was ruled by a purely republican government. It could no longer count on the steady support of the socialist movement for Caballero hoped to seize power after a republican failure and his use of extreme language terrified the middle class. His old fear of losing influence to the Anarchists was now compounded by the growing influence of the Communists, who were attracting many of the militant Socialist youth. The moderate Socialists, led by Prieto, disagreed strongly with Caballero's tactics and thus on the eve of the Civil War the world of labour, in Carr's phrase, 'displayed a chaotic incoherence'.

In contrast, the forces of the extreme right were united, from the Falange to the Traditionalists (the diehard Catholic reactionaries). They all believed that Spain was being ruined and betrayed by the Republic and there seemed ample evidence to support this view as violence increased. Revolutionaries legally convicted of crimes were amnestied and a clamour arose for revenge on the authorities who had detained them. One of the most stupid moves by the government was the ousting of Zamora as president in May, his place being taken by Azana. As Stanley Payne has explained, Zamora's removal 'ended the last guarantee for impartial constitutional government and made the exercise of public power in Spain a monopoly of the Left'.

However, for the alienated forces of the Right to create a successful counter-revolution, a positive move was required from the generals. They disliked the prevalent disorder but as they were divided on the question of which régime should replace the Republic, they hesitated to act. The government, aware of the army's hostility, transferred important generals to posts outside Spain, Goded being sent to the Balearic Islands and Franco to the Canaries. This was a fatal move for as Raymond Carr notes, 'discontent was tightened into a plan of revolt by the government's defensive action against the military malcontents'. General Mola, who had been sent to Navarre, became the chief conspirator establishing links with the Falange and other right-wing groups.

By July 1936 a civil war was almost inevitable. Much blame for this situation must lie on the middle-class republicans who had not carried out impartial government but had attacked the Right and pandered to the Left. The murder on July 13 of Calvo Sotelo, who had replaced Robles as leader of C.E.D.A., was the final incident which sparked off an uprising. Never before in the history of a west European parliamentary régime had a key opposition leader been murdered in cold blood by the state police. The act was a reprisal for the murder of a young Republican soldier by the Falange, but it convinced the Right that order could only be restored by the overthrow of the Republic. General Franco flew to Morocco on July 18 to lead the Army of Africa in a revolt.

Predictable and understandable as this development was, it must be condemned on grounds of morality and political wisdom. In the words of Brenan, 'with a little patience the Right would have gained much of what it sought without a war, for the Popular Front was breaking up rapidly through its inner disorders and a revolution from the Left had already been tried and had failed. But the Nationalist leaders had had their heads turned by Nazi Germany: they wanted nothing less than a complete victory with the annihilation of their enemies.' The result was a ruinous and bloody civil war.

The Course and Consequences of the Civil War

In the early days of the war neither side acted with decision. President Azana and his government underestimated the commitment of the army leaders to rebellion and hesitated to arm the workers, which would mean more power being ceded to the streets. The key to rapid army success lay in the seizure of the big cities but many army units failed to move promptly. As a result, major cities like Madrid, Barcelona, Valencia and Bilbao remained in Republican hands and both sides had lost any possibility of a quick victory.

With the government paralysed, revolutionary terror was unleashed by the Left with indiscriminate killing and church-burning by the C.N.T. rank and file, which confirmed the hostility of the upper middle classes. But terror was practised by both sides in what was to be a cruel and wasteful war. The execution by the Right of Lorca, Spain's outstanding contemporary poet, was symbolic of the waste while the cruel character of the fighting is well drawn in Hemingway's *For Whom the Bell Tolls*. The scene where villagers beat bourgeois prisoners with flails and throw them over a cliff fully reflects the realities of the period. At the same time virtues of courage and sacrifice were also in evidence.

By the end of July, the rebels (Nationalists) had gained control of northern Spain except the areas around Bilbao in the extreme north and Barcelona in the north-east. The Republicans controlled southern Spain with the important exceptions of Seville, Granada and Cadiz. Franco, soon accepted by the Nationalists as Commander-in-Chief of their forces, hoped to end the war quickly by capturing Madrid using the Army of Africa. Delays by the Nationalists allowed Republican resistance to stiffen and Madrid was to hold out until 1939, its defence by the Republicans being in Carr's words 'the central epic of the war'. When the Italian forces sent by Mussolini to aid Franco advanced on Madrid, the International Brigade (volunteers from abroad) counter-attacked at Guadalajara, causing chaos in the Italian motorised divisions. After this defeat, Franco realised that a decisive battle at Madrid would not occur in the immediate future and was forced to carry on a war of attrition, assuming that the Republican armies would collapse before the Nationalists.

The Republicans attempted to stave off defeat by a series of offensives to relieve the Northern Front and Madrid. These were successful in saving Madrid until 1939 but could not halt the decisive offensive by the Nationalists in conquering Republican held territory in the north in 1937. Total air superiority was enjoyed by the Nationalists, as was vividly highlighted by the bombing of Guernica. This factor, combined with faulty organisation on the Republican side, led to the fall of Bilbao. By October the whole of the northern coast with its industrial potential was in Franco's hands.

The Nationalist commander's hopes of an immediate offensive in Madrid were thwarted by a Republican offensive at Teruel in December which disrupted his concentration of forces. Franco countered this disappointment by a drive to the sea towards Valencia in March 1938, a move which took the Republicans by surprise at a time when they were still exhausted by the Teruel offensive. They attempted to halt Franco's advance on Valencia by a brilliantly planned attack at the battle of the Ebro in July. After initial successes, their efforts faltered and Franco bled the opposition to death by repeated attacks on a narrow front. Air superiority was again vital as it reversed the ratio between attack and defence casualties. The Republican armies in Catalonia subsequently collapsed and in January 1939 the Nationalists entered Barcelona.

Now came the final drama of the war and with it tragic irony. Colonel Casado, the pro-Anarchist commander of the Republican Army of the Centre, quarrelled with the Communists and bitter fighting broke out in Madrid. When it ended the Republicans were in no state to defend the capital. When Madrid fell in March, the Civil War was over.

Three factors chiefly explain the Nationalist victory: (1) Franco's own contribution; (2) the divisions among the Republicans; and (3) the greater foreign aid given to the Nationalists. Francisco Franco was a strict and dedicated professional soldier who won a reputation for courage and efficiency in the Foreign Legion. In 1931, he was Director of the Saragossa Military Academy and up to this point had refused to take sides in politics. The Republicans, in their zeal to reduce the army's influence, closed down Franco's Academy and his dislike of the Republican régime was deepened by the October Revolution of 1934, which he crushed ruthlessly. After he was sent to the Canaries in 1935 he was prepared to take up arms against the Republic.

Once the war started Franco soon became supreme commander of the Nationalist war effort, as the Army of Africa which he commanded was the real core of Nationalist strength. In 1937, his supporters demonstrated their confidence in him by making him head of state. In some ways he was fortunate in that potentially serious rivals—Goded, Sanjurjo and Mola—were all killed early in the war. But Franco was an able soldier who resembled Montgomery in his patience and in the way he conserved the lives of his men. German officers found him too cautious but he replied that to hurry would mean the deaths of more Spaniards. His troops repaid his concern for their welfare by giving him unquestioning loyalty.

On the political front his own calm authority and the support of the Church prevented splits in the Nationalist coalition, which was made up of a motley group of Falangists, Carlists, Monarchists, the army and the Church. He was determined to make Spain a one-party state and after José Antonio's execution by Republicans in 1936, he forced the Falange and the Carlists to merge. 'The political synthesis which he achieved among his followers was the chief factor in giving him ultimate victory,' writes Hugh Thomas. Nor should Franco's diplomatic skill be underestimated; he succeeded in gaining invaluable German and Italian help without any real surrender of Spanish sovereignty.

In direct contrast, the Republicans came near to destroying themselves before they achieved any efficient direction of the war and the old rivalries which continued to fester were always likely to erupt again at crucial periods. When the war commenced, both the C.N.T. and the Communists indulged in terrorism which made it impossible for the Republican government to organise a serious war effort.

Caballero became Prime Minister after Azana's retirement and he managed to persuade the C.N.T. leaders to join the government but the coalition was always an uneasy partnership. Anarchists refused normal military discipline and kept back arms for use against their so-called allies. Their attempts to collectivise farms and factories alienated the peasantry and the middle classes and resulted in a big increase in Communist strength. The Communists had moderated their policies to facilitate collaboration with other groups so that they now appeared as the loyal supporters of a broad-based democratic front. Unfortunately, they could not desist from attempts to gain control of the Republican armies and they roused the anger of the C.N.T., the Socialists and the Republicans.

These divisions prevented the Republic from turning popular enthusiasm for the Republic to good account. The militia remained merely the improvised forces of the labour organisations captained by those who could seize weapons and impose their claim to leadership by force of personality. Militia columns often broke before trained troops and when bombed were seized by collective panic. Competition between the rival groups led to inefficient allocation of scarce military supplies. In contrast, Franco's African Army, a decisive factor in the war, was well disciplined and well equipped; it felt at home in the difficult mountain terrain over which many of its actions were fought. It was able to shield the rest of the Nationalist forces while they were trained and equipped and by 1938 the Nationalist strength was 500,000 men.

The third crucial factor, foreign aid, was clearly in Franco's favour as the Western democracies were determined to stay neutral. Fear of a general war, Chamberlain's desire for Italian friendship and the Conservative government's dislike for 'Red' Spain committed Britain to neutrality and pressure was brought to bear on Blum's government in France to follow a similar course. Therefore effective aid for the Republican side came only from Russia in the form of advisers, raw materials and tanks. Useful though this aid was, it was deliberately limited by Stalin, who merely aimed at a continuation of the war rather than a full Republican victory so that the European powers could not unite against Russia at a time when the purges were being carried out; the number of Russians sent to Spain, therefore, did not exceed 2,000.

Both Hitler and Mussolini thought that the Nationalist victory would be swift and gave aid to Franco in the belief that they would gain his alliance on the cheap. In the end the Italians sent 50,000 men, over 700 aircraft and 950 tanks. The Germans sent far fewer men, about 16,000, but qualitatively their help was more valuable than Italy's. Their Condor Legion comprised 11 aircraft squadrons which played a decisive role at key engagements like the Ebro. Germany also sent a tank battalion which was used for training purposes. In the long run it was the continuity of German and Italian aid that tipped the scales in Franco's favour.

European opinion was antagonised by the many atrocities in the war, especially the bombing of civilians. The destruction by German planes of the Basque town of Guernica resulted in the deaths of 1,600 people and the event was permanently enshrined in Picasso's painting. What was particularly horrifying was that the largest single category of deaths was due to executions and reprisal killings.

For Spain herself the Civil War was tragic: 600,000 people were killed, large areas of the country were in ruins and Spanish society remained bitterly divided. Spain was now to experience a régime of order; the Republican armies were demobilised and the Nationalists systematically wiped out opponents by execution. To Franco the Republican incorporation of the mass of the Spanish people into political life seemed misguided as it tore apart the fabric of national unity. Under his rule Spain was not to be allowed the luxury of politics and his dictatorship became the most powerful Spanish government since the reign of Philip II in the sixteenth century. The régime was consolidated by eight years of political proscription, which Gabriel Jackson has described as 'awe-inspiring in its lack of pity and lack of imagination'. Only with the approaching defeat of the Axis powers in 1944 did the mass executions end.

Franco's Rule in Spain

Once the war was over, Franco's dictatorship faced grave problems—the decline in national wealth, the hostility of much of the population, potential divisions among the Nationalists and before long the danger of involvement in the wider European struggle. On the other hand, Franco enjoyed great personal power; he enjoyed the prestige of being the successful war leader; rivals had been eliminated in the Civil War and the majority of the nation, exhausted by three years of war, were in no mood to contest his rule. The General was determined to continue his authoritarian rule and refused to consider the restoration of the former king, Alfonso. Franco's native caution made him consider all interests in the Nationalist coalition and he gave places in his cabinet to members from all the different groups.

Franco was equally concerned to stay neutral in the European war and signed a treaty of friendship and non-aggression with Salazar's Portugal, which had sent 20,000 troops to help him during the Civil War. In 1942, the two régimes formed an Iberian Bloc, the aim of which was the preservation of the neutrality and independence of the Peninsula. With the German victories of 1940, Franco made a number of moves to conciliate Hitler. The Germans were provided with submarine facilities in Spanish ports and Serrano Súñer, a Fascist who believed that Germany would inevitably dominate the continent, became Foreign Minister. However, Franco was too skilful and cautious a diplomat to be drawn into full intervention in the European war, apart from providing 20,000 troops to fight on the Russian front after June 1941. Hitler did in fact meet Franco in October 1940 to draw Spain into the war but for once he met his match. Franco countered his every argument and Hitler was so exasperated that he later remarked that he 'would rather have three or four teeth yanked out than go through that again'.

In time, the Fascist members of the government, like Súñer, were weeded out and in 1945 a national assembly with limited powers was introduced. A proclamation of civil liberties was also made which Payne describes as 'another dab of icing on the cake of dictatorship'. These moves were partly for foreign consumption at a period when Franco feared some Allied action against Spain. They had no effect on foreign opinion; Spain was virtually isolated apart from the friendship of Portugal and Peron's Argentina.

Franco kept his nerve in this difficult period, aided by police control of the divided Left, and the loyalty of the army. In 1947 he held a plebiscite on the Law of Succession, which defined Spain as a kingdom with the dictatorship fulfilling the role of a regency. Franco reserved himself the right to name his successor, a right which he delayed exercising until 1969 when he named Don Juan Carlos, grandson of Alfonso XIII, as future king.

The intensification of the Cold War led to a distinct improvement in Spain's diplomatic position. Franco now appeared respectable as the general who had defeated the Communist menace and Spain was seen as an important cog in the collective security system of Western Europe. In 1951, the United States established military bases in Spain in return for economic aid, which by 1965 had reached approximately 1,800,000,000 dollars. In 1955, Spain was able to gain entry to the United Nations.

As Fascist influences declined in the 1950s, Franco increased the role of the army leaders and the Church. A semi-secret Catholic lay order, *Opus Dei*, came into the limelight; influential in the universities its aim was to increase the power of the Roman Catholic Church and its members gained posts in the 1957 cabinet. The army had doubts about its position removed in 1962 when Lieutenant General Grandes was appointed Vice-Premier.

Though the difference between the Spanish standard of living and that of most of Western Europe probably grew under Franco's rule a rise took place in real incomes. Unemployment was kept low by massive emigration of workers to the more advanced states while the country benefited from the development of tourism. Improved material standards combined wtih the wishes of most of the population for order and peace. Most Spaniards felt that never again must a civil war be allowed to break out in Spain. Yet extremist political organisations still existed and in 1967–8 workers succeeded in mounting major demonstrations in the chief towns, the Basque provinces and Catalonia. In September 1975, the execution of Basque nationalists provoked international criticism of the regime.

In November, Franco himself died at the age of 82. His pragmatic dictatorship had never been seriously threatened. He always drew a cross-section of opinion into his government and his personal power remained great to the end, backed by the army and a Civil Guard of 800,000 men. Overshadowing Spain now is the future stability of the country. On the surface the forces of the Right appear sufficiently organised and powerful to prevent any disturbances though the Left may well attempt to emulate the success of the Portuguese revolutionaries. The Right has the difficult task of learning to live without Franco. A sick joke current at the time of his death illustrates the point: the Spanish cabinet is in session when word reaches it that Franco has died. An anxious discussion follows until someone says, 'Yes, but who's going to tell him?'

Further Reading

Brenan, G., *The Spanish Labyrinth*, Cambridge University Press, London, 1950.
Carr, R., *Spain 1808–1939*, Oxford University Press, London, 1966.
Payne, S., *Franco's Spain*, Stanford University Press, Stanford, 1966.
Thomas, H., *The Spanish Civil War*, Penguin, Harmondsworth, 1968.

Questions

1. What long-term factors have precluded the establishment of stable parliamentary government in Spain?
2. Account for the outbreak of the Civil War in 1936.
3. For what reasons did the Nationalists emerge victorious from the Civil War?
4. What can be said for and against Franco's rule in Spain since 1939?

CHAPTER FIFTEEN

THE FOREIGN POLICY OF THE THIRD REICH 1933–39

The Area of Debate

A. J. P. Taylor's book, *The Origins of the Second World War* (1961), aroused fresh argument on why war broke out in 1939. Taylor maintained that Hitler was in many ways an ordinary German statesman who wished to restore Germany's position in Europe. It was the opportunities presented to him by other statesmen, not Hitler's aggression, that allowed him to gain control of Austria and Czechoslovakia in 1938. Hitler, argued Taylor, did not want a general war in 1939 and it was a surprise to him that the Western powers sided with the Poles after Germany attacked Poland in September. Thus to Taylor the war broke out by accident.

The Taylor thesis provoked spirited comment from a number of historians, including Hugh Trevor-Roper, Tim Mason and Christopher Thorne. They emphasise the expansionist aims of Nazism, the heavy rearmament in Germany between 1933 and 1939 and the importance of the Hossbach Conference in 1937 when, in Mason's words, 'the latent expansionism of the Third Reich ceased to be latent and became explicit'.

What were Hitler's Aims?

From his earliest days with the Nazi party, Hitler was always passionately interested in foreign affairs. In *Mein Kampf* much space is devoted to them and it seems probable that the views expressed were sincerely held and reveal Hitler's true intentions. Hitler had three major objectives: (1) he wished to overturn the shameful Versailles Treaty which meant winning Germany's right to rearm and the recovery of the lands lost in 1919—the Saar, Alsace–Lorraine, German colonies and above all the areas lost to Poland; (2) he wished to extend the frontiers of Germany to include all people of German race, especially the Germans of Austria and Czechoslovakia; (3) the first two objectives were in a sense only steps on the road towards the real goal, which was to make the Germans the dominant race in Europe at the expense of the racially 'inferior' peoples in the east.

Hitler, in Norman Rich's phrase, was a 'thoroughgoing Malthusian' and feared the time when Germany could no longer feed her growing population. Therefore Germany must expand for survival as she was surrounded by inferior races who might combine to destroy her. Thus was justified the doctrine of '*lebensraum*', or living-space, at the expense mainly of the Poles and the Russians. 'History proves,' wrote Hitler, 'that the German people owes its existence solely to its determination to fight in the East and to obtain land by military conquest. Land in Europe is only to be obtained at the expense of Russia. The German Reich must therefore follow in the footsteps of the Teutonic Knights in order to guarantee the nation its daily bread through occupation of Russian territory.' Of course, there would be no incorporation of non-Germans in this larger Germany; that had been the error of the British and the Spanish in their Empires. The inferior inhabitants were to be made useful or removed.

The struggle would also be turned against the Jews. As William Carr has shown, Hitler lived in a nightmare world of his own making where sinister Jewish wire-pullers lurked behind every movement of which he disapproved, from Freemasonry to Marxism. He saw the Jew as a member of a lower race that lived like a parasite on higher races, spreading doctrines like democracy or Bolshevism. This made Hitler even more decided on attacking Russia and explains why he assumed that Russia was 'ripe for dissolution' when in fact she was on the road to becoming a great industrial power.

Hitler believed that struggle was inevitable and humanity mere weakness. His ideas can be described as a kind of crude Social Darwinism and had been picked up in the gutters of Vienna; but his foreign policy can only be understood as an expression of his racialist philosophy. The work of Fritz Fischer has revived the old argument about the continuity of German foreign policy from William II to Hitler. Similarities obviously exist if one bears in mind Hitler's first and second objectives, but the differences are as striking as the similarities. The aims of Imperial Germany pale into insignificance compared to the appalling ruthlessness of the Nazis with their emphasis on race and aim to enslave the peoples of Eastern Europe. 'In this very real sense,' as William Carr asserts, 'one can still maintain that Hitler's policy was uniquely different from that of preceding régimes.'

Hitler believed that Imperial Germany had committed a grave error in alienating Britain by chasing colonies and building a large navy. Underestimating Britain's concern for Europe, he believed that he could win her friendship by waiving colonial and naval ambitions, and he hoped also to gain Italian cooperation. France would then be helpless and Germany would be free to strike at Russia in the east. Of course, these ideas did not represent a blue-print for aggression. Hitler was at the mercy of events like other statesmen and had to alter course from time to time as events unfolded, but he was the supreme opportunist who exploited to the full the opportunities that were now to occur.

The Years of Caution (1933–35)

Germany's diplomatic position on Hitler's accession was superficially unpromising. She was disarmed, lacked allies and was still surrounded by members of the French alliance system—Belgium, Czechoslovakia, Poland and France herself. The hostility of Soviet Russia could be assumed on ideological grounds while Mussolini's Italy was concerned about the German threat to Austrian independence.

The Versailles Treaty had limited Germany's armed forces to 100,000 men and, despite von Seeckt's secret rearmament, the army consisted of only 10 divisions when Hitler came to power. It was his first task to resurrect the army but such a policy might lead to French intervention while it was being accomplished. Therefore a cautious and pacific foreign policy was absolutely necessary so that rearmament could continue without hindrance.

This situation explains the surprising moderation which Hitler displayed in the early years. He was always talking peace and his speeches were masterpieces in the art of propaganda. The Germans attended the Disarmament Conference and accepted British proposals for a general reduction in armaments knowing full well that the French would refuse to agree. The French refusal gave Hitler the pretext which he needed to leave the conference on grounds of inequality of treatment and in October Germany also left the League of Nations, a move justified by a plebiscite.

In January 1934, Hitler was able to demonstrate his 'peaceful' intentions by concluding a 10-year non-aggression pact with Poland. This was a complete break with Weimar foreign policy and seemed to have three advantages: (1) it was a breach in the French alliance system; (2) Hitler saw Poland as a potential ally against Russia; (3) the pact was also a temporary expedient to forestall any Polish attack on Germany. What Hitler failed to realise was that the pact would accelerate a rapprochement between France and Russia and in fact these two countries signed a non-aggression pact in February.

Despite this, rearmament was well under way by the end of 1934. In December 1933, the army put forward plans for a peacetime army of 21 divisions by 1937, and a period of service reduced from 12 years to one year so that reserves could be built up. More than 50,000 men were recruited in April 1934, but Hitler was not satisfied and in October another 70,000 men were recruited, bringing the total strength of the army to 240,000; to this figure could be added 200,000 policemen trained as infantrymen. By the end of 1934 Germany had created an airforce of 2,000 planes.

That Germany's diplomatic position was still one of insecure isolation was demonstrated by events in Austria in 1934. Hitler had a special affection for Austria and assumed that with the help of the Austrian Nazis he would soon assimilate his native country into Germany. The Austrian Chancellor Dollfuss countered Nazi violence in 1933 by banning the Austrian Nazis and he solicited the support of France, Britain and Italy. Hitler lost interest, but in July 1934 the Austrian Nazis provoked an uprising which, though it was suppressed, led to the death of Dollfuss. The powers reacted strongly, especially the Italian government which sent four divisions to the Brenner Pass as a gesture of support for Austria. Hitler was forced to repudiate all connection with the conspiracy and realised that the union of Austria and Germany was out of the question until Germany was stronger.

Nevertheless, the year 1935 saw a radical improvement in Germany's diplomatic position. In January a plebiscite was held in the Saar, as agreed at Versailles, and it resulted in a 90 per cent vote in favour of return to Germany. Next came Hitler's first major gamble in international affairs. After the Austrian fiasco he was anxious to introduce conscription and expand the army to 36 divisions. Despite the protest of the army leaders at the pace of the expansion, he announced the re-introduction of conscription in March. Foreign reaction was what he expected. Britain, France and Italy protested at this unilateral breach of the Versailles Treaty but took no action to prevent it. True, European opinion seemed to harden against Hitler. In April the foreign secretaries of Britain, France and Italy met at Stresa, condemned the German action, reaffirmed their loyalty to the Locarno treaties and repeated their declaration on the need for Austrian independence. To this Stresa 'front' was added in May a pact between France and Russia pledging mutual assistance against unprovoked aggression. Russia also concluded a similar pact with Czechoslovakia, promising support against aggression on condition that France honoured her pledges first. Hitler was not, however, overawed by these developments. He intuitively perceived that this apparent unity of opinion against him was flimsy. He realised the mutual suspicion between Russia and the Western powers, the longing of the democracies for peace, and the feelings of sympathy that existed in Britain over the German position. The unity, he felt, would not last long and he was soon proved correct in his analysis.

In June came a major German success when an Anglo–German naval agreement was signed which limited German tonnage to 35 per cent of that of Britain and her Commonwealth. The limitation was no hardship for Germany because it would take her some time to reach the 35 per cent ceiling anyway. The treaty itself is evidence that a rapprochement with Britain was one of Hitler's long-term aims and only in 1937 did he conclude that a full alliance with her could not be secured.

Britain's failure to consult her partners, France and Italy, about the naval agreement gave a disastrous impression of bad faith and gravely sabotaged the Stresa Front. It was, writes Norman Rich, 'a horrendous diplomatic blunder for in effect it recognised Germany's right to rearm and consequently its right to break international treaties forbidding such rearmament'. Worse was to follow, for the Stresa Front collapsed completely in the autumn when Britain and France imposed sanctions on Italy following her attack on Abyssinia. The Western democracies succeeded in getting the worst of both worlds; their imposition of sanctions alienated Italy but their failure to take any really effective action against Mussolini dealt their prestige, and that of the League of Nations, a fatal blow. Hitler noted the passivity of the Western powers and all he was required to do to strengthen Germany's diplomatic position was to remain neutral in the dispute. Attention was drawn away from Europe to African affairs, and the Italians, offended by Britain and France, began to draw nearer to Germany. The fragile unity was shattered and the way lay open for further German advances.

New Opportunities (1936–37)

At the beginning of 1936 Hitler could survey the European scene with great satisfaction. The Stresa Front had collapsed and in France a weak caretaker government was in office. Convinced that no state would oppose him, Hitler felt that the time was ripe for the remilitarisation of the Rhineland, especially as enthusiasm for the Nazi régime was on the decline in Germany. Therefore in February a plan was drawn up for contingents of the German army to reoccupy the Rhineland with orders to make a fighting withdrawal if the French intervened. Hitler used the ratification of the Franco–Soviet agreement by the French Chamber of Deputies in late February as a pretext for his troops to enter the Rhineland in March, asserting that the pact was incompatible with the Locarno agreements. As usual, he played on his opponents' desire for peace by immediately offering a non-aggression pact to Belgium and France.

The move was a huge gamble for France and Poland could launch 90 divisions against Germany, as his generals pointed out; yet the gamble succeeded. The British government under Baldwin was more concerned at checking any action that the French might take than in condemning this latest German breach of the Versailles Settlement. In *The Times*, a leader article saw the crisis as 'A chance to rebuild'. Lord Lothian expressed the British view when he commented, 'After all they are only going into their own back garden.' The French government was most reluctant to act on its own and in any case was informed by the defeatist French military that an offensive operation against the German troops in the Rhineland was impossible. 'The Rhineland crisis,' says Donald Watt, 'showed weakness to be embedded in the national will of France.' By her failure to act, she virtually admitted that she was no longer willing to defend the security system which she had been at pains to build since 1918. Sunk deep in a Maginot mentality, French governments from this point on tended more and more to follow British policies.

The League of Nations had achieved much in the 1920s, but was shaken already by the Japanese invasion of Manchuria in 1931 and the Italian aggression in Africa in 1935. It now was further undermined by Hitler's illegal action. The smaller powers lost faith in the League and they sought security either in neutrality or by attempting to court Germany. Belgium, for example, though still a member of the League of Nations, refused any longer to be a guarantor of the Locarno Treaties. Most significant of all, the remilitarisation of the Rhineland opened the way for all Hitler's later outrages. In his prophecy that the powers would not move against him, he was proved right and his generals were proved wrong. His confidence increased greatly and he felt able to tell the German people, 'I go with the assurance of a sleepwalker on the path Providence dictates.' For the next two years he would still need to exercise caution while Germany constructed her Rhineland defences. Then in the event of another conflict German forces would be poised directly on the French border, while conversely the French would be deprived of their former advantage of being able to strike at Germany through a demilitarised zone which was also Germany's industrial heartland.

The year 1936 continued to bring success to the Germans. In July an Austro–German agreement was signed. The German government recognised Austria's sovereignty but in return Austria promised to maintain a foreign policy based on the principle that she was a German state and also to give Austrian Nazis a share of political responsibility. In the next year and a half the Germans used the agreement as a lever by which pressure could be applied on the Austrian government. In August, the Nazis won considerable prestige by the way in which they organised the Olympic Games held in Berlin. In November, Ribbentrop, who, like Mussolini, had a mania for pacts signed the Anti-Comintern Pact with Japan in which the partners pledged themselves to defeat the Communist world-conspiracy. Italy joined the pact in the following year.

The most important German move after the Rhineland escapade in 1936 was the promise to help General Franco when the Spanish Civil War broke out in July. Germany stood to gain in several directions from such action. In the next three years she sent military supplies and men including the famous Condor Air Legion, thus gaining useful experience in the training of men and the value of equipment such as tanks in battle conditions. Intervention in the war also gave Germany access to Spanish mineral resources and would counter the threat of a Communist success in Spain. Franco's victory would be a 'Fascist' victory and would give France another frontier to defend in time of war. As the Italians sent large numbers of troops, they were more embroiled in the Spanish Civil War than the Germans and therefore were less likely to oppose German aims in Austria. At the same time the two 'fascist' powers were now clearly on the same side and in November Mussolini referred to their two countries as the 'axis' powers. Hitler hoped that Germany and Italy would form such a powerful front that Britain would be forced to come to terms with the dictators. With this end in view, he sent Ribbentrop to Britain as ambassador in August. 'Arrogant, vain, humourless and spiteful, Ribbentrop was one of the worst choices Hitler ever made for high office,' writes Alan Bullock. It is hardly surprising that the British government did not respond to his overtures for mutual support against Communism.

Gathering Momentum (1937–39)

The adoption of the Four-Year Plan in 1936 is highly significant as a mark of Hitler's determination to prepare Germany for war. It was appropriate that his choice as supervisor of the plan was Göring, who was regarded as the party's strong man. The plan itself fell short of its objectives. There was no total mobilisation of the economy and inefficient small units of production were not eliminated, but this does not invalidate the thesis that Hitler saw autarchy as assisting the rapid expansion of the armed forces for short campaigns with limited objectives. When Schacht protested that arms cuts were necessary Hitler and Göring brushed his advice aside. When they faced opposition from the steel bosses, the Nazi leaders set up a state-owned steel corporation, later known as the Hermann Göring Works.

In November 1937, the military implications of the new policy were spelt out by Hitler at the Hossbach Conference. Five others were present besides Hitler himself and Colonel Hossbach, whose minutes provide us with our information. They were the War Minister, von Blomberg, the Commander-in-Chief of the army, von Fritsch, the Commander-in-Chief of the navy, Raedar, the air force chief, Göring, and the Foreign Minister, Neurath. Hitler declared that Germany needed 'living-space' but would have to reckon with the opposition of two 'hate-inspired antagonists', Britain and France. Germany's military superiority would last until 1943–45 after which her enemies would begin to catch her up and therefore he was resolved to solve Germany's problem by that period at the latest. If France was torn by internal strife or clashed with Italy in the Mediterranean, the opportunity must be taken to overrun Czechoslovakia and Austria. Hitler did not believe that the Western powers would oppose this.

The significance of the meeting, as we have seen, has caused controversy among historians. Its importance may be gauged by the fact that Hitler wished it to be regarded as his last will and testament in the event of his death. 'In its explicitness and its anti-Western rather than anti-Bolshevik framework here was a significant moment in the development of Nazi expansionism,' writes Christopher Thorne. It is no accident that those who protested at Hitler's plans—Neurath, Blomberg and Fritsch—were soon dismissed and replaced by more pliable servants. Strategic plans for war, formerly defensive in character, now aimed at a pre-emptive strike at Czechoslovakia to forestall any effective action by that power in the event of a war in the west. Thus the harangue of November 1937, in the words of E. M. Robertson, marked 'a real turning point in Hitler's pre-war policy'.

With the Rhineland fortified, Hitler felt that he could adopt a more violent foreign policy and, as he said at the conference, he wished to strike down his opponents before Germany's military advantage disappeared. But other factors probably played a large part in his thinking. The international situation was now favourable as closer relations with Italy developed, as France appeared to drift towards civil war, and as the purges in the Red Army appeared to make Russia a negligible factor. The conference also reveals Hitler's disillusionment with Britain as hopes of an alliance with her faded. His own hypochondria is important; he was always preoccupied with his own mortality and wished to accelerate events while he still enjoyed good health. Finally, he was concerned that the German people appeared to be more interested in social and economic matters and what interest they had in foreign affairs was waning. Committed to rearmament, Hitler knew that he could not satisfy the hopes of the people for higher living standards. Therefore the only way in which unity could be preserved and the weakening of the régime prevented was by an active foreign policy. As Mason has shown, 'the Third Reich had either to set itself new tasks by expanding or ... cease from being totalitarian'.

Appeasement

One of the reasons for the Nazi commitment to a more violent foreign policy in

1937 was the assumption of British hostility. It is therefore most ironic that in May of that year the statesman most associated with appeasement of Hitler, Neville Chamberlain, became Prime Minister, replacing the indolent Baldwin who had evinced little interest in foreign affairs. 'Appeasement' is still a term of abuse, signifying to many people a policy born of cowardice and stupidity. The writer deplores such a facile view while recognising that Chamberlain did possess faults. He was certainly arrogant. Comparing him to Baldwin, Taylor says of Chamberlain that he was 'a harder, more practical man, impatient with the drift in foreign affairs and confident that he could stop it'. He was also intolerant of opposition and refused to listen to the advice of colleagues like Eden who advised caution in his attempts to deal with Hitler. He became blinded to reality by regarding appeasement of Hitler as a mission. He therefore ignored unpalatable facts like the sufferings of the Czechs. So desirous was he of peace that he convinced himself that Hitler could be trusted and as a result the Munich settlement, in Christopher Thorne's phrase, became 'a study in self-delusion'. Finally it may be said that Conservatives like Chamberlain had a blind spot about Soviet Russia, whose power they underrated and whose ideology they detested. Chamberlain wrote in his diary in March 1939, 'I must confess to the most profound mistrust of Russia. I have no belief whatever in her ability to maintain an effective offensive, even if she wanted to.'

Yet what moved the British Prime Minister was a horror of war and the feeling that in any future conflict the devastation would be greater than ever before. The potential of the bomber had been dramatically demonstrated at Guernica in the Spanish Civil War. War, the ultimate evil, must therefore be avoided at all costs by the peaceful elimination of German grievances. 'To this enterprise,' writes F. N. Northedge, 'Chamberlain brought great assets and vices which were the reverse of the assets. He was courageous, energetic, dedicated, austere. No one could doubt that his hatred of war was deeply felt or that he would exert himself to the utmost to avert it. His mind was lucid, logical, tenacious, capable of seeing the drift of an argument or the implication of a proposal with lightning speed.'

Chamberlain then was a humane individual; he was also following a rational policy. Britain in the 1930s lacked the power to rule her global Empire, which in the Far East was threatened by Japan. Only by concessions in Europe which would secure peace could the reality of British weakness be hidden. With most German governments such a policy could have borne fruit but the novel extremism of the Nazi state made its foreign policy incompatible with that of Britain's. Thus the ultimate failure of Chamberlain's policies was inevitable but it is most doubtful whether any British government could for long have remained at peace with the Third Reich. Perhaps Chamberlain should have realised how unscrupulous Hitler was earlier than he did but the German leader, who possessed great charm and magnetism when he wished, fooled many intelligent people in his time.

The *Anschluss*

Perhaps the most un-Wilsonian article in the Versailles Settlement was that forbidding the union of Austrian Germans with Germany. All shades of political opinion in Austria resented the clause and the difficult post-war years only aggravated this feeling. Only after Hitler came to power did Pan-German sentiment lose ground. The Austrian government should at this point have combined with the Socialists to crush the Austrian Nazis but in fact one of the last acts of Dollfuss was to crush the Socialists in the civil war of February 1934, a policy that could only strengthen the Austrian Nazi position. After the Austro–German agreement of 1936, Austrian Nazis like Seyss-Inquart entered the government, thus further undermining its real independence.

At the same time, a decline was taking place in Austria's external protection. In the abortive Nazi coup of 1934, Mussolini had stood firmly behind Austria; by 1937 Italy and Germany were drawing together and it was clear to the Nazis after Mussolini's visit to Germany in September that the Italian leader would not again oppose German aims in Austria. In Britain and France feeling was widespread that Germany could not be prevented from swallowing Austria in the near future. In November, Lord Halifax visited Germany as Chamberlain's emissary and told the Nazis that the British government desired a peaceful correction of German grievances; specific mention was made of Austria as well as Czechoslovakia and Danzig. Such well-intentioned naivety was of course an invitation to Hitler to indulge in diplomatic blackmail.

It now appeared to the German leader that the passage of time would bring Austria into Germany and he told Göring in September 1937 that Germany should avoid any explosion of the Austrian problem in the foreseeable future, but should continue to seek an evolutionary solution. That he did not rule out a swift stroke if the opportunity occurred was then made clear at the Hossbach conference in November and by early 1938 both Göring and Ribbentrop were urging him to seek an early solution to the Austrian problem.

An opportunity now arose for Hitler that sprang directly from the subversive activities of the Austrian Nazis. In January 1938, Austrian police raided Nazi headquarters in Vienna and discovered plans for an uprising the repression of which would provide the pretext for intervention by the German army. Realising the threat to his country's independence, the Austrian Chancellor Schuschnigg decided to seek a meeting with Hitler in an attempt to check the unrest and gain time until the international situation improved in Austria's favour. When he visited Hitler at Berchtesgaden on February 12, he received a rude awakening. Displaying himself as the gangster he was, Hitler subjected the Chancellor to a torrent of abuse in which he condemned the high treason of Austrian history. Before he left, Schuschnigg was forced to sign an agreement which provided for the alignment of the foreign policies of Austria and Germany, complete freedom for the Nazis in Austria and the appointment of Seyss-Inquart as Minister of the Interior and another Nazi, Glaise-Horstenau, as War Minister.

Schuschnigg's behaviour on his return home was initially acquiescent. He did nothing to mobilise foreign support for Austria in case such action might enrage Hitler—'a madman with a mission', as Schuschnigg described him. He also complied with the terms of the agreement, bringing Seyss-Inquart into the cabinet as Minister of the Interior with authority over the police. Hitler for his part believed that more concessions could be wrung out of the Austrian government and still wished to follow an evolutionary absorption of Austria.

Then in March Schuschnigg decided belatedly on an act of defiance with an intensity born of despair. Realising that time would mean more Nazi control, he called on his countrymen on March 9 to vote on the following Sunday for 'a free and German, independent and social Christian and united Austria'. This plebiscite was an attempt to destroy Hitler's argument that the majority of the Austrian people wanted union with Germany. Hitler was taken by surprise and was furious at Schuschnigg's temerity especially as the Chancellor's announcement was greeted with enthusiasm in Austria. It seemed likely that the plebiscite would result in a vote of confidence for Schuschnigg and Hitler was determined to prevent it. The German army was ordered to prepare an improvised invasion of Austria and when Austrian Nazis managed to force Schuschnigg into resigning, Hitler acted. On March 12, German troops moved into Austria to be greeted with applause. Hitler decided that instead of a union of states under common leadership, Austria would be a province of the Third Reich.

The European powers acquiesced in the aggression. France was without a government during this vital period while Chamberlain was more interested in dealing with future questions. The British government did protest at the use of force against an independent state but Neville Henderson, the British ambassador to Germany, took away any impact that this might have had by agreeing that Schuschnigg had acted with precipitate folly. Hitler's main anxiety was over the possibility of Italian action. He need not have worried; Mussolini had not forgotten the Western disapproval of his Abyssinian adventure and refused to contemplate the idea of any cooperation with the Western powers against Hitler. Hitler's gratitude to Mussolini for his non-intervention was genuine and long-lasting.

As a result of the *Anschluss*, the balance of power in south-eastern Europe moved sharply in Germany's favour. Control of Austria gave the Germans domination of the Balkans and the strategic position of Czechoslovakia became grave, for Germany could now threaten her from three directions. Germany also gained 100,000 men for her armed forces and useful economic resources, mainly in steel capacity, iron ore mines and Austria's foreign exchange reserves. Hitler was elated by the ease of his victory and turned next to the Czechs.

Munich

Of the new states created after the First World War, Czechoslovakia alone had been successful. The country possessed an advanced economy and the constitution, which gave universal suffrage, created a genuine parliamentary régime in which the rights of the minority nationalities were safeguarded. The new republic was fortunate in its presidents Thomas Masaryk and, from 1935, Eduard Beneš.

On the other hand, the racial problems of the new state remained serious. The rural Slovaks wished for more autonomy within Czechoslovakia and their relations with the urban Czechs were uneasy. More vociferous than the Slovaks were the 3 million Sudeten Germans who continually complained of injustices inflicted on them by the Czechs. In 1933, Konrad Henlein founded the Sudeten German Party which came to be a fifth column; it was in all essentials a Nazi party and began to demand more independence for Germans as a prelude to incorporation into the Third Reich. Hitler encouraged the activities of the Sudeten German party, subsidising its efforts at the rate of 15,000 marks a month. He had an intense hatred of the Czechs, a legacy of his Vienna days when Czech rivalry seemed to threaten German dominance in the Habsburg Empire. Post-war Czechoslovakia was doubly obnoxious to Hitler because it was democratic and a part of the Versailles Treaty. It was also the key to Eastern Europe and must be destroyed.

The *Anschluss* inflamed the situation. The Czech government felt that its defences were now outflanked and that it would be more susceptible to economic pressure. For his part Henlein felt bold enough to spell out his demands at Karlsbad in April 1938. He still demanded autonomy rather than complete independence but he wanted a revision of Czech foreign policy and freedom for the Sudeten Germans to adhere to German ideology. He was under orders from Hitler to step up his demands periodically so that no negotiated settlement could be arrived at with the Czech government.

The German menace was underrated by Beneš. He felt that if Czechoslovakia were threatened, the Western powers in their own interests would be bound to stand by her. 'As a supposition,' remarks Christopher Thorne, 'it was entirely reasonable and entirely erroneous.' To be sure, Czechoslovakia seemed secure; all parties had a high regard for her army and fortifications while France was pledged to assist her if she were attacked.

Yet Czech security was illusory. In France, Daladier was now Premier and Bonnet was Foreign Secretary. Both were appeasers who felt that Czechoslovakia could not be saved and they were glad to see the British take the initiative in the events that were now to unfold. Chamberlain's government was eager to thrust Beneš towards agreement with the Sudeten Germans as part of a comprehensive programme of appeasement, after which a new Concert of Europe of the four great powers—Britain, Germany, Italy and France—could be re-established. It was widely felt in British government circles that in the interests of European peace the Czechs must be coerced or abandoned. As for Russia, her treaty of 1935 bound her to help Czechoslovakia only if France acted first and in any case the Polish and Rumanian governments made it clear that they would refuse the necessary passage to Russian troops through their countries. The Soviet government did wish to help Czechoslovakia but when Litvinov, the Commissar for Foreign Affairs, approached the Western powers on the question, he found them most unresponsive. Chamberlain still hoped to draw Mussolini away from Hitler rather than cooperate with a Communist régime whose army was of doubtful value after the recent purges. The British and the French held talks in April and agreed to give strong advice to Beneš to make all necessary concessions to the Sudeten Germans. At the same time, the German government was given private assurance that it would with a little patience gain all that it desired in the Czech question.

In May came an unexpected rebuff for Hitler. Two Sudeten Germans were shot by the Czech police and as rumours spread of German troop movements, the Czechs mobilised. Both Western powers warned Germany against making any aggressive move against Czechoslovakia which infuriated Hitler as in fact no German troop movements had taken place and the foreign press crowed over what they regarded as a German defeat. Now Hitler's desire to crush the Czechs became something of a personal vendetta. At the end of May he confirmed his 'unalterable intention to smash Czechoslovakia by military force in the near future'. Operation Green, which provided for the seizure of Bohemia and Moravia, had already been worked out in detail. It was now envisaged that it would take place in September and 12 German divisions were stationed on the Czech frontier.

During the summer, negotiations between the Czech government and the Sudeten German party dragged on without result. This impasse, together with the May scare, made Chamberlain all the more anxious to see a speedy agreement reached. He sent Lord Runciman as mediator in the dispute, a high-handed move which shocked the Czechs. Despite favouring the Sudeten German, Runciman was unable to solve the deadlock, even though Beneš made concessions in August that met all the Karlsbad demands. With Hitler preparing Operation Green and the Hungarian and Polish governments claiming Slovakia and Teschen respectively, the threat to Czechoslovakia was mounting. In early September the crisis seemed near breaking point. Hitler ordered Henlein to break off negotiations with the Czech government and on September 12 made an inflammatory speech at Nuremberg in which he referred to the Sudeten Germans as 'neither defenceless nor deserted'. This was a direct incitement to the Sudeten Germans to instigate riots which led to a proclamation of martial law by the Czechs and Henlein's flight to Germany, where he now openly proclaimed the desire of his people to return to the Reich.

The crisis impelled Neville Chamberlain to make the dramatic move of offering to fly to Germany to see Hitler. When the two men met at Berchtesgaden, Hitler insisted that the Sudeten Germans must be incorporated into the Reich but promised to stay his hand until Chamberlain, who agreed in principle to the move, had consulted his colleagues and the French. The British premier received the impression that Hitler 'was a man who could be relied on when he had given his word'. By September 21 the Western powers had 'persuaded' Beneš to promise the cession to Germany of those areas of Czechoslovakia with more than 50 per cent Germans.

Chamberlain then met Hitler again at Godesberg on September 22 and was stunned to learn that the German leader was unwilling to accept the Czech concessions on the pretext that Czech brutality made an immediate German invasion necessary. At their previous meeting it had been understood that any German occupation would only take place after due negotiations with the Czechs and other interested powers. Hitler demanded that the problem must be settled by October 1. War was now near, for Hitler wanted a military triumph and he kept the tension screwed up by a speech on September 26 full of burning invective against Beneš. However, on September 28 he agreed to accept a conference on the matter. On the previous day an armoured division had passed through Berlin before silent crowds and this apathy displayed by the German public, combined with Italian representations, probably made Hitler change his mind. In any case, it was apparent that he would make considerable gains at any conference.

In Britain, Chamberlain had broadcast to the nation on September 27 and referred to the Czech crisis as 'a quarrel in a far away country between people of whom we know nothing'. Nevertheless, the forces were put on a war footing. The news that Hitler had agreed to a conference reached the Prime Minister as he was speaking to the Commons. His announcement of Hitler's concession made virtually the whole House of Commons cheer in hysterical relief.

The conference, to which the Czechs and the Russians were not invited, was duly held at Munich between Germany, Britain, Italy and France. Agreement was reached by September 30. The Sudetenland was to be occupied by the Germans by October 10 up to a line determined by an international commission. After Polish and Hungarian claims were settled, the four powers would guarantee the remainder of the Czech state. Before he left, Chamberlain persuaded Hitler to sign a declaration affirming the intention of Britain and Germany never to go to war with each other again and on his arrival home he told an enthusiastic crowd, 'I believe it is peace for our time'.

The consequences of Munich were immense. Czechoslovakia lost Teschen to Poland and South Ruthenia to Hungary. Germany gained virtually all the Czech fortifications and territory, which included 800,000 Czechs. Czechoslovakia lost 11,000 square miles of territory and 70 per cent of her iron and steel capacity, including the Skoda arms factory at Pilsen. She was now helpless and her army of 35 divisions was removed from the scales of European power, which moved decisively in Germany's favour.

The Western capitulation to Hitler had serious consequences in other ways. The Soviet government now believed that France and Britain would always be weak and unreliable and it began to entertain seriously the idea of doing a deal with Germany. As Hildebrand says, 'the foundations of the Nazi–Soviet Pact of the 23rd of August, 1939, were laid in Munich'. Western inactivity was also noted by the Japanese government and it was soon to announce plans for a New Order in East Asia. Hitler's prestige rose to new heights in Germany though he was angry at being robbed of his military triumph. 'That fellow Chamberlain has spoiled my entry into Prague,' he muttered. However, he now felt sure that the democracies would never oppose him and aimed to absorb the rest of Czechoslovakia in the near future. Finally, Hitler's success at Munich disheartened the German opposition to his rule led by Beck, Halder and Canaris.

The Final Disillusionment

Munich had demonstrated how stubbornly Chamberlain was prepared to pursue his mission of peace but his faith in Hitler was soon to be shattered. Germany repeatedly procrastinated over signing the guarantee of the remainder of the Czech state. Chamberlain and Halifax hoped to moderate Hitler by persuading Mussolini to counsel caution. With this end in view, they visited Rome in January 1939 but they merely won Mussolini's contempt and further inclined him towards a full military alliance with Germany.

Meanwhile the rump state of Czechoslovakia found that its real freedom of action was negligible. The Slovaks were now demanding more autonomy and in March their leaders Tiso and Durcansky went to Hitler for help in the matter. Seeing a further opportunity for undermining the Czech state, Hitler bullied the Slovak leaders into drawing up a draft declaration of independence and an appeal for German help. With the situation deteriorating, the aged President Hacha of Czechoslovakia visited Hitler on March 15 to see what could be preserved. He was so violently upbraided by Hitler that he fainted. When he recovered he was made to sign an agreement putting Czechoslovakia in Hitler's hands to preserve order. German troops now moved into Bohemia and Moravia while Hungarian troops moved into Ruthenia. On March 16 Tiso requested Germany to assume a protectorate over Slovakia. Again Hitler was able to claim to have acted within the bounds of legality as he merely 'complied' with the requests of the Czechs and Slovaks. There was no question of Western intervention despite the guarantees made at Munich. Yet Hitler's latest act had at last aroused not only the British government but the Commons and the public as well.

That the dictators would only understand force seemed fully proved by two further aggressions. In late March, Germany seized the Lithuanian port of Memel and Hitler visited it on the battleship *Deutschland*; it was to be his last bloodless territorial gain. The recent German successes had incensed Mussolini, who remarked querulously that 'every time Hitler occupies a country he sends me a message.' In the words of Christopher Thorne, 'it remained only for jackal to ape its master'. Mussolini, eager to win back the approval of the Italian public by a new success, sent troops into Albania in April on the pretext of restoring order.

Danzig and War

The next German target was only too clearly Poland. The loss to Poland of

Danzig, the Polish Corridor and part of Silesia was more resented by Germans than any other part of the Versailles Treaty. Ribbentrop raised the Danzig and Polish Corridor questions in October 1938. As the Poles refused to concede anything, his tone, at first friendly, became threatening and in early 1939 tension between the two countries increased. Therefore in April the British proposed an unconditional defence pact with Poland followed by similar pledges to Rumania and Greece. Chamberlain's promise to Poland was striking in that for the first time Britain was guaranteeing a state in Eastern Europe. Hitler was enraged but still regarded the British guarantee as bluff, and indeed the irony of the situation was considerable for the British were guaranteeing the country they were least able to help effectively. Hitler now allowed the tension to relax so that the British and the French might scale down their obligations to Poland.

What was really required for an effective guarantee of Poland was alliance with Soviet Russia, which was now courted by both sides. Negotiations between the Western powers and Russia began in April but were carried on with a lack of sincerity by both parties. Stalin suspected the West of trying to engineer a Russo–German war and kept alive the possibility of an agreement with Hitler. The Western powers wanted a superficial rather than a real agreement with Russia merely to impress Hitler, as they still disliked the whole concept of a Communist alliance. Thus it was that the British showed no sense of urgency in the negotiations, even sending a mission to Russia by sea in August. The Russian Foreign Minister now was Molotov, who wanted a firm British commitment or nothing. Negotiations finally broke down on August 21 over the Polish refusal to allow the Red Army into Poland in the event of a German attack. The Polish hatred of Russia was intense. 'With the Germans we risk losing our liberty,' said Beck, the Polish Foreign Minister, 'With the Russians we lose our souls.' Learning the wrong lesson from the mistakes of the Czechs, he was resolved to refuse any concessions to either Germany or Russia.

Faced with Polish intransigence, Hitler decided in April to smash Poland in the near future and Operation White, the plan for the invasion of Poland, was prepared to take effect on September 1. His confidence grew in May with the conclusion of a firm alliance with Italy, the Pact of Steel. Based on the German draft, the pact pledged the two nations to support each other if one 'became involved in hostilities with another Power or Powers'. It was in effect an offensive alliance though Ribbentrop assured the nervous Italians that there would be no war for four or five years. In fact, the day after the pact was signed Hitler harangued his generals on the need to smash Poland at the first suitable opportunity. By August it was clear to Mussolini and Ciano how far they have been duped by the Germans. Ciano wrote in his diary of a meeting with Ribbentrop at which the German Foreign Secretary declared that even the cession by Poland of Danzig and the Polish Corridor would not suffice. '"We want war," he said gazing at me with his cold metallic eyes.'

War was made virtually certain by an event that astonished the world—the conclusion of the Nazi–Soviet Pact in August. The West had assumed that such a pact was impossible in view of Hitler's long-standing hatred of Bolshevism. 'The factor they overlooked,' explains Alan Bullock, 'was Hitler's utter lack of scruple and his skill as a power politician.' He did not relinquish his longer-term aim of attacking Russia but he saw that a temporary alliance would assist in the destruction of Poland. The two countries had begun to move closer together after Munich, on Soviet initiative, and by May 1939 serious negotiations were under way. By

August the Russians were offering a non-aggression pact though they wished for a careful discussion of details first. This did not suit the Germans who, in view of the September deadline for their invasion of Poland, were in a fever of impatience to settle the matter fully. Ribbentrop persuaded Hitler on August 20 to send a telegram to Stalin requesting permission for the German Foreign Secretary to go to Russia to sign the pact. The Russians agreed and the pact was signed on August 23. Hitler's need for a rapid conclusion of the pact and his fear that Russia might come to an agreement with the West enabled Stalin to drive a hard bargain. Finland, Estonia, Latvia and Eastern Poland were to be in the Russian sphere of influence while Lithuania and Western and Central Poland would be in the German sphere of influence.

Hitler declared that the pact was his master-stroke which would enable him to eliminate Poland without the intervention of the Western powers who would now, he assumed, realise that the Polish position was beyond help. The Russians, in fact, were gambling on the opposite and Stalin warned Ribbentrop that 'Britain would wage war craftily and stubbornly'. The Russian leader hoped that the pact would avoid the old Soviet nightmare—a combined European attack on Russia. Thus Ulam believes that 'the agreement and the steps leading to it represent the quintessence of Stalin's diplomacy'. Some historians, however, condemn the Russian move as appeasement of Hitler and point to the way it made war inevitable. 'Stalin gave the green light to aggression in 1939,' asserts Snell, who argues that the pact not only sealed Poland's fate but brought nearer a German attack on Russia.

Hitler's determination to attack Poland was now firm and August 26 was the date fixed for the invasion. Two disappointments in fact made him delay for a few days. Against his expectations, the British ratified the Anglo–Polish treaty and Neville Chamberlain reiterated his determination to stand by the Poles. Then the Italians, realising the implications of the Nazi–Soviet Pact, told Hitler that they could only support Germany in a general war if they received huge stocks of war materials. Hitler's nerve was shaken but not broken; he postponed the attack until September 1 in a final attempt to undermine British support for Poland by offering supposedly more moderate terms to the Poles. This guile failed to work and on September 1 German troops invaded Poland on the pretext of Polish frontier violations which were in fact rigged by the Nazis themselves. The French and British governments after some hesitation demanded the evacuation of Polish territory. As no Germany reply was received, the two Western powers declared war on September 3. It is significant that there were no scenes of enthusiasm in Berlin or elsewhere like those of twenty-five years before.

Germany was quite well prepared for war by the autumn of 1939. The peacetime strength of the army had reached 52 divisions, which on general mobilisation could be expanded to 103 divisions. She now possessed a considerable navy and 3,000 aircraft. After Hitler's diplomatic successes, the morale of the German armed forces was now high. Yet Hitler would have been wiser to slow down his triumphal progress. By 1938 he had transformed Germany's international position and could have consolidated his gains. Instead he pressed on and drove other European powers into a reluctant coalition against him. It was this inability to stop that was to destroy him but, as Alan Bullock says, he was 'already on the way to that assumption of his own infallibility which marked the deterioration of his judgment'.

Further Reading

Bullock, A., *Hitler: A Study in Tyranny*, Penguin, London, 1969.
Carr, W., *Arms, Autarky and Aggression: A Study in German Foreign Policy 1933–1939*, Edward Arnold, London, 1972.
Rich, N., *Hitler's War Aims*, Andre Deutsch, London, 1973.
Robertson, E. M. (ed.), *The Origins of the Second World War*, Macmillan, London, 1971.
Taylor, A. J. P., *The Origins of the Second World War*, Penguin, Harmondsworth, 1963.
Thorne, C., *The Approach to War 1938–1939*, Macmillan, London, 1967.

Questions

1. What were the chief aims of Hitler's foreign policy?
2. To what extent and for what reasons did Hitler accelerate the tempo of his foreign policy in 1937?
3. What can be said for and against Appeasement?
4. Why did the Second World War break out in 1939?

CHAPTER SIXTEEN

THE ORDEAL OF TOTAL WAR 1939–45

The Early German Victories (1939–40)

On the outbreak of war Germany was stronger than any other belligerent power, for as A. S. Milward has pointed out, 'no nation had ever previously spent so vast a sum in peacetime on preparation for war'. Hitler could mobilise approximately 5 million men though he did not enjoy numerical superiority. Against his 105 divisions, the French could muster 94, the Poles 40 and the British 4. Germany's advantage lay in her more modern equipment, particularly the 6 armoured (panzer) division in which were incorporated most of her 3,200 tanks. The French and the British had the same numerical strength but their tanks were inferior to those of Germany.

The two sides had similar numbers of planes but the German Luftwaffe was organised to support advancing ground forces and its light bombers and fighters were of high quality. The British fighters—the Spitfire and the Hurricane—were good but their bombers lacked sufficient range while the French airforce in general was out of date. Only on the sea did the Western powers enjoy real superiority over Germany.

Germany's opponents made a cardinal error in assuming that the new war would resemble the First World War in that the Germans could be ground down by a war of attrition. They were soon to see the error of this assumption. In ten days the German armies had reached Warsaw after the Luftwaffe had prepared the way by destroying the Polish air force and disrupting communications. The fate of the Poles was sealed when on September 17 the Russian armies struck from the east, and by the end of the month all Poland had been overrun. Giving another sign that peace with Britain was a long-held desire, Hitler called on the Western powers to accept the situation and come to terms but his peace offer was ignored.

There now occurred a period of inactivity on the Western front which has won the contemptuous description of the 'phony war'. Instead of launching an offensive, the Western powers stood on the defensive behind the fortifications of the Maginot Line and Hitler was given time to shift his troops from the east to the western front, which had previously been lightly fortified. He had envisaged a German offensive in the west in November but it was to be rescheduled 29 times, a vivid example of Hitler's incapacity for making a firm decision.

The centre of interest now shifted east to the Baltic. In November, Russia attacked Finland and by March 1940 had imposed harsh terms on the Finns who had to cede Karelia, territory to the south and west of Lake Ladoga, and islands in the Gulf of Finland; yet the Finns fought with courage and inflicted heavy casualties on the Russian troops, an achievement which made Hitler even more disdainful of Russian fighting capacity.

Meanwhile, Germany and her opponents had been attempting to persuade the Scandinavian states to take a more active interest in the war but they stuck resolutely to neutrality. The British First Lord of the Admiralty, Winston Churchill, wanted the Norwegian coast mined to prevent supplies of iron ore going to Germany. By the time the Cabinet approved the plan it was too late. Germany derived 51 per cent of her iron ore from Sweden and Norway, and in April 1940 German troops invaded Denmark and Norway to safeguard these supplies. Again Hitler refused to listen to the objections of his generals, who opposed the dispersion of German troops. Denmark was forced to surrender within hours but the Norwegians resisted with Allied help. The British took Narvik in June and sunk three German cruisers and 10 destroyers but the larger objective—the interruption of supplies of iron ore to Germany—was not gained. With Hitler's offensive in the west in June, the British had to abandon Narvik and Norway fell under Nazi control.

By May, Germany had massed 134 divisions on the western front against 94 French and 10 British divisions, to which were added 22 Belgian and 8 Dutch divisions when the Low Countries were invaded. The German advantages in armour and planes were to prove decisive. Franco–British relations were far from harmonious, with continual French demands for more British troops and planes in France. On May 10, the German offensive in the west began with a drive into the Netherlands and the Dutch surrendered in five days after the bombing of Rotterdam had killed 900 civilians. German troops also moved into Belgium and in a surprise move German armour crossed the Meuse to strike through the Ardennes. By May 20 Guderian's mechanised columns had smashed through the French lines at Sedan and reached the Channel. The Allied armies were now in chaos and in June the British government had to authorise its Commanding General Gort to evacuate his troops from Dunkirk. In an operation lasting eight days, 200,000 British and 130,000 French soldiers were rescued from the Dunkirk beaches by a motley collection of naval craft. Hitler neglected an opportunity to send in German tanks to finish off the Allied troops because he assumed that the task could be left to the Luftwaffe. As Gordon Wright has noted, his error 'enabled a salvage operation of inestimable military and psychological importance to be carried out'. After it a new mood of national unity prevailed in Britain.

But nothing could save France. On June 16, the French government, now under Marshal Pétain, asked Germany for armistice terms which were signed a week later at Compiègne in the same railway car used for the German capitulation in November 1918. Hitler literally danced for joy. His terms were deliberately moderate for he hoped to keep a French government nominally in control of much of France. Therefore the Germans only occupied the north-west of France, leaving the Vichy régime in control of the remaining three fifths of the country. Hitler was now at the peak of his career and, as Alan Bullock has explained, he is entitled to the major share of the credit for the victories of 1940 because he had perceived the reality of French weakness and forced his generals against their wishes to undertake an offensive using the most modern techniques of warfare.

The Battle of Britain

Hitler confidently expected that the British would be forced to sue for peace now that their situation appeared hopeless. In this he was to be disappointed for the British now possessed a charismatic war leader in Winston Churchill. It has perhaps become all too fashionable to write off Churchill's achievements but they were considerable. He became Prime Minister in May after the failure of the Norwegian campaign had led to the fall of Chamberlain. Churchill brought a new urgency to government and after the evacuation at Dunkirk his resolution was clear to all. 'We shall fight on the beaches, we shall fight on the landing-grounds, we shall fight in the hills; we shall never surrender.'

Churchill soon won an astonishing personal popularity with the British public through his broadcasts, which succeeded because they were both rhetorical and cheeky. With his speeches, his cigar and his unconventional dress, his appeal to the man in the street was tremendous. As Henry Pelling has said in a recent biography, 'Churchill's most endearing quality was his evident humanity. This reflected or seemed to reflect the mood of the people in the country; there was nothing of the remote intellectual about him.'

As supreme director of the war, Churchill possessed great power, a situation that eliminated the emasculating quarrel between soldiers and civilians of the First World War. The task of supervising the conduct of the war imposed a heavy burden on the British Premier. As A. J. P. Taylor has noted, 'in this turmoil of activity he made some great mistakes and many small ones. The wonder is that he did not make more. No other man could have done what he did, and with a zest that rarely flagged.'

When the British failed to oblige him by a prompt capitulation, Hitler reluctantly began to prepare a plan for the invasion of Britain. For such a plan to succeed, control of the air was essential. The Luftwaffe commander, Göring, cockily promised that the R.A.F would soon be destroyed and that an invasion of Britain would be simple. In August, the greatest battle in air history, the Battle of Britain, began with 13 German divisions at French Channel ports ready for Operation Sea-Lion. The Luftwaffe had stationed in France 1,200 bombers and about 1,000 fighters against a British fighter strength of 900, but the Spitfires and Hurricanes were faster and more heavily armed than any German plane except the Messerschmitt 109 which lacked their range. The R.A.F.'s radar provided an early warning of German attacks and its radio ground-control systems permitted the best use of British planes.

Göring's blunders also improved Britain's position. Instead of concentrating on fighter bases and radar stations, he ordered the Luftwaffe to bomb inessential targets like London. Thus though the British lost 650 planes, German losses were even heavier at about 1,100 planes, and on September 17 Hitler postponed Operation Sea-Lion indefinitely. The Battle of Britain was a triumph of foresight and organisation over improvisation and sloppy thinking. It saved Britain from invasion and as Churchill said of the R.A.F., 'Never in the field of human conflict was so much owed by so many to so few.'

The Invasion of Russia

In July 1940, Hitler told his generals that he had decided to make war on Russia as soon as the strategic position allowed it. He originally envisaged an offensive in the autumn but realised that the date would have to be postponed until a proper plan had been worked out. His staff tried to persuade him to invest German forces in the Mediterranean where Mussolini, having massed troops in Libya, was planning to attack the British in Egypt. As Alan Bullock comments, Hitler 'declined to look at the Mediterranean as anything more than a sideshow which could be left to the Italians with a stiffening of German troops. It was to prove one of the supreme blunders of his strategy.' By May 1941 the plans for the invasion of Russia, Operation Barbarossa, were near completion.

Several reasons impelled Hitler towards a campaign in Russia. He believed that the British had stayed in the war only because of the hope of Russian aid at some time in the future. Therefore, he told his generals, Russia must be smashed in order to obtain security in the west. Another advantage would arise out of a Russian defeat: by increasing the power of Japan in the Far East it would effectively neutralise Britain's other hope, the United States. Hitler did in fact nurse hopes of a simultaneous attack by Japan and Germany on Russia but the Japanese government was now more interested in southern Asia and was in any case too wily to do Germany's dirty work for her!

Another reason for Hitler's desire to attack Russia was his belief that the Russians would never tolerate a definitive German victory in the west. He had no confidence in Stalin's good faith and Russian actions since September 1939 convinced him that Russia would try to obstruct a full German victory. Not only had the Russians invaded Finland; by their diplomatic pressure on Rumania, Bulgaria and Turkey they had become the bitter rivals of the Germans in the Balkans. In June 1940, Rumania had been forced to cede Bessarabia and Northern Bukovina to Russia and these gains meant that Russia became an even greater threat to the Rumanian oil-fields. True, the Russians were fulfilling their obligations in supplying Germany with stocks of raw materials, but in Hitler's view the arrangement had two flaws. The Russians might well cut off deliveries to Germany at any time that suited them and they demanded prompt payment in the form of armour and munitions which one day would almost certainly be used against German troops.

Overriding all other factors was Hitler's obsession with *Lebensraum*. The Nazi–Soviet Pact had always been a temporary expedient as far as he was concerned, just as total control of all western Russia had been his ultimate objective. 'Hitler invaded Russia,' asserts Alan Bullock, 'for the simple and sufficient reason that he had always meant to establish the foundations of his thousand-year Reich by the annexation of the territory lying between the Vistula and the Urals.'

Operation Barbarossa was planned for May 1941 but an important delay occurred, partly caused by the attempts of the Italians to gain some of the glory. In September 1940, the Italian army in Libya drove back the British forces 60 miles into Egypt and Mussolini was so elated by his success that he was rash enough to attack Greece in October as a counter to growing German influence in the Balkans. From this point on the Italians experienced only disaster. They were sharply checked in Greece and lost most of their fleet at the hands of the British at the battles of Taranto and Cape Matapan. In December, Italian forces in North Africa were routed by a British counter-attack led by Wavell and 130,000 Italians were taken prisoner. Mussolini was forced to accept German help in Africa and German forces led by Erwin Rommel beat the British back into Egypt in April 1941.

Before Barbarossa could be launched Hitler believed that it was necessary to remove the threat to the German flank caused by Mussolini's failure to crush the Greeks, who were now receiving British aid. Pressure was put on the Bulgarian and Yugoslavian governments to permit the transit of German troops through their respective countries for deployment against the Greeks. Both finally acquiesced but in Yugoslavia the surrender to German bullying provoked a palace revolution and a repudiation of the agreement with Germany. In rage Hitler ordered the invasion of Yugoslavia in April and German forces destroyed organised resistance in 11 days. A week later Greece surrendered and British forces there had to be evacuated. The two operations have often been held responsible for the six-week delay in the invasion of Russia but in fact German preparations for the offensive were not complete by May.

Hitler assumed that the German *blitzkrieg* would work as successfully in

Russia as it had in the west. He did not bother to lay plans for a winter campaign or even lay up stores of winter equipment or clothing. By June 1941 about four million men, 3,300 tanks and 5,000 aircraft were ready to invade Russia. When Operation Barbarossa commenced on June 22 the Russian forces were taken by surprise. By mid-July the Germans were two thirds of the way to Moscow, having captured more than a million prisoners. In the north, Leningrad came under siege and in the Kiev region a Russian army of 600,000 was surrounded. When Kiev fell in September the drive towards Moscow was continued.

For many of these disasters Stalin must be held responsible. He refused to believe Allied and Russian reports that Hitler was about to strike because he assumed that a German attack would only come when Britain was defeated. No plans had been made for a strategic withdrawal to take advantage of Russia's greatest resource, space. In fact, Stalin ordered his troops onto the offensive so that they were more easily encircled by the invaders. Russia seemed near collapse: 1,200 planes had been destroyed within hours of the German attack and within a few months 2·5 million men had been lost out of a total force of 4·5 millions. Stalin's nerve appeared to go and, in Ulam's words, in the early period of the war 'he left the country rudderless'.

The situation was saved by the flow of Russian troops from the Far East, by fatal German delays in August in maintaining the offensive, and by the rain, mud and ice of the Russian winter which brought German armour to a standstill. When Hitler ordered a final effort to take Moscow in 1941, the Russians counter-attacked magnificently in December with 100 divisions skilfully led by Zhukov, probably the best general in the war. The Führer had fallen into the trap of allowing the Russians to retreat and draw his armies further and further into their vast hinterland. Now he ordered that the German forces should not retreat but stand fast regardless of losses. On this score he was undoubtedly correct for a retreat in winter conditions would have degenerated into a rout. His order caused conflicts with the generals, and with the resignation of Brauchitsch and the dismissal of Guderian and Runstedt, the army lost its top professional commanders.

Meanwhile, the European war had become a truly global war. On December 7, Japan made a surprise attack on the American naval base of Pearl Harbour and precipitated a Pacific war. Hitler without hesitation declared war on the United States, an act that calls for some explanation as up to this point Hitler had shown caution in his dealings with the Americans despite their increasing aid to Britain. It is sometimes argued that he had no conception of the economic and military potential of the United States. More plausibly, he realised that Roosevelt, who was already giving all aid short of war to Britain and Russia, was only waiting for the right opportunity to intervene in the European war and that in the near future some incident would give the president a suitable pretext. Hitler had also promised the Japanese in November to join in a war against the United States; he kept his promise in the vain hope that the Japanese would not only help him against Russia but tie down the Americans in the Pacific as well. Finally, he saw that an early declaration of war would allow German aircraft and submarines to strike at American shipping before America's defences had been properly organised. But whatever the reasons, historians for once concur in condemning the enormity of Hitler's error in declaring war on the United States. Bullock describes it as 'the greatest single mistake of his career' while Rich asserts that Hitler had now 'created a situation which virtually guaranteed Germany's ultimate defeat'.

For a season the consequences of Hitler's errors were hidden by new victories.

In the Far East, Japanese forces seemed invincible as they took the Philippines, Malaya and many Pacific islands. Hitler believed that the Japanese entry into the war would dry up the flow of American aid to Britain and Russia so that he could finally destroy Russia in 1942. Despite his failure to concentrate on the Moscow region where the strongest Russian forces were encamped—he also struck at Leningrad and the Caucasus in an effort to seize the oil-fields—his forces gained huge successes. Two Russian armies were encircled and German forces advanced deep into southern Russia. In North Africa Rommel, having suffered reverses in the winter, renewed his offensive in Libya and by taking Tobruk in June threatened Cairo and the Suez Canal. In the autumn of 1942, the Axis powers seemed close to victory on all fronts but appearances were deceptive.

The Sinews of War

Imperceptibly the fortunes of war were already turning against Germany through Hitler's failure to achieve the efficient mobilisation of all Germany's resources for the war effort. This was in stark contrast to Britain, where after Dunkirk the ground was prepared for the most thoroughly coordinated war economy of any warring nation. The British were regimented in a way that the Axis leaders never dared ask of their own people—in the direction of labour, in the rationing of food, through the imposition of high taxation. The American historian Gordon Wright asserts that 'operating by consent rather than compulsion, utilising a partially antiquated industrial complex and working with limited resources, the British government managed to convert a loosely articulated peacetime economy into a fully mobilised economy for total war'. One statistic vividly illustrates this achievement: from 1940 to 1942 the British production of tanks and aircraft surpassed that of Germany, where the highest level of war production was not reached until 1944.

The Soviet efforts to mobilise for total war were equally impressive. The third Five-Year Plan had resulted in new industries in the Urals and western Siberia and by June 1941 the eastern regions of Russia were producing 39 per cent of her steel and 35 per cent of her coal. But for this powerful new industrial base, secure from enemy attack, the German offensive might well have succeeded.

Russia still faced an appalling situation for the German troops overran the older industrial regions and war production was cut by over half by December 1941. The crisis was surmounted by titanic efforts: 1,560 factories were transferred from the threatened areas in the west to the Volga and the Urals; 2,250 completely new plants were built between 1942 and 1944 so that the output of tanks rose to 2,000 a month and aircraft production from 1,000 to 3,000 a month. The contribution of British and American aid was also important, mainly in the form of vehicles, foodstuffs and clothing.

The Soviet régime made great efforts to mobilise its manpower by the direction of labour to the east. Improved management and the high morale of a nation fighting for survival resulted in greater productivity after 1942. The greatest flaw in the economy continued to be agriculture where, despite the use of young people and women to fill the gaps in the labour force, the Soviets relied heavily on imported foodstuffs from their Western allies. Like the British, the Russians held down consumption by rationing and high taxation. By the later stages of the war the Russians could deploy on the eastern front twice as many soldiers as the Germans and possessed 8,000 tanks to Germany's 2,300, despite the concentration of two thirds of all German forces in the east.

Only slowly did Hitler consent to full mobilisation of the German economy for war. After the successful Russian resistance in late 1941, he ordered vast increases in arms and the size of the army in January 1942. His Minister of Armaments and Munitions, Albert Speer, was talented and managed to treble arms production in the next two years. He did this despite the rivalry of competing agencies, chiefly the army's War Economy Branch, Göring's Four-Year Plan Office and Himmler's S.S., which was a particular hindrance in its barbarous and wasteful use of labour. Speer also clashed with the Nazi *gauleiter* Fritz Sauckel, who headed the manpower agency, and the labour shortage was never really solved. Speer believed that foreign workers could best be used in their own countries but Sauckel insisted on transporting them to Germany. Speer's reliance on the industrialists met sharp criticism from many Nazis who wanted stricter party control of the economy and they also resisted his attempts to hold down consumption.

Considering these obstacles, Speer's achievement in trebling arms production was impressive. His authority over aircraft production remained limited and bombers continued to be built instead of the more necessary fighters. When he did gain a measure of control in 1943, he raised the production of planes from 2,300 to 3,538 in little over a year, despite Allied bombing and shortage of materials. In the end even Speer could not work a miracle in the face of harsh economic realities. Germany was facing a coalition vastly superior in manpower, industrial potential and scientific knowledge.

Hitler's New Order

By 1942 the Nazi empire covered most of Europe, which would enjoy, boasted Hitler, a new order for a thousand years. He now had a unique opportunity to implement his long-harboured objectives to make the German race absolutely supreme in Europe. The conquered areas were to be colonised by Germans and the indigenous population cleared out. Responsibility for this task lay with Himmler's S.S. and early in the war a million Jews and Poles were removed from Poland to make room for German settlers. After the invasion of Russia, vast new possibilities were opened up. Some Slavs would be kept as a source of cheap labour; most would be expelled to Siberia and central Asia. Fortunately, there was time only for a few scattered colonial experiments before the tide of war turned in 1943. A practice was made of selecting 'racially valuable' members from the Slav races with the intention of making them good Germans.

To counterbalance the superiority of the Allied economies, the Germans resorted to the simple process of commandeering all the raw materials, food and manpower in the conquered areas. As Göring remarked with refreshing honesty, 'I intend to plunder and plunder copiously'. That the conquered races might starve was a matter of complete indifference to Himmler and Hitler. German rule was worst in the east where mass confiscation was practised by the S.S., whereas in the West some veneer of legality was preserved.

One of the most acute problems which Germany faced was the labour shortage, exacerbated by the failure to use female labour on any large scale. Foreign workers were shipped into Germany to meet the shortage. At the peak of this exploitation, more than 7 million foreign workers were stationed in Germany while another 7 million were working for the German war effort in their native countries. Yet the Nazi inefficiency and tyranny made poor use of potentially enormous economic assets and shattered the myth that totalitarian states organise for war more effectively than do the democracies. It seems incredible that despite the acute labour shortage 3 million out of 4 million Russian prisoners-of-war died of ill-treatment in German camps.

There was indeed a striking contradiction in Nazi policies. While striving for economic growth, they could not free themselves from their heinous racial doctrines which, when implemented, robbed Germany of its necessary labour force. When Poland was purged of its political élite by execution, gaol or deportation, one German field marshal protested at such methods. 'Wars are not won with the methods of the Sally Army,' Hitler retorted.

Nazi behaviour was particularly atrocious in Russia. 'This is a war of extermination,' Hitler told his military advisers in 1941, and Himmler instructed his S.S. on the necessity of destroying 30 million Slavs to make room for German colonists in the east. 'The Russians,' Goebbels noted in his diary, 'are not people but a conglomeration of animals.' The Nazi atrocities in Russia were both criminal and stupid. More generous behaviour might have induced many Russians, especially in the Ukraine, to welcome the German invaders and support them against the detested Soviet régime. Nazi barbarism made the Russian people fight with heroic zeal, as exemplified at Leningrad which withstood a German siege of 890 days.

If any resistance was met in any occupied country the Germans did not hesitate to impose collective punishments, as at Oradour in France where the entire population of the village was murdered for an act of sabotage committed elsewhere. When the S.S. chief Heydrich was assassinated in Czechoslovakia in 1941, the Nazis killed 15,000 Czechs and the villages of Lidice and Lezaky were destroyed.

The nadir of Nazi genocide was seen in the treatment of the Jews. From 1933 pressure on them had mounted in Germany as Hitler's Brownshirts organised a boycott of Jewish shops and daubed Jewish stars on the shop windows. In 1935 were enacted the Nuremberg Laws which reduced Jews to the status of second-class citizens. In November 1938, the Brownshirts burned down 267 synagogues and 815 Jewish stores in the affair known as the 'Crystal Night': 36 Jews were killed and the Jewish race was heavily fined for causing trouble. Gradually Jews were excluded from education, the civil service and businesses. Those Jews who could, now left the country.

Persecution grew worse with the outbreak of war and in September 1941 Jews were ordered to wear a hexagonal star made of yellow material and bordered in black, inscribed with the word *Jude*. The use of the Star of David as a stigma was typical of Nazi vindictiveness but worse was to come. Göring instructed Heydrich to submit plans for a final solution to the Jewish problem. The Reichsmarshal meant only evacuation to the east but the doctrinaires around Himmler worked out plans for the extermination of the whole Jewish race. The S.S. combed Europe for Jews, took them to a remote place, made them dig their own graves and strip naked. Then they were mown down by machine-gun fire and buried in a mass grave.

This was too slow for the zealous Himmler and mass extermination camps were set up, notably at Auschwitz and Buchenwald. Here the Jews were given poison gas in chambers disguised as shower rooms. The S.S. administrators kept copious records of these foul murders. An office was founded to collect and package all the possessions of the dead—their clothing, gold teeth and hair. Thus the Jews were not only exterminated as if they were vermin; they were used as raw material for the war effort. Gerald Reitlinger puts the cost of the Final Solution in human lives at between 4,200,000 and 4,600,000 Jews and to this figure should be added about 3 million people of other races who became victims of Nazi savagery in the camps.

The German Resistance to Hitler

The German resistance in the words of A. J. Ryder was 'a tragedy within a tragedy'. Those Germans who felt obliged to oppose Hitler faced an agonising crisis of conscience because their actions could so easily be interpreted as treason. Such a moral dilemma meant that German resistance remained divided and ineffective and in any case many potential anti-Nazis had been imprisoned before the war started.

Opposition to Hitler in Germany came from five directions. (1) On the Left, Socialists and Communists began underground groups, the most successful of which was '*Rote Kapelle*', a Communist spying organisation. (2) Members of the General Staff like Halder and Beck grew increasingly uneasy under Hitler's rule and were supported by a number of civilians, chiefly the ex-Lord Mayor of Leipzig, Gördeler. (3) A similar group developed inside the Military Intelligence Department of the O.K.W. (Combined Services) and included Admiral Canaris and General Oster. (4) Among the students the most notable group was the White Rose in Munich, led by Hans and Sophie Scholl, who both paid with their lives for their courage. (5) Finally, a group grew up around Count von Moltke called the Kreisau circle. It included Bonhoeffer and many gifted men from diverse backgrounds. A member of the group, Count Claus von Stauffenberg, was finally chosen to assassinate Hitler and after several near misses, an attempt was made in July 1944 but Hitler by a lucky accident escaped death. His vengeance was barbaric. Several of the instigators of the plot, including Stauffenberg, were summarily shot; others were given a slow hanging with cords suspended from meat-hooks after torture and trial before Freisler in the People's Court. More than 4,000 people lost their lives as a result of the July plot, including Rommel, who was given the choice of trial or suicide and opted for the latter.

The Collapse of Hitler's Empire

The American Contribution

By the end of 1941 the entry of the United States into the European war had become imminent as the American government had stepped up its aid to Britain on a massive scale in the previous two years. Her European allies were thankful that despite Pearl Harbour Roosevelt insisted on giving priority to the European theatre of the global conflict for America's huge production potential was always likely to ensure the defeat of the Axis. Her economy when fully mobilised for war was to produce 75,000 tanks, 10 million tons of merchant shipping and 120,000 aircraft a year. Fifteen million American men and women were enlisted in the war effort. Yet the American entry into the war had another major consequence; it marked another stage in the decline of Europe which became more and more dependent on decisions made in Washington.

The War at Sea

It was fortunate that Hitler had shown little concern or comprehension of naval warfare and as a result had constructed only a small submarine fleet of 56 craft. These alone began to inflict alarming casualties on the Allies and between June

1940 and December 1941 Britain lost more than one third of her merchant tonnage. The Allied need to help the Russians by the Arctic searoute to Murmansk gave the Germans new opportunities for destruction and a shortage of merchant ships threatened because most of the American mercantile marine had to be assigned to Pacific duties. In 1942 Hitler, now converted to the idea of submarine warfare, had over 300 U-boats built and they inflicted appalling casualties on Allied shipping. In 1942 more than 6 million tons of shipping were lost and in March 1943 new record losses were experienced with 97 ships lost in 20 days.

The Battle of the Atlantic was, however, already turning in the favour of the Allies through the tenacity of British merchant seamen and improved use of the convoy system. American yards were producing ships faster than the U-boats could sink them and new techniques were developed to combat the submarines, including the use of long-range aircraft (the Liberators), aircraft carriers and centrimetric radar. In April 1943, Allied losses were halved and in May the Germans lost 41 U-boats, a blow from which their naval effort never really recovered.

In comparison to the U-boats, German surface raiders achieved little and in time were hunted down by the Royal Navy. In September 1939, the pocket battleship *Admiral Graf Spee* was damaged by British warships and her commander scuttled her in the River Plate. In May 1941, the mighty *Bismarck*, having sunk Britain's most famous battleship, the *Hood*, was herself destroyed by the combined efforts of British planes and ships. In December 1943, *Scharnhorst* was sunk by torpedoes and in April 1944 the *Tirpitz*, having been immobilised by British midget submarines, was destroyed by aircraft in a Norwegian fjord.

The War in the Air

One of the most controversial issues in the Second World War has been the strategic bombing of Germany. After German air raids on British cities in 1940, the R.A.F. retaliated in kind by area bombing at night in the hope of undermining German civilian morale. Churchill and the head of Bomber Command, Sir Arthur Harris, felt that attempts to destroy vital German resources like synthetic oil plants by precision bombing were impracticable. From 1942 Lancaster heavy bombers began to pound German cities, the climax being the raids on Hamburg which caused firestorms and made a million people homeless. Germany civilian morale did not crumble, however, as in time air raids became accepted as a matter of course.

The American attempts to make daytime raids on precise targets led to alarming casualties. In the raid on the ball-bearing plants at Schweinfurt in October 1943, 148 bombers were lost. The situation was to some extent transformed by the use of the P-51 Mustang fighter. Powered by an Anglo-American Rolls-Royce Packard engine, it was not only the best single-seat fighter in the war but could be equipped with long-range fuel tanks so that it could escort bombers all the way to Berlin. German fighters were eliminated from the skies and American bombers disrupted Germany's supplies of synthetic oil.

The extent of the damage done to Germany's war effort has been a matter of debate. German war production continued to rise until late in the war (1944) but Germany did became starved of petrol and many newly constructed planes lay idle for this reason. One and a half million people were required to repair the damage to communications and Ruhr industry in general. Perhaps Albert Speer should have the last word on the subject; he was of the opinion that American attacks on key industrial targets were a serious cause of the breakdown of the German industry in the final stages of the war.

The War on Land

In November 1942 there occurred three clear signs that the war was moving into a new phase. After a period of efficient preparation General Montgomery's Eighth Army shattered the Axis forces at El Alamein in Egypt, after Rommel's supply lines across the Mediterranean had become overstretched and increasingly harassed by the British. This battle has always been remembered with affection in Britain and the Commonwealth and was a great tonic after years of defeat. It made secure Montgomery's reputation as the best British field-commander since Wellington.

The Russians meanwhile had become restless at what they regarded as Western sloth and clamoured for a second front in Europe. The British refused an American suggestion for a small cross-Channel operation of 6 divisions on the grounds that it would hardly draw German troops away from the Russian front as there were 33 German divisions in the west anyway. Still, a diversionary action to help the Russians was required and Churchill proposed a surprise descent on Morocco and Algeria. In November an Anglo-American armada landed in North Africa and, with Montgomery's forces pressing from the east, moved on Tunis. By May 1943 the fighting in North Africa was over though the campaign has its critics who condemn it for delaying the cross-Channel invasion by its consumption of time, men and materials. On the other hand, Italy was now within easy reach and the Desert War cost Germany and Italy about 1 million soldiers killed or taken prisoner.

A third triumph marked Allied progress in November 1942. The German armies in Russia had driven far towards the Caucasus oilfields but in the way lay Stalingrad on the lower Volga. Obsessed by its name Hitler did not choose to bypass it and in September his troops had entered the city. They found themselves facing ferocious resistance from the Russian forces who were being regularly reinforced. Hitler refused to allow his commander-in-chief, von Paulus, to withdraw and, as a consequence, when three Russian armies counter-attacked in November they were able to trap 330,000 Axis troops in a pincer movement. After fierce fighting for 10 weeks, the remnants of the German army, about 100,000 men, were forced to surrender. Like El Alamein, Stalingrad proved that the German armies were far from invincible and, as Michael Howard has remarked, if ever there was a decisive battle in history it was Stalingrad. It demonstrated the extent to which Hitler's daring and determination had degenerated into blind overconfidence and belief in his own infallibility. As Alan Bullock explains, 'This was the reverse side of the strength which he derived from his own belief in himself—and it was the weakness which was to destroy him, for in the end it destroyed all power of self-criticism and cut him off from all contact with reality.'

By May 1943 the British and American leaders, to Stalin's chagrin, decided that a cross-Channel invasion would have to wait until 1944. As an alternative Churchill proposed an immediate attack on Italy where Mussolini's power was now patently crumbling. The British argued that such a campaign would knock Italy out of the war, clear the Mediterranean for Allied shipping and provide bases for aerial bombardment on Germany and the Rumanian oil-fields. In July, the Allies landed successfully in Sicily, a development that paved the way for the fall of Mussolini. His successor Badoglio wasted little time in bringing Italy onto the side of the Allies.

The German response was to seize control of nearly all the Italian peninsula and the Allies who had landed on the Italian mainland in September faced a long and bloody campaign to dislodge an enemy who for some time enjoyed numerical superiority. Only in June 1944 was Rome taken and it was April 1945 before the German hold on Northern Italy was broken. Nevertheless, the costly campaign contributed to ultimate victory in three ways. It eliminated Italy from the war and provided aerodromes from which the Allies could bomb the Balkans, central Europe and southern France, but most important of all it pinned down 25 German divisions in Italy and a similar number of troops in the Balkans against a possible Allied attack there, including forces that would otherwise have been used in Russia.

On the Russian front, the early months of 1943 saw German troops on the retreat but they were still strong enough to launch their third summer offensive in July. Their offensive was routed at Kursk, the scene of the greatest tank battle in history until the Middle East war of 1973. The heavy Stalin and medium T34 tanks were more than a match for the German Tiger tanks, a sign that the Russian armaments industry had overtaken that of Germany. By the end of 1943, two thirds of Russian territory occupied by the Nazis had been liberated. In 1944, Russian forces swept into Poland, Warsaw was taken and by the end of the year Germany itself was threatened. Russian forces had also rolled through Rumania and Bulgaria though their advance was checked in Hungary.

At Teheran in November 1943 the three major Allies had at last fixed the date of the cross-Channel invasion of Normandy, which would be supported by an attack on the south coast of France. The preparation for the D-Day invasion was enormous; it was hoped to land 200,000 men with their equipment in the first two days, with the landing of another 440,000 men in the next nine days. On June 6, 1944, five seaborne and three airborne divisions were landed in Normandy and four beachheads established without any serious hitches. By the end of July the Allies had broken out from these beachheads and by the end of August Paris had been liberated. The landing on France's southern coast was also successful in August so that for a time it was hoped that the war would end in 1944.

General Montgomery at this point pressed hard for a powerful dash to Berlin across the Rhine but an attempt to outflank Germany's Siegfried Line by dropping airborne troops in Arnhem in September failed. This convinced the Commander-in-Chief of the Allied forces, Eisenhower, that a broad front advance was safer than Montgomery's plan. In any case, he believed that the offensive would have to pause so that his forces could be reinforced.

In December 1944 came the last desperate German fling of the war, a thrust through the Ardennes spearheaded by a powerful tank force which it was hoped would split the Allied forces and take Antwerp, the main Allied supply port. This 'Battle of the Bulge' led to temporary routing of the six divisions which lay in the way of the German attack but in the end the Germans lost 600 tanks. The Allied advance continued on all fronts in February 1945. To the disgust of the British, Eisenhower would not make the capture of Berlin a top priority and the honour of taking the German capital fell to the Russians when in April they launched a great final assault with 1½ million troops. Hitler and Goebbels committed suicide and early in May the German forces surrendered unconditionally. Victory over Japan was not long delayed; in August, after President Truman authorised the dropping of atomic bombs on Hiroshima and Nagasaki, the Japanese government surrendered and the global war was over.

The Consequences of the War

Despite all the suffering, the Second World War was worth fighting if only because it led to the destruction of a régime that could perpetrate the horrors of Belsen and Auschwitz, a régime indeed that was the greatest threat to European civilisation so far encountered. For this reason A. J. P. Taylor believes that the Second World War was that rarity, a just war: 'Despite all the killing and destruction that accompanied it, the Second World War was a good war.'

The conflict also brought certain indirect benefits, for the requirements of total war necessitated great advances in science and in state planning. In Britain, for example, the Beveridge Report of 1942 laid down the guidelines for the creation of the Welfare State, and state socialism, allied with American aid, was to be a major factor in Europe's rapid material recovery after the war. Even the invention of nuclear weapons with all their potential evil has benefited mankind. By multiplying man's power to destroy his own kind, they have made the consequences of another war so horrifying that they have so far been an effective deterrent and contributed to peace.

Against these benefits must be set the evil results of the most destructive war in all history which, in Gordon Wright's phrase, 'speeded the downward spiral of European power and influence'. More than 30 million people were killed in the holocaust; over half were Russians but it was Poles who suffered the highest casualty rate of all. They lost nearly 6 million of their people, 15 per cent of the entire population. The slaughter was accompanied by an uprooting of peoples unprecedented in European history. Between 1939 and 1947, 16 million Europeans were forced to leave their homes and move to other regions.

The destruction of material assets was enormous and Europe seemed destined for some years to endure poverty and starvation. In contrast, the extra-European powers appeared immensely strong. The United States had suffered relatively few casualties and the war had stimulated her true revival from the depression years of the 1930s. Russia too had demonstrated her immense military might and it was clear even by 1945 that these two super powers would now enjoy a preponderant influence in European affairs. Their rivalry, which was to become the most important feature of the postwar decades, was soon to split Europe into two ideological camps.

The war also transformed the relations of European states with their colonies. Japanese victories in Asia over European armies fatally undermined the prestige of colonial powers like France, Britain and the Netherlands. Colonial nationalism in Asia and Africa was stronger than ever before and the peoples of these continents would no longer tolerate a position of subjection.

Finally, the atrocities of the war provoked doubt and despair about the very nature of the human race. The Final Solution was not the work of Germans alone. The Danes, Norwegians and Hungarians tried to protect their Jews but in the Netherlands, Rumania, France and Russia locally recruited collaborators astonished the Germans by the virulence of their anti-Semitic sentiments. The guilt was appallingly widespread. 'In the end,' says Norman Rich, 'one of the saddest features of the Nazi experience is that out of all the suffering, the bloodshed and the destruction which Nazism inflicted on the world, the Nazi movement contributed nothing to human culture and civilisation. Nothing except a terrible lesson about how fragile and vulnerable human civilisation is.' The old Europe had gone for ever, the architect of its ruin being Hitler, the most barren and repellent figure in human history.

Further Reading

Bullock, A., *Hitler: A Study in Tyranny*, Penguin, Harmondsworth, 1969.
Pelling, H., *Winston Churchill*, Macmillan, London, 1974.
Rich, N., *The Establishment of the New Order*, Andre Deutsch, London, 1974.
Taylor, A. J. P., *The Second World War*, Hamish Hamilton, London, 1975.
Wright, G., *The Ordeal of Total War 1939–1945*, Harper Torchbooks, New York, 1968.

Questions

1. Account for the ease of German victories in the early part of the war.
2. Why did Hitler attack Russia in 1941?
3. What were the main features of the New Order?
4. Why did the Allies win the Second World War?
5. Do you agree with Taylor's view that the Second World War was a 'good' war?

CHAPTER SEVENTEEN

POST-WAR DEVELOPMENTS

The Onset of the Cold War

The Grand Alliance

When the Nazis attacked Russia in June 1941 both Churchill and Roosevelt arranged to send aid to the Russians. Churchill remarked to his secretary, 'If Hitler invaded Hell I would make at least a favourable reference to the Devil in the House of Commons.' In the course of the war the decisions of the Grand Alliance—the United States, Russia and Britain—determined the territorial and political structure of post-war Europe.

Western relations with Russia were never really cordial and were clouded by mutual suspicion. The two Western powers nevertheless sent massive aid to Russia and, according to Snell, 4,400 tanks and 3,100 planes had reached Russia by mid-1942. Stalin demanded more Western action, in particular the opening of a second front. The Russian leader was most suspicious that the West were deliberately delaying this move in the hope of seeing Russia permanently weakened by the German attack. To reassure the Russians, Churchill offered a formal alliance and at the Casablanca conference in January 1943 the two Western leaders insisted that Germany would have to surrender unconditionally. Stalin was not noticeably appeased by their declaration and when he was informed that the Normandy operations would be delayed until 1944 he hinted that Russia might be forced to make a separate peace with Germany. There seems little doubt that his confidence in his allies was severely strained.

At the Teheran conference in November 1943 relations between the allies improved. The Western leaders made a definite promise that the Normandy invasion would take place in May 1944 and in return Stalin promised to make war on Japan once Germany was defeated.

As the war went on, the meetings of the Big Three revealed a growing discrepancy between Stalin's aims and those of the Western statesmen. Churchill and Roosevelt had met off the coast of Newfoundland in August 1941 to draft the Atlantic Charter, a general statement of principles on which a post-war settlement might be based. Both powers disavowed any national gain or the implementing of any territorial changes contrary to the wishes of the inhabitants. All peoples would have the right to choose their own forms of government in a new world of economic cooperation. The aggressive nations would be disarmed and a general system of security created. In January 1942, these principles were embodied in a Declaration of the United Nations which all governments at war with Germany signed.

With the advantage of hindsight we can appreciate that Stalin could never be persuaded to subscribe to the principles of the Atlantic Charter though he subscribed to them on paper. His objective was Russian control of all eastern Europe and to his diplomacy he brought his greatest gifts of patience, tenacity and shrewd appreciation of the strength and weaknesses of his partners in the Grand Alliance. He was assisted by the attitude of Roosevelt. Unlike Churchill, the American trusted Stalin and hoped to play the mediator between the British and the Russians. He was deeply convinced that the most serious problem for the post-war world was not Soviet strength but British Imperialism. He told Mikolajczyk, 'Of one thing I am certain, Stalin is not an Imperalist.' While he was President the Americans showed relatively little concern for Poland or, in the military sphere, the need for the West to gain Berlin.

As the war continued, Stalin's diplomatic position improved and by 1945 the Red Army was in occupation of most of Eastern Europe. The differences between the Allies now became acute. At Teheran a cordial atmosphere had reigned but at the next two important meetings of the Big Three—at Yalta in February and at Potsdam in July—the cracks in the Grand Alliance could not be papered over.

The Major Areas of Disagreement

Many issues divided the Western powers from Russia. They quarrelled with the Soviets over the structure of the new United Nations Organisation, in which Russia was to repeatedly abuse her right of veto in the Security Council. They rebuffed Stalin's suggestion that Russia should join in the occupation of Japan after Japan's surrender in August 1945. The growth of Russia's influence in the Balkans broke agreements with the Western powers, provoked furious rows at Potsdam and led to British intervention in Greece in 1944 and 1947. But the problems that divided the West and Soviet Russia above all others were Poland and Germany.

Poland was the first issue that revealed the inability of the Allies to compromise and it became, in Snell's phrase, 'a touch-stone of Greater Power relationships'. The West and the Soviets disagreed sharply on the question of Poland's post-war frontiers and government. Britain had officially gone to war to defend Polish independence and wished Poland to recover her lost territories and have an independent government. The Russians were not prepared to return their gains made at Poland's expense but would allow Poland to receive compensation at Germany's expense. Stalin was inflexibly opposed to the creation of any anti-Soviet government in Poland.

At Teheran in 1943 an agreement on the Polish boundaries was reached. Russia would retain her gains, with Poland gaining much of East Germany up to the Oder and East Neisse rivers. No agreement was reached on the nature of the post-war Polish government. Britain and the United States favoured the London-based Polish government in exile. As the London Poles were opposed to giving up any territory to Russia, Stalin refused to recognise them and set up another Polish group, the Union of Polish Patriots.

The hostility of the London Poles towards Russia had increased after the discovery by the Germans in 1943 of a mass grave in Katyn Forest in which were buried the bodies of several thousand Polish officers captured by the Russians in 1939. Relations between the London Poles and Russia deteriorated even more after the Warsaw Rising in 1944. The Russians refused to help the rising and even prevented the Western allies from using Russian airfields to drop supplies to the Poles.

The attitude of the London Poles to Russia was understandable but hardly politic as it was always likely to encourage Stalin to take a harder line. In December 1944, the Union of Polish Patriots, now the Lublin Committee, proclaimed itself as the provisional government and in January 1945 Stalin recognised it, much to the anger of the West. At Yalta a new agreement was reached. The Lublin Committee was to form the nucleus of a Polish government with Russia guaranteeing free elections and the inclusion of the London Poles in the new government. These guarantees were never implemented.

Germany was an even more serious problem than Poland because the issues at stake were much greater. The power that controlled Germany would control the whole continent of Europe. At Yalta it was agreed that Germany and Berlin would be divided into four Allied zones controlled by Britain, Russia, the United States and France. As Berlin was surrounded by the Soviet zone, it was to be the source of several crises in the next few years.

The Soviets and the Western powers were soon at loggerheads over the treatment Germany was to receive. The Russians wanted Germany permanently crippled while the West wanted her domination broken without leaving the continent under Russian sway. The Russians demanded huge reparations and ravaged their own zone when the West suggested more modest payments. The amount of German territory that should go to Poland was still in dispute. At Potsdam the Russians insisted that the Polish-German border should now run along the Oder-West Neisse line, an agreement giving more territory to Poland than had the Teheran agreement.

What Stalin really desired was a partition of Germany, with the Rhineland and Bavaria being separated from the rest of the country. The Western powers had themselves considered such schemes earlier in the war but were unwilling to implement them in 1945. At Potsdam the Big Three agreed to treat Germany as a unit with the frontiers of 1937. Ironically Stalin still achieved his objective. In time a de facto partition of Germany into two states was accomplished by Russia's refusal to merge her zone of occupation with the Western zones to form a united Germany.

Europe in Two Blocs

In March 1946 Churchill, in a speech at Fulton, Missouri, commented, 'From Stettin in the Baltic to Trieste in the Adriatic, an iron curtain has descended across the continent.' At the time many in the West thought that he was exaggerating the Russian menace but later events appeared to prove the accuracy of Churchill's opinion. The Soviets consolidated their hold over nearly all Eastern Europe and fears that Greece and Turkey were in danger led to the enunciation of the Truman Doctrine in 1947. President Truman declared that the security of Greece and Turkey was vital to American national interests and began a substantial programme of aid. Soon both blocs had formed alliance systems, N.A.T.O. and the Warsaw Pact. In 1950, the Cold War 'hotted up' with the invasion of South Korea by Communist North Korea. Only after Stalin's death in 1953 were the first hesitant steps towards better relations taken.

Was the Cold War Inevitable?

By the very completeness of its victory, the decline of the Grand Alliance became inevitable. Only mutual fear of Germany had kept such contrasting partners together for so long and once the German threat receded then so the unity of the Allies dissolved as well. Indeed, it is remarkable that the coalition was maintained until the end of the war.

The main reason for conflict must be sought in the character of the state systems. Suspicion of the West was built into the Soviet system and it was inherent in the character of Stalin. He remarked to one of Tito's colleagues, Djilas, 'Churchill is the kind who, if you don't watch him, will slip a kopek out of your pocket. Roosevelt is not like that. He dips in his hands only for bigger coins.' Collaboration with the West after 1945 would have involved the risk of Russia being opened to Western influences which would have eroded the strength of Stalin's totalitarian régime. It was a risk Stalin was not prepared to take. He even rejected Marshall Aid, after which step, as Ullam says, 'both sides became frozen in mutual unfriendliness'.

A clash with the West was likely for a second reason. As Feis and Ulam have emphasised, Stalin was a Great Russian nationalist. One of the supreme motives behind his war aims and peace plans was a Russian domination of Europe more complete than that achieved by the tzars. No demonstration of Western goodwill could have overcome this blend of suspicion and ambition in Stalin. Nor would a tougher policy towards Russia have been possible in 1945. The publics in the West would not have tolerated a new confrontation with an ally nor could the Western powers have negotiated from a position of strength. Territories in dispute were occupied by Russian troops and the use of the atom bomb was unthinkable.

No doubt the Soviet threat was exaggerated in the West. Russia emerged from the war gravely weakened and the Russian army was reduced to less than 3 million by 1948 from more than 11 million during the war. Though Stalin was determined to expand his influence he did not wish to incur the risk of war. The reality of Russian weakness was not appreciated in the West, where it was widely believed that massive Soviet armies were ready to march to the English Channel. Yet Western apprehension was understandable. The war had eliminated Germany and left Russia as the only Great Power on the continent. George Kennan was in essence correct when he stated in 1947 that the main aim of Soviet policy was to 'make sure that it has filled every nook and cranny available to it in the basin of world power'. He advocated that the West carry out a long-term policy of containing Communism in the hope that in time the Soviet régime would either mellow or break up.

Kennan's policy of containment still makes sense in a European context. The Cold War is still being waged but it is now no longer a two-sided but a triangular phenomenon. The split between Moscow and Peking has created a new Cold War. As the West and the Soviets moved closer in the 1950s, Russia and China moved further apart and since 1964 Sino-Soviet relations have been bitter (see Chapter Nineteen).

Prosperity in Western Europe

The Reasons Behind European Recovery

After the Second World War had reduced much of Europe to ruins, the economic recovery of Western Europe after 1945 was both startling and unique as its peoples experienced ever-mounting affluence. The aggregate Gross National Product of Western Europe measured at constant prices was more than two and a half times higher in 1963 than it had been in 1939. The transformation was not immediate. The early years after the war saw many West European countries enduring hardship caused by the war. Only in 1948 did real recovery begin with the proper application of genuine remedies like the programme of American aid. By the early 1950s the fact of European recovery was evident as West European countries enjoyed a period of sustained and powerful expansion with impressive growth rates. Though some deceleration of economic growth occurred in the late 1950s it was only temporary and further robust advance occurred in the 1960s. 'For all its variations in pace,' comments Postan, 'the ascent of the European economy after 1945 was both steeper and smoother than at any other period in modern history.' Europe no longer seemed doomed as in the inter-war years to suffer the alternations of boom and slump.

Six main reasons may be put forward for this apparent economic miracle: (1) the survival of capital from the war; (2) changes in government policies; (3) the existence of a large pool of labour, (4) developments in world trade; (5) American aid; and (6) technological and scientific advance.

(1) The war years had not been years of complete economic waste but a period when scientific and engineering advances had prepared the way for potential growth in the future. The needs of war had led to huge amounts of public and private investment in industries serving the war effort. Therefore by the end of the war, even devastated Germany had actually increased her capital stock. In many countries, much of the damaged equipment could be brought back into operation and converted to peaceful uses at relatively small cost.

(2) Economic recovery was also stimulated by developments in government thinking. The dangers of mass-unemployment had been proved in Germany before the war and the need for full employment was genuinely appreciated. Economists had provided the means for implementing full employment policies, notably J. M. Keynes in his epoch-making *General Theory of Employment*, which for some time appeared a panacea for all economic problems. Keynes proposed in his book that governments could eliminate unemployment by variations in tax rates and their own expenditure.

It was essential for public order that governments did act positively to stem unemployment in the post-war period. Expectations of fast economic growth had been engendered among their peoples, who now came to expect perpetually improving material standards. This, as David Landes says, was the greatest change of all, a revolution of expectations and values. To meet this demand for affluence, governments were obliged to develop welfare measures like the Beveridge Report in Britain, which was based on the Keynesian assumption that effective demand should be maintained at a height necessary to secure full employment. To meet the costs of such social reform and other obligations, governments became committed to achieving high growth rates.

Individual governments began to introduce new bodies whose sole object was the planning of economic development. In France an ambitious national plan was drawn up in 1946. Inspired by Monnet, it aimed at a national product equal to 1929 by 1948 and 25 per cent higher by 1950 by providing France with a modern energy and transport system. The planners had considerable powers through their control of available capital and they put it to use in the areas where it would produce the highest returns. By 1952 French output stood 8 per cent above 1929 and therefore the planning may be considered successful as output in 1946 was only a fraction of what it had been in 1929. State intervention was even more marked in Austria and Italy.

(3) An influential school of economists, including W. A. Lewis and Charles P. Kindleberger, has argued that the existence of a large supply of labour was an important factor in the recovery of the European economy. That such a supply existed is undeniable. It stemmed from the high rate of natural increase, from the huge number of refugees and from the migration of agricultural workers to the towns. The newcomers, it is argued, contributed to European expansion by adding to output and by their willingness to move to those branches of industry that were rapidly expanding. The availability of cheap labour encouraged investment by en-

suring that wages would lag behind prices and that costs would remain competitive in the world market. In an age of technology with its simplification of tasks, the new workers could perform a useful function even if they lacked training. The criticism that can be made of the 'pool of labour' theory is that industrial development came first and then called up labour, not the reverse.

(4) For European economic recovery to be sustained it was necessary that the whole world economy after 1945 should be expanding. Thus European countries for selfish and unselfish reasons contributed to the economic development of underdeveloped countries, their annual payments rising from 2,000 million dollars in the early 1950s to about 16,000 million dollars in the early 1960s. Though the benefits accruing were only partly economic, the spending helped to sustain world demand for European products. World demand was also increased by a shift in the terms of trade. In the inter-war years the price of raw materials fell compared to that of industrial goods. As a result, overseas countries were too poor to buy European goods. After 1945 this tend reversed; the terms of trade moved in favour of the primary producers and overseas demand for European industrial products increased.

The implementing of liberal commercial policies since 1945 has been put forward as a crucial factor in European recovery. Before the war, commercial policies had become more restrictive with even Britain, the champion of free trade, turning to protection in 1932. Since 1945 the freeing of international trade has been the avowed target of a number of international organisations like the O.E.E.C. and the E.E.C. By the 1960s considerable progress had been made in the reduction of tariffs and quantitative restrictions.

The effects of free trade were several. The foreign trade of European countries could grow more quickly and this in turn contributed to European economic growth by promoting the flow of resources to exporting industries and improving personal incomes. The increase in foreign trade encouraged specialisation in industries like chemicals, aircraft and motor-cars in a situation where the domestic market alone was too small to support such projects. Only with the international market in mind could large firms like I.C.I. and Volkswagen expand and at the same time gain the attendant economies of scale.

(5) Much more important than some of the above factors were the contributions made by the United States. In June 1947, the American Secretary of State, George Marshall, announced a programme of aid to restore the ailing European economies. Though Churchill called the move 'one of the most unsordid acts of history', it was by no means wholly altruistic because it served American interests. It came three months after Truman had offered to support free peoples threatened by Communism and the Marshall Plan was really a branch of the American policy of resisting Communism. The United States government realised that a prosperous Europe would be the best possible barrier to Communism. It would also provide a market for American exports and a field for American investment. At the same time, the Marshall Plan may be seen as another step by the United States towards the fulfilment of her new world responsibilities.

Whatever the motives, the American aid made an invaluable contribution to European recovery. Between the end of 1947 and June 1950 nearly 10,000 million dollars were made available to the most needy countries for investment and in that period output of goods and services rose by 25 per cent. It was the timing of Marshall Aid that was so critical. Post-war problems had made 1946–7 lean years indeed and therefore as David Landes explains Marshall Aid 'played a decisive role in shifting the economies of Europe from a rut of dislocation and crisis to that path of independently sustained growth they have followed ever since'.

The United States contributed in two further ways to European recovery. Her military aid to West European countries and the expenses of American forces in Europe helped to close the dollar gap while the world's most affluent country was influential as an example. With her high living standards the United States became an object of emulation and the desire to catch up the Americans provided an impulse to European growth.

(6) The progress of many of the most important industries was assisted by vast scientific and technological advance. Oil, natural gas and nuclear power have become substitutes for coal. Large chemical firms like Bayer, an offshoot of I. G. Farben, began to produce over 12,000 different items as many new synthetic products replaced other materials. Light engineering, stimulated by the war, has provided whole new ranges of durable consumer goods. Manual tasks have been reduced in industry and agriculture as automation eliminated much of the strain, though not the monotony, from work.

With scientific and technological advances assuming such importance, research and development have become essential emphases in modern industry. They do not of themselves assure economic growth because there are too many slips between the idea and its realisation. Nevertheless, the technological and scientific advances have been so considerable that they are perhaps the most important reason for European recovery and constitute a second industrial revolution.

Economists often seek one fundamental cause which makes everything else operate. The historian distrusts this approach as he seeks to understand the complexities of a given problem. An analysis of postwar expansion shows that it is the product of a number of factors and their importance varies with the particular national economy one is assessing.

The Changing Shape of the West European Economy

Significant changes in the economy and society of Western Europe have taken place in the period after 1945. Its population rose from 264 million in 1940 to 320 million by 1970. Before the war, with a decline in both the birth and death rates, Europe had become a preponderantly middle-aged continent but with the war a baby boom occurred in Western Europe and a rapid growth of the population resulted. The population increase was particularly striking in France, for so long a country with a static population.

Agriculture shared in the general prosperity of the period with a spectacular rise in mechanisation. The increased use of fertilisers, especially in the Netherlands and Denmark, was even more important in raising yields per acre. It was the increased productivity of agricultural labour that released much of the labour force for use in industry or services. All over Europe the proportion of the population employed in industry rose but the proportion employed in the tertiary sector, services, rose even more. In contrast, only 17 per cent of the working population in Western Europe were employed in agriculture in 1965 compared with the figure of nearly 50 per cent in 1914. An even greater fall in the agricultural sector would have occurred but for government policies designed to protect agriculture. Even so, Europe is well on the way to becoming an urban continent.

Fundamental changes occurred in industry. As in agriculture, they were a case of pre-war trends accelerating. One of the main trends was an increase in the size and a corresponding reduction in the numbers of firms in the key industries.

Dramatic increases in the scale of output resulted from the growth of combined huge firms like I.C.I. and the three successors to I. G. Farben in Germany, Hoechst, Bayer and B.A.S.F. Small firms still showed a capacity for survival, many growing up to serve the needs of the large organisations. Garages, for example, mushroomed to service the motor car.

Another striking feature was the development of public ownership. In France, the state gained control of the railway, electricity, gas, television, petroleum and car industries. An even greater degree of nationalisation was experienced in Austria and Italy. West Germany tended to be the exception to the rule as Volkswagen and electrical undertakings were returned to private ownership. When one adds to nationalisation the more traditional activities of the State in controlling the armed forces and the social services, then the extent of State intervention has become considerable. The governments of Western European countries were employing about 40 per cent of the labour force by the 1960s.

Current Problems

So consistently high has aggregate demand been that the recurrent problem in nearly all European countries has been inflation. Until the 1960s price rises were relatively modest; the United Kingdom retail price index rose only 82 per cent between 1948 and 1961. By 1975 the rise in prices had reached the rate of 25 per cent per annum and showed no signs of abating. Only in Germany has inflation been contained with any success. The situation is serious for whereas moderate inflation may well be conducive to economic growth, price rises have now reached the point where they create serious distortions in the economy.

The latest phenomenon has been a novel combination of inflation and unemployment, as West Europe has experienced its deepest recession since the war. The vast rise in the price of primary products, especially oil, has belatedly proven the truth of Keynes' prophecy that progressive industrialisation would cause primary products to be relatively scarce and dear and manufactures more abundant and cheap. Europe's imports therefore cost more in terms of the goods it can offer in exchange and for the next few years, until the availability of North Sea oil, Europe will have to export a larger share of its output to buy the same volume of imports. An obvious danger exists that real incomes may decline.

Unfortunately, the benefits of the increased price of oil will go to a few Arab countries and bring about another danger predicted by economists in the 1950s. The terms of trade have not moved sufficiently in favour of primary producers in general and they too are suffering from the increased cost of oil. Their ability to buy manufactures may well decline, thus reducing the trade of the industrialised countries. Perhaps the importance of this factor can be exaggerated because the ability of Western countries to take in each other's output has increased since 1945. Even so, it is clear that the miracle of European growth is over, at least for the present.

The Demise of Colonialism

Nothing in the history of the colonial empires was more remarkable than the speed with which they disappeared. In 1939, 500 million people in Asia and Africa were ruled by Europeans. By 1970 the number had fallen to 21 million and with the 1974 revolution in Portugal leading to the independence of Angola and Mozambique, old-style colonialism has practically ceased to exist. The rapid loss of their colonial empires threw into sharper relief the changed position of European states in the world. They had become second- or even third-rank powers, a fact of life driven home by the Suez Affair which can be regarded as the last gesture of British Imperialism.

In Asia the British rapidly granted independence to India, Pakistan, Burma and Malaya after the war. The Dutch were in no position to reoccupy their Far Eastern possessions and the Dutch East Indies became Indonesia in 1945. It was, however, France which suffered the most disastrous retreat in Asia. An attempt was made to create a Federation of Indo-China to include Laos, Cambodia and Vietnam. The resulting struggle with Ho Chi Minh's Communists led to the calamitous French defeat at Dien Bien Phu in 1954.

The defeat of France in Indo-China made the retention of her African empire infinitely more difficult. In fact, as far as Africa was concerned, the retreat from empire, in Fieldhouse's phrase, changed from a measured crawl to an uncontrolled gallop. Tunis, Morocco, Algeria, French West Africa and French Equatorial Africa had all gained their independence from France by 1962. Meanwhile, the British had pushed their more advanced African colonies towards self-rule. Ghana (the former Gold Coast) became independent in 1957, followed by Nigeria in 1960. As the 1960s progressed, all Britain's former African possessions gained self-government including Kenya, Uganda and Zambia (the former Northern Rhodesia).

It is still difficult to account for this rapid pace of decolonisation because the events are too recent and no one explanation fits all cases. Certainly both the United States and Russia were hostile in sentiment and policy towards colonialism and obstructed the attempts by European powers to re-establish colonial control after 1945. American policy was negatively hostile as seen in the reluctance of the United States to answer French appeals for help in Indo-China. Material help was given, but Eisenhower was unwilling to intervene directly by using American troops. The Russians were positively hostile to Western imperialism and through the Cominform a coordinated Soviet offensive was launched in Asia. Soviet aid was a significant factor in Ho Chi Minh's success in Indo-China.

Of more importance than the hostility of the super-powers was the change in the influence and attitudes of the colonial powers themselves. The coercive power of European states had declined due to the effects of two world wars. In 1945 they were so exhausted and bankrupt that their priority was domestic reconstruction. If empire was to be retained only at the cost of further imperial wars, then for most European governments the price was too high. Again the case of Indo-China furnishes the most vivid example of this mood. This apparently unending war, in which the average Frenchman had little interest, imposed an intolerable psychological strain on France. The sense of relief once total withdrawal had been decided upon in 1954 was reflected in the vote of the French Assembly which approved the Indo-China settlement by 471 votes to 14.

In any case, European opinion had become more responsive to the principle that colonial peoples should be encouraged to seek independence. Before 1939 Imperial rule still seemed morally justifiable provided that its methods were benevolent. The war changed this self-confidence as German imperialism within Europe aroused horror. Yet even before the war it had been appreciated in British government circles that India would have to become independent. The Labour Prime Minister between 1945 and 1951, Clement Attlee, had served on the Simon Commission of 1928 which investigated Indian affairs and he had become convinced that the British must leave India. His views were paralleled in other West European countries and as a result Europe emancipated many of her colonies long before she was forced to do so.

Japanese victories in Asia over the white races during the war had profound implications for the future of Western colonialism. At the height of her power, Imperial Japan controlled Indo-China, Malaya, Burma, the Philippines, the East Indies and Thailand. A Greater East Asia ministry was created to exploit the conquered territories and the harsh rule implemented by the Japanese did much to arouse East Asian nationalism. At the same time the Japanese paid lip-service to the principle of independence and a number of concessions were given to their new possessions after the tide of war had turned in favour of the Allies. As Richard Storry explains in *The History of Modern Japan*, 'the granting of even sham independence to the occupied countries of Asia . . . meant that it would be morally impossible for the Western colonial nations to refuse them real independence once Japan was defeated. . . . Thus Japanese victories, by destroying the mystique of White supremacy, and Japanese policies, by according to the occupied territories at least the outward form of independence, greatly hastened the birth after the war of the new nations in South and South-East Asia.'

Finally, the new strength of colonial nationalism made a rapid end to the European empires likely once the war had ended. D. K. Fieldhouse suggests that this colonial nationalism had three roots. (1) It existed continuously from the moment of occupation in areas like Hindu India and Moslem North Africa where non-Christian and non-European cultures survived. (2) It was stimulated by an infusion of European ideas and practices. European ideals of liberty, equality and independence were incompatible with colonial rule and made the colonial peoples resent their subordination. (3) European rule affected most aspects of colonial society and many of the fundamental changes that occurred were resented. For example, large-scale industry and mining produced shanty towns and with them a rootless proletariat.

Where two or more of these influences coincided, as in India and Indonesia, strong national movements arose. India, by extracting concessions before 1939 and by gaining independence in 1947, proved colonial nationalism to be a formidable force which could no longer be ignored. By the time he visited Africa in 1960, Harold Macmillan, the British Prime Minister, felt it necessary to comment on the new power of African nationalism. 'The most striking of all impressions I have formed since I left London a month ago is the strength of this African national consciousness. In different places it may take different forms. But it is happening everywhere. The wind of change is blowing through the continent.'

It is still too early to draw up a final balance-sheet for the period of European imperialism. In defence of the Imperial experiment it may be suggested that living standards in many colonies have risen through European rule higher than they would otherwise have done. Secondly, the people of Asia and Africa were introduced to the European ideals of equality and independence. Finally, the European empires provided for many years a framework of political stability over much of the globe.

There were two chief drawbacks to Imperial rule. It destroyed the old social and political institutions in many colonies and left a dangerous vacuum in colonial societies. Secondly, it failed to give the colonies adequate education for independence and the history of many former colonies since independence has been one of political chaos and economic decline rather than progress. Particularly saddening has been the failure of parliamentary government in the former colonies as many African countries have succumbed to dictatorship.

The Movement for European Unity

The Organisation for European Economic Cooperation

The idea of European unity is centuries old. As far back as 1650 William Penn had called for a European parliament and in the period between the two World Wars Briand had striven in vain to implement the idea. After the holocaust of the Second World War it was widely believed that Europe could only be rebuilt by a cooperative effort in an age when the small nation-state was no longer a viable unit. The onset of the Cold War gave a decisive impetus to turning these beliefs into practice.

With the proclamation of Marshall Aid in 1947, the Organisation for European Economic Cooperation (O.E.E.C.) was established. Its first task was the delicate one of dividing American aid among the member states. This objective was successfully achieved over a three-year period. The second principal activity was the liberalisation of trade, the free flow of which had been severely limited by many restrictions in the post-war period. As tariff reductions were the concern of G.A.T.T., the O.E.E.C. concentrated on other barriers to free trade, principally quantitative restrictions. Within six years trade between European nations doubled. A third area of activity lay in finance. To improve the system of payments between member states, a European Payments Union was created in 1950 to institute a general multilateral system of payments.

Some members wished to push ahead and develop a European customs union, a move opposed by Britain because of her close ties with the Commonwealth. Despite this disappointment, the O.E.E.C. flourished. By 1959 it had 18 members including Spain and since then the United States, Canada, Japan and Australia have joined to convert the organisation into a more global institution. The word 'Europe' has been dropped and it has become the Organisation for Economic Cooperation and Development (O.E.C.D.), reflecting one of the major problems of our time—the economic development of underdeveloped countries.

The Council of Europe

Economic institutions have played the most important part in the moves towards European integration after the war but they have tended to concentrate on specialised functions. A more comprehensive attempt to unite Europe has been attempted under the Council of Europe, established in 1949 by 10 West European states. Again the British attitude at the time profoundly disappointed other European states. Though Britain became a founder member, Attlee's Labour government regarded the Council of Europe with the utmost reserve. The British were not attracted by the abstract idea of European unity, a concept they distrusted as a potential infringement of sovereignty. At this stage, too, it was felt that Britain's true interests lay more with the Commonwealth and the United States than with Europe.

Nevertheless, the Council expanded its membership to 17 countries by 1971. With its headquarters in Strasbourg, it has two central organs, a Council of Ministers composed of the foreign ministers of the member states and an Assembly whose members are elected by the parliaments of the member states. The Assembly is not a parliament as such, for it has no authority to legislate for the member states. If a two-thirds majority of the Assembly is in favour, it can make recommendations to the Council of Ministers which in turn can make recommendations to the member states. Real power has therefore so far eluded the Council of Europe as individual states guard their sovereignty.

The Council has been useful as a policy-formulating body, sponsoring some important treaties like the European Convention for the Protection of Human Rights and Fundamental Freedom. In the first 20 years it has concluded more than 70 agreements, mainly on matters relating to welfare, and it is still regarded as the nucleus of a European parliament.

The European Economic Community

The European Economic Community, or Common Market, owed its birth and progress to a number of sentiments intensified by the war. The German occupation left behind it a sense of common destinies and a desire for a larger union. Further inspiration came from the menace of Communism but also from a wish to catch up the United States. Economic unification was seen as a more practicable step than political unification, which it was hoped would develop naturally in time.

The first success for the apostles of economic union was the economic integration of the Low Countries, with Belgium, the Netherlands and Luxembourg forming the Benelux Union in 1948. At the same time French statesmen, notably Jean Monnet and Robert Schuman, were active in promoting European integration. In 1951 the heavy industries like coal and iron came under the control of a European Coal, Iron and Steel Community which established a common market in these products and a common programme of expansion. In the 1950s, supranational machinery was set up to supervise the work of this organisation. Again, while many European countries expressed an interest in joining, the British preferred to stay aloof.

The evolution of a common market in coal and steel was of profound importance in preparing the way for more fundamental attempts to establish a European Community. In 1955, delegates representing Belgium, West Germany, France, the Netherlands, Italy and Luxembourg met at Messina and agreed to form the European Economic Community. The constitution and programme were worked out in the next 18 months and in March 1957 the Treaty of Rome, setting up the E.E.C., was ready for signature. It established a customs union of the six countries concerned, pledged to reduce, and by 1969 abolish, all tariffs on their mutual trade. However, this was only the initial objective of the E.E.C. for in the preamble to the Treaty of Rome was stated the intention to establish the foundations of an ever closer union among the European peoples. Therefore from the start the political concept of European union underlies the whole endeavour. The aim is to end historic rivalries in a fusion of essential interests and therefore the title 'Community' is a more appropriate one than 'Common Market'. The aim of the Community is not merely the establishment of free trade in a common market but the harmonious development of all economic activities, a rising standard of living and closer relations between member states. Obstacles to the free movement of persons, services and capital were to be abolished and a common agricultural policy was to be inaugurated. Other aims were the improvement of working conditions, the use of a European Investment Bank and the expansion of trade with overseas countries.

By 1963 the Community had progressed satisfactorily in its aim to initiate free trade. Quotas had been abolished and tariffs had been cut to 60 per cent below their 1957 level. External tariffs (tariffs on trade with countries outside the Community) were also lowered. With a total population of 165 million people, the E.E.C. had emerged as the world's greatest trading power and it represented two thirds of Western Europe's resources.

Slower progress was made in freeing the movement of capital and labour and in establishing a common agricultural policy. The Community's agricultural policy has aimed at providing the consumer with security of supply at stable prices while giving the efficient farmers the confidence to provide the food needed and a market of 250 million people in which to sell it. The ultimate objective was to allow free trade in all goods, including agricultural produce. Yet before the formation of the E.E.C., all the six governments had helped their own farmers in different ways, often against each other. Therefore the task of developing a common agricultural policy was always difficult. Only slowly did the Six move towards common price levels for agricultural products, with frequent arguments over the financing of the Community's agricultural policy.

Meanwhile the British, largely in response to the formation of the Community, took the lead in 1959 in forming the European Free Trade Association (E.F.T.A.), composed of seven countries outside the Common Market (Britain, Switzerland, Austria, Portugal and the Scandinavian countries). It was realised by the countries in E.F.T.A. that if their exports to the Six were subject to import duties which did not apply to imports from countries within the Community, the consequences would be serious. The object of E.F.T.A. was to establish a free market between its members by the gradual abolition of tariffs and most other obstacles to trade, though quantitative restrictions remained and unlike the Community there was no common external tariff between E.F.T.A. partners.

In some ways E.F.T.A. was successful. Its member states represented a total of 95 million customers and its foreign trade was greater than that of the United States and almost as great as that of the Community. Yet for Britain it soon became clear that membership of E.F.T.A was no substitute for membership of the E.E.C. Industrial production among the Six was increasing nearly three times as quickly as in Britain in the late 1950s and this impressed the Conservative government in Britain. The Community constituted an expanding economy of 165 million people while in E.F.T.A. Britain had partners with a population of only 40 million people, most of the states already conceding low tariffs. Therefore in July 1961 the Macmillan government announced that it wished to initiate negotiations with the Six about joining the Community. By the end of 1962, negotiations appeared near completion but in January 1963 General de Gaulle came down firmly against British entry.

The Community and de Gaulle

The French government were prepared to accept the economic advantages of the Community provided that special provisions were made for the protection of French agriculture. General de Gaulle himself was adamant that Europe should remain a group of sovereign states (led by France) whose identity would not be submerged in any supranational organisation. During his period of power he was to hamper the development of European unity in two ways.

His attitude to British membership was inflexible. There is no doubt British interest in the E.E.C. was genuine as links with the Commonwealth loosened. Perhaps the British negotiators made an error in insisting on certain conditions before entry, primarily the safeguarding of agriculture, trade with the Commonwealth and the future of Britain's partners in E.F.T.A. This led to lengthy negotiations and gave de Gaulle an opportunity to assert his will. In January 1963, he announced at a press conference that Britain was not yet ready to join the Community but his real motive was his fear that Britain would become a serious rival to France inside the Community. France's partners favoured British entry but were not consulted by the general before he applied his veto which provoked a crisis in the affairs of the Community. As A. H. Robertson explains, 'France was criticised by her partners on the grounds that once the decision to open negotiations had been taken unanimously it was contrary to the spirit if not to the letter of the Rome treaties that one member should go back on that decision contrary to the wishes of the others.' However, the alternative was an E.E.C. without France, and France's partners yielded.

When the Wilson government applied for membership in 1966, it was no more successful than the Conservatives. Again the British overtures were rejected largely because of de Gaulle's attitude. To demonstrate France's independence of the United States was the keynote of his foreign policy and he disliked Britain's 'special relationship' with the Americans and Anglo-American cooperation in the field of nuclear research.

The general's second attack on European unity was aimed at the structure of the E.E.C. itself. The two main decision-making organs of the Community were the Council of Ministers and the Commission, the former composed of the foreign ministers of the Common Market countries with a voting system giving more votes to large countries than to small ones. In the Commission a more supranational approach was adopted, the 'Eurocrats' of the Commission representing the common interests of the organisation. The national governments had already begun to view the work of the Eurocrats in Brussels with suspicion. They feared that this supranational authority, already possessing 3,000 personnel by 1962, was becoming too powerful and were apprehensive that a new technocratic élite was being created whose first loyalty was to the E.E.C., not to their own country.

De Gaulle was particularly hostile to the attempts of the Commission to increase its power. In 1965 he took a dislike to the Commission's proposals on agricultural policy and threatened to withdraw France from the Community unless a solution acceptable to France was adopted. His real aim was to weaken the strength of the Commission and forestall any possibility of France being outvoted by her partners. Even the Germans were angered at the general's outrageously high-handed approach and in the end the French made some concessions on agricultural policy, but de Gaulle's real objective was achieved. All important decisions were in future to be decided by the foreign ministers and the Commission's authority was weakened. The general's vanity may have temporarily strengthened French prestige but it weakened Europe. The process of European unity was delayed by a decade and only after de Gaulle's retirement could it again move forward.

New Horizons

With the accession to the French presidency of Pompidou in 1969, the European climate changed. In December the Six decided to hold negotiations with other countries with a view to enlarging the Community and in 1970 negotiations began with Britain, Ireland, Denmark and Norway. Britain, Ireland and Denmark joined the Community in 1972 though the Norwegian people rejected membership in a referendum.

In 1974, the British elections resulted in a Labour government pledged to fundamental renegotiation of Britain's terms of entry to the Community and the putting of the results to the whole British people. Therefore 1975 proved to be crucial to the survival of the Community. Already strains between the original members had become evident, caused primarily by new economic problems like the oil crisis and the unique combination of rising unemployment with rampant inflation. The danger of protectionist policies by member states against each other grew—with, for example, the French objecting to the huge exports of Italian wine to France. Such a development threatens the whole spirit of the E.E.C.

However, the future prospects of the Community improved in June when the Labour government, having renegotiated the terms, put the issue in the hands of the British people through a referendum. The result was a massive 'Yes' to staying in by 17 million votes to 8 millions and Wilson hailed the vote as 'the end of fourteen years of national argument'. It seems probable that Britain is now rooted in the Community and will play a growing role in all the E.E.C. institutions. Only time will tell. One thing is certain: for all the difficulties that have arisen in the evolution of the E.E.C., notably over agriculture and the need for democratic control of the Commission, there is no denying the success of this great experiment in European cooperation.

The North Atlantic Treaty Organisation

The menace which West European countries believed lay behind the Iron Curtain accelerated moves to strengthen their defences. The French proposed a predominantly European scheme but the United States, Britain and the Commonwealth pressed for a form of Atlantic Union. This was surely more realistic. The time had passed when Europe could defend itself and the United States was needed to play the leading role in a new defence force.

The groundwork for this new force was laid in Brussels in 1948, and in 1949 a treaty was signed setting up the North Atlantic Treaty Organisation (N.A.T.O.). It was primarily a treaty of collective self-defence in which it was understood that if any N.A.T.O. member was the object of an armed attack, the other members would afford it all military and other aid. Within a few years the United States, Britain, Canada, the Benelux countries, Norway, Iceland, Denmark, Greece, Turkey, Italy, West Germany, France and Portugal had all joined the organisation. The decision to join in N.A.T.O. marked a revolutionary step forward in American foreign policy. Since the days of George Washington the United States had avoided entangling alliances; by signing the N.A.T.O. treaty the American government made a definite commitment to safeguard European security.

Two important developments in N.A.T.O. were provoked by the outbreak of the Korean War, which drew attention to the danger of war in Europe and the inadequate state of the West European defences. The Americans, who had been bearing the burden of re-equipping European armies, now pressed for the integration of N.A.T.O. forces under a centralised command with the inclusion of West German units. The first phase of this development went smoothly enough. In 1950, Eisenhower was appointed as Supreme Allied Commander of all N.A.T.O. forces and established his military headquarters known as S.H.A.P.E. (Supreme Headquarters Allied Powers Europe) near Paris. Under his central direction regional commands were later established for Northern, Central and Southern

Europe. The evolution of this rather complex structure was a remarkable example of the new spirit of cooperation.

The question of German rearmament was a much thornier problem. Understandably, the French were deeply apprehensive at the dangers of reviving German militarism but in October 1954 they accepted a British proposal for West German membership of N.A.T.O. combined with certain assurances for France. Both Britain and the United States promised to keep their forces on the continent for an unlimited period.

By 1957 N.A.T.O. was able to claim that its forces for the defence of Europe had increased fourfold and that these forces had become more effective in fire power, planning and standardisation of equipment. Yet in many respects the organisation fell short of expectations and faced many difficulties. Its original aim was to provide a force of 96 divisions to combat any Soviet attack on Western Europe, and this was never achieved. More seriously, after the relaxation of tension after Stalin's death in 1953, the whole cohesion of the organisation deteriorated. Member states were variously involved in areas of the world other than Europe—the United States in Korea, Britain in the Middle East and France in Algeria and Indo-China. At times, as in the Suez crisis of 1956, N.A.T.O. members were in open disagreement with each other, the Anglo-French attack on Egypt coming under direct American condemnation.

A fundamental long-term strain on the N.A.T.O. alliance lay in the area of nuclear strategy. It was only natural that the European members resented American nuclear supremacy, which though it was a valuable deterrent meant that N.A.T.O. was dominated by the United States. In any crisis the Americans would decide whether or not to use nuclear weapons to help Europe and the European states were bound to question the extent to which the Americans were really committed to Europe. The American government in its turn was reluctant to let European countries have control over nuclear weapons because of the risk that they might be used in relatively unimportant local conflicts which could trigger off a nuclear war. With Britain and France already developing their own nuclear weaponry, the American fears of a proliferation of nuclear arsenals were realistic.

The British and American governments managed to reach some agreement on this vexed question. At Nassau in December 1962 Macmillan and Kennedy hammered out an arrangement by which the British abandoned their plan for Skybolt missiles in return for American Polaris missiles to be used in British nuclear submarines. The United States went further in 1964 in proposing the creation of a multilateral nuclear force (M.L.F.) consisting of 25 surface vessels, each equipped with eight Polaris missiles and manned by crews of mixed nationalities so that her partners in N.A.T.O. could enjoy some participation in the operation of a nuclear force. The plan seemed to cause more division than unity in the N.A.T.O. alliance and was dropped. The French President, de Gaulle, opposed the M.L.F. on the grounds that it would in fact reinforce the American domination of N.A.T.O. He refused to accept Polaris missiles or participate in the formation of a multilateral fleet, affirming his belief in the viability of national nuclear deterrents.

De Gaulle disliked the whole structure of the organisation with its American leadership and the placing of French forces under a Supreme Allied Commander who was not French. In 1966 he withdrew French forces from N.A.T.O. and the headquarters of the organisation had to be transferred at great expense from Paris to Brussels.

There can be no complacency about N.A.T.O.'s future effectiveness. It now has 300 committees and like U.N.O. is a bureaucracy of byzantine proportions with 23,000 experts being consulted every year. So far in the organisation's history, a real emergency has not arisen but it is questionable whether all its members would support it in the event of a crisis.

In recent years understandable alarm has been expressed at the weakness of N.A.T.O. in conventional arms compared to the Soviet camp which has carried out a massive programme of rearmament. N.A.T.O. possesses only 63 divisions compared to the 102 divisions of the Warsaw Pact countries (the Soviet bloc's equivalent of N.A.T.O., comprising Russia, East Germany, Poland, Czechoslovakia, Rumania, Bulgaria and Hungary). Against the Warsaw Pact's 21,000 tanks, N.A.T.O. can put into the field only 7,000 tanks. Indeed, this gap between the two blocs may widen as a number of N.A.T.O. countries, including Britain, wish to implement cuts in their defence budget.

A more economical and perhaps more effective defence system might be achieved by the standardisation of weaponry but this is an explosive political issue. In 1975 the French government waxed furious at a decision by Belgium and other N.A.T.O. allies to buy American F16 planes in preference to the French Mirage fighter in what was called the 'arms deal of the century'. In the Warsaw Pact countries standardisation is complete but N.A.T.O. countries compete with each other to supply arms. This leads to much waste of research resources and hampers the efficiency of the fighting units themselves. For example, N.A.T.O. countries have 31 different anti-tank weapons in use when the ideal number would be five. As a recent American report has stressed, N.A.T.O. is not getting enough 'bang for its buck'.

Perhaps the most serious question mark hanging over N.A.T.O. is the strength of the American commitment. The value of N.A.T.O. to the United States was questioned in the late 1960s when it became clear that the nation's resources were being strained by global involvements. The number of American troops in Europe was reduced and the United States government has repeatedly stressed that the European members of N.A.T.O. should assume a greater share of the burden of European defence. After her recent humiliations in Vietnam, the danger that the United States might return to her old isolationist policies cannot be dismissed lightly.

Further Reading

Feis, H., *From Trust to Terror: The Onset of the Cold War 1945–1950*, Anthony Blond, London, 1970.

Fieldhouse, D. K., *The Colonial Empires*, Weidenfeld and Nicolson, London, 1966.

Landes, D. S., *The Unbound Prometheus*, Cambridge University Press, London, 1969.

Laqueur, W. Z., *Europe Since Hitler*, Penguin, Harmondsworth, 1972.

Postan, M. M., *An Economic History of Western Europe 1945–1964*, Methuen, London, 1967.

Robertson, A. H., *European Institutions*, Stevens, London, 1973.

Snell, J. L., *Illusion and Necessity—The Diplomacy of Global War*, Houghton-Mifflin, Boston, 1973.

Questions

1. Was the onset of the Cold War inevitable?
2. Account for the prosperity enjoyed by Western Europe in the post-war period.

3. Why was the process of decolonisation so rapid after 1945?
4. How much progress towards real unity has Western Europe made in the post-war years?
5. What major problems face N.A.T.O. today?

CHAPTER EIGHTEEN

WESTERN EUROPE SINCE 1945

France Since the Second World War

The Fourth Republic

With the fall of France in June 1940 there came to the fore a little-known brigadier general, Charles de Gaulle. Born in 1890, he had fought in the First World War, being taken prisoner at Verdun. Arrogant and unorthodox, his relations with his superiors were normally bad and he only became a colonel in 1938. He was a brilliant military thinker and wrote a prophetic book on tank warfare. Having fought well during the Battle of France, he became the leader of the Free French and returned to Paris in triumph in 1944. He restored order and constituted a new government composed of members from 13 different parties.

It is difficult to be neutral about de Gaulle. Walter Laqueur rightly refers to his 'colossal egocentricity and his dictatorial and capricious style even when he was at his best'. Possessed by overweening self-confidence, he was convinced that his historical mission was to restore France's prestige and great power status. His experience during the war when the Allies refused to regard him as the legal head of the French government in exile offended his self-esteem and made him a difficult colleague for Roosevelt and Churchill to work with.

France herself faced grave problems. She was expected to make a real contribution to the war effort when in fact she was on the brink of anarchy. A difficult issue was that of the punishment to be meted out to collaborators. They were more severely purged than in most other countries. Almost 2,000 death sentences were carried out but to this figure should be added 4,500 collaborators killed by partisans. With the pre-war leaders discredited, the Communists, led by Thorez, were now the strongest party with nearly a million members. De Gaulle disliked them because of their links with Russia and refused to grant them any key positions in his cabinet.

In October 1945, elections were held for a new Constituent Assembly whose chief task was to write a constitution for the Fourth Republic. Three parties—the Communists, the Socialists and the M.R.P. (*Mouvement Républicain Populaire*)—won 75 per cent of the vote and wanted to adopt measures depriving future presidents of the Republic of all authority. De Gaulle, who had advocated a strong presidency, resigned in protest in January 1946. He felt sure that his hour would come again when the political parties had discredited themselves. If he hoped for an early return to power, he was disappointed. The French people showed profound indifference to this departure, an intolerable affront to his proud spirit. He returned to the family home at Colombey and in vain attempted to prevent the adoption of the new Constitution, but in October 1946 the French people voted in favour of virtually the same political system as before the war. They did so with some apathy for 9 million abstained from casting their vote.

Political Instability

France's economic progress during the years of the Fourth Republic was not matched by any similar development in her political institutions. With parties on the Left and Right that were enemies of the régime—the Communists and de

Gaulle's *Rassemblement du Peuple Français* (R.P.F.) respectively—government relied on frail coalitions of Socialists, Radicals and members of the *Mouvement Républicain Populaire* (M.R.P.). Between 1946 and 1958 there were 25 different governments and, as Denis Brogan has written, such a system 'made for an amiable form of parliamentary life but destroyed the voter's sense that he was voting for anything or anybody in particular, or that his formal representatives, once they were elected, were responsible to him or to anybody.' Gradually public confidence in the régime was eroded.

The only new party proper was the M.R.P., led by Georges Bidault and Maurice Schumann and founded in 1944 to spread Christian democratic consciousness. Throughout the Fourth Republic it played an important role in politics and was represented in most of the cabinets. Bidault was Prime Minister in 1946 and in 1949–50, while Schumann held that office in 1947 and 1948. The M.R.P. was a party of the left in favour of nationalisation and it tried to act as a bridge between the Communists and their enemies. However, the unremitting hostility of the Communists prevented any real cooperation.

The real decline of the party started in 1947 when de Gaulle made a bid for power. He declared that parliament had ceased to be representative of the people and demanded a change in the constitution. In April he announced the formation of the R.P.F., which he hoped would be a national movement above the party system. Biographers of de Gaulle like Alexander Werth and Brian Crozier believe that this episode in his life does de Gaulle little credit. His oratory, the mass rallies and the exposure of the Communist threat recall only too well certain features of Fascism. Nevertheless, the success of the R.P. F. in the municipal elections in October was startling as it gained 40 per cent of the total vote. The General, posing as the man of storms who would rescue France from the troubles of the Fourth Republic, seemed in a position to overturn the parliamentary system but he hesitated, believing that the time was not yet ripe for any extreme move. Though the R.P.F. won 121 seats in 1951, it ebbed away in the following years. It lacked its own press and there was no television, which was to help de Gaulle in 1958. To his disgust, the R.P.F. began to join in governments and play the parliamentary game. Once again, as Brian Crozier remarks, de Gaulle suffered the agonies of a mere spectator at great events. The Fourth Republic showed some resilience in surviving its crises and he announced his retirement for a second time, maintaining that he would only return to politics in the event of a really serious situation. By 1957 he was virtually a forgotten man.

Meanwhile, the Republic stumbled into fresh problems. Governments were so short-lived that they achieved little and public discontent manifested itself in the growth of a new mass movement on the extreme right, Poujadism. The movement was headed by a small town demagogue, Pierre Poujade, who led a personal crusade against taxation and bureaucracy. He rallied the support of small shopkeepers and farmers who detested central government interference and the power of labour and big business. Other elements in Poujadism were anti-Semitism, xenophobia and Imperialism. In 1956, the Poujadists polled 2·6 million votes and won 52 seats. The movement added to the troubles of the divided centre parties whose vote the Poujadists reduced.

However, it was in Indo-China that France's worst disaster occurred. In 1946 the Communist and Nationalist leader Ho Chi Minh and his military commander Vo Nguyen Giap started their long-planned campaign for Vietnamese independence using the Communist organisation, the Vietminh. Ho Chi Minh was to fight first the French and then the Americans until his death in 1969, his dream of a Communist Indo-China finally being realised in 1975.

The French stuck doggedly to their objective of holding Indo-China until 1954. Then a disastrous decision by General Henri Navarre led to a complete collapse. Navarre tried to draw the Vietminh into battle at Dien Bien Phu but as it was in a hollow surrounded by hills the French found themselves surrounded by Vietminh artillery and could only be supplied by air. After a long siege, Dien Bien Phu fell in May and France's will to continue the war was broken. Pierre Mendès-France became Prime Minister with liquidation of the war as his principal objective. By July an armistice was arranged, and the French withdrew from Indo-China, which was divided into North and South Vietnam. The war, which lasted seven and a half years, had cost France 92,000 dead and 114,000 wounded. The defeat in the Far East had a profound impact on France's hold over her North African empire and by 1956 Morocco and Tunisia had been granted virtual independence.

The Fifth Republic

The Fourth Republic never won the respect of the majority of Frenchmen because it patently failed to provide political stability, yet it took another great colonial crisis to undermine it. In 1954 a revolt broke out in Algeria and soon 350,000 French troops were fighting in the colony against 150,000 members of the Algerian Liberation Movement (F.L.N.). The war itself split French society deeply. Many Frenchmen opposed any retreat from Algeria for it was not only part of metropolitan France but the home of 1 million French people. By the fourth year of the war it was becoming clearer that a negotiated peace would have to come. The French Right and the Algerian French were determined to resist this and set up the O.A.S. (*Organisation de l'Armée Secrète*), which like the F.L.N. indulged in acts of terrorism in France and Algeria. When in May 1958 it was rumoured that the Pflimlin government was considering a settlement with the Algerian rebels, the French army in Algeria, determined that there should be no second Dien Bien Phu, came out in open revolt and demanded that de Gaulle be called to head the government.

De Gaulle, who had himself almost despaired of ever returning to power, suddenly became the central figure in the crisis. As the Algerian situation worsened, his leadership alone seemed essential if civil war were to be avoided. The General was now a more cunning and subtle politician than in 1947; instead of trying to add to the Fourth Republic's problems he was shrewd enough to wait until power was offered to him. He merely issued the statement that he held himself ready to take over the powers of the Republic if needed. The Pflimlin government, unable to deal with the army rebels, resigned on May 28 and President Coty called on de Gaulle to avert civil war. The general accepted on condition that he was given a free hand to draft a new constitution for approval by popular referendum. In early June the Assembly accepted his terms and by its surrender assisted him in destroying the Fourth Republic by a bloodless revolution.

The new Constitution incorporated de Gaulle's own political theories as the president was to be vested with wide powers. He was to have the right to appoint the prime minister and dissolve parliament. Effective control over defence and foreign policy lay in his hands. He was to be elected by the people for seven years and could make use of the popular referendum, thus further reducing the importance of parliament. In September, after de Gaulle had made shrewd use of the television network, nearly 80 per cent of metropolitan France approved the new constitution.

In the winter months of 1958–9 a reorganised two-house parliament (National Assembly and Senate) was elected and de Gaulle was chosen as President by an electoral college of 80,000 delegates from local councils. For the parliamentary elections dedicated Gaullists regrouped to form a new party, the Union for the New Republic (U.N.R.), which became the ruling party of the Fifth Republic, helped by the new voting system under which France was divided into 465 constituencies. Each party could nominate a single candidate for each constituency but he could be elected on the first ballot only if he obtained half the votes. If he failed to do so, there would be a second ballot. As de Gaulle anticipated, the system encouraged non-Gaullist candidates to drop out after an initial stalemate in the first ballot and voters in general voted for Gaullist candidates in the second ballot. Thus in the first ballot in November only 39 out of 465 candidates were elected but in the second ballot a massive switch to the Gaullists occurred. The outcome, as Dorothy Pickles has noted, was 'probably the most unrepresentative Assembly in French history'. The U.N.R., though only polling about one quarter of the votes, composed nearly half the new National Assembly. Loyal colleagues were now appointed by de Gaulle to high position; Michel Debré became Prime Minister until 1962, when he was replaced by Georges Pompidou.

Algeria

The new President's overriding initial task was to find a solution to the Algerian question. The war in Algeria had a peculiarly vicious character about it. As Alfred Cobban writes, 'the Algerian nationalists intensified their campaign of largely indiscriminate murder, while the army organised underground counter-terrorist services. Terrorism was met by counter-terrorism and torture by torture.' The cost in lives and resources sickened the French people who were weary of decades of futile colonial wars.

The Algerian war then was the supreme test of de Gaulle's political ability. The army and settlers in Algeria had supported his return to power for the specific purpose of keeping Algeria French. De Gaulle, who had not committed himself on the question, would have liked a victory by the French army but was realistic enough to see that it was impossible. His thinking on the issue evolved until he was determined to give independence to Algeria. Brian Crozier sees another motive in the President's mind. He was so possessed by a burning ambition to restore French greatness and break the American leadership in Western international affairs that he wished for the most speedy end to the Algerian problem, which had become a tiresome distraction for him.

In September 1959, de Gaulle publicly grasped the nettle by offering Algeria self-determination within four years of the restoration of peace. The declaration accelerated the process of polarisation in Algerian politics. In January 1960, the French settlers and army in Algeria attempted a second revolt after de Gaulle had recalled General Massu for declaring that the French army would never leave Algeria. This rebellion collapsed quickly but in April 1961 more serious trouble occurred when the O.A.S., led by two generals, Salan and Jouhaud, seized power in Algeria. De Gaulle did not flinch in the face of this daunting challenge; in the words of Crozier, he met it 'by an inflexible display of personal authority'. He appeared on television in his general's uniform and, condemning the rebels for their stupid adventure, forbade all Frenchmen to carry out their orders. The rebellion lost impetus and by the end of the month most of its leaders had been arrested.

The O.A.S. now went underground and devised new murderous tactics by which they hoped to kill the President and keep Algeria French. At least four attempts were made on de Gaulle's life between September 1961 and August 1962. A bloody campaign of urban terrorism led to many deaths but it did not prevent a 90 per cent vote in favour of Algerian independence when a referendum was held on the issue in 1962. Agreement with the F.L.N. was finally reached and Algeria became independent, but only at heavy human cost: 800,000 of the 900,000 European Algerians felt it expedient to seek refuge in France and 10,000 Moslems who had served in the French army were massacred by the new Algerian government. De Gaulle must take part of the blame for these excesses because in his haste to be rid of the Algerian burden, he virtually gave the country away.

Nevertheless, as Brian Crozier has admitted, 'that he was able to part with Algeria without a civil war in France was a great though negative achievement which in all probability would have been beyond the capacity of any other leader France possessed'. The General was now at the height of his power and prestige. France for the first time since the war seemed to have effective leadership which was welcome after the chaotic politics of the Fourth Republic. De Gaulle reaped the benefits of the work of predecessors as the economy improved; yet even in 1962 a slow erosion of the Gaullist régime was beginning. The General's main interests lay in the defence and foreign policy and his actions in those fields had no relevance to the needs of ordinary Frenchmen. Support drained from the Gaullists and in the Presidential elections of 1965 de Gaulle was elected by only 54 per cent to the socialist Mitterand's 46 per cent.

De Gaulle's Foreign Policy

It was soon clear when he came to power for a second time that de Gaulle's views on Europe were rigid and uncompromising. His desire to restore French greatness and break American influence in Europe amounted to an obsession. He nursed a bitter resentment against Britain and the United States because in his view they had treated him with a lack of due regard. 'Yalta,' asserts Crozier, 'was the intolerable lump that stuck in de Gaulle's throat.' He could never forgive the Anglo-Saxons for keeping him out of the conference that was to determine the shape of the post-war world. In any case, he stood uncompromisingly for French self-interest and believed that his country had few common interests with Britain and the United States. It was, as Walter Laqueur reminds us, an essentially eighteenth-century concept of international politics with ideology playing little if any part in it. He dismissed as imaginary the Soviet threat to Western Europe and his attitude to N.A.T.O. and the E.E.C. proves that he saw no necessity for Atlantic or European unity.

A conflict of views with the Americans was therefore almost inevitable. In the General's mind, France was a world power whereas the Americans regarded France as merely one of the great European powers. Therefore he determined to demonstrate France's capacity to be independent of the United States. In March 1959 he withdrew French naval units from N.A.T.O. Mediterranean Command and established a pattern which was to be repeated in the next few years. He was in fact touching on a real issue—the extent of America's commitment to the defence of Europe which is still concerning West European states now. The general believed that only a strong European power could assure European security and he insisted that France should have her own nuclear deterrent, the '*force de frappe*'. Yet he was ignoring the realities of power; the French nuclear deterrent, though it cost 1,000 million dollars a year, was of little military value and only a concerted effort by several European powers together could really strengthen the continent. De Gaulle sabotaged such efforts.

The General's European policy was based on friendship with West Germany. In return for his support of the Germans against the Soviet bloc, he expected West German cooperation with his own plans for French domination of the Common Market and independence of the United States. Other European states were not consulted.

After the solution of the Algerian question, de Gaulle felt sufficiently confident to make more grand gestures. In 1965, France left S.E.A.T.O., the south-east Asian equivalent of N.A.T.O., and ceased to participate in any N.A.T.O. manoeuvres. In 1966, France withdrew from N.A.T.O. altogether, with the general attempting to forge new links with Russia. In 1964, he visited Russia and Kosygin returned the visit. De Gaulle referred to the new alliance between the countries but the prestige he gained was largely spurious. The Russians certainly did not regard France as a super-power and in any emergency she would have to be defended by the Western Alliance. The practical limits of French power were well illustrated by the loss of influence in Algeria, which came more and more under Russian rather than French control after independence.

The events of 1968 in France not only revealed the brittleness of de Gaulle's rule there but the absurdity of his foreign policy as well. With the unrest undermining the franc, France needed massive foreign help, especially from West Germany and the United States. Perhaps the general began to realise the unreality of his own policies for his actions became those of an embittered and frustrated man, as seen in his brutal rejection of Britain's membership of the Common Market and his exclamation of '*Vive le Quebec Libre*' to encourage French separatists during a visit to Canada in 1967. In trying to carry out a foreign policy based on 'grandeur', as Crozier comments, de Gaulle was 'never to acquire the means commensurate with his ambitions'.

The French Revolution of 1968 and de Gaulle's Resignation

The period of the 1950s and early 1960s was a relatively quiet one in Western Europe. The various régimes seemed stable as unions and students appeared to have little interest in politics. Thus the wave of student revolts which affected the whole of Europe in 1968 astonished the continent. Perhaps it should not have done; a new generation had grown up discontented with the sterility of modern society.

The unrest was most serious in France, where the student population had risen from 122,000 in 1939 to 643,000 in 1969, with consequent problems over accommodation and the relevance of academic courses. The government did little for the students and for many of the student fraternity the President seemed to be an anachronism. The first notable event was a strike by students and teachers at Nanterre in November 1967. In February 1968, the Paris students went on strike and use was made of Molotov cocktails. The French students' union was now in the hands of a militant group including Cohn-Bendit and in May really serious trouble occurred with huge demonstrations leading to clashes between police and students as the latter attempted to take over the university buildings.

The violence of the police swung public opinion behind the students. Unemployment, too, contributed to the unrest. Though the number of unemployed was only 450,000 it was rising sharply and causing alarm. On May 13, hundreds of thousands of Parisians demonstrated against the régime and all over France action committees were created as workers joined the movement. The Sorbonne was occupied and on May 17 ten million workers went on strike. De Gaulle, who was on a state visit to Rumania, had to interrupt his grand foreign policy and return home.

France was not, however, in the throes of a revolution though the troubles revealed the profound discontent of many French people at the authoritarian pretentiousness of de Gaulle's government and its failure to deal with social and academic problems. The régime seemed in danger as the parties of the Left joined the movement and the C.G.T. won substantial pay awards at the end of May which the rank and file turned down.

Yet the movement lacked any real unity; the radical slogans of Cohn-Bendit and his associates antagonised wide sections of the French public. Fervent assertions through irritating chants took the place of rational discussion and the search for truth. There was much talk about destroying the régime but a palpable lack of constructive thinking about what to put in its place. In the end the great majority of the population in France and elsewhere were bound to repudiate extremists like Cohn-Bendit, Tariq Ali or Rudi Dutschke. Most people, including the workers, had a stake in the maintenance of law and order and disliked the student predilection for violence and destruction.

An opportunity existed, therefore, for de Gaulle to reassert his authority. Having assured himself of the loyalty of the French army, he announced on May 30 that he would not resign and called for the defence of the Republic against the threat of Communist dictatorship. The general's verbal magic was again effective. A million of his supporters now demonstrated in his favour and gradually the occupied factories and universities were evacuated by workers and students.

Though he survived the events of May 1968, de Gaulle's prestige was destroyed. That he was taken by surprise is an indictment of his rule; he was too remote from real life and had no interest in the conditions under which ordinary French people lived. Problems like inadequate housing and social services had been ignored. His overbearing paternalism, especially in his use of the judicial machine and the constitution, was intensely irritating, as was his increasingly theatrical and eccentric handling of foreign affairs.

The General sought to restore his prestige by implementing changes in the Senate and by the creation of regional councils. However, by deciding to hold a referendum on these reforms and by announcing that he would regard the referendum as a vote of confidence, he took an unnecessary risk. In April 1969, while nearly 11 million French people supported the reforms, over 12 million voted against them. True to his word, the General resigned. In exposing himself to public rejection, he had again demonstrated his taste for the theatrical. The French nation greeted the news of his departure with some relief for the feeling had grown that he had outlived his usefulness. De Gaulle settled down to writing. He died in November 1970 and was buried at Colombey-les-Deux-Eglises.

Brian Crozier is right when he states that 'the fame of de Gaulle outstrips his achievements'. Between 1940 and 1945 he launched the Resistance and restored the Republic. In his second period in power he can be credited with two undeniable achievements: the constitution of the Fifth Republic and the solution of the Algerian question. The constitution has proved itself a durable instrument under de Gaulle's successors and France has been given generally effective government. That the Algerian settlement was achieved without a civil war was a masterly performance though the General's impatient shedding of the problem increased the price in human terms that had to be paid.

Against these achievements must be set the neglect of social problems and the absurdity of his foreign policy, which was divisive and weakened N.A.T.O. and the E.E.C. Perhaps he hung on to power for too long; he should have retired in 1965 when he was still popular, having rid France of the Algerian burden, but though he possessed charisma and intelligence he behaved as if he were living in a previous century. In the end he wasted his talents; he could have contributed to a more united Europe in full partnership with the United States. Instead, as Crozier reminds us, he chose to make repeated gestures of petulance and defiance that weakened the West without compensating advantages to France.

French Politics after de Gaulle

De Gaulle had changed the system whereby the president was elected by an electoral college, replacing it with election by direct popular vote. It was this system of election by universal suffrage which brought to the presidency the affable and shrewd Georges Pompidou. He had been a teacher and banker for much of his life but he became de Gaulle's second prime minister in 1962, holding the premiership until 1968 when he became the scapegoat for the 1968 Revolution. He was popular with the U.N.R. because he paid attention to the wishes of members of parliament. Though less abrasive than the General, he was no figurehead president.

Pompidou was more favourable to British entry to the Common Market and in 1972 held a referendum in France on the question of Britain's entry which was approved by a decisive majority. Unlike de Gaulle, he was interested in domestic issues and tried to implement a new social policy—almost a new 'social contract'. He was less autocratic than the General, seeing his role as one of steering on many issues affecting the nation's welfare. Therefore it tended to be on financial matters that he intervened most. De Gaulle in 1968 had refused to devalue the franc on grounds of prestige. Pompidou less than a year later reversed this decision.

Pompidou did not strive for the grand manner in foreign affairs as had de Gaulle. While he followed the main tenets of de Gaulle's foreign policy, he worked towards warmer relations with the United States. At the same time his government retained the desire to maintain France's and Europe's independence of the United States so that Europe under French leadership might appear as an alternative to the two power blocs. Thus Pompidou retained France's nuclear deterrent and tried to create a special position in the Middle East by selling arms to the Arab states in return for secure supplies of oil.

In April 1974 this skilful and patient politician died of a rare kind of leukemia. He was succeeded by Valéry Giscard D'Estaing, who narrowly beat the socialist Francois Mitterand in the presidential elections. Giscard d'Estaing's achievement in becoming President without a mass party (he was not a Gaullist) is proof of his political talents and personal magnetism. His record as Finance Minister from 1962, when he helped to control inflation, particularly contributed to his success. Only 48 when he became president, Giscard is the youngest French president in 80 years, which gives him something of a Kennedyesque image. Though a member of the French aristocracy, he has adopted a more relaxed informal style of presidency than de Gaulle's, believing it important to establish direct links with the man in the street.

Giscard is conducting foreign policy more graciously than de Gaulle but the substance is the same because France's determination to display independence of the United States is rooted in French politics. He has, however, proved flexible over Britain's wish to renegotiate the terms of the Common Market.

Describing himself as a liberal traditionist, Giscard sees his role as one of modernising France's political and cultural life on the stability bequeathed by de Gaulle and Pompidou. With foreign affairs in a satisfactory state he intends to devote more time to domestic politics. He has lowered the voting age to 18 and pressed for a law liberalising abortion. He is seeking to increase worker participation in industry and intends to launch an attack on tax fraud and evasion by a general tax on capital gains.

West Germany Since 1945

Germany in 1945

May 1945 was the darkest hour in German history. The state that had dominated Europe lay in ruins, divided into five occupation zones. Such was the destruction that it seemed inconceivable that the country would ever revive. In addition, the Russians aimed at a punitive squeezing of Germany and stripped their zone of its industrial equipment. The Western powers saw the ultimate folly of such a policy in a situation made fantastically difficult by the refugee problem. From the territories lost to Poland and Czechoslovakia were expelled about 13 million Germans, two thirds of whom settled in the Western zones. Their conditions were appallingly hard and the process of assimilation necessarily prolonged.

In this grim situation the immediate task of the occupying powers was to keep the basic necessities of life going. A shortage of healthy Germans hampered this work. Three million Germans had been killed in the war, two million were disabled and millions more lingered in hospitals and prisoner-of-war camps.

In the Western zones, democratic parties again emerged. The Christian Democratic Union (C.D.U.) replaced the Centre party, which had lost prestige by its failure to oppose Hitler. The C.D.U. was a more interdenominational party than the Centre party had been and stood firmly for denominational schools, religious education and general conservative principles. Its leader was the ex-Lord Mayor of Cologne, Konrad Adenauer. The Social Democrat party (S.P.D.) was led by Kurt Schumacher and, as before 1933, was divided into hard-line Marxists and gradualists. The third important party, a long way behind the other two, was the Liberal Free Democratic party (F.D.P.), an alliance of business and the intelligentsia. The Communist party (K.P.D.) failed to make headway in Western Germany as it was seen to be the tool of the Russians.

In the summer of 1946, the British accepted an American proposal for the economic merger of their two zones which became effective in January 1947. In retrospect this came to be interpreted as a move towards dividing Germany permanently. In fact, the Russians and French were invited to join the scheme and refused. Yet the need for cooperation between the zones was essential because of Germany's desperate economic situation. Output in 1946 was one third of the 1936 total with acute food shortages, especially in the urbanised British zone where there were 260,000 cases of tuberculosis. Britain herself was short of food but had to divert grain to Germany at the cost of bread rationing at home. In the hard winter of 1946–7 fuel shortages caused much suffering. With the influx of refugees and 5 million Germans made homeless through bombing, accommodation was a huge problem. Everything was in desperately short supply and a black market grew up. Since the paper currency was virtually worthless, payment on the black market was in cigarettes. A packet of 20 American cigarettes was worth 150 marks, which put the occupying forces in a powerful buying position. Germany seemed spiritually and economically bankrupt.

One of the most delicate tasks of the military government was the rooting out of Nazism. The occupying powers agreed on the objective but the process itself was difficult. Eight million people had belonged to the Nazi party and it was often impossible to determine the extent of an individual's devotion to the Nazi doctrines. In the American zone, 800,000 people received penalties of varying severity, in the British zone 156,000 were removed from office and in the Russian zone nearly 500,000 people were dismissed according to official figures.

The trial of 24 top Nazis was conducted at a special international court which sat at Nuremberg from November 1945 to August 1946. Twelve Nazis received the death sentence though Ley and Göring committed suicide. Many other Germans who had served the Nazi regime—generals like Manstein and industrialists like Krupp—were tried for crimes against humanity. In the end, 600 people were executed and over 4,000 imprisoned. Though a witchhunt was avoided, this justice could not be exact. As time passed and with the onset of the Cold War a more tolerant attitude began to prevail.

A. J. Ryder reminds us that with all its flaws the process of denazification was essential. 'It was both a moral imperative and a matter of commonsense that the new régime should depend on civil servants, teachers, judges, policemen and journalists who had not actively supported Hitler's ideology.' The process was in fact incomplete; two thirds of the judges and nearly all the staff in the Foreign Office in the Federal Republic in 1950 had held office during the Third Reich. Yet denazification was a substitute for the revolution which Germany never had.

The German Phoenix

By 1947 the harsh realities of the Cold War were forcing the Western powers to reappraise their German policies. It was seen that Germany must be helped to pay its way and contribute to the reconstruction of Western Europe. In September 1946 James F. Byrnes, the American Secretary of State, told an audience at Stuttgart that the British and American zones would merge to help the recovery of the German economy and that the German people would be given more self-government.

In the Anglo-American zone (Bizonia) an elected economic council with its own executive was set up. In practice, the executive was filled by Christian Democrats because the S.P.D. leader, Schumacher, preferred total opposition to any compromise. This was a tactical error as his rival Adenauer was able to increase his influence.

Gradually the West German economy revived after 1947, the announcement of Marshall Aid in June providing it with the essential injection of capital. A new bank was created, later to become the Deutsche Bundesbank, but the key move was a drastic currency reform in June, 1948, 10 old marks being exchanged for one new mark. The reform led to an immediate economic revival as the German people now had confidence in the currency. The Christian Democrats believed in competition and freedom for industry from economic controls. Their economics expert, Professor Ludwig Erhard, described his policy as a social market economy because public resources were used for social purposes while industrial output left in private hands would, he believed, expand to meet the demand. He made sure that Marshall Aid was used for industrial investment and the foundations for Germany's future prosperity were laid. Between June 1948 and December 1949, industrial production rose 125 per cent. The West German economic miracle was under way and by 1953 living standards were higher than in 1938.

It was this economic revival that provoked the Russians into bringing pressure on the West at its weakest point—Berlin. In June 1948 all land traffic from the West to Berlin was stopped, the purpose being to starve the city into surrender. The Western reply to this Soviet coercion was to supply Berlin by an air-lift and in the course of 200,000 flights West Berlin was supplied with 1½ million tons of goods. The Soviet government had two alternatives: it could either attack the West's planes or end the blockade. As the former alternative could have led to war, Stalin lifted the blockade in May 1949. The uneasy joint government of Berlin was ended and in 1950 West Berlin became a semi-autonomous city state, sharing in the prosperity of Western Germany. In practice it has been part of the Federal Republic and has become a symbol of freedom for refugees fleeing from Russian tyranny.

The Creation of the Federal Republic

The failure to reach an agreement with the Russians over uniting Germany led the three Western powers to promote the creation of a democratic West German state which, it was hoped, would strengthen Europe economically and militarily. In June 1948, the three military governors called on the West German state governments to convene a constituent assembly. In September, a committee chosen from the state parliaments drew up the Basic Law which laid the foundations of a constitution. A major issue was the degree of central government power and the rights of the individual states. In the end, after hard bargaining, the Social Democrats gained the financial supremacy of the central government while cultural policy remained the preserve of the state governments. The main legislative body was to be the *Bundestag*, with nearly 500 members elected by universal suffrage for four years. The upper house, the *Bundesrat*, was to number 45 members composed of representatives of the state governments.

The creators of the Basic Law worked sensibly to avoid the weaknesses of the Weimar constitution. The powers of the president were limited; unlike Hindenburg he was not to be the commander-in-chief of the armed forces nor was he to possess any emergency powers. One of his principal functions was to appoint the chancellor, who must have the confidence of the *Bundestag*. An attempt was made to combine the advantages of the British system of voting for known candidates in single-member constituencies with those of proportional representation whereby each party receives exactly as many seats as its total of voters entitles it to. Under the post-war German system each voter has two votes, one for a specific candidate and one for a party list so that half the members of the *Bundestag* are chosen in one way and half by the other. Any party failing to win three seats directly or at least 5 per cent of the total votes cast forfeits its right to be represented, a move to prevent the proliferation of small parties which had been a feature of the Weimar period.

Important powers were given to a Federal Constitutional Court which could pronounce on the legality of political parties and condemn any threat to the rule of law. In 1956, it declared the German Communist party to be unconstitutional and it has been a pillar of the new state. The new constitution has worked well through the common-sense of its creators, the ability of political leaders and the consensus which the Federal Republic has enjoyed and which was conspicuously lacking in the Weimar Republic.

In August 1949, Germany's first general election was held with no party gaining an overall majority. The Christian Democrats gained 139 seats, the Social Democrats 131 and the Free Democrats 52, with the extremist parties winning very few seats. Adenauer became the chancellor of a coalition government with the Free Democrats. Erhard was given the post of Economics Minister while the Free Democrat Theodor Heuss became the Federal Republic's first President. The election results were a grave disappointment to Schumacher's S.P.D. but though a man of immense courage the socialist leader had been too uncompromising and very difficult to work with. Another reason for the S.P.D. defeat was the loss of the Protestant East Germany, which meant that nearly half the population were Catholics.

Now began the Adenauer era. Born in 1876, the new Chancellor was deeply rooted in the Catholic faith and had been dismissed as Lord-Mayor of Cologne by the Nazis in 1933. Serious, resolute and astute he stood for much of what most German wanted—liberal economic policies after years of state interference, Christian standards after years of Nazi barbarism and international cooperation after a period of fanatical nationalism. He did not believe in full parliamentary democracy as in his view it had contributed to the destruction of the Weimar Republic. As Laqueur remarks, 'Adenauer's style of work was paternalistic, if not authoritarian.'

Adenauer's stable government and his obvious desire for a rapprochement with Germany's hereditary enemy, France, soon led to an improvement in his country's international status, with Germany joining the Council of Europe and the Schumann Plan. The Chancellor gained the confidence of the Allies in general because he refused to negotiate with the Russians over German reunification. Therefore by 1952 the Allies ended the occupation régime entirely and the Federal Republic was recognised as a completely sovereign state. A more contentious issue was German rearmament. In 1950, N.A.T.O. decided that for the sake of West European security, the rearmament of West Germany was essential. The decision caused an uproar in France and Britain as well as in West Germany, but nevertheless the Federal Republic joined N.A.T.O. and contributed contingents of troops. Special care has been taken to avoid the creation of any military élite. The *Bundestag*'s Defence Committee has kept a careful watch over the army, though as it has never reached its original target of 500,000 men it would appear that German youth are not attracted by the ethos of the barrack square.

During the 1950s Adenauer steadily pursued his two major objectives in foreign policy: reconciliation with France and close cooperation with the United States. The Federal Republic's entry into the E.E.C. by the Treaty of Rome fulfilled his dream, especially as a close colleague Professor Hallstein was the first President of the E.E.C. Commission. The burning question of the Saar which had divided France and Germany since the First World War was settled in 1957 by the return of this territory to the Federal Republic after France had again tried to absorb it.

The Federal Republic's relations with the United States became extremely cordial. Both countries loathed Communism and the Federal government refused to recognise either Poland's right to Germany's eastern lands or the legality of the East German government on the grounds that it was a puppet régime imposed by the Russians. Even if the West Germans had adopted a more flexible approach to the Communist bloc it is unlikely that the two Germanys could have been united. The Russian attitude to German unity hardened in the 1950s and in November 1958 Khrushchev created a crisis by demanding that the Western occupation of Berlin must be ended in six months. Though this crisis fizzled out the East German government built the Berlin Wall in 1961 to prevent refugees escaping from East to West Berlin. The Wall was a terrible symbol of East Germany's tyranny and many who attempted to escape were shot down.

The new parliamentary democracy was soon proved to be a most stable régime. The number of effective parties had fallen to three by 1961, with only the F.D.P. preventing the formation of a complete two-party system. Adenauer's C.D.U. again formed a coalition government in 1953 but in 1957 it gained a clear majority. In 1961 the C.D.U. suffered reverses but was still able to hold on to power in another coalition with the Free Democrats.

In his last two years of power between 1961 and 1963, Adenauer's reputation suffered a decline. His decision to run again for the chancellorship in 1961 at the age of 85 was resented even by some of his own party because it was felt that he was trying to keep out Erhard, whose talents he rather despised. A second reason for Adenauer's decline was a grave political crisis in October 1962. The weekly news magazine *Der Spiegel* criticised the West German army's reliance on America's nuclear deterrent and its lack of good conventional weapons. In high-handed fashion the government arrested the proprietor and defence editor of the magazine on a charge of high treason and broke into the magazine's offices at the instigation of the minister of defence, Franz Josef Strauss. When the charges against *Der Spiegel* could not be substantiated, the government appeared ridiculous. At the behest of the Free Democrats Adenauer had to dismiss Strauss and promise to retire in 1963.

This anti-climax to his career should not blind us to Adenauer's place in German history. He was, asserts A. J. Ryder, the greatest German statesman since Bismarck. Both were strong personalities who loved power and could be unscrupulous, yet both demonstrated high skill as diplomats. Like Bismarck, Adenauer was no democrat; he treated his colleagues as subordinates and showed little respect for the *Bundestag*, from which he withheld information. At times his conservative policies seemed negative. Far too little attention was paid to education and his foreign policy can be criticised as rigid because he refused to make any move towards reconciliation with East Germany. But it may be argued with equal force that Adenauer's authoritarian brand of democracy was the right form of transitional government for Germany in this period. If at times he was inflexible, he was also at other times subtle and sensitive—for example, in the way his government paid compensation of 3,450 million pounds to the Jews for their sufferings under the Nazis. Adenauer was a master in the exercise of legitimate power and if his government was dull, it gave many Germans a security and contentment they had never before experienced.

The Economic Miracle

The term 'economic miracle' has become a cliché but when applied to West Germany it still retains some validity. From 1950 to 1964 the country's gross national product rose threefold, faster than any other European state. After 1950 over half a million new dwelling units were built every year and by 1960 West Germany was producing 50 per cent more steel than united Germany had before the war. The symbol of German recovery was the Volkswagen car and by 1961 over a million German cars had been exported. The standard of living was transformed, with consumption per head trebling between 1950 and 1964. The boom was export led and in the early years domestic consumption was kept down to enable a high percentage of the gross national product to be spent on capital formation.

An important reason for West Germany's success was relatively harmonious labour relations: 1923 was still not forgotten and organised labour was willing to practise wage restraint in the interests of controlling inflation. German unions also numbered only 16, which has contributed to an absence of demarcation disputes. Worker participation too has contributed to stable labour relations. Hans Böckler, chairman of the General Trades Union, favoured worker participation in industry and Adenauer, with whom Böckler was on good terms, was willing to concede to the unions on the matter. In 1951 and 1952 laws were passed laying down that half the supervisory council in each firm was to consist of workers. In practice, the workers have a considerable say in conditions of work and still leave management to the managers, but their new status has helped morale.

The relative backwardness of German agriculture was solved by the consolidation of small units and mechanisation. As a result, less than one person in 10 now works on the land compared to one person in five in 1950. In 1964, a much smaller number of farm workers produced 50 per cent more food than before the war. 'It is not too much to describe these changes as an agrarian revolution,' asserts A. J. Ryder.

The stream of farm workers to the towns was one reason for the absence of inflation. So was the huge influx of refugees who were continually increased by people fleeing from the Russian zone; between 1949 and 1962 more than 3 million entered West Germany from the East. A third source of fresh labour has been the guest worker; more than 2 million workers from the poorer parts of Europe like Italy, Yugoslavia and Turkey flocked to West Germany to enjoy the higher wages of that thriving economy.

The period has not been one of unblemished economic progress. By the 1960s German economic growth slackened and in 1966–7 came a serious recession with almost 700,000 unemployed. German self-confidence was shaken as many Germans found it difficult to forget the crisis of 1929 to 1933. Certain areas like nuclear power, electronics and education have been neglected and this may well be a sign that a certain complacency has crept into German life.

Brandt and Détente

Adenauer's resignation in 1963 ushered in an unsettled period in German politics. Erhard, Adenauer's successor as chancellor, faced a number of problems and showed a lack of decisiveness in coping with them. He was pulled both ways by the French show of independence from the United States and by 1966 faced growing unemployment. The Free Democrats disliked the tax increases in the 1966 budget, lost confidence in Erhard and withdrew from the coalition, a move that forced Erhard's resignation in November. The two main parties now formed a Grand Coalition with the Christian Democrat Kiesinger as Chancellor and Willi Brandt, the socialist Mayor of West Berlin, as Foreign Minister.

The decision of the Social Democrats to join in such a coalition was a turning-point in their history. Since the creation of the Federal Republic they had endured a long period in the political wilderness and had lost their best leaders, Schumacher and Reuter. The new leaders of the party, like Brandt, believed that Schumacher's hard-line approach was out of date and in 1959 the S.P.D. adopted the new Godesberg programme, declaring itself to be a people's, not a class, party. It accepted the economic formula of as much competition as possible, as much planning as necessary. It ended its old hostility to the churches and its opposition to rearmament. The S.P.D. was now only slightly left of centre and the gap between itself and the C.D.U. was much smaller. Nevertheless, the Grand Coalition was an uneasy combination and by its very nature was bound to be a temporary expedient. In the 1969 elections the S.P.D. for the first time gained more votes than the C.D.U. and joined in a coalition with the F.D.P., with Brandt as the new Chancellor.

Brandt was a firm believer in the need for reconciliation with the Communist countries of Eastern Europe, a policy known as '*Ostpolitik*'. Erhard's government had first moved towards more cordial relations with Eastern Europe in 1966 and when Brandt became Foreign Minister in December of that year, he continued to seek a rapprochement. The Russian invasion of Czechoslovakia in 1968 delayed reconciliation but Brandt persevered, and when he became Chancellor in 1969 he defined his aims as better relations with all the East European states, including East Germany. A man of sincerity with an impeccable record as an opponent of Nazism, Brandt was helped by the election of a fellow Social Democrat, Gustav Heinemann, as President. Heinemann's courage and integrity as minister of justice had won respect and he was more tolerant of Communism than many of his colleagues.

Now *Ostpolitik* made some headway. In 1970 the Federal Republic concluded treaties with Russia and Poland in which the signatories renounced the use of force and confirmed the Oder-Neisse line as the de facto frontier between Poland and East Germany. In 1971, a compromise agreement on Berlin was reached. Russia acknowledged that access to Berlin was still a four-power responsibility and relaxed the rules so that West Berliners could visit their relations on the other side of the Wall. In seeking this new relationship with Eastern Europe, Brandt showed considerable courage. His real objectives were long-term; ultimately he hoped that *Ostpolitik* would result in a united Germany. In the short term this was out of the question, bearing in mind East Germany's strategic importance to Russia.

That *Ostpolitik* was also a risky policy became evident in May 1974, when a tired and discouraged Brandt suddenly resigned. The ostensible reason was the scandal that followed the arrest in April of Günter Guillaume, a close personal aide, who confessed to being an East German spy. Yet Brandt's own reputation was strong and he could have blamed the country's security police for the scandal, but he believed that ultimate responsibility lay with himself.

Other reasons explain his resignation. In 1972 he had led the S.D.P. to its greatest electoral victory winning 45·8 per cent of the vote, but from then on he faced a series of disappointments. His attempts to implement reforms in education and taxation were frustrated and even his triumphs in *Ostpolitik* were criticised. His government only narrowly escaped defeat in the *Bundestag* when the Federal Republic's treaties with Russia and Poland were ratified in May 1972. Brandt was accused of giving more to the Communists than he had obtained. Depressed at the prospects of parliamentary government in a world of big corporations and other interest groups, Brandt was already close to giving up the chancellorship when Guillaume was arrested.

If Brandt's career is over he will go down as a man whose domestic policies failed but he will be remembered as an architect of peace for the way in which he strove to implement *Ostpolitik*. His treaty with Russia, renouncing force, led to the establishment of diplomatic relations with every East European country except Albania. Trade and cultural ties between West Germany and the Soviet bloc have begun to grow, though the Guillaume affair has naturally raised doubts about the sincerity of the Russian response to Brandt's initiatives.

Brandt has been succeeded by Helmut Schmidt, who has begun the task of pulling the Social Democrats out of their recent gloom. He is an abrasive, blunt dynamic personality with a nickname in Germany of 'Schmidt the Lip'! He appears a tougher and more efficient individual than Brandt and so far has shown due caution in dealing with the Soviets. Schmidt's main concern has been the economy. The recession in West Germany in the winter of 1974–5 has been deeper than expected with 1·2 millions unemployed and about 700,000 on short time. The government attacked the unemployment problem vigorously with a number of reflationary measures. A capital expenditure programme was launched with help for firms carrying out new investment and giving jobs to the unemployed. The appreciation of the currency and the relatively modest wage settlements have kept inflation at under 6 per cent. Nevertheless, the West German economic miracle seems largely over; profitability in German industry has declined, the symbol of this development being the huge losses incurred by Volkswagen in 1975.

Uneasy Democracy in Italy

Italy in 1945

The era of Fascism left few permanent marks on Italian life and the part played by Italians in their own liberation produced a tremendous feeling of national exhilaration. Though their efforts had been confined mainly to northern Italy, they amounted, as Elizabeth Wiskemann reminds us, to a second Risorgimento in which all classes had taken part. In a few weeks after the Allied landings in 1943, the political parties and unions revived. Badoglio's government was replaced in June 1944 by Bonomi's coalition cabinet in which the strongest element was a revived Populist party. It was now called the Christian Democratic party, uniting in its ranks people of very different political persuasions from the moderate Left to the far Right. The Socialists were split as usual; now the divisive issue was whether or not to develop close collaboration with the Communists. The Communists themselves were now a formidable force. In the cold Palmiro Togliatti they possessed an able leader and their membership rose to over 2 million.

The future of the monarchy was the chief early problem requiring a solution. Its association with Fascism had robbed the House of Savoy of its prestige, especially as Fascist government had brought the miseries of a lost war and occupation by the vindictive German ally. Victor Emmanuel III resigned in favour of his son Umberto II but a general referendum on whether the monarchy should be retained could not be avoided. In June 1946, 54 per cent of Italians voted for a republic and Umberto left Italy. Though the vote was close, the controversy died a relatively easy death.

There was no such easy solution to the other problems facing Italy. Bonomi's government showed little will in purging Fascist elements or tackling the awesome task of economic reconstruction. Liberation thus became an anti-climax and a mood of hopelessness and cynicism replaced the earlier optimism. The situation seemed ripe for a major Communist bid for power and no doubt the Communists later regretted that they did not seize power by revolution in 1945, when they were enjoying high prestige for their role in the resistance. Such an attempt, however, might well have provoked British or American intervention as had occurred in Greece.

In June 1945, the inactive Bonomi government was replaced by one led by Parri, the picturesque leader of the Radical Action party. Parri's attempts to initiate progressive reform caused the Christian Democrats to turn against him and his government fell in December.

The Era of de Gasperi

The fall of Parri brought in the rule of the Christian Democrats under the shrewd, honest Alcide de Gasperi. At first his coalition government included Socialists and Communists, but in 1947 he resigned and formed a new government from which the Communists found themselves excluded for the first time since the war. Under Saragat's chairmanship the Constituent Assembly worked out the new constitution of the republic. In the first elections under the new system in 1948, the Christian Democrats gained an overall majority, winning 305 out of 574 seats. De Gasperi continued his alliance with the Republican, Liberal and Social Democratic parties in a stable coalition which lasted nearly five years.

For the Left, the results of the 1948 elections meant that they were destined for a long period in the political wilderness. The Socialist party had already split over the question whether to continue cooperation with the Communists or maintain their own political freedom of action. In 1947, Giuseppe Saragat formed a new party, the Social Democratic party, which took part in government. The larger and more left-wing group, the Socialist party under Pietro Nenni, drew even nearer the Communists and remained in opposition. The conflict between Nenni and Saragat was a deep, ideological gulf which weakened the political system by increasing the apparent strength and unity of the Communists.

De Gasperi did not find his coalition governments easy to handle. The party had a strong conservative wing but also included Catholic trade unionists who wanted to transform the movement into a genuine labour party. The tug-of-war between the wings often paralysed its attempts at reform and only part of the credit for the economic recovery of the 1950s should go to the government.

Nevertheless, de Gasperi was persistent, conciliatory, moderate and sincere. He avoided purely Christian Democrat cabinets and any subservience to the Roman Catholic Church. A believer in the European idea, he took Italy into N.A.T.O. and made her an active member of the Council of Europe and the Coal and Steel Community. De Gasperi actually visited the South and in 1950 his government launched important schemes to help that area. His clever, arrogant colleague Amintose Fanfani made the only genuine effort before 1970 to provide housing, though his presence made the task of holding the coalition together more difficult.

The elections of 1953 reflected the political flux raised by these reform projects. All the government parties lost ground, with the Christian Democrats losing 80 seats to their right-wing opponents, the Monarchists and the neo-Fascist M.S.I. (*Movimento Sociale Italiano*). De Gasperi could not form a new coalition and was forced to resign; he retired from politics and died in 1954. It seemed a tragic end to all his labours, yet the foundations for future economic progress had been laid and, as Elizabeth Wiskemann points out, de Gasperi 'had probably achieved, with his slender resources, as much as was then possible in the way of both social reform and the preservation of personal liberty; he had brought Italy back into the comity of Western Europe'.

A long period of immobility and instability now ensued, extending into the next decade. Vital legislation on education and housing was obstructed by party factions allying with the permanent Communist opposition. In the decade after de Gasperi's death there were no fewer than 12 governments.

The Opening to the Left

Some revival of the system occurred as a result of the elections in 1958, which saw moderate opinion rally to the Christian Democrats while the Monarchists and the M.S.I. lost ground. With only 42 per cent of the vote, the Christian Democrats were still dependent on the backing of one or two other parties and after a period of political stagnation what was really required was the creation of a centre-left coalition. From 1956 on the possibilities of such an arrangement had begun to improve. Nenni and his Socialists had begun to reconsider their position after Khrushchev's revelations and the events in Hungary (see Chapter Nineteen). They became increasingly tired of rather negative opposition and became more moderate. In 1962, they supported Fanfani's coalition government, though they were not part of it. In return, Fanfani promised reform of regional administration and the nationalisation of electricity.

After the 1963 elections the political system stabilised even though the Communists won a record number of 166 seats; the party was particularly strong in central Italy, the so-called Red Belt. Now the left-wing of the Christian Democratic party combined with Nenni's Socialists and Saragat's Social Democrats in a new coalition headed by Aldo Moro. This development had been helped by the conciliatory attitude of the reforming John XXIII, who became Pope in 1958. Unlike his predecessor Pius XII, he was not intransigently hostile to the Left.

The Moro government temporarily restored some stability to Italian politics. Moro himself possessed prodigious verbal skill which he used to avoid precise definitions or commitments, a useful gift in such a coalition government. Little tangible was achieved but, as Elizabeth Wiskemann comments, 'a very slight leftward tendency was generally maintained which was to the country's advantage'. In 1966, after 19 years of separation, the Socialists and Social Democratic parties reunited with Nenni as chairman. Their unity was rather fragile, the Nenni Socialists, for example, remaining in the Communist-dominated trade union organisation, the *Conferazione Generale Italiana del Lavoro* (C.G.I.L.). The two parties in any case had only 95 seats in the Italian parliament, barely half the Communist figure.

The Long Crisis

Despite its strength, the Moro coalition failed to deal with urgent matters like taxation, education or civil service reform. Its one major achievement was old age pensions. Therefore a sense of failure and frustration began to surround the centre-left coalition. In the 1968 elections, the Communists increased their number of seats to 177 and became the second largest party, attracting the votes of immigrant southern workers and disenchanted youth. In summer 1969 the fragile socialist alliance split apart and brought the government down, the Social Democrats forming a new party ironically named the Unitarian Socialist party (P.S.U.). Unrest grew as students rebelled against similar academic conditions as had students in France. Thus 1969 was a year of agitation on an unprecedented scale, with Italian students creating a far closer alliance with the workers than their counterparts in France or Germany. There was a great increase in violent strike activity as the trade unions, growing in confidence, fought major firms like Pirelli and Fiat. The union struggles were not solely about wages. In November 1969 a massive general strike was over the housing problem.

In these conditions, attempts to recreate a durable centre-left coalition by Christian Democrats Rumor, Moro and Fanfani were difficult. In March 1970, Rumor did manage to lead a government for a 100 days in which a cautious divorce bill was finally passed. Parliament's decision on this grave issue was confirmed by a referendum in May 1974, despite the opposition of the Church.

Nevertheless, a grim atmosphere of violence pervaded Italian life in the early 1970s. In July 1970 there began what became seven months of civil war at Reggio di Calabria, a sign of the South's bitter discontent. The growth of the neo-Fascist party (M.S.I.) was alarming; in 1972 it became the fourth largest of Italy's 21 political parties and clashes between the Fascists and the Left led to many bomb outrages and kidnappings. The long political crisis weakened the Italian economy. By 1974 the economic miracle was evidently well and truly over as the growth rate slackened, inflation rose to 25 per cent and unemployment reached nearly 1 million. The whole political system seemed near collapse as a balance of payments crisis coincided with three rapid government crises. In December some calm was restored as a minority government led by Moro survived with the tacit support of the Left.

Italy today may be seen as the classic case of the multi-party system in contemporary Europe. There are seven main parties—Communists, Socialists, Social Democrats, Republicans, Christian Democrats, Liberals and neo-Fascists—with a number of smaller parties. As no one party normally succeeds in winning a majority of the popular vote, government has been based on a coalition of the centre parties and has been marked by cabinet instability. With 40 governments since the fall of Fascism, one is tempted to compare Italy today with the French Fourth Republic or even Italy before Fascism. The same sense of prolonged crisis and frustration is evident, arising from the deep ideological divisions of the electorate.

For two reasons, however, the present Italian system does possess a certain stability. One is the strength of the Christian Democratic party, which has polled about 40 per cent in all the postwar elections and has therefore been the hub of all the coalition governments. It has attempted to be all things to all voters and has given the democratic centre some durability. However, the position of the party has been eroded by recent election results. In the regional elections of June 1975, the Christian Democrats, with 35·9 per cent of the vote, gained a bare lead over the Communists, who made their biggest advance in any election since the war in gaining 33·5 per cent of the vote. To win back lost voters the Christian Democrats will have to tackle Italy's problems more convincingly. The next important elections are in 1977 and the Italians have shown that they are not afraid to vote the Communists into power.

Perhaps the participation of the Communists in government would not be the disaster that people on the Right fear. In some respects the Left has acted most responsibly in the last few years, being a second reason for the survival of the system. Communist, Socialist and Catholic trade unionists have subordinated their political differences to join together in vigorous campaigns on important social issues like housing and health. The Communists have proved effective local administrators in 21 cities and have deservedly won much respect from moderates, though their long-term objectives are still regarded with suspicion, especially after recent events in Portugal. Their Secretary, Enrico Berlinguer, did offer to join in a 'historic compromise' with other political parties but in 1974 the secretary of the Christian Democrats, Fanfani, refused to consider an alliance, at attitude which he might well be forced to reconsider.

Despite these two factors the future of Italian democracy is in some doubt. The system has so far been judged with indulgence after 20 years of Fascism but if it does not do more to satisfy the aspirations of the people it will continue to lurch from crisis to crisis as urgent problems are neglected. Perhaps one can find consolation in the adaptability of the Italians. Though their system is untidy, it is one with which they have learned to live. As their outstanding historian Gaetano Salvemini once remarked, 'the Italian situation is always desperate but normal'.

Italy's Economic Miracle

The Italian economy failed to revive as rapidly as expected after 1945. It wilted in the face of inflation, the dislocation of the transport system and the return of millions of prisoners-of-war. Projects of currency reform were defeated and in the winter of 1945–6 industry was almost at a standstill. The failure to carry out radical reforms produced a bitter climate of agitation and industrial unrest between 1946 and 1948 as the C.G.I.L. expanded its membership to over 5 million.

Italy therefore became the last major European country to benefit from the economic boom of the 1950s, but after the stormy post-war years the economy achieved something of the same economic miracle as Germany. With a growth rate of almost 6 per cent it has enjoyed one of the highest growth rates of any industrial country and in the early 1960s it was expanding more rapidly than Japan. Italy's achievements have been outstanding in cars, office machinery and in the electrical industry. By 1967 one third of all European refrigerators were of Italian origin.

Certainly external factors such as the growth of world trade and international aid go a considerable way in explaining the revival of the Italian economy. Between 1945 and 1950 Italy received 3,500 million dollars of aid through the United States and the Marshall Plan.

A number of internal factors contributed to the miracle. The loss of her colonies not only spared Italy the humiliation that decolonisation brought to Britain and France; the country was free of the heavy expenses in which its colonies had always involved it. Of more importance has been government economic policy, which has been positively interventionist. To Luigi Einaudi must go the credit for inaugurating such policies. In 1947 he restricted credit to combat runaway inflation but gave generous credit facilities to firms with competitive potential. Other firms had to sell out or go 'bankrupt'. The logical result by the mid-1960s was that nearly one third of Italian industry was owned by the government, including five of the country's nine largest companies. Given the many unsolved social and economic problems in Italy, state intervention is likely to increase.

A third factor has been the energy supply. Italy's great economic weakness until the middle of the twentieth century was her lack of coal, iron, gas, and oil. In 1949, however, oil was struck in the Po valley and in 1953 in Sicily, while supplies of natural gas have been located at Lodi and near Ferrara. Gas became Italy's vital source of energy and a public corporation was developed under the able Enrico

Mattei to use energy sources in the national interest.

Industrial advance up to 1960s was helped by the relatively low wage rates and the plentiful supply of cheap labour from rural areas, though this situation has changed with the high wage increases of the last few years. Entry to the E.E.C. began to bring advantages after 1958. Unemployment was mitigated as many Italians went to work in West Germany and Switzerland, sending home remittances which helped Italy's financial situation favourably. Tourism was of even more benefit, 31 million people visiting Italy in 1969.

The powerful surge of industrialisation from the 1950s has caused a transformation of Italian society by changing the distribution of the active population. Between 1951 and 1964 alone the proportion of the labour force engaged in agriculture fell from 43 per cent to 26 per cent, while the proportion engaged in industry rose from 31 per cent to 41 per cent. 'The whole feeling of Italian life changed,' asserts Elizabeth Wiskemann. 'Not only was the sharp edge of poverty blunted but the structure of Italian society, still relatively static even in the north, suddenly melted and became fluid.'

This social and economic advance should not be exaggerated. The depressions of the 1970s have revealed the fragility of Italian industry. Many inefficient small firms remain and even the giant corporations have failed to carry out sufficient research. Unemployment has not ceased to be a major problem; the policy of investing in capital-intensive industries meant that job hunger has continued for much of the period since 1945. In the 1950s it reached the figure of 2 million and has recently risen again to 1 million after falling to less than half a million in the mid-1960s.

Therefore Italy's economic miracle has been an incomplete development. The government has to relaunch investment, which has flagged since 1963, a daunting task, since to accumulate the necessary capital it must reduce the real wages of the Italian public. One final feature of the miracle should be noted: it has aggravated the chasm between the North and the South, which remains to a large extent embedded in desperate poverty.

The South

Italy is still a state comprising two societies: the dynamic North and the stagnating South. The South's stagnation can be explained by three causes. It endures unfavourable natural conditions—for example, a lack of water and mineral resources. Its geographical setting militates against its advance; it is remote from the industrially advanced countries of Europe which have stimulated industrialisation in the North. The consequences of unification hurt the South as it faced the full force of Northern competition. The reaction of the Southern peasantry took two forms—violence and emigration. In the first 25 years since the war, 6 million people left the South and in 1970 the riots in Reggio Calabria proved the intensity of Southern discontent.

The Italian government has reacted with some energy to implement land reform and in 1950 a Southern Development Fund was created by the de Gasperi government to initiate public works in the South. The policy did not hit at the roots of the problem—namely, the lack of industry—but in the 1960s some grandiose industrial projects were completed. The steel works at Taranto and the Alfasud car factory near Naples are outstanding examples. Firms like Pirelli and Fiat have found it advantageous to locate new plant in the South, where they enjoy financial incentives, plentiful supplies of labour and a lack of strong union opposition.

In 1971 the government initiated a new attack on the Southern Question by authorising the Southern Development Fund to spend more in the next two years than it had spent in the previous 20 years. In the short run, however, it is impossible to be optimistic about the South's future. Much of the money spent on the South has been wasted because rational planning has been subordinated to the wishes of local vested interests. The modern industries that have come to the South are 'cathedrals in the desert', because they are capital intensive and have not provided Southern workers with employment.

Many Southerners who have moved to Northern Italy have ended up in miserable conditions, living in shanty towns without running water, electricity or medical services and experiencing discrimination. In the long run the internal migration may make Italy a more united society but in the short run it has made the South a wasteland and choked the Northern cities with new social problems. Italy remains, in Elizabeth Wiskemann's phrase, 'an extraordinary mixture of developed, developing and undeveloped'.

Further Reading

Cobban, A., *A History of Modern France* (Volume 3), Penguin, Harmondsworth, 1970.
Crozier, B., *De Gaulle: The Statesman*, Methuen, London, 1974.
Laqueur, W. Z., *Europe Since Hitler*, Penguin, Harmondsworth, 1972.
Ryder, A. J., *Twentieth Century Germany from Bismarck to Brandt*, Macmillan, London, 1973.
Wiskemann, E., *Italy Since 1945*, Macmillan, London, 1971.

Questions

1. Account for the instability of French politics during the Fourth Republic.
2. What were de Gaulle's chief objectives and to what extent did he succeed in achieving them?
3. Explain why parliamentary government has been so stable in Western Germany since 1945.
4. How far have Italian governments solved the major problems confronting them since 1945?

CHAPTER NINETEEN

THE SOVIET ORBIT 1945–75

The Final Years of Stalin (1945–53)

Despite his failure to prepare Russia against the impending German attack in 1941, Stalin emerged from the war with increased stature as a leader. The Russian defeats early in the war were so enormous that he appeared to be the only man capable of saving his country from the Nazi menace. Therefore, as Ulam explains, Stalin was 'outrageously the beneficiary of the magnitude of the disaster'. The Russian people supported him, despite his crimes and errors, as the only barrier against complete collapse.

In many ways Stalin was a mediocre war leader. He was a military dilettante whose choice of generals like Timoshenko was usually poor and he interfered with the work of his most able commander, Zhukov. Again he was saved from the consequences of his own shortcomings by the even grosser errors of Hitler. Stalin did score real triumphs in the field of diplomacy, where he displayed patience and tenacity, and also succeeded in creating an image of himself as the patriotic generalissimo of unyielding willpower.

Russia too emerged from the war with increased stature as one of the world's two super-powers, deservedly so as she had borne the greatest share of the burden in the European war. Yet the cost was enormous; about 20 million Russians had died and many cities had been reduced to ashes. Agricultural production was only 60 per cent and steel production only 50 per cent of their pre-war levels. Soviet citizens had been compelled to undergo more hardship than almost any other country in Europe.

If the Russian people or Stalin's colleagues hoped for a breathing-space at the end of the war they were soon disillusioned. In Ulam's phrase, he strove to rule as ubiquitously as before. He appreciated Russia's real weakness and wanted his country to catch up with the West before the Americans realised their power and used it. Totalitarian terror was again to be imposed. Russians disloyal enough to be taken prisoner were to be treated with exemplary severity. More than 5 million Soviet citizens still lived west of the Soviet borders at the end of the war and at Yalta the Allies agreed that they should be repatriated. Truly horrible events occurred as a result of this arrangement. Nicholas Bethell in his book *The Last Secret* has shown how many Russian soldiers had to be forcibly repatriated because they knew that a hideous fate awaited them in Russia. Many committed suicide after killing their families rather than return; even more were shot out of hand on their arrival in Russia.

It is clear that time had not mellowed Stalin's lust for power; rather it had eroded his patience and made him more eager to humiliate others. He was angry at growing old and distrusted his subordinates, fearing that he might become their prisoner through illness, as had happened to Lenin. Fear of those closest to him is a despot's occupational disease, Adam Ulam reminds us. Stalin hated his colleagues not only as potential rivals but as a potential successors. Therefore Zhukov, who had brought him victory, was soon consigned to professional obscurity and his contribution to that victory written off. The faithful Molotov was not only replaced as Foreign Minister by Vyshinsky in 1949 but had to stand by as his wife Pauline was sent into exile.

The Cultural Offensive

During the war Russian citizens had gained greater freedom and many of them had been abroad and seen the relatively liberal conditions in the West. Stalin feared that foreign political and cultural ideas would make returning Russian soldiers a potential revolutionary force. Russia had also acquired some 22 million new citizens by her gain of the Baltic republics, Bessarabia, Bukovina, Eastern Poland, South Sakhalin and part of East Prussia. The returning soldiers and new citizens were to be indoctrinated or reindoctrinated and in the summer of 1946 an ideological campaign started, led by Andrei Zhdanov. The campaign was provoked partly by Stalin's personal whim but also by a hard serious calculation. Russians had to be taught to despise foreigners with their dangerous ideas on political and cultural freedom, for otherwise the strength of the totalitarian régime in Russia would be eroded.

The leading figures in Russian cultural life again found themselves under fire, including Anna Akhmatova, one of the greatest Russian poets of her generation. The most important Russian composers Prokofiev and Shostakovich were criticised as degenerates, Zhdanov contemptuously comparing Shostakovich's music to the dentist's drill. Even the film director Eisenstein was not safe from attack. Russia's leading economist, Eugeni Varga, was disgraced for suggesting that an imminent economic crisis in the West was not inevitable.

Propaganda became more intense and ideological control much stricter, a great effort being made in education. The number of students in higher education rose from 800,000 before the war to 1,200,000 in 1946. They were taught that Russia was superior to the West in science and indeed all other fields as well. 'The all-pervasive, absurd and mendacious propaganda was an insult to the intelligence and the maturity of Soviet citizens,' comments Laqueur. It was in the atmosphere created by such propaganda that the most famous scientific fraud of modern history was perpetrated. Trafim Lysenko, with the backing of Stalin and Zhdanov, preached that environment, not heredity, transformed and made man, inducing in one individual in his lifetime changes that could be transmitted to that individual's descendants. Russian scientists who attempted to object to Lysenko's theories were victimised by the loss of their jobs and laboratories. In Stalin's last years anti-Semitism was increasingly practised; Stalin always disliked the Jews because of their cosmopolitan attitudes and they were harried out of intellectual life. The purges went on after Zhdanov's death in suspicious circumstances in 1948, hundreds of people being dismissed from official positions.

Communist Expansion in Eastern Europe and Asia

The Russian successes during the war gave the openings to Communist parties loyal to the Soviet Union to increase their influence throughout Europe. The two countries which were exceptions to the rule were Greece, where the Communists were checked by British intervention in December 1944, and Yugoslavia, where Tito took a strongly independent line. In the rest of Eastern Europe local Communists came to power backed by the might of the Russian armies. In former Axis satellites like Rumania, Bulgaria and Hungary, Communist régimes could simply be imposed on the native populations but in the cases of Poland and Czechoslovakia a more delicate approach was required. Polish Communists were particularly dependent on Russian help because of the traditional Polish hostility to Russia, recently increased by the Russian refusal to help the Warsaw rising. In Czechoslovakia, the Communists moved cautiously, taking part in Beneš' People's Front government and gaining control of crucial ministries.

In each of the European countries, the Communists had to overcome opposition which was centred in the peasant parties and the Christian Churches. This task was made more difficult by the conduct, or rather misconduct, of the Russian troops. In Poland, Mikolajczyk and the People's Party came under increasing pressure and, in fear for his life, the leader was forced to escape abroad. In Czechoslovakia, free elections were held in 1946 in which the Communists gained 38 per cent of the vote; it was only in 1948 that the Communists proceeded to more extreme measures. The only non-Communist minister, Jan Masaryk, son of the founder of the republic, died after falling from a window in most dubious circumstances, and Beneš resigned as President in June.

With the political opposition crushed, the new Communist régimes felt able to implement a social revolution by collectivising agriculture and nationalising industry. For a time they had broken up large estates for the benefit of the peasantry, whose cooperation they needed. Now the trend was reversed and it must be assumed that it was against the wishes of the majority of the population. Where the East European countries did learn from the Russian experience was in their slower pace of economic changes, which avoided any repetition of the massacres in Russia in the 1930s. As a result, by no means all farming was collectivised in East Europe even by the mid 1950s.

In Yugoslavia, Tito continued his defiant and independent attitude which angered Stalin. The Russian leader continued to hope that Yugoslav Communists would depose Tito so that Yugoslavia could be brought into line with other satellites. He made a grave error in failing to appreciate Tito's strong grip on his country. The Yugoslav leader was capable of acting ruthlessly, and had quickly eliminated non-Communists like General Mihailovic, who was executed in July 1946. But Tito's position in the Yugoslav Communist Party was unrivalled because of his part in the epic wartime resistance. Therefore the denunciation of the Yugoslav leader by the Cominform (the revived Comintern) and by *Pravda* that he was guilty of failing to implement Communist programmes had no success whatever. The criticism was in any case untrue. Tito collectivised agriculture in Yugoslavia more rapidly than did leaders in other East European countries and only after his quarrel with Stalin did he become relatively moderate and liberal. In 1951, Tito accepted aid from the West and since then has tried to institute a decentralised Communism with a human face. At the time of writing, Tito still ruled Yugoslavia. He has been ruthless in suppressing Croatian nationalism but has followed relatively liberal economic policies. He has repeatedly stated his determination that Yugoslavia should be socialist yet non-aligned, a clear warning to Russia against any interference in Yugoslav affairs.

Tito's defiance of Stalin made the Russian more determined to complete his stranglehold over other East European countries, and purges of party members occurred in all the satellites. The Church came in for attack, the most notorious case being the treatment of Cardinal Mindszenty of Hungary, who was arrested and tortured. In East Germany, Walther Ulbricht became the key man in Stalin's plans. An energetic organiser, his loyalty to Russia was never in doubt. Having harassed other political parties out of existence, Ulbricht's Communists launched a major programme of economic change. The repression of the régime, combined with Russian economic exactions, made it loathed by the people of East Germany. Many voted with their feet by fleeing to the West and in just over a decade the population of East Germany fell from 19 to 17 million. The drain of manpower, much of it young and skilled, was a further burden on the country's economy. In 1949, East Germany was formally proclaimed as the German Democratic Republic. The rulers of East Germany hoped to make their country comparable or indeed superior to the Federal Republic but they failed in this objective, the building of the Berlin Wall in 1961 being a tacit admission of their failure.

In Asia, as in Europe, the Communists had achieved a prominent position in resistance movements during the war. At the end of the war they were able to take power in China, North Vietnam and North Korea, with the important difference that apart from North Korea they were not installed by Russian troops. The Chinese Communists did, however, receive much aid from Russia at a time when the United States withheld arms from their Kuomintang rivals. In 1950 the new Chinese leader, Mao Tse-tung, visited Moscow and signed a Sino–Soviet treaty by which the two countries became allies, Russia promising to supply industrial equipment to China. Relations at this point were still cordial as China depended on Russian aid but already China had indicated her intention to be treated as the equal of the Soviet Union rather than her satellite.

The Cominform now became the spearhead of a Communist offensive in Asia and it planned several armed risings in that continent from 1948. In India, the Philippines, Burma, Malaya and Indonesia, Communist risings were checked. In Indo-China, Ho Chi Minh's Communists defeated the French and won control of Northern Indo-China. The high point of the Communist offensive was in Korea, where in June 1950 North Korea launched an attack on South Korea. When United Nations forces had driven back the North Koreans, Chinese 'volunteers' joined in to help the Communist cause. Though the Korean war ended in stalemate, the prestige of Russia and China was enormous in the 1950s and the war had proved that American troops were not invincible.

The Soviet Economy

The loss of 20 million people and the destruction in west Russia meant a heavy task of reconstruction. In spite of these difficulties, economic progress was rapid after 1945, with coal output doubling and steel, oil and electricity output almost trebling in seven years. By 1950, asserts Alec Nove, the U.S.S.R. had a stronger industrial structure than before the war. But the Russians failed in their primary objective, that of catching up the United States, which Khrushchev said would be achieved by 1970, Russia's G.N.P. being only half that of the United States.

Stalin's economic system after 1945 was a war economy imposed in peacetime with tight controls and a channelling of resources to heavy industry. Though a welcome improvement in real wages took place after 1947, the standard of living remained among the lowest in Europe with an intolerable housing shortage caused by disgraceful neglect of the problem. Public affluence was a contrast to private squalor. Enormous power stations were established in Stalingrad, the Volga-Don Canal was built and many targets set down in a new Five-Year Plan started in 1946 were reached. At the same time, the average Russian family still lived in one room, had little food and very drab clothing.

Agriculture had been neglected to provide labour and capital for heavy industry and after Stalin's death in 1953 it became a priority, with Khrushchev having a special interest in its advance. Virgin lands in western Siberia were cultivated, higher prices were paid to collective farms and farmers were given more freedom to work their private plots. After a disastrous grain harvest in 1953 of only 82 million tons, the new policies combined with good weather to produce a record harvest of 170 million tons in 1967. Improvements in livestock were less impressive. Khrushchev himself pressed for an increase in the size of collectives by amalgamation of farms. The real purpose for this was political; the formation of even larger units in agriculture would strengthen the Party's control over the peasantry.

The pressures on Soviet leaders were considerable after Stalin. They felt obliged to make an attempt to improve living standards and the construction of new houses doubled between 1955 and 1958; but at the same time they still wished to make a forced march to a mature industrial economy while keeping up with the military and space programmes of the United States. Thus the Soviet government was drawn into attempting to do too much in too many directions at the same time. Defence spending rose by one third in the years 1959 to 1963 and in consequence the targets of the Seven-Year Plan begun in 1959 were not reached in agriculture and some industries, though key industries like steel made considerable progress.

The End of Stalin

The war saw a vast increase in the membership of the Communist party from 3·4 million to 6·3 million and in 1952 Stalin made important changes in its structure. The Central Committee was almost doubled in size and the Politburo was renamed the Praesidium, with 25 members. Prominent new members of the Praesidium were Beria, Malenkov, Bulganin, Kosygin and Khrushchev. They were Stalin's trusted henchmen and there is no evidence that they opposed his ruthless measures. In 1952, at the first Party Congress since 1939, it was clear that Malenkov was now the heir-apparent.

Stalin's last months were accompanied by strange events that have never been fully explained. In January 1953, *Pravda* announced that nine doctors, six of them Jewish, had been charged with murdering leading Russian politicians through medical mistreatment. Beria and Malenkov were accused of lack of vigilance in failing to detect the plot. New purges were expected but at this critical juncture Stalin suffered a severe stroke and died on March 5. He died unmourned, for absolute power had turned him into a monstrous tyrant who built a system of terror and a structure of personal power unprecedented in modern history. The tragedy is, as Ulam reminds us, that Soviet Russia today is still much more Stalin's than Lenin's in spirit.

The Khrushchev Years (1953–64)

On the death of Stalin it appeared for a short while that Malenkov would inherit the dead dictator's position but a period of collective leadership ensued. Malenkov, Beria and Molotov formed a triumvirate and appeared to hold the reins of power. Criticism of Stalin in this period was implied rather than explicit but Beria's announcement in April that the doctor's plot was a hoax and his criticism of harsh police activities were startling. An impression of confusion had now been created in the Soviet leadership which encouraged demonstrations in Russia and other countries in the summer. In June 1953, a strike by East Berlin building workers sparked off a revolt which was only crushed by the intervention of Russian troops. Mass executions followed the crushing of a prisoners' strike in Vorkuta concentration camp in Northern Russia. Meanwhile, the power struggle continued behind the scenes, coming into the open in December when it was announced that Beria and six of his supporters had been executed for being capitalist agents. There need be no tears for Beria; his record as Chief of Police had been particularly vicious.

It was now that Khrushchev rose to prominence. He was born in 1894 and joined the Communist party in 1918. Despite being an uneducated coalminer, he showed talent for management and in 1939 became a member of the Politburo. In 1949 he became secretary of the Central Committee with a reputation on agricultural matters. His increased influence was demonstrated in 1953 by his condemnation of the record of the collectives and his call for agricultural reform. In 1954 he directed that new areas of Asiatic Russia be used for grain and by 1956 90 million extra acres were under cultivation.

Apart from this, Khrushchev was shrewd enough to remain in the background in the immediate period after Stalin's death. Now First Secretary of the Party, he was able to fill key positions with his own supporters. Thus when his rivalry with Malenkov came into the open in January 1955, he was able to force Malenkov's resignation as Chairman of the Council of Ministers. Malenkov, after confessing his inexperience and taking the blame for the unsatisfactory state of agriculture, was succeeded by Marshal Bulganin. He and Khrushchev were to share power in the next few years with Khrushchev the more dominant personality.

The new Soviet leaders made a number of moves to re-establish Russian power in Eastern Europe. In July 1953, the Hungarian premier Matyas Rakosi had been replaced by the more liberal Imre Nagy. In 1955, the Russians forced out Nagy and brought back Rakosi. In May 1956, the signing of the Warsaw Pact strengthened the Russian position in Eastern Europe generally as satellite armies were placed under Russian command. An attempt was also made to restore relations with Yugoslavia, with both 'Mr B. and Mr K.' visiting Belgrade.

The Russian leaders were also prepared to make some moves to the West. In May 1955, Russia signed the Austrian peace treaty and her troops evacuated Austria. In July came a summit meeting at Geneva attended by Britain, France, the U.S.S.R. and the United States. The main issues discussed were German reunification and European security in general. The cordial relations that were created became known as the 'Geneva spirit' and the more flexible Russian foreign policy strengthened the international prestige of the Russian leaders. In reality, the Geneva conference, in Ulam's phrase, 'underlined the new form of impasse in East–West Relations'. The more friendly relations made the chances of war appear remote and therefore there was no need for either side to make concessions. Geneva may have helped to lessen international tension but it could find no solution to the problems of disarmament or the German question.

The most startling breach with the past was Khrushchev's secret speech at the Twentieth Party Congress in February 1956, when he revealed many of Stalin's worst crimes. His motives for such a move require some explanation. In Donald Treadgold's view, 'he was trying to exorcise the incubus of his dead master, whom he had loyally served for so long, because of the massive unpopularity of all Stalin stood for among the Soviet people, yet he wished to avoid calling into question the structure of the whole régime or opening the way to public queries about the role of the leaders of 1956 during the commission of the crimes that he detailed'. Khrushchev still believed that Stalin had performed great services to Russia but he called the party to eradicate the cult of personality and restore Leninist principles of 'Soviet socialist democracy'.

His disclosures had a shattering effect on Communist governments in other countries. The Italian Communist leader Togliatti was prompted to state that Communism had now to become polycentric. It had to be tailored to the needs of individual countries rather than to directives emanating from one centre, Russia. These directives, Togliatti believed, should no longer be obligatory. He was not alone in this belief.

Revolution in the Soviet Orbit

The year 1956 was a watershed in postwar politics for both the Soviet bloc and the West. For the West, the Suez fiasco proved that Britain and France were no longer Great Powers, whereas in the Soviet orbit trouble flared up in Poland and Hungary. Hopes of a genuine relaxation of Russian rule had been aroused by the Khrushchev revelations and when these hopes were disappointed, protests mounted. In June, Polish workers clashed with the police and 100 people were killed. In August, Wladyslaw Gomulka, who had been Poland's chief Titoist, was reinstated. In October, Russian intervention seemed likely after Khrushchev and Gomulka had a stormy interview at which the Russian threatened the use of Soviet troops. Nevertheless, he showed restraint as Gomulka tried to calm the Polish people. Time was to show the wisdom of Khrushchev's attitude for the new Polish régime became a pillar of Soviet orthodoxy, Gomulka only falling from power in 1970 after riots at Gdynia.

Much more serious trouble was encountered in Hungary. In October 1956, a student demonstration was held in Budapest, the students demanding the withdrawal of Russian troops from Hungary, the reinstatement of Imre Nagy and free elections. The Hungarian secret police and Russian troops attacked the students, who were joined by the Hungarian army as fighting spread all over the country. On October 17, a new government which included non-Communists was formed with Nagy at its head. The next day a ceasefire was announced and Russian forces withdrew from Budapest. However, early in November Russian troops returned and after bitter fighting installed a new régime under Janos Kadar. Nagy and his colleagues fled to the Yugoslav Embassy for asylum. When they left it under a Kadar pledge of safe conduct they were imprisoned and executed in 1958. By then 200,000 Hungarians had fled to the West. In time, by a strange irony Kadar made Hungary a freer country than Gomulka's Poland.

The view is sometimes put forward that the Suez crisis benefited the Russians by distracting attention away from the Hungarian tragedy and preventing help from being sent to the Hungarians, but this is surely erroneous. Neither the United Nations nor the United States would have directly challenged Russia, one of the world's two super-powers. Nor was the force of world opinion likely to deter the Soviet leaders from checking Hungarian deviation. As Walter Laqueur remarks, 'world opinion does not count for much in Moscow's eyes if basic Soviet interests are involved'. Khrushchev believed that the passage of time would make the world forget Hungary and he was right.

The Hungarian tragedy was, however, a blow at Khrushchev's own position and he seemed likely to lose power as his chief rivals—Malenkov, Molotov and Bulganin—tried to force him out of office. They underestimated his tenacity and their failure to oust him meant their dismissal from full membership of the Praesidium. Khrushchev's victory was owed partly to the backing of Zhukov and the army but also to the fact that his supporters had a majority in the Praesidium. In 1958, Bulganin was deposed as Premier and Khrushchev held the top posts in both the party and government as Stalin had done. Rivals like Molotov, who became ambassador to Mongolia, were virtually exiled. No doubt they could console themselves with the thought that in Comrade Stalin's time a harsher fate would have awaited them!

The element of destalinisation in Khrushchev's rule should not, however, be exaggerated. His régime was more humane than Stalin's but it was still authoritarian. Artists might have more freedom to express themselves but there were severe limits beyond which they were unwise to transgress. When Boris Pasternak was awarded the Nobel Prize in 1958 for his novel *Dr Zhivago*, Khrushchev compelled him to refuse it. In 1963 the Russian leader denounced abstract art and modern literature as well as carrying out a campaign against religion which led to the closing of half the churches in Russia. On the other hand, Khrushchev allowed Alexander Solzhenitsyn to publish *One Day in the Life of Ivan Denisovich*, a horrifying picture of Stalin's concentration camps.

Relations with China and the United States

Soviet relations with China deteriorated rapidly during the Khrushchev years. His denunciation of Stalin angered the Chinese Communist leaders, who believed in rigid adherence to the Stalinist type of government. Khrushchev's belief in coexistence also alienated the Chinese for they hoped that with the Soviet launching of sputniks in 1967 the Communist world offensive could be intensified. In a sense the two countries were bound to become hostile because they both desired the leadership of the Communist world. In the words of Walter Laqueur, 'the conflict was not over the correct ideological interpretation of Marx and Lenin but over national interests, autonomy and big power aspirations'.

The Chinese were furious when Khrushchev became the first head of any Russian government to visit the United States. The Russian leader visited President Eisenhower at Camp David with a huge retinue befitting a tzar. The two statesmen planned another summit meeting for 1960 but it never took place because of the U-2 incident. When this American reconnaissance plane was brought down over Russia, Khrushchev demanded an apology which Eisenhower refused. Nevertheless, the Russian still condemned the Chinese for their opposition to 'détente' and in July 1960 he cut off Soviet military and economic aid to China.

Relations with the West also remained poor. Khrushchev supported Fidel Castro's new Communist régime in Cuba and the question of the Berlin Wall divided the two blocs. In 1962, the Russian leader suffered a severe diplomatic defeat which he brought on himself. Misjudging the will of the new American president, John F. Kennedy, Khrushchev was tempted into attempting to install Soviet missiles in Cuba. The American met the Soviet move with a firm ultimatum and the world held its breath as the long-feared clash of the two super-powers appeared imminent. Fortunately, Khrushchev's good sense finally prevailed; he yielded to the ultimatum and withdrew the missiles. A more peaceful Soviet policy was now pursued. In 1963, the Washington–Moscow 'hotline' was established and a treaty banning further nuclear tests except underground was signed.

The Cuban affair was the perfect opportunity for the Chinese Communists to criticise Soviet policy for lack of wisdom and also for cowardice in surrendering to American pressure. By 1964 Mao was calling Russia an Imperialist state and China's ally in Eastern Europe, Albania, also heaped abuse on the Russian leader. Clearly the day when Russia directed world Communism was gone and polycentrism (a number of different centres of Communism) had come to stay.

The Fall of Khrushchev

The Cuban affair was a personal disaster from which Khrushchev never really recovered, but domestic affairs were also eroding his power. In 1963, the failure of the grain harvest necessitated the import of foreign grain while Khrushchev's cuts in military expenditure offended the powerful military lobby. His attempt to divide the party into an industrial and an agricultural branch was unrealistic and was abandoned. General irritation grew with the unpredictable and irrational style of his government. Therefore in October 1964, while Khrushchev was on vacation, his enemies proclaimed Brezhnev as first party secretary and Kosygin as head of the Soviet government. It was explained that Khrushchev had resigned through old age and poor health. Soon attacks on him began. *Pravda* condemned his 'hare-brained schemes', and his 'bragging and bluster'.

Khrushchev was a crude but colourful character. At times his behaviour was absurd, as witness his action at the United Nations in 1960 when he took off his shoe and banged it on the table during Macmillan's speech. Even so, his bluster was preferable to Stalin's purges and in retrospect the Khrushchev years seem relatively good ones for Russia with considerable economic progress and more cultural freedom. He was, in Laqueur's phrase, 'an agent of freedom and progress in Soviet postwar history', yet his period in office also demonstrated the tragic dilemma of Soviet rulers. While wishing to improve the lot of the Soviet people by a more humanitarian Communism, he was afraid that excessive concessions would threaten the very survival of the Soviet system. His successors have faced the same dilemma and their solution has been a rather more severe style of government.

The Era of Brezhnev and Kosygin

Brezhnev and Kosygin have for the last decade proved to be prudent, cautious rulers. They have made few important initiatives in domestic affairs, apart from gradually stopping destalinisation and rehabilitating Stalin himself. For a time a more liberal approach was tried in economic policy. Individual enterprises were given more power to plan and produce with a view to profit-making. This applied not only to industry but to the collectives, where there was a renewed stress on smaller units. From 1966 attempts were made to provide for a higher rise in consumer goods than in capital goods and indeed the standard of living has risen in Russia.

The régime has attracted an unfavourable press in the West by its intolerance of creative work or of the right of protest. In 1966, Andrei Siniavsky and Yuli Daniel were sent to a forced labour camp for having novels and essays published in the West. Recently Andrei Sakharov, one of Russia's greatest nuclear physicists, has come under increasing official pressure for protesting at this injustice and other abuses in the Russian system. The case of the ballet dancers Valery and Galina Panov, who had to leave Russia to practise their art, was a vivid illustration of the dead hand of Soviet rule.

The most famous victim of Soviet intolerance has, however, been Alexander Solzhenitsyn. A former army officer interned for eight years in a forced labour camp, he described his experiences in a powerful autobiographical novel, *One Day in the Life of Ivan Denisovich*. The existence of the camps had never been admitted in print before and the novel caused a sensation. The author was awarded the Nobel Prize in 1970 and though he was warned off going to Sweden to receive it, he did not refuse it either. He came under increasing official pressure and was expelled from the Union of Soviet Writers.

In 1974, the West was treated to his long-awaited *Gulag Archipelago* which, unlike earlier works, contains no element of fiction. It was a harrowing account of the horrors of the penal camps and Solzhenitsyn's own fate at the hands of the authorities. As Leonard Schapiro has commented, 'it is dynamite so far as the Soviet authorities are concerned since it undermines whatever legitimacy the present régime may have'. There was no place in Russia now for Solzhenitsyn. In 1974 he was exiled to the West.

The Far East

The new régime's most permanent and urgent problem was the new hostility of China. The day after Khrushchev's fall the Chinese leaders were able to announce that they had exploded their first nuclear device, a development that worried the Russians more than the West. Soviet aid to North Vietnam was disliked by the Chinese government, as was Kosygin's mediation in the dispute between India and Pakistan in 1966 which gave Russia great prestige in Asia.

Such Soviet initiatives formed one of the causes of China's Cultural Revolution. The Chinese leaders feared a growth of opposition at home and a number of prominent Chinese were purged with the help of the Red Guards. These puzzling events can be seen as an attempt by Mao to maintain his power and revive the militant spirit of Chinese Communism, thus avoiding the revisionism of Soviet Russia. The Cultural Revolution caused a complete end to Sino–Soviet friendship and, as a number of border incidents ensued, Moscow's attitude became more threatening. Though relations improved temporarily in 1970, they remain tense. The Chinese no longer regard Russia as a Communist state at all. In their view Russia is a 'social Fascist' state and a much greater threat to China than Western countries with whom the Chinese have sought better relations in the 1970s.

With world Communism in such disarray, the Russian leaders have been fortunate in that they have been able to discount any threat from the West. Strains have been evident in N.A.T.O. while the United States has been racked by racial problems, the Watergate scandal and defeat in Vietnam.

Czechoslovakia

The true nature of the present Soviet régime was tragically illustrated by the events in Czechoslovakia in 1968. Discontent had grown there with the brutal rule of Antonin Novotny and in January 1968 he was replaced as First Secretary of the Czech Communist party by Alexander Dubcek. Now came the 'Prague Spring' as Dubcek's more liberal régime granted freedom of the press and civil liberties, including the right of other parties to exist. Dubcek and his colleagues were aiming at a more human and democratic socialism and the new course enjoyed wide popular support.

Despite Dubcek's protestations of loyalty to the Warsaw Pact, the Soviet government was now alarmed and in July it warned the Czechs not to leave the road to socialism. Meetings between the two governments were held in late July and early August and it appeared that Russia and other Communist states accepted the Dubcek programme. Then on August 20, Soviet and other Warsaw Pact troops invaded Czechoslovakia and replaced Dubcek with Gustav Husak. In September, Brezhnev laid down his views on the Soviet action in Czechoslovakia and they have become known as the 'Brezhnev Doctrine'. Brezhnev asserted that he was against interference in the affairs of other states except when a threat to socialism arose in a Communist country. Then, maintained the Russian leader, it becomes a matter of concern for all socialist countries.

As in the case of Hungary in 1956, a storm of criticism arose abroad but again, as time passed, the world forgot. In 1976, Husak was still in power in Czechoslovakia and has humiliated Dubcek, reducing him to the status of a mechanical engineer.

The Soviet invasion of Czechoslovakia had a profound effect on European politics. Czechoslovakia was the one East European country with democratic traditions but its 'Prague Spring' coincided with a hardening of Soviet policies. Albania and Rumania had already demonstrated their independence of Russia and the Russians were determined to prevent any more deviation in the Soviet camp. In this they were supported by several of the hard-line leaders in the other satellites, notably Ulbricht and Gomulka. Once again coercion was seen as the real basis of Communist rule though further disunion was created in the Communist camp as Yugoslavia, Albania and China all condemned the Soviet action.

For the West the crisis showed that true coexistence with Soviet Russia was still far from being realised and N.A.T.O. was given a new lease of life. It is clear that the Russians will use force if any of their satellites in Eastern Europe appear likely to deviate from the Russian view of Communism, and therefore the Brezhnev doctrine implies that a Communist seizure of power in any country is an irreversible event. Gradual change in Eastern Europe is now unlikely as Soviet hostility to political systems different from its own remains constant. The limits of 'détente' are clear as the Cold War appears likely to continue for an indefinite period despite the rather specious results of the recent Helsinki agreements.

Russia in 1975

The Western view of Russia three quarters of the way through the twentieth century is infinitely depressing. It is fair to say that in many respects the Soviet government has become tzarism writ large. In its own way it is as expansionist as tzarist Russia ever was and cannot avoid the temptation of indulging in intrigues against the West, as witness its aid to North Vietnam and its fishing in the troubled waters of the Middle East on the side of the Arabs. As in tzarist days, writers and thinkers find themselves excluded from any say in the way their country is run. The leadership still insists on ideological uniformity because to grant real cultural freedom would risk opening the flood gates of political liberty. The tension between the intelligentsia and the political leadership seems likely to worsen as the Soviet government persecutes any group which seeks to retain an identity of its own like the Jews.

Soviet society is as class-ridden as Russia in the nineteenth century. An élite exists composed of party members, government officials and senior members of the armed forces. The stultifying hand of the bureaucracy is everywhere causing inefficient allocation of resources. With independent thought stifled, no way exists by which these faults can be remedied. More than any other country, Russia is dominated by its secret police, the K.G.B. (the initials in Russian for 'Committee of State Security'). John Barron in his book, *The K.G.B. The Secret Work of Soviet Agents*, has demonstrated the wide activities of this organisation not only in Russia but in the world at large.

Finally, one may suppose that a difficult period lies ahead for the Russian state. The present leadership is aging and Brezhnev has been reported ill on several occasions. With the present Russian society inspiring little enthusiasm, future leaders will face demands for a more progressive government which will provide higher living standards and more liberal policies.

Further Reading

Laqueur, W. Z., *Europe Since Hitler*, Penguin, Harmondsworth, 1972.
Nove, A., *An Economic History of the U.S.S.R.*, Allen Lane, London, 1972.
Treadgold, D., *Twentieth Century Russia*, Rand, Chicago, 1972.
Ulam, A., *Expansion and Co-existence. The History of Soviet Foreign Policy 1917–1967*, Secker and Warburg, London, 1968.
——, *Stalin*, Allen Lane, London, 1974.

Questions

1. What can be said for and against Stalin's rule in Russia between 1939 and 1953?
2. In what ways were the Khrushchev years beneficial to Russia?
3. Analyse the decline in Sino-Soviet relations since 1945.
4. To what extent have Soviet Russia and the West reached a position of genuine coexistence in the 1970s?

CONCLUSION

EUROPE IN 1979

It would be reasonable to assert that Europe's immediate future will be a difficult one. The continent is divided into two armed alliances and freedom is severely limited in Eastern Europe. Though more free and prosperous, Western Europe has yet to find an answer to the stultifying effects of a mass culture that caters for the lowest common denominator. The energy crisis and inflation threaten a real cut in the standard of living in the next few years.

Social problems abound. Europe is now an urban continent and governments face new tasks in the creation of a healthy environment with the motorcar threatening the cities of Europe with total paralysis. Nor must it be assumed that higher living standards have made Europeans happier. Increased leisure has resulted in boredom while the anonymity of big city life has resulted in alienation. Figures for drug addiction, suicide and crime continue to rise steeply. The permissive society and the decline in church attendance have eroded the certainties of the old moral codes. Post-war Europe has seen a great expansion in education but there has remained the question of 'education for what?' Many students may be educated to discontent in a materialistic age which appears to lack ideals.

The extra mobility of labour, beneficial in some ways, has led to new forms of exploitation. Guest-workers from southern Europe have become a vital part of the labour force in Western Europe and it is estimated that there will be 22 million guest-workers in the E.E.C. by 1980. They have experienced language difficulties, atrocious living conditions and discrimination. In a depression they are the first to be dismissed.

Yet every age is beset with problems. If the age of European political predominance has ended, then at least European civilisation is still a model for the rest of the world. The recovery of Europe after 1945 has been splendid and, unlike past ages, the prosperity has been shared by large sections of the population. It is to be hoped that Europe will continue to demonstrate the same vitality in the face of new challenges.

MAPS

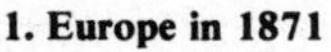
1. Europe in 1871

2. The Balkans: 1880–1914

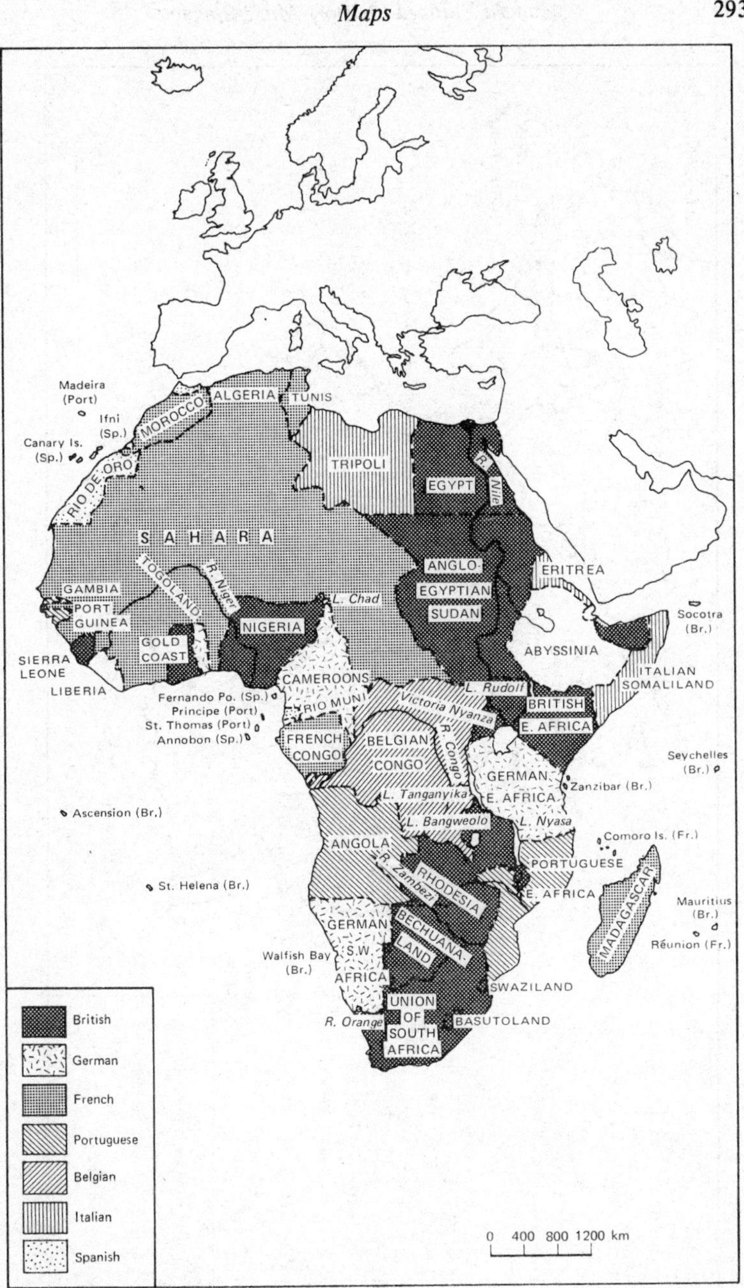

3. Africa in 1914

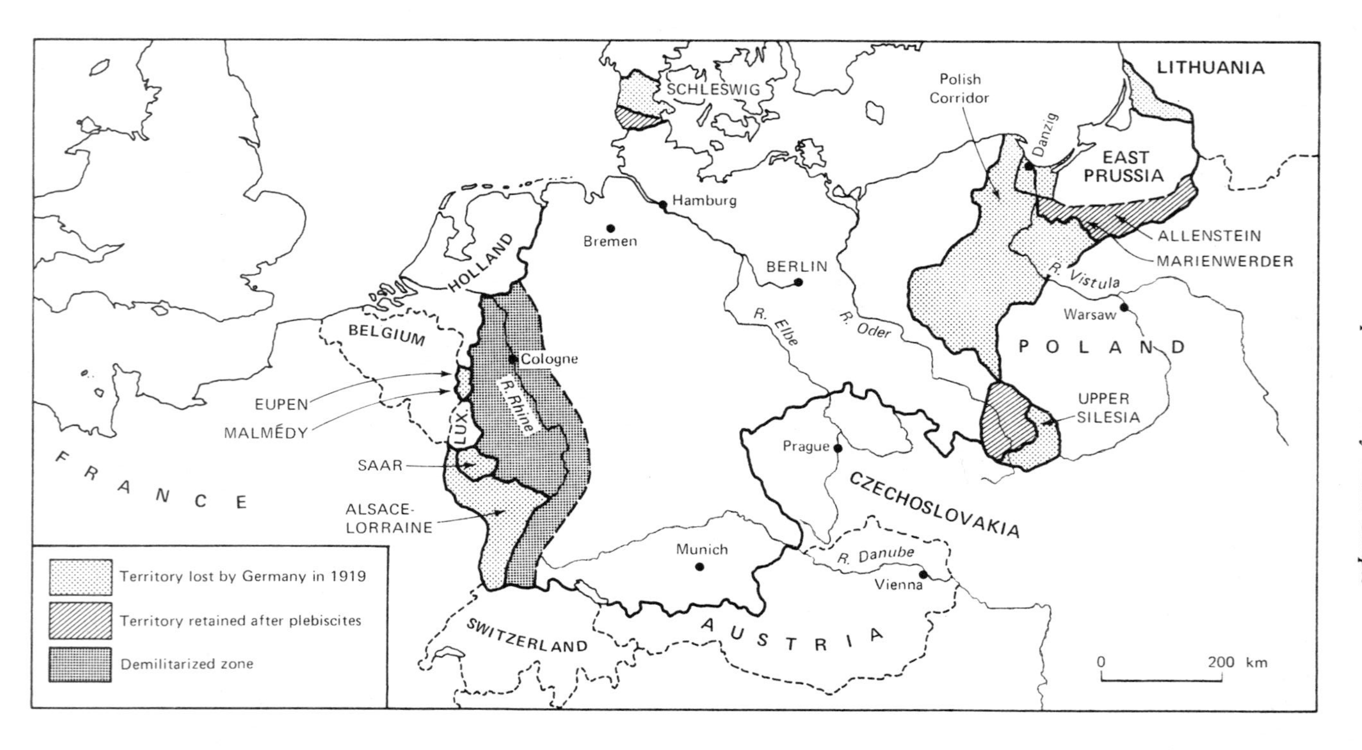

4. Europe in 1919

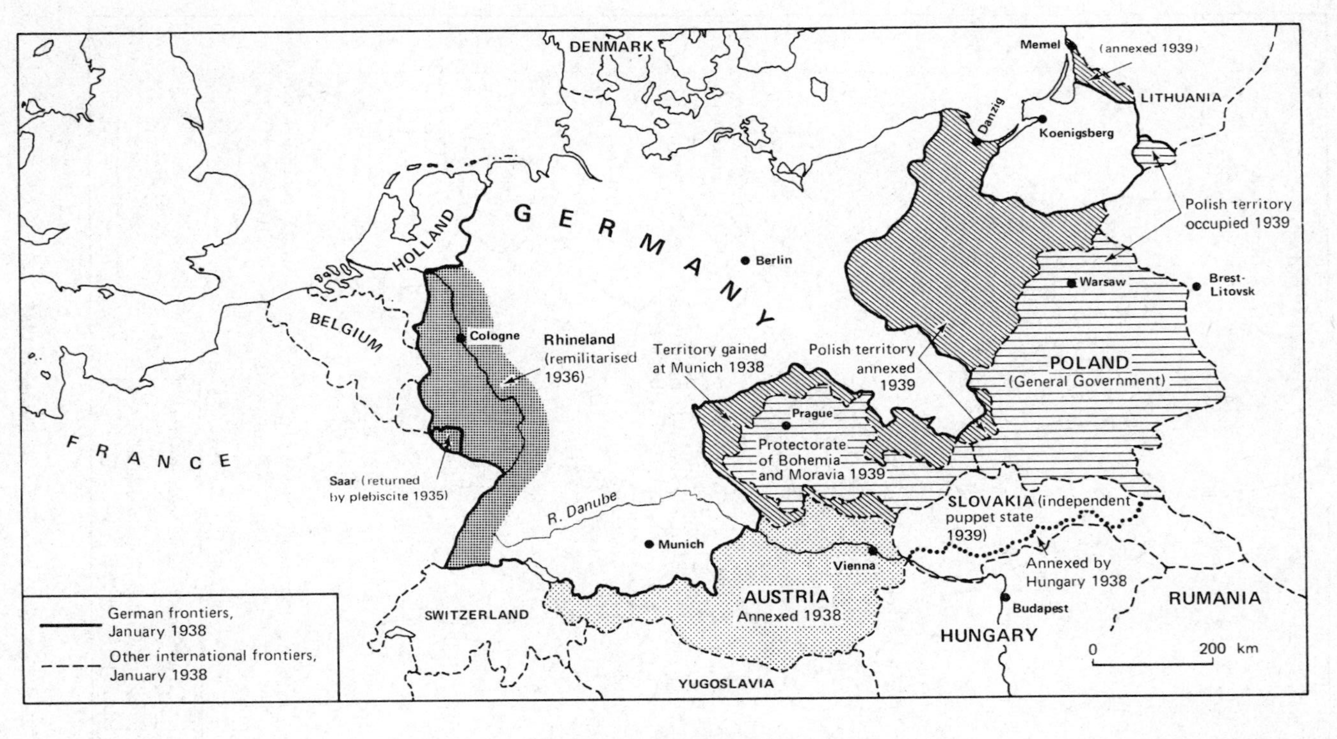

5. German expansion: 1933–40

6. Europe in 1945

INDEX

Index